Y0-BYW-404

DISCARDED

MILLENNIALISM AND SOCIAL THEORY

MILLENNIALISM
AND SOCIAL THEORY

Gary North

Institute for Christian Economics
Tyler, Texas

Copyright, Gary North, 1990

Library of Congress Cataloguing-in-Publication Data

North, Gary.
Millennialism and Social Theory / Gary North
p. cm.
Includes bibliographical references and index.
ISBN 0-930464-49-4 : $14.95
1. Millennialism. 2. Sociology, Christian. 3. Eschatology.
4. Dominion theology. I. Title.
BT891.N67 1990
236'.9–dc20 90-47609
CIP

Institute for Christian Economics
P. O. Box 8000
Tyler, Texas 75711

This book is dedicated to the five billion people alive today who will perish for all eternity, one by one, over the next 80 years, unless: (1) the Holy Spirit makes an historically unprecedented positive move; and (2) the Church of Jesus Christ at long last begins to get its act together. The exponential curve of souls has now appeared. Either heaven starts to fill up in earnest or hell does.

MAY 1991

HERMAN

"Have I got time for a cup of coffee?"

TABLE OF CONTENTS

Q. 191. *What do we pray for in the second petition?*

A. In the second petition, (which is, *Thy kingdom come*,) acknowledging ourselves and all mankind to be by nature under the dominion of sin and Satan, we pray, that the kingdom of sin and Satan may be destroyed, the gospel propagated throughout the world, the Jews called, the fulness of the Gentiles brought in; the church furnished with all gospel-officers and ordinances, purged from corruption, countenanced and maintained by the civil magistrate: that the ordinances of Christ may be purely dispensed, and made effectual to the converting of those that are yet in their sins, and the confirming, comforting, and building up of those that are already converted: that Christ would rule in our hearts here, and hasten the time of his second coming, and our reigning with him for ever: and that he would be pleased so to exercise the kingdom of his power in all the world, as may best conduce to these ends.

Larger Catechism
Westminster Confession of Faith (1646)

We who are reckoned as "conservatives" in theology are seriously misrepresented if we are regarded as men who are holding desperately to something that is old merely because it is old and are inhospitable to new truths. On the contrary, we welcome new discoveries with all our heart; and we are looking, in the Church, not merely for a continuation of conditions that now exist but for a burst of new power.

J. Gresham Machen (1932)*

---

*Machen, "Christianity in Conflict," in Vergilius Ferm (ed.), *Contemporary American Theology* (New York: Round Table Press, 1932), I, pp. 269-70.

PREFACE

What is the biggest problem facing the world today? Is it the weather? Are we facing a new ice age? (Oops. Sorry. Scratch that. That was 1973's looming apocalypse. I meant global warming!) Is it that burning fossil fuels creates the greenhouse effect? Or is it rather the high price of fossil fuels, which is pressuring us to consume less of them? Is it atomic power (today, the only economically feasible technological alternative to fossil fuels)? Is it the hole in the ozone layer? Is it acid rain? Is it the proliferation of nuclear weapons? Is it chemical and biological warfare? Is it international terrorism? Is it AIDS? Is it abortion?

Or might it be none of the above?

I have a traditional answer to this question. Why traditional? Because the question is itself traditional. The answer to this question has been the same from the day that Cain killed Abel. *The biggest problem facing the world is that the vast majority of the people in this world are headed straight to hell.* If "the world" means the people who live on planet earth, then this is the number-one problem on earth. It can be solved in only one way: a huge, rapid, historically unprecedented wave of conversions to saving faith in Jesus Christ.

Christians say that anything that happens to an individual on earth is insignificant, compared to his eternity. But is this really true? It is *not* true, but this is how Christian evangelists have traditionally described the problem. The problem is not stated correctly. One event that happens to a person on earth is vastly more important than anything that happens to him in eternity: his acceptance or rejection of Jesus Christ as his personal Lord and Savior. This event can take place only *on earth and in history*. "And as it is appointed unto men once to die, but after this the judgment" (Heb. 9:27). This covenantal (judicial) decision will *determine* where the person spends eternity, so it has to be far more important than eternity itself. After all, something that Adam and Eve did on earth and in history got humanity into this frightful legal position in the first place.

Jesus was quite clear about what is most important in life and death, and why:

> Verily, verily, I say unto you, He that heareth my word, and believeth on him that sent me, hath everlasting life, and shall not come into condemnation; but is passed from death unto life (John 5:24).

"Is passed from death unto life": this is the heart of the matter.

When we say to someone, "You're history," we mean it is all over for him in our eyes. When, at the moment of a person's death, God says, "You're history," He really means "You're eternity." It is all over for him in God's eyes. These are the only eyes that really count. So, the greatest problem facing the world today is the same old problem: most people have not accepted Jesus Christ's atoning work on the cross as their only legitimate, acceptable payment to a God of wrath. (How about you?)

Today, the numbers of people on earth are staggering. Between five billion and six billion people are now alive. These numbers are expected to grow, short of some unforeseen calamity like a plague or world war. But if the gospel continues to be rejected by at least 90% of these people, as is the case today, then most people are facing a gigantic calamity that only Christians accurately foresee. They are headed for eternal wrath.

Here is the question of questions: "Are the vast majority of these people inevitably doomed to hell?" Put another way: "Are the vast majority of these people *predestined by God* to hell?" We cannot lawfully answer this question; only God knows. "The secret things belong unto the LORD our God: but those things which are revealed belong unto us and to our children for ever, that we may do all the words of this law" (Deut. 29:29). But there is nothing in the Bible that tells us that we should assume that the vast majority of them are inevitably doomed. We must work and pray on the assumption that something can be done and *will* be done by God to overcome this seemingly unsolvable problem: getting the gospel to these people in time. And by the words "in time," I mean *in history*. I mean in my generation.

A Question of Time

It is common in evangelical circles to say that "this world is running out of time." This another way of saying, "The lost are running out of time." Yes, time is indeed running out, just as fossil fuels are running out, but when? In ten years? A thousand years? Ten thousand years? It makes a big difference. The question that we need to get answered is this: "Is time running out for the people alive today?" And the answer is categorically *yes*. The average life span for people living in industrial nations is about 75 years. If a child gets by his first five years, this figure goes above 80 years. In underdeveloped nations, the life span is less, especially for newborn children. So, I can confidently say that time is running out for these people, and my answer does not depend on any theory regarding the timing of Jesus' Second Coming.

The Church of Jesus Christ now faces a major problem. It is the same old problem that it has always faced, but today the stakes are far higher because the number of souls on the line is so much larger. These people are spiritually dead. If they do not respond favorably in history to the gospel of Jesus Christ, they will remain spiritually dead for all eternity. They will not die spiritually; they are *already* dead spiritually. They enter history with God's declaration of "Guilty as charged!" against them. This is their legacy from Adam, their spiritual birthwrong.

I contend in this book that the concern of most evangelical Christians is misplaced today. For over a century, their primary theological concern has been the dating of the Second Coming of Christ. Speculation regarding this event, and Christians' appropriate response to it, has governed both the worldview and actual strategies of the majority of those denominations (mostly headquartered in the United States) that call themselves evangelical. In short, various theories of the Second Coming of Christ, especially its dating (supposedly imminent), have overshadowed the uncontestable *fact* of world population growth and its implications for world evangelism.

When the highly debatable timing of a future event becomes more important to a person than his response to a visible, measurable, threatening event in the present, we call that person out of touch with reality, if not mentally deranged. But when millions of Christians regard the dating of the pre-tribulation Rapture as more important than the Church's efforts at evangelism, or worse, when they tie these evangelism efforts primarily to the dating of this future eschatological event, we have called this "understanding the times." When missions fund-raisers come into churches and tell their members to give more to missions because "when that last person is converted to Christ who is scheduled for salvation, Jesus will come again to Rapture His Church," the missions board has missed the point. (I actually heard such an appeal for funds in a Reformed Presbyterian Church, Evangelical Synod – a very peculiar use of the doctrine of predestination.) The idea behind the conversion to saving faith in Jesus Christ is to transform the way men live and die, not to end history. Jesus said, "I am come that they might have life, and that they might have it more abundantly" (John 10:10b). We are to be overcomers in life, not "overleavers."

Evangelism Explosion (Thermonuclear)

It is my hope and prayer that the spread of the gospel of salvation will take a "quantum leap" in my generation, or at least in the generation immediately behind me. It is my hope and prayer that presently lost people's positive response to the gospel will reach unprecedentedly high percentages in my generation. This means that I am praying for an unprecedented *historical discontinuity*: a worldwide reversal of the growth of Satan's earthly kingdom in my generation. I do not mean a reversal of merely his external kingdom; I mean his spiritual kingdom. Satan's kingdom has both aspects: spiritual and institutional. It is both supernatural and historical.

What this book argues is this: *so is God's kingdom.* This is a simple thesis on the surface, yet complex beneath. While most Christians will nod their heads in agreement to the question, "Does God's kingdom have an institutional aspect to it?", since they are members of His Church, when asked about the specifics of God's institutional kingdom outside the Church and family, they grow vague. This is a serious problem. While I do not believe it is the biggest problem there is, it is an aspect of that larger problem of world evangelism.

It is an aspect of the question, "How should we then live?" This question is basic to personal salvation. "If ye love me, keep my commandments" (John 14:15). "If ye keep my commandments, ye shall abide in my love; even as I have kept my Father's commandments, and abide in his love" (John 15:10). "And hereby we do know that we know him, if we keep his commandments. He that saith, I know him, and keepeth not his commandments, is a liar, and the truth is not in him. But whoso keepeth his word, in him verily is the love of God perfected: hereby know we that we are in him" (I John 1:3-5). It could not be any clearer. We must keep His commandments.

But what are these commandments? Do they lose all of their authority outside the door of the local church and Christian home? Or are there commandments that are supposed to govern all of our thoughts and actions in every sphere of life? If the answer to this last question is *yes*, then the next question is obvious: "What *are* these commandments?" Also the following question: "Where do we find these commandments?"

If the answer is, "No, God's commandments do not govern all of our thoughts and actions," then this question should be obvious: "Then why does God judge us for whatever we think, say, and do?" Jesus warned: "But I say unto you, That every idle word that men shall speak, they shall give account thereof in the day of judgment" (Matt. 12:36). Paul warned: "For we must all appear before the judgment seat of Christ; that every one may receive the things done in his body, according to that he hath done, whether it be good or bad" (II Cor. 5:10). Also, Paul said, "Casting down imaginations, and every high thing that exalteth itself against the knowledge of God, and bringing into captivity every thought to the obedience of Christ" (II Cor. 10:5). Are these thoughts only those that pertain to personal salvation, the Church, and the Christian family?

If God threatens to brings sanctions against us, then He must have ethical standards governing His sanctions. After all, He is not a capricious God. But where do we find God's standards (laws)? In the Bible, right? But some Christians answer *no*, or at least, "not only the Bible." Then I ask: "Does the Bible have answers for *all* our fundamental moral questions?" I also ask: "Does the Bible supply us with the presuppositions necessary to conduct all of our scientiffic and intellectual investigations?" If the answer to both questions again is *no*, then the Bible is turned into (1) a supplementary handbook to man's autonomous moral insights, based on universal natural law, or else (2) a handbook on personal mysticism. Possibly it becomes both. In fact, it is neither.

This book is written to promote belief in the sovereignty of God's law, not man's law. It is written to promote evangelism, not mysticism.[1]

Beyond Mysticism

Here is what this book is all about: a discussion of the Bible as the sole authority that should govern our opinions about everything. I contend that the Bible is authoritative in every field.[2] But Christian scholars from the very early days of the Church have insisted on placing Greek philosophy (the original secular humanism) above the Bible, or at least side by side the Bible. But the Bible says concerning itself that nothing is equal to it. "All scripture is given by inspiration of God, and is profitable for doctrine, for reproof, for correction, for instruction in righteousness" (I Tim. 3:16). The Bible corrects all other books, thoughts, and actions. So, to place anything side by side the Bible is to place it *above* the Bible. Yet this is what Christian philosophers have been doing for almost two thousand years.[3]

We have already concluded that the Bible does speak to every area of life. (Haven't we? Of course we have. So, let us go for-

1. It is a companion volume to Kenneth L. Gentry's book, *The Greatness of the Great Commission: The Christian Enterprise in a Fallen World* (Tyler, Texas: Institute for Christian Economics, 1990).

2. Gary North (ed.), *Biblical Blueprints Series*, 10 vols. (Ft. Worth, Texas: Dominion Press, 1986-87).

3. Cornelius Van Til, *A Christian Theory of Knowledge* (Nutley, New Jersey: Presbyterian & Reformed, 1969).

ward.) *The Bible therefore "lays down the law" for every field: family life, sociology, health, economics, education, politics, biology, geology, and even mathematics.*[4] The experts in each of these fields, as well as all the others, are required by God to go to the Bible in search of their particular field's operational first principles, as well as for some of the actual content (facts) of their fields. They do not lay down the law to the Bible. Their particular fields of study do not dictate to the Bible the theory and content of truth.

This means that the Bible is relevant for social theory. So, where are the books that explain what the biblical view of social theory is? There have been hybrids in history, of course, such as Scholasticism's attempted fusion of Stoic natural law theory and the Bible. More recently, there has been liberation theology's attempted fusion of Marxism and biblical rhetoric. But there is only one self-conscious body of literature that relies solely on the Bible in order to establish its first principles of social theory: theonomy or Christian Reconstruction. This book is my attempt to show you why this is the case.

A Brief Word of Encouragement to Secular Academics

Because of the title of this book, there may be a few secular academics who decide to read it. These days, millennialism has become a "hot topic" in academic circles. Already, this Preface has lost some of these readers. They have closed the book in disgust. "Why, this book is written by a Bible-believing Christian! Furthermore, I was expecting a detailed study that would include references to at least 73 recent articles in German theological journals."

Look, I am on my way to heaven. I am not about to read 73 (or even ten) scholarly articles by liberal German theologians.[5] In the realm of academics, such a task is about as close to hell on earth as anyone can come. Besides, the reason why some

---

4. Vern S. Poythress, "A Biblical View of Mathematics," in Gary North, (ed.), *Foundations of Christian Scholarship: Essays in the Van Til Perspective* (Vallecito, California: Ross House Books, 1976).

5. There is one exception: Henning Graf Reventlow, author of *The Authority of the Bible and the Rise of the Modern World* (London: SCM Press, [1980] 1984), which I regard as one of the half dozen most important history books written since World War II.

English-speaking scholar wants a book summarizing the latest findings of German theological scholarship (which will be completely refuted by other German theologians within five years) is so that *he* does not have to wade through the stuff, even if he reads German fluently, which he probably doesn't.

The secular scholar may also ask himself: "Why should I read a polemical book by one Christian against other Christians?" Well, for one thing, *to gain new insights*. After all, prominent historians today read the polemical books of previous Christians (for example, the output of the English Puritans' pamphlet wars of 1640-60) in order to find out what was going on. Why not read today's polemical pieces a couple of hundred years before they, too, become "hot topics" for future historians? Why not find out early what is going on?

A word of encouragement: I did not just recently fall off an academic turnip truck. There is meat here. I am applying some fundamental biblical themes to the modern academic world of social theory. This project may scare away the average Christian, who will regard it as far too worldly, but it should not scare away a serious academic. For instance, can you define social theory? I provide a unique operational definition in Chapter 2. It will help anyone to make sense out of the present debates over social theory and social systems. (Look, do you *really* want to read Talcott Parsons?)[6]

So, stay with it. You will learn about some of the most fundamental issues in the Bible, and why the vast majority of Bible-believing Christians today pay no attention to them.

6. One of the signs that I was "in too deep" in researching my doctoral dissertation was that Talcott Parsons started making sense to me. I knew it was time to wrap it up.

INTRODUCTION

And we have seen and do testify that the Father sent the Son to be the Saviour of the world (I John 4:14).

It has been almost two thousand years since the birth of Jesus Christ, Savior of the world. This world is not yet saved. The question is: Why not?

There are several possible Christian answers, all of which have been offered by Christians in the past:

1. It is not God's time yet.
2. The Church is not ready yet.
3. Saving this world must wait for the millennium.
4. This world will never be saved, because:
    a. the millennium is exclusively spiritual;
    b. the promised victory is exclusively spiritual; and
    c. most people will not experience it.

What is also remarkable – or not so remarkable, as this book will demonstrate – is that two millennia after the Incarnation of God's Son in history, His followers have no idea what a saved world ought to look like. They have no blueprint for a uniquely biblical social order. There is no comprehensive body of materials that would point to a solution to this question: "How would a Bible-based society differ from previous societies and present ones?" Hardly anyone is even asking the question.

Hardly anyone ever has.

A few people are asking it: liberation theologians (Marxist-socialists) and Christian Reconstructionists (social neo-Puritans). Both schools of thought are far outside the mainstream of the

Christian Church. (Anyway, the Reconstructionists are.)

There are several reasons for this lack of interest in social theory. I explore some of them in this book. A basic reason is that the Church has yet to come to any agreement on many of the fundamental issues of the faith. There is agreement on the doctrines of the Trinity and the Incarnation, which were put into their basic formulation by the Church councils of Nicea (325), Constantinople (382), Ephesus (431), and Chalcedon (451). The Athanasian and Nicene creeds are products of this early agreement. The Church international believes that the Second Person of the Trinity, equal with the Father and the Holy Spirit, became flesh in the form of perfect humanity, in union but without intermixture. There is also agreement on the final judgment. At the resurrection of all men, Christ will separate the sheep from the goats, with the goats sent into eternal fire. There will be no second chance for the goats.

The areas of disagreement are quite extensive. Christians have come to no agreement regarding such basic biblical themes as these: the proper structuring of Church authority (hierarchy); the nature of the moral law and its relation (if any) to Old Testament law; the nature of the sanctions that God brings in history; and the nature and timing of the millennium.

Another reason for the lack of interest in social theory is that Christians still do not agree on the fundamental message of the Bible. This may sound fantastic, but it is actually the case. If you were to ask ten Christians what the message of the Bible is, cover to cover, you would probably get ten different answers. They would be related to Jesus Christ in some way, or to His salvation, but they would not be the same answer. I am not speaking of phrasing: I mean different answers.

Try this experiment. Write down in one sentence what you believe is the most fundamental theme in the Bible, from Genesis to Revelation, including even the Book of Esther, which does not mention the name of God. Then compare your answer to the one I offer on the next page. Remember: keep your answer to a single sentence. (Minimize the semicolons, please.)

Here is the correct answer, in six words:

"The transition from wrath to grace."

It sounds so simple. It *is* simple. Children can understand it. It is also frighteningly comprehensive and complex. It includes everything. Theologians can barely understand it. (Few do, as I hope to show in this book.) It is *the* theme of the Bible. There is no more fundamental theme that is pursued explicitly from beginning to end: not the glory of God, not the sovereignty of God, not even the mode of baptism. The one theme that unites all passages in the Bible is God's grace to mankind in providing the means of deliverance from God's wrath to God's blessing.

The New Testament's emphasis is *personal* deliverance from *eternal* wrath to eternal blessing. The Old Testament's emphasis is *corporate* deliverance from *temporal* wrath to temporal blessing. These dual emphases do not cancel out each other. The theme of eternal personal deliverance is not entirely absent from the Old Testament, and the theme of corporate historical deliverance is not entirely absent from the New Testament. But each Testament has a particular emphasis. *Neither emphasis denies the other*. (The Church, rest assured, has not agreed on this.)

Deliverance in History

God made promises to the Israelites, just before they covenanted with Him, and just before He gave them His law:

> And Moses went up unto God, and the LORD called unto him out of the mountain, saying, Thus shalt thou say to the house of Jacob, and tell the children of Israel; Ye have seen what I did unto the Egyptians, and how I bare you on eagles' wings, and brought you unto myself. Now therefore, if ye will obey my voice indeed, and keep my covenant, then ye shall be a peculiar treasure unto me above all people: for all the earth is mine: And ye shall be unto me a kingdom of priests, and an holy nation (Ex. 19:3-6).

The Egyptians had come under God's wrath. The Israelites had been delivered from Egyptian slavery. It could not have been any clearer. Here was a God who could and would fulfill His promises to His people *in history*.

He asked them to tie themselves to Him in a covenant: *a*

perpetual legal-personal bond. They did. They came under the terms of this covenant. It was ratified again by their children just before they entered the Promised Land. They had to obey.

> Behold, I set before you this day a blessing and a curse; A blessing, if ye obey the commandments of the LORD your God, which I command you this day: And a curse, if ye will not obey the commandments of the LORD your God, but turn aside out of the way which I command you this day, to go after other gods, which ye have not known. And it shall come to pass, when the LORD thy God hath brought thee in unto the land whither thou goest to possess it, that thou shalt put the blessing upon mount Gerizim, and the curse upon mount Ebal (Deut. 11:26-29).

National obedience would bring national blessings. These blessings are summarized in Leviticus 26:3-12 and again in Deuteronomy 28:1-14. National transgression would bring national cursings (Lev. 26:14-39; Deut. 28:15-68).

The nation would inevitably disobey, God told Moses.

> And the LORD said unto Moses, Behold, thou shalt sleep with thy fathers; and this people will rise up, and go a whoring after the gods of the strangers of the land, whither they go to be among them, and will forsake me, and break my covenant which I have made with them. Then my anger shall be kindled against them in that day, and I will forsake them, and I will hide my face from them, and they shall be devoured, and many evils and troubles shall befall them; so that they will say in that day, Are not these evils come upon us, because our God is not among us? (Deut. 31:16-17).

Nevertheless, there was always this hope before the people, the hope of guaranteed deliverance through national repentance.

> If they shall confess their iniquity, and the iniquity of their fathers, with their trespass which they trespassed against me, and that also they have walked contrary unto me; And that I also have walked contrary unto them, and have brought them into the land of their enemies; if then their uncircumcised hearts be humbled, and they then accept of the punishment of their iniquity: *Then will I remember my covenant with Jacob*, and also my covenant with Isaac, and also my covenant with Abraham will I remember; and *I will*

> *remember the land.* The land also shall be left of them, and shall enjoy her sabbaths, while she lieth desolate without them: and they shall accept of the punishment of their iniquity: because, even because they despised my judgments, and because their soul abhorred my statutes. And yet for all that, when they be in the land of their enemies, *I will not cast them away*, neither will I abhor them, to destroy them utterly, and to break my covenant with them: for I am the LORD their God (Lev. 26:40-44). (emphasis added)

We see in the Old Testament a series of devastating national cursings, yet also restorations. God's people obey and are then blessed. Then they forget who God is and what He has done for them. He brings them under His wrath. Here is *continuity*: the enjoyment of blessings, which in turn leads to forgetfulness and sin. Here is also *discontinuity*: the destruction of their daily routines of sin and rebellion by God's direct intervention into history. God's positive sanctions of blessing (continuity), if used to further sin, will call forth His negative sanctions of cursing (discontinuity). *The progressive expansion of God's blessings in history will not be allowed by God to subsidize a continual expansion of sin.*

> Beware that thou forget not the LORD thy God, in not keeping his commandments, and his judgments, and his statutes, which I command thee this day: Lest when thou hast eaten and art full, and hast built goodly houses, and dwelt therein; And when thy herds and thy flocks multiply, and thy silver and thy gold is multiplied, and all that thou hast is multiplied; *Then thine heart be lifted up, and thou forget the LORD thy God*, which brought thee forth out of the land of Egypt, from the house of bondage; Who led thee through that great and terrible wilderness, wherein were fiery serpents, and scorpions, and drought, where there was no water; who brought thee forth water out of the rock of flint; Who fed thee in the wilderness with manna, which thy fathers knew not, that he might humble thee, and that he might prove thee, to do thee good at thy latter end; *And thou say in thine heart, My power and the might of mine hand hath gotten me this wealth.* But thou shalt remember the LORD thy God: for it is he that giveth thee power to get wealth, that he may establish his covenant which he sware unto thy fathers, as it is this day. And it shall be, if thou do at all forget the LORD thy God, and walk after other gods, and serve them, and worship them, I testify against you this day that *ye shall surely perish.* As the nations which the LORD destroyeth before your face, so shall ye perish; because ye

would not be obedient unto the voice of the LORD your God (Deut. 8:11-20). (emphasis added)

New Heaven and New Earth

There was also a promise of covenantal fulfillment *in history*: the beginning of God's New Heaven and New Earth. The pattern of continuity and discontinuity will cease. The following prophetic passage refers to a future, still unfulfilled period of earthly blessings.

> For, behold, I create new heavens and a new earth: and the former shall not be remembered, nor come into mind. But be ye glad and rejoice for ever in that which I create: for, behold, I create Jerusalem a rejoicing, and her people a joy. And I will rejoice in Jerusalem, and joy in my people: and the voice of weeping shall be no more heard in her, nor the voice of crying. *There shall be no more thence an infant of days, nor an old man that hath not filled his days: for the child shall die an hundred years old; but the sinner being an hundred years old shall be accursed.* And they shall build houses, and inhabit them; and they shall plant vineyards, and eat the fruit of them. They shall not build, and another inhabit; they shall not plant, and another eat: for as the days of a tree are the days of my people, and mine elect shall long enjoy the work of their hands. They shall not labour in vain, nor bring forth for trouble; for they are the seed of the blessed of the LORD, and their offspring with them. And it shall come to pass, that before they call, I will answer; and while they are yet speaking, I will hear (Isa. 65:17-24). (emphasis added)

This prophecy has to refer to history, for it says that there will be sinners practicing evil and "children" dying at age one hundred. In the midst of evil, righteous people shall flourish. History, not heaven alone or the post-resurrection world alone, is the realm of the New Heaven and New Earth. *The transition to this externally blessed realm is historical.*

Will God remember sin? Not judicially. (Obviously, God does not develop a case of total amnesia.) His grace in history is sufficient.

> The LORD is merciful and gracious, slow to anger, and plenteous in mercy. He will not always chide: neither will he keep his anger

> for ever. He hath not dealt with us after our sins; nor rewarded us according to our iniquities. For as the heaven is high above the earth, so great is his mercy toward them that fear him. As far as the east is from the west, so far hath he removed our transgressions from us. Like as a father pitieth his children, so the LORD pitieth them that fear him (Psa. 103:8-13).

A day is coming when men's *cultural deliverance* will be so widespread, because of men's *widespread repentance*, that God will bring unprecedented blessings in history.

What, then, of eternity?

Deliverance in Eternity

Jesus came to placate God's wrath. He lived a perfect life, died at the hands of sinners, and rose again. He ascended into heaven. Sinful men's debt to God has been paid. They can appropriate this payment as their own. On this legal basis, and only on this legal basis, men can find deliverance from God's eternal wrath to come. This deliverance begins in history. This is the New Testament's version of the fundamental biblical theme of the transition from cursing to blessing.

It is clear that in the Old Testament, the discontinuities of this transition – captivity and deliverance – were historical. What about the discontinuities in the New Testament?

It is also clear that the ultimate discontinuity in this life is the transition from God's wrath to His grace. *This is a far greater discontinuity than mere physical death.* It takes place in history.

> The Father loveth the Son, and hath given all things into his hand. He that believeth on the Son hath everlasting life: and he that believeth not the Son shall not see life; but the wrath of God abideth on him (John 3:35-36).

God's free gift of eternal life is offered in history (and only in history), and it is accepted in history (and only in history).

> And as it is appointed unto men once to die, but after this the judgment: So Christ was once offered to bear the sins of many; and unto them that look for him shall he appear the second time with-

out sin unto salvation (Heb. 9:27-28).

What this means is simple to state: *eternal deliverance takes place in history*. The problem is, Christian theologians have not taken this principle seriously outside of the doctrine of soteriology (salvation), narrowly defined as soul-saving alone.

The Ultimate Discontinuities Are Historical

There are three great discontinuities in history: (1) Adam's fall, which was the judicial basis of mankind's transition from grace to wrath; (2) the Incarnation of the Second Person of the Trinity in human flesh; and (3) Jesus Christ's separation from God the Father on the cross. Compared to these three events, all other historical *and cosmic* discontinuities are minor. While most Christians would agree with this in principle, they are still almost hypnotized by those passages that describe the discontinuity between this world and the final judgment. They regard the coming fiery transformation of the skies as the really big event – in their own thinking, dwarfing the death of Christ.

The order of magnitude separating the death of Christ from the final judgment is much greater than the order of magnitude between this world and the post-resurrection world. How can I be so sure? Because I recognize that the order of magnitude separating (1) Adam's *legal status* before God immediately prior to his fall from (2) his legal status immediately after was far greater than the order of magnitude separating (a) the pre-fall physical world from (b) the post-fall physical world. *Transgressing God's one law in Eden was a monumental discontinuity*. God's curse on the world was merely God's negative physical sanction. God's common grace to Adam and the creation, made possible because of Christ's payment to God on the cross, allowed God to reduce His negative physical sanctions on both Adam and the environment. God's negative physical sanctions were minimal compared to Adam's transgression. Therefore, *compared with the death of Christ*, the future positive physical sanctions of final judgment and the post-judgment world will also be minimal.

Let me put this a different way. The order of magnitude of the separation of Jesus Christ from God the Father at the cross was analogous to the separation of heaven from hell or the post-judgment perfection of the New Heaven and New Earth from the perfection of the lake of fire (Rev. 20:14-15). This is the *judicial* difference between "saved" and "lost." Compared to this, the physical circumstances of Christ's bodily return to earth are minimal. Therefore, the magnitude of the *judicial transition* from wrath to grace in history far overshadows the *physical transition* from this world to the next.

Adam's physical death was a covenantal result (sanctions) of his transgression in history. Jesus' physical resurrection was a covenantal result of His perfect atonement in history of God's wrath. It is not physical death that stands as life's greatest discontinuity. *The greatest discontinuity in life is the judicial transition from wrath to grace.* Jesus made this plain when He told men what to fear most:

> And fear not them which kill the body, but are not able to kill the soul: but rather fear him which is able to destroy both soul and body in hell (Matt. 10:28).

Each person's discontinuity from grace to wrath is judicial and automatic. Everyone is born under the judicial curse against Adam. This is the doctrine of original sin. Thus, there is no major transition from covenant-breaking in history to hell. There is no judicial transition. Eternity in the lake of fire is merely an extension of life lived apart from God's redeeming grace in history. In short, *deliverance in eternity begins in history.*

The Church has always said that it believes this. Nevertheless, the Church has only rarely applied this most fundamental of all biblical themes to its overall theological system. *Specifically, churches have refused to apply this principle to eschatology.* One thing that churches agree on today is that man's covenantal-judicial deliverance in history must be understood as strictly spiritual-personal and in no sense social. The judicial transition from wrath to grace supposedly applies only to the individual soul, not to the physical body or the body politic.

What, then, of the Old Testament? Is it simply "God's Word, emeritus"? For the major theme of the Old Testament is *God's social and institutional deliverance of His people in history*. Does the New Testament abandon this perspective? Or does it simply not emphasize it, *taking for granted our acceptance of the Old Testament's message of comprehensive deliverance in history*?

The answers to these questions have divided the Church for almost nineteen hundred years. We need to get agreement.

Conclusion

This book is a reassessment of three covenantal themes: biblical law, God's sanctions in history, and the millennium, though primarily the latter two. I begin with this obvious New Testament teaching: the fundamental transition from *personal* wrath to grace is historical, not post-final judgment. What I try to show is that the Bible teaches that *this fundamental historical transition from wrath to grace is also social and cultural*. The post-judgment New Heaven and New Earth will be an extension of the historical New Heaven and New Earth, as surely as each redeemed person's resurrected body will be an extension of his historical body. *There is therefore a very significant continuity between this world and the world to come*. This is true of both aspects of both worlds: saved vs. lost. The implications of this statement are monumental, as I hope to show in this book.

There is a coming discontinuity called the final judgment, but compared to the discontinuity in history from God's wrath to God's grace (Christ's atonement and His saints' personal regeneration), it will be a comparatively minor affair. Lots of trumpets and noise, plus a few million (or a few billion) people flying upward all at once, but hardly anything on the order of magnitude of the *judicial discontinuity* of personal regeneration in history: "Therefore if any man be in Christ, he is a new creature [creation]: old things are passed away; behold, all things are become new" (II Cor. 5:17).

If I am wrong about this, then the crucifixion was a gigantic error, a case of overkill. It was an historical event, and it has cosmic implications. But if the post-historical cosmic *results* of the crucifixion are more important – more of a discontinuity – than God's negative sanctions against Jesus Christ on the cross, then what was the purpose of the Incarnation? Why didn't the entire legal transaction between Father and Son take place in heaven? Why did Jesus Christ have to utter the most terrifying words in history? "My God, my God, why hast thou forsaken me?" (Matt. 27:46b).

Any attempt to elevate the coming transition, from this world to the next, above the historical discontinuities of Adam's fall, the Incarnation, and Christ's crucifixion, is deeply misguided theologically. Such a view of the past relegates history to a secondary consideration. If history is secondary, then the Incarnation and crucifixion are also secondary. No Christian would admit this openly, of course, yet virtually all of them psychologically accept it as an operational fact of life. Most Christians, no matter what they say about the centrality of the crucifixion and its soul-transforming results, do not really believe it. They regard Jesus' Second Coming at the final judgment (or to begin the millennial age) as by far the most spectacular discontinuity.

The error in such thinking is to regard the *cosmic results* of judicial (covenantal) transactions as more important than the judicial transactions themselves. This places far too great an emphasis on the material aspects of salvation and not enough on the judicial. (Notice, I did not say *spiritual*. I am not here contrasting the spiritual aspects of life with the material; I am contrasting the *judicial-covenantal* aspects with the material.) God the Father took His Son to the cross *in history* primarily to settle a *judicial debt* that had been contracted in history. The goal of the cross was only secondarily to restore a fallen cosmos, either in history or eternity. Adam's transition from grace to wrath (Gen. 3:6-7) preceded God's curse on Adam and the cosmos (Gen. 3:17-19), which was secondary to it; similarly, Jesus' crucifixion preceded His bodily resurrection and the beginning of the restoration of the cosmos. In short, keeping God the Father happy with man was of far greater importance than restoring the creation. But this does not negate the reality of that restoration, both in history and eternity. That restoration is as real as the original cursing of it by God in the garden.

I do not want to leave the impression that I regard the coming restoration of all things at the final judgment as merely equal in magnitude to God's original curse of the earth. It is far greater. But consider what this means. It is greater because *God's blessings are more fundamental than God's cusings*. His wrath is terrible; His grace is far greater. We must not argue for the equal ultimacy of grace and wrath, if by this we mean equal effect. They are equal in duration, not equal in effect. While most Christians say they believe this (presumably all Christians do believe it), they do not believe it *with respect to history*. They are inconsistent. This book is my attempt to restore consistency in their thinking.

The fundamental discontinuities in God's providential decree (including the post-resurrection world) are judicial-covenantal, not physical-cosmic. The modern evangelical Church does not really believe this, even though officially, most of its theologians would agree, if pressured to respond. But no one pressures them to respond. The issue never occurs to anyone. This is because the modern Church believes far more in the future *cosmic* discontinuity of the Second Coming of Christ than in the combined *historic and trans-historic* discontinuities of personal and then social transformation. The modern Church optimistically looks up far more often than it optimistically looks forward.

With this perspective in mind, consider the theme of this book: the relationship between God's historical sanctions and the biblical doctrine of the millennium.

1

ESCHATOLOGY AND THE MILLENNIUM

[W]hat is the future of the idea of progress? Any logical answer must be that the idea has no future whatever if we assume the indefinite, prolonged continuation of the kind of culture that has become almost universal in the West in the late twentieth century. If the roots are dying, as they would appear to be at the present time, how can there be shrub and foliage? But is this contemporary Western culture likely to continue for long? The answer, it seems to me, must be in the negative – if we take any stock in the lessons of the human past. . . . [N]ever in history have periods of culture such as our own lasted for very long. They are destroyed by all the forces which constitute their essence.

Robert Nisbet (1980)[1]

Nisbet's words serve as both a warning and a prophecy, although he has never been a big fan of secular prophets. He has too much faith in the unforseen and unforeseeable events of history to take seriously the doctrine of historical inevitability.[2] But he believes that the West is today facing a major crisis, and at the heart of this crisis is modern secular man's loss of faith in historical progress. The idea of progress has been at the heart of Western civilization, he believes: from the Greeks (a controversial assertion) to the present. Now this ancient faith is waning. The question is: Will it continue to wane? Where there is an *if*, there can be no inevitability. *If* this loss of faith continues, it will have terrible consequences for Western civilization. He

---

1. Robert Nisbet, *History of the Idea of Progress* (New York: Basic Books, 1980), pp. 355-56.

2. Nisbet, "The Year 2000 and All That," *Commentary* (June 1969).

does not believe that this loss of faith will continue, assuming that Western Civilization survives. But if it does persist, Western civilization as we know it today will not survive.

I think he is incorrect about the Greeks' commitment to the idea of historical progress, as I have explained elsewhere.[3] He is eminently correct with respect to the post-Reformation West. The fundamental ideas undergirding a doctrine of historical progress are these: (1) a sovereign predestinating agent who (or impersonal force that) guarantees the linearity of history (anti-cyclicalism); (2) cultural and social authority based on a representative's publicly acknowledged legitimacy, which in turn is derived from his (or their) access to (3) the wisdom revealed by the sovereign agent or force, meaning detailed knowledge of permanent standards of evaluation ("Progress compared to what?"); (4) culture-wide cause-and-effect relationships (challenge and successful response); and (5) compound growth over long periods of time (technical knowledge, tools, and the division of labor). If any one of these five premises is abandoned, the entire system collapses theoretically, and will therefore eventually collapse historically.[4] Today, all except linear history are being called into question. In short, point one – historical linearity – does not necessarily imply historical progress. There can be linearity downward into the void. Modern physical science, for example, points directly to such a decline.[5]

---

3. Gary North, *Moses and Pharaoh: Dominion Religion vs. Power Religion* (Tyler, Texas: Institute for Christian Economics, 1985), ch. 17. In many of his works, the Benedictine historian of science Stanley Jaki [YAHkee] has made the case far more persuasively than I have. Jaki has focused on the importance of the idea of linear history for the development of science, though not the idea of progress as such. See especially Jaki, *Science and Creation: From eternal cycles to an oscillating universe* (London: Scottish Academic Press, 1974).

4. This assertion of the unity of theory and practice is itself a fundamental aspect of Western social theory.

5. If scientists announce the discovery of physical evidence of a coming "big collapse" of the cosmos that will someday complement the "big bang" of creation, producing yet another "big bang," cyclicalism will receive a scientific shot in the arm. At present, few scientists believe that there is sufficient matter in the universe to produce a "big contraction." The linearity of history is therefore still presumed scientifically: the heat death of the universe (entropy's effect). This does not produce optimism; on the contrary, it affirms an ultimate cosmic pessimism. Gary North, *Is the World Running Down? Crisis in the Christian Worldview* (Tyler, Texas: Institute for Christian Economics, 1988), ch. 2.

It is not a controversial observation to say that the origin of the idea of progress in history was uniquely biblical.[6] This Christian concept was stolen and then secularized by Enlightenment thinkers in the seventeenth and eighteenth centuries.[7] They proclaimed another transcendental sovereign (or sovereigns) besides the biblical God to guarantee the linearity of mankind's history. They identified new enlightened representatives to replace the officers of existing churches and states. They found new law-orders and new sanctions in history. But most of them retained deep faith in historical continuity: the compound growth of mankind's knowledge and his tools of dominion.[8] What must be clearly understood is that the Enlightenment's idea of progress, like the Christian doctrine, involves far more than faith in the linearity of history.

Basic to the Christian idea of progress is not simply the idea of linear history (Augustinianism) – point one – but also the idea of a coming earthly millennium that is the product of actions in history: *human actions coupled with God's sanctions in history*. Without a very specific form of millennialism, namely, *covenantal postmillennialism*, there can be no *consistent* Christian idea of historical progress. What I hope to demonstrate in this book is that there are conflicting views of Christianity's millennial faith, and they produce rival views regarding progress. They also produce rival approaches to the question of social theory. The generally preferred approach is no approach at all.

General Eschatology

This book is an introductory study of the relationships among three ideas: millennialism, God's sanctions in history, and social theory. Everyone knows what sanctions are: rewards and punishments. But prior to about 1950, comparatively few secular scholars would have known what millennialism is, let alone how central it has been to the thinking of various late-medieval sects and Protestant Christianity since the end of the

6. It is this that Nisbet denies by attempting to trace the idea back to the Greeks.
7. Nisbet, "The Year 2000 and All That," *op. cit.*
8. An eighteenth-century exception was the skeptic, David Hume.

sixteenth century,[9] especially American Protestant evangelicals in the twentieth century. (One group that immediately acknowledged and praised this early European connection was the Communist movement.)[10] Slowly but surely, humanist scholars have begun to understand millennialism's importance. They have begun to document the fact that there have been significant relationships in Western history between millennial speculation and social change.[11] They are far more aware of these historical events than most Christians are.

Millennialism is a subset of eschatology. Eschatology is defined as "the doctrine of last things." It generally refers to the individual's death and final judgment: heaven and hell. It also deals with corporate final judgment at the end of time.

> When the Son of man shall come in his glory, and all the holy angels with him, then shall he sit upon the throne of his glory: And before him shall be gathered all nations: and he shall separate them one from another, as a shepherd divideth his sheep from the goats: And he shall set the sheep on his right hand, but the goats on the left. Then shall the King say unto them on his right hand, Come, ye blessed of my Father, inherit the kingdom prepared for you from the foundation of the world (Matt. 25:31-34).

The warning is clear: there are no second chances ahead.

---

9. Igor Shafarevich, *The Socialist Phenomenon* (New York: Harper & Row, [1975] 1980), ch. 2.

10. *Ibid.*, p. 214.

11. Ray C. Petry, *Christian Eschatology and Social Thought: A Historical Essay on the Social Implications of Some Selected Aspects in Christian Eschatology to A.D. 1500* (New York: Abingdon, 1956); Norman Cohn, *The Pursuit of the Millennium: Revolutionary messianism in medieval and Reformation Europe and its bearing on modern totalitarian movements* (2nd ed.; New York: Harper Torchbooks, 1961); Sylvia L. Thrupp (ed.), *Millennial Dreams in Action: Studies in Revolutionary Religious Movements* (New York: Schocken, 1970); Ernest Lee Tuveson, *Millennium and Utopia: A Study in the Background of the Idea of Progress* (New York: Harper Torchbooks, 1964); Bernard Capp, "The Political dimension of apocalyptic thought," in C. A. Patrides and Joseph Wittreich (eds.), *The Apocalypse in English Renaissance thought and literature* (Ithaca, New York: Cornell University Press, 1984); Ernest Lee Tuveson, *Redeemer Nation: The Idea of America's Millennial Role* (University of Chicago Press, 1968). On late nineteenth-century America, see Jean B. Quant, "Religion and Social Thought: The Secularization of Postmillennialism," *American Quarterly* (Oct. 1973); James H. Moorhead, "The Erosion of Postmillennialism in American Religious Thought, 1865-1925," *Church History* (March 1984).

There is no system of reincarnation or karma. "And as it is appointed unto men once to die, but after this the judgment" (Heb. 9:27). There is also no nothing ahead – no "soul sleep" or annihilation. Christianity preaches the fire next time.

> And I saw a great white throne, and him that sat on it, from whose face the earth and the heaven fled away; and there was found no place for them. And I saw the dead, small and great, stand before God; and the books were opened: and another book was opened, which is the book of life: and the dead were judged out of those things which were written in the books, according to their works. And the sea gave up the dead which were in it; and death and hell delivered up the dead which were in them: and they were judged every man according to their works. And death and hell were cast into the lake of fire. This is the second death. And whosoever was not found written in the book of life was cast into the lake of fire (Rev. 20:11-15).

The eschatological questions of death, final judgment, and eternity have been generally agreed upon throughout Church history. The familiar creeds, East and West, mention some version of these phrases: ". . . from whence He will come to judge the quick [living] and the dead," and ". . . the resurrection of the dead and the life everlasting." In this sense, general eschatology does not serve as a major differentiating factor in Church history. Millennialism does.

Millennialism Defined

It is this narrower eschatological topic that has received increased interest by historians. It has also become the focus of interest for modern evangelicals. Eschatology proper – death, final judgment, and eternity – is of less interest to secular scholars than millennialism is. It is also of little interest to evangelicals today, since they assume that their personal eternity is secured. The "hot topic" today is millennialism, not the far hotter and more permanent topic of the lake of fire.

There are three basic views of a millennial era of blessings: premillennialism, amillennialism, and postmillennialism. (The premillennial dispensational view is sometimes considered a fourth view.)[12] They are three completely irreconcilable viewpoints. Nevertheless, they overlap in curious ways.

Premillennialism

The premillennial view teaches that Jesus Christ will return to earth in history to set up a visible kingdom that will last one thousand years. Then will come the final judgment. This is a literal interpretation of the prophecy in Revelation 20:

> And I saw an angel come down from heaven, having the key of the bottomless pit and a great chain in his hand. And he laid hold on the dragon, that old serpent, which is the Devil, and Satan, and bound him a thousand years, And cast him into the bottomless pit, and shut him up, and set a seal upon him, that he should deceive the nations no more, till the thousand years should be fulfilled: and after that he must be loosed a little season (Rev. 20:1-3).

Premillennialism has had a checkered history. It has been called *chiliasm*, from the plural of the Greek work for thousand: *chilia*. Many people in the early Church held this position, but Augustine rejected it. So did the major Protestant reformers. Most evangelicals today are premillennialists.

A variant of premillennialism, called dispensationalism, is dominant in modern fundamentalism, and has been since the late nineteenth century. This viewpoint was first developed sometime around 1830.[13] It focuses its attention today on a coming Great Tribulation for the state of Israel which will begin seven years before Christ returns to set up His earthly millennial kingdom.[14] Most dispensationalists are pre-tribulational. This pre-tribulational eschatology teaches that Christians will be

---

12. Robert G. Clouse (ed.), *The Meaning of the Millennium: Four Views* (Downers Grove, Illinois: InterVarsity Press, 1977); Millard J. Erickson, *Contemporary Options in Eschatology: A Study of the Millennium* (Grand Rapids, Michigan: Baker, 1977).

13. Clarence B. Bass, *Backgrounds to Dispensationalism: Its Historical Genesis and Ecclesiastical Implications* (Grand Rapids, Michigan: Eerdmans, 1960); C. Norman Kraus, *Dispensationalism in America: Its Rise and Development* (Richmond, Virginia: John Knox Press, 1958); Dave MacPherson, *The Great Rapture Hoax* (Fletcher, North Carolina: New Puritan Library, 1983).

14. Hal Lindsey, *The Late Great Planet Earth* (New York: Bantam, [1970]).

"Raptured" secretly (!) out of the world to heaven seven years before Jesus returns to establish His visible kingdom on earth. As soon as the Church is gone, the seven years of the Great Tribulation for Israel will begin. There are also mid-tribulational and post-tribulational dispensationalists, but their numbers have always been few.[15]

The main eschatological hope of most dispensationalists has been the coming Rapture ("caught up"), when Christians will be removed bodily from the growing crises of history. They believe that Christians will be spared the miseries of Armageddon. Christians who live until the Rapture will get out of life alive.

Amillennialism

Amillennialism is commonly believed to have been the dominant millennial viewpoint in Western Christendom since the beginning of the Middle Ages.[16] It interprets the prophesied one thousand years of Revelation 20 as symbolic of the whole Christian era. The millennial kingdom of God is spiritual, yet not entirely spiritual, for it includes Christian families and orthodox churches. It will never attain dominance in cultural or political matters, however. The city of man and the city of God are always distinct. There will be no meaningful progress in history, except for ecclesiastical progress. This limited form of progress will not be accompanied by a widespread acceptance of the gospel. There will, if anything, be an increasing rejection of the gospel over time. There will at best be improvement in Christian creeds, Church order, and family government. This view is held by Roman Catholics, Lutherans, and modern Continental (Dutch) Calvinists on both sides of the Atlantic.

Both Augustine and Calvin have reputations as having been amillennialists. That Augustine was basically postmillennial in his perspective was not clear to those who followed him, nor to modern historians. The influence of his less millennially focused

---

15. Richard Reiter, *et al.*, *The Rapture: Pre-, Mid-, or Post-Tribulational?* (Grand Rapids, Michigan: Zondervan Academie, 1984).

16. Whether Charlemagne and Pope Gregory VII believed it is a question worth investigating.

City of God has been so overwhelming that his earlier writings, especially his six volumes of commentaries on the Psalms, have been neglected. It is in his exposition of Psalm 110 that we see his vision of world dominion by Christians. His less precise, more symbolic references to time and eschatology in *City of God* prevailed in Western Christianity throughout the medieval period. Calvin's writings suffer from a similar ambiguity. There are both postmillennial and amillennial passages in his writings, but the influence of the *Institutes of the Christian Religion*, which is comprehensive but less detailed on matters of eschatology, has led even the Calvinists to neglect his Bible commentaries and other theological works in which his historic optimism is readily apparent.[17]

Postmillennialism

Postmillennialism has features of both premillennialism and amillennialism. It shares with amillennialism a commitment to historical continuity. Both views insist that Jesus will not return to earth physically to establish a millennial kingdom. It shares with premillennialism a commitment to the earthly fulfillment of many of the Old Testament's kingdom prophecies. Postmillennialism's hermeneutic (principles of biblical interpretation) is neither exclusively literalistic nor exclusively symbolic. (For that matter, this is also true of dispensationalism's hermeneutic; it only appears to be literalistic.)[18]

Postmillennialism had its greatest historical impact from the early Puritan era through the North American religious revival known as the First Great Awakening (1735-55).[19] It dominated conservative American Presbyterian theology, North and South,

---

17. Gary North, "The Economic Thought of Luther and Calvin," *Journal of Christian Reconstruction*, II (Summer 1975), pp. 104-6. Greg L. Bahnsen has catalogued many of Calvin's postmillennial statements: Bahnsen, "The *Prima Facie* Acceptability of Postmillennialism," *ibid.*, III (Winter 1976-77), pp. 69-76.

18. Kenneth L. Gentry, Jr., "Consistent Literalism Tested," *Dispensationalism in Transition*, III (Sept. 1990), published by the Institute for Christian Economics.

19. Symposium on Puritanism and Progress, *Journal of Christian Reconstruction*, VI (Summer 1978); Iain Murray, *The Puritan Hope: Revival and the Interpretation of Prophecy* (London: Banner of Truth Trust, 1971).

during the nineteenth century.[20] It faded in popularity during the First World War. It has begun to revive within Calvinist circles since the early 1970's as a result of the U.S.-based Christian Reconstruction movement (social neo-Puritanism) and the British-based Banner of Truth publishing organization (pietistic neo-Puritanism). It is presently gaining a toehold in American charismatic circles, primarily as a result of David Chilton's *Paradise Restored*.[21]

Like amillennialists, postmillennialists interpret symbolically the one thousand years of Satan's bondage, with "millennial" referring to the entire era between the ascension of the resurrected Christ to heaven and the final judgment. Yet, like the premillennialists, some (though not all) postmillennialists also take the one thousand years literally: a unique era of spiritual and cultural blessings within the overall millennial era, blessings which God will grant because of massive, worldwide conversions to faith in Christ as Savior and Lord. The basic postmillennial point is this: *there will be a long era of earthly millennial blessings in the future*. Jesus will return bodily to judge the world postmillennially: after the era of millennial blessings is over.

A key passage for postmillennialism is Paul's citation of Psalm 110. Psalm 110 reads: "The LORD said unto my Lord, Sit thou at my right hand, until I make thine enemies thy footstool. The LORD shall send the rod of thy strength out of Zion: rule thou in the midst of thine enemies" (Psa. 110:1-2). Paul writes:

> For as in Adam all die, even so in Christ shall all be made alive. But every man in his own order: Christ the firstfruits; afterward they that are Christ's at his coming. Then cometh the end, when he shall have delivered up the kingdom to God, even the Father; when he shall have put down all rule and all authority and power. For he must reign, till he hath put all enemies under his feet. The last enemy that shall be destroyed is death (I Cor. 15:22-26).

---

20. Princeton Theological Seminary, the bastion of conservative Presbyterianism, was overwhelmingly postmillennial: J. A. Alexander, Charles Hodge, his son A. A. Hodge, and B. B. Warfield. See also James B. Jordan, "A Survey of Southern Presbyterian Millennial Views Before 1930," *Journal of Christian Reconstruction*, III (Winter 1976-77).

21. David Chilton, *Paradise Restored: A Biblical Theology of Dominion* (Ft. Worth, Texas: Dominion Press, 1985).

Postmillennialism is divided into two camps: pietistic postmillennialists and covenantal postmillennialists. The former view is the postmillennialism of Augustine, Jonathan Edwards, eighteenth- and nineteenth-century revivalism, and late nineteenth-century American Presbyterianism. It is not tied to a specific view of law and society.[22] Covenantal postmillennialism is the postmillennialism of the New England Puritans and the modern Christian Reconstruction movement. It defends the continuing authority of biblical law and its cultural and civil sanctions. It sees the expansion of God's kingdom in history as an outworking of widespread conversions to saving faith in Jesus Christ, coupled with an extension of the Old Testament civil case laws.[23] It proclaims a kingdom established by God in history, but *judicially and representatively*: through saving faith.

The Millennium: Discontinuity

Millennialism for contemporary evangelical Christians is a topic of great personal interest but of little social interest. In fact, the more seriously the two ecclesiastically dominant forms of millennialism are taken, the less seriously both social theory and social activism are taken. This is the thesis of this book.

Premillennialism

The dispensational, premillennial Christian, living (as Timothy Weber has put it) in the shadow of the Second Coming,[24] is able to persuade himself that he is not necessarily going to die; he could soon be "Raptured" to heaven, and surely will be Raptured before Armageddon occurs, according to Scripture. Thus, the closer Armageddon appears to draw near, the more certain is the imminence of the Christian's "blessed hope": the Rapture. The worse the newspaper headlines, the brighter the outlook of the dispensationalist. Bad news means that "Jesus

22. See Chapter 10: "Pietistic Postmillennialism."

23. Gary North, *Tools of Dominion: The Case Laws of Exodus* (Tyler, Texas: Institute for Christian Economics, 1990).

24. Timothy P. Weber, *Living in the Shadow of the Second Coming: American Premillennialism, 1875-1925* (New York: Oxford University Press, 1979).

must be coming soon." The escape hatch from history looms!

The dispensationalist is convinced that escalating social problems are signs of the approaching conflagration, so they will soon no longer be his problems. The more complex and seemingly unsolvable the problems are, the less interest the dispensational, premillennial Christian has in solving them. A world of unsolvable problems is a world that is clearly speeding to the day of release for Christians: the "secret" Rapture into the world beyond the clouds.

The blessed hope for premillennial Christians is their personal ability to escape the cynical reality of the old slogan, "Nobody gets out of life alive." They also want to overcome that other dilemma: "Everybody wants to go to heaven, but nobody wants to die." Premillennial, pre-tribulational dispensationalism's doctrine of the "any moment" Rapture – the Church's literal lifting up to heaven, an event which has no intervening Bible prophecies remaining to be fulfilled – and historic premillennialism's doctrine of the Second Coming of Christ to set up His earthly kingdom immediately (without a subsequent seven-year Great Tribulation on earth) are both manifestations of a psychological quest to escape the universal negative sanction of physical death. But more than this: *they are both manifestations of a desire to escape personal and corporate responsibility in an increasingly complex and threatening world.*

Amillennialism

Amillennial Christians share this same motivation. They, too, teach a version of the doctrine of the "any moment" Second Coming of Christ. No prophecy remains to be fulfilled between this moment and the Church's cosmic deliverance. Unlike the premillennialists, amillennialists believe that there will be no millennial era of earthly blessings; Christ will come at the final judgment. But there is no fundamental difference between them with respect to *the cosmic, discontinuous nature of their hoped-for deliverance*. Amillennial Christians hope and pray that history will end soon, and in the meantime, they, like their dispensational brethren, remain inside what are effectively psychological and institutional ghettos.[25]

As residents of psychological and institutional ghettos, few American evangelical Christians have any self-conscious interest in social theory, although they almost intuitively adopt certain traditional views about society. They have adopted what is sometimes called the American civil religion.[26] It is based on concepts of natural law and political pluralism. This civil religion is self-consciously neutral with respect to specific religious confessions. No one is asked to believe in God in order to participate in politics, or even to swear in a court of law.

This traditional social outlook is strongly reinforced by the prevailing views of the millennium. American Christians' very lack of interest in social theory, like the views of society which they almost intuitively hold, is a direct result of the exegetically opposed yet socially similar eschatologies that they hold dear: premillennialism and amillennialism. Both views lead to a denial of the possibility, or at least the relevance, of social theory.

The Millennium: Continuity

The acceptance of the general Christian eschatological view regarding death and resurrection has consequences for one's view of time: linear rather than cyclical. This has been evident throughout Western history. But eschatology is more than personal death and resurrection. It also raises the question of progress. This is especially true of the doctrine of the earthly millennium. This has become a major dividing issue among

---

25. Christian Reformed Church theologian and Westminster Theological Seminary president R. B. Kuiper warned his fellow Dutch-Americans: "By this time it has become trite to say that we must come out of our isolation. . . . Far too often, let it be said again, we hide our light under a bushel instead of placing it high on a candlestick. We seem not to realize fully that as the salt of the earth we can perform our functions of seasoning and preserving only through contact." R. B. Kuiper, *To Be or Not to Be Reformed: Whither the Christian Reformed Church?* (Grand Rapids, Michigan, Zondervan, 1959), p. 186.

26. Russell E. Richey and Donald G. Jones (eds.), *American Civil Religion* (New York: Harper & Row, 1974). See also Sidney E. Mead, *The Lively Experiment: The Shaping of Christianity in America* (New York: Harper & Row, 1963); Robert N. Bellah, *The Broken Covenant: American Civil Religion in Time of Trial* (New York: Seabury Crossroad, 1975). For a warning, see Herbert Schlossberg, *Idols for Destruction: Christian Faith and Its Confrontation with American Society* (Washington, D.C.: Regnery Gateway, [1983] 1990), pp. 250-59.

Christians. It literally defines some Christian groups; their members see their life's work in terms of a millennial theory.

Amillennialism

In the West, speculation regarding the earthly millennium was for centuries considered controversial and unproductive. Ever since Augustine switched from premillennialism to a non-apocalyptic view of the future,[27] the Church, both East and West, has tended to downplay millennial speculation. Such speculation has long been seen by the Roman Church as leading to mischievous consequences, especially the phenomenon that is usually derided as "enthusiasm," meaning emotionalism, the creation of new independent sects, and even social revolution.[28] This opinion has been shared by Lutherans, Anglicans, and other churches.

Because of this official ecclesiastical and academic hostility to millennial speculation, people in the pews have historically been more concerned about the personal and eternal side of eschatology and less interested in the various *institutional and judicial continuities* that relate today's events and historical processes to a future millennium and then to the end of time. Heaven rather than history has been the focus of concern. Personal ethics rather than social ethics has been regarded as primary. Liturgy has been regarded as vastly more important than social action. How one prays in public has been regarded as more important than how or where one works.

Postmillennialism

The postmillennialist sees the history of the Church as a progressive, continuous application of the Great Commission and its cultural implications. It views evangelism as more than the mere sharing of the message of personal salvation. It sees history as the progressive *discipling* of humanity. It teaches that

---

27. ". . . I myself, too, once held this opinion." Augustine, *City of God*, XX:7 (Modern Library edition), p. 719.

28. Ronald Knox, *Enthusiasm: A Chapter in the History of Religion* (New York: Oxford University Press, 1950).

Jesus Christ gave His Church a *corporate* assignment in history: the Great Commission.

> And Jesus came and spake unto them, saying, All power is given unto me in heaven and in earth. Go ye therefore, and teach all nations, baptizing them in the name of the Father, and of the Son, and of the Holy Ghost: Teaching them to observe all things whatsoever I have commanded you: and, lo, I am with you alway, even unto the end of the world. Amen (Matt. 28:18-20).

If this international discipling of the nations must be completed prior to the Second Coming of Christ – a denial of the "any moment" Second Coming – then this raises an inevitable question: *"What is the specific nature of the work that has been assigned to the saints by God?"* Second, is this task exclusively one of soul-saving or is it also to become culture-transforming? If the answer to the second question is "the latter," as this book argues that it is,[29] this raises a number of specific problems for philosophers, strategists, and leaders in the Church, such as: "What kind of social order is explicitly Christian?" "What personal and institutional efforts are legitimate in achieving these ends?" "How comprehensive is the lawful authority of the institutional Church in pursuing its goals?"

Theologians have seldom devoted much time or energy to answering these questions. From time to time, however, Western society has been swept by great waves of new eschatological speculation about the necessary earthly preparations for the coming millennium, and these periods have been noted by the uprooting of existing conventions and institutions.

The Idea of Progress

The question of continuity between the present and a future earthly millennium inevitably raises the question of historical progress. Is there meaningful progress in history? No one living in the modern world denies some kind of progress, unless he

---

29. See also Kenneth L. Gentry, Jr., *The Greatness of the Great Commission: The Christian Enterprise in a Fallen World* (Tyler, Texas: Institute for Christian Economics, 1990).

has adopted some version of Hinduism's doctrine of *maya*: the illusion of material reality. Very few of us want to return to a pre-industrial world without the basic amenities of civilization: anesthetics, electricity, telecommunications, air conditioning, and rapid transportation.

But is technological-economic progress really meaningful? Do scientific inventions change the nature of man? Does per capita economic growth change the fundamental questions of death, judgment, and eternity? Christians know the answer: *no*. So, when pressed regarding the reality of historical progress, most Christians return to the broader issue of eschatology and away from the millennium. They will explain their denial of historical progress by an appeal to the unchanging issues of general eschatology. But this shift from narrow millennialism to general eschatology is deceptive. In reality, they still cling to a particular view of the Second Coming of Christ. Most Christians presume the absence of spiritual (and therefore meaningful) progress in history because most Christians have a discontinuous view of the Second Coming of Christ. This victorious, visible coming from on high supposedly will not be influenced by the prior success of Christians in applying God's law to historical circumstances. Premillennialists and amillennialists deny that there will be this kind of cultural success prior to Christ's Second Coming: either at the beginning of the millennium (premillennialism) or at the end of history (amillennialism).

They will admit to ecclesiastical progress. Ask Christians if there has been progress in revising the creeds, and they will say yes, unless they are either Greek Orthodox, who deny the legitimacy of post-medieval creeds, or members of some Anabaptist sect that denies the legitimacy of creeds altogether. But most Christians assume that creedal improvement affects only the institutional Church, not society at large. Creedal progress is not seen even as an aspect of social progress, let alone a contributing cause. This presumes a fundamental relationship in history: *the social irrelevance of the historic Christian creeds*. It presumes that there is no continuity between the Church's creeds and civilization. Yet it is this which must be proven first, not presumed. It is Christian Reconstruction's contention that *there can be no civilization without a creed.*[30] Creeds are therefore inescapable concepts. It is never a question of "creed vs. no creed." It is always this question: "Which creed?"

Creeds have consequences. Christian creeds include certain presuppositions about law, judicial cause and effect, and time. These views may be more implicit than explicit, but they exist.

Conclusion

The idea of eschatology is fundamental to Christianity and therefore to Western history. So is millennialism. Modern secular historians understand this far better than Christians do. But eschatology in the broadest sense is not a significant differentiating doctrine within Christianity. It is the far narrower idea of millennialism that is differentiating – in fact, highly divisive.

In most eras in Western history, millennialism has not been emphasized. This was especially true in the early medieval era, A.D. 500-1000.[31] But emphasized or not, a particular view of the millennium will become dominant within any particular Christian denomination or culture. In principle, there cannot be eschatological neutrality, meaning millennial neutrality, any more than there can be neutrality in any other area of life. There can be personal indifference or ignorance, but there cannot bc neutrality. Everything is under the decree of God, and God is not neutral. When we identify an inescapable concept, any assertion of neutrality is deceptive: either deliberate deception or self-deception. Millennialism is an inescapable concept. It therefore has consequences. These consequences include the formation of attitudes toward the development of social theory.

The main dividing issues are these: historical continuity vs. discontinuity; the role of biblical law in extending God's earthly kingdom; the role of God's sanctions in history; the role of the Holy Spirit in history; and the limits of the Great Commission.

---

30. R. J. Rushdoony, *Foundations of Social Order: Studies in the Creeds and Councils of the Early Church* (Fairfax, Virginia: Thoburn Press, [1968] 1978).

31. In a book of over 400 pages, Petry devotes fewer than ten pages to early medieval eschatology, A.D. 500 to 1000. The individuals he cites are for the most part minor figures in Church history. Petry, *Christian Eschatology and Social Thought*, pp. 114-20.

Secondarily, there is the issue of time remaining before Jesus returns bodily to earth. While neither premillennialism nor amillennialism teaches a specific timetable regarding the return of Christ to earth, their adherents generally believe that time remaining is very short.[32] Their cultural battle cry is this: "Come quickly, Lord Jesus." The postmillennialists' cry is this: "Come quickly, but only after your Church has achieved its role in fulfilling the Great Commission." The differences between the two battle cries are enormous. The first is either a call to retreat from most of the battlefields of life, or else a call to launch a kamikaze-type attack against the prevailing humanist culture. The second is a call to historical victory. The first tends to dissuade its adherents from producing detailed social theories. The second may or may not, depending on the adherents' view of law and historical sanctions.

32. The doctrine of the "any-moment coming" of Christ officially precludes our identification of any contemporary event as a fulfillment of prophecy. Nonetheless, dispensationalists througout the twentieth century have identified contemporary events as fufilled prophecies. See Dwight Wilson, *Armaggeddon Now! The Premillennarian Response to Russia and Israel Since 1917* (Grand Rapids, Michigan: Baker, 1977).

2

WHAT IS SOCIAL THEORY?

Christianity has often been accused of being too "otherworldly" in that it has failed to offer viable political, economic, judicial, and social programs for the world order. The teaching of Jesus that his kingdom "is not of this world" has been interpreted to mean that earthly life must merely be endured, and that Christians cannot expect to accomplish lasting reform before the return of Christ. But does the New Testament really offer no guidance for shaping political or economic policy? Does it contain no judicial or social precepts that may be applied in today's societies? True, neither Jesus nor Paul spoke in detail of political or economic ideologies. But since both spoke out of a Jewish background and context, direct allusions may have been unnecessary. Christians must understand that their faith is rooted in Old Testament Judaism and that the Mosaic Covenant and Law (which contain highly specific political, economic, and social precepts) can give guidance even today.

Larry Postan (1990)[1]

Mr. Postan is not a well-known author, but his assessment of the theological problem is correct. His topic is the growth of Islam and the reasons for it. He is a professor of missions at Nyack College. He is concerned about the weakness of gospel efforts in the face of worldwide successes in direct evangelism by Islam. He sees a major flaw in contemporary Christian evangelism that is leaving it vulnerable to the counter-claims of Islam. The average age of each convert to Islam is 31; in contrast, the average age of Christian converts is 16. This is significant. As he says, "for every year the non-Christian grows older than 25, the odds increase exponentially against his or her ever becoming a

1. Larry Postan, "The Adult Gospel," *Christianity Today* (April 20, 1990), p. 25.

Christian."[2] What we need, he says, is an adult gospel.

He lists five reasons why Westerners choose Islam over Christianity. The fourth is important for this chapter.

> Fourth, Islam is practical. It is considered a this-worldly religion in contrast to Christianity, which is perceived as abstract to the extreme. Muhammed left his followers a political, social, moral, and economic program founded on religious precepts. Jesus, however, is said to have advocated no such program; it is claimed that the New Testament is so preoccupied with his imminent return that it is impractical for modern life.[3]

I wrote in the Preface that my concern is evangelism. The typical fundamentalist response is this: "If your concern is with evangelism, why are you wasting your time writing about social theory? What has economics got to do with evangelism?" That depends. If you are evangelizing children, not very much, at least not directly. But what if you are evangelizing adults? Then such things matter a great deal. If they do not matter on the front end of the gospel presentation, they matter on the back end, when the person asks: "Now what am I required by God to do?" If the evangelist's answer is, "Pass out gospel tracts," it is far too limited an answer. God requires a great deal more.

Only for those adult Christians who want to continue to live as children does the message of contemporary pietism have a strong appeal. Sadly, their name is legion. They have defined Christian evangelism too narrowly. They have defined it in terms of their immediate emotional needs, not in terms of the biblical doctrine of God's comprehensive redemption. They have not understood true biblical evangelism: *personal regeneration leading to social transformation*. To begin to understand biblical evangelism, we should begin with Moses' words to the generation that was about to conquer the land of Canaan.

> Behold, I have taught you statutes and judgments, even as the LORD my God commanded me, that ye should do so in the land

2. *Ibid.*, p. 24.
3. *Idem.*

> whither ye go to possess it. Keep therefore and do them; for this is your wisdom and your understanding in the sight of the nations, which shall hear all these statutes, and say, Surely this great nation is a wise and understanding people. For what nation is there so great, who hath God so nigh unto them, as the LORD our God is in all things that we call upon him for? And what nation is there so great, that hath statutes and judgments so righteous as all this law, which I set before you this day? Only take heed to thyself, and keep thy soul diligently, lest thou forget the things which thine eyes have seen, and lest they depart from thy heart all the days of thy life: but teach them thy sons, and thy sons' sons; Specially the day that thou stoodest before the LORD thy God in Horeb, when the LORD said unto me, Gather me the people together, and I will make them hear my words, that they may learn to fear me all the days that they shall live upon the earth, and that they may teach their children (Deut. 4:5-10).

Evangelism is comprehensive. It must produce positive fruits. These fruits are not merely personal. Like the Queen of Sheba who journeyed to Israel because of Solomon's legendary abilities as a civil judge, so are other non-believers expected to see and praise God's social laws because of their visible results.

This view of evangelism is hated by the vast majority of those who call themselves Christians. It is ridiculed as if it were some sort of rejection of the Bible. Writes Peter Masters, heir of Spurgeon's pulpit at the Metropolitan Tabernacle in London: "Reconstructionists teach that the great commission of Christ to His disciples goes beyond the work of evangelism. In their view it includes this quest for the social-political dominion of the world; the persuading of all nations to submit to the rule of Israel's ancient laws."[4] At least he was kind enough and precise enough to use the word, "persuading," rather that "forcing," etc.

Notice his phrase, "beyond the work of evangelism." Into this brief phrase is packed an entire worldview, the worldview of Christian pietism. Evangelism is narrow, he presumes. To discuss men's requirements to obey the laws set forth in the Old Testament is necessarily to discuss social transformation. These laws deal with all aspects of society.[5] In Masters' view, all such

4. Masters, "World Dominion: The High Ambition of Reconstructionism," *Sword & Trowel* (May 24, 1990), p. 13.

5. R. J. Rushdoony, *The Institutes of Biblical Law* (Nutley, New Jersey: Craig Press,

discussions are peripheral to evangelism. If pursued in detail, they become obstructions to evangelism, he and all pietists believe. But social theory is only possible if men are willing to pursue such questions in great detail. This is why pietism, with its narrow definition of evangelism, is hostile to social theory.

Defining Social Theory

Social theory is more difficult to define than is eschatology. Social theory is the view that men adopt to explain how society operates, or better yet, how it holds together. It is the question of the nature of *the social bond*.[6] Every social theory must offer answers to at least five fundamental questions: (1) What provides legitimacy to any given institution or complex system of institutions? (2) What system of authority binds people and institutions together in their cooperative ventures? (What do we mean by "institution"?) (3) What are the rules and regulations of the social bond, and how are they discovered and applied to specific cases in history? (4) What are the sanctions that individuals and institutions legitimately bring against deviants and outsiders? (5) What is the view of time (continuity) that binds men and institutions to both the past and the future?

Point five is the issue of eschatology. Man's past, present, and future are covenantally intertwined. Christianity has always affirmed the linearity of history: creation, fall, redemption, and the final judgment. Western Christianity, especially Puritanism, has at times also affirmed the possibility of progress within this linear temporal process: history can be "linear upward." The widespread public acceptance in the West of the twin concepts of scientific progress and economic growth was closely related to the spread of Puritan postmillennial eschatology.

It was a secularized version of this Puritan vision of progress that was adopted by Enlightenment humanism: progress without God's sovereignty, authority, law, historical sanctions, or final judgment. The past was seen as being pregnant with the future.

1973).

6. *The Social Bond* was Nisbet's choice for the title of his textbook on sociology (New York: Knopf, 1970).

This humanist vision is now fading. Nisbet is probably correct regarding the cause of the late twentieth century's loss of faith in progress: "There is by now no single influence greater in negative impact upon the idea of progress than our far-flung and relentless jettisoning of the past."[7] The humanists also failed to understand why disrespect for the past would lead to loss of faith in the present: *we are all becoming part of the past*. We, too, will be jettisoned by future generations. Our works and dreams will be cast out of future men's thinking. We will be consigned, as Communist Leon Trotsky put it, to the ash can of history. So, what kind of commitment to such future ingrates can modern man be expected to reveal? Very little. Millions of people today are increasingly ready to abort the future, as well abort the yet unborn who would otherwise become the future.[8] Western society has become increasingly present-oriented, with fateful consequences for Western culture. Present-orientation is a denial of the very foundations of Western culture: respect for the past and faith in the future.

The Three Views of Society

There are three, and only three, fundamental views of the underlying nature of the social bond. Each of them reflects a particular view of the cosmos, which in turn undergirds the particular view of society. These views are organicism, contractualism, and covenantalism. The first two have been dominant in Western philosophy and social thought. The third, being uniquely biblical, has been ignored.

Organicism. This is by far the most widespread view in man's history, though not in the modern West. Society is viewed as an

---

7. Robert Nisbet, *History of the Idea of Progress* (New York: Basic Books, 1980), p. 323.

8. I realize that there is a counter-tendency in the ecology movement: to preserve the environment for future generations. The implicit motto of many in this diffuse movement is this: "Save baby seals, not unborn humans!" First, this attitude is anti-human. It is a commitment to an animist Mother Nature rather than to God's environment, including people made in His image. Second, it is a call to stop economic growth, which raises many questions and emotional commitments besides a mere commitment to future generations. There can be present-oriented hidden agendas wrapped securely in the call to save the earth for future generations.

organism, just as the cosmos is: a growing thing that has the characteristic features of life. The model institution of the organic society is the family, which is closely associated with physical birth, cultural and physical nurturing, and death. This organic view of society is often associated with the concept of a hierarchical chain of being that links God, man, and the cosmos.[9] It is also associated with magic and with magic's fundamental principle: "As above, so below." Man supposedly can manipulate any aspect of the cosmos (macrocosm) by manipulating representative features (microcosm). The crudest manifestation of this philosophy is the voodoo doll. Philosophically, this view of society is associated with *realism*: an underlying metaphysical unity transcendent to mere individuals. Organicism is divided into two major historical streams: familism (medieval) and statism (Greco-Roman).[10]

Contractualism. This is the dominant view of the modern world, although its philosophical roots go back to the Middle Ages (e.g., William of Occam). Society is based either on a hypothetical original contract among men in pre-historic times or on a constitution of some kind. The primary model is the State, not the family, although in some modern social philosophies, the free market is the model. The familiar phrase associated with this outlook is "the social contract." Men in the distant past voluntarily transferred their individually held political sovereignty to the State, which now maintains social order. Each social institution is governed by the terms of an original contract, whether mythical or historical. The social bond is based exclusively on voluntary legal contracts, hypothetical or historical, among individuals. Philosophically, this view of society is associated with *nominalism*: the denial of any underlying metaphysical reality or transcendent social unity apart from the thoughts and decisions of individual men. Contractualism is

9. Arthur O. Lovejoy, *The Great Chain of Being: A Study of the History of an Idea* (Cambridge, Massachusetts: Harvard University Press, [1936]).

10. In English political thought, the archetype organic treatise is Robert Filmer's defense of patriarchal-monarchical absolutism, *Patriarcha* (1680). It was important primarily because it called forth John Locke's response, *First Treatise of Civil Government* (1690): contractualism.

divided into two major historical streams: individualism (right-wing Enlightenment)[11] and collectivism (left-wing Enlightenment).[12] The former is evolutionary in its view of society; the later is more revolutionary.

Covenantalism. This is not a fusion of organicism and contractualism; it is a separate system. It views society as a complex system of legal bonds, with God as the ultimate Enforcer of these covenants and contracts. There are only four covenants: personal (God and the individual); ecclesiastical (sacramental), familial, and civil. These final three are monopoly institutions founded directly under God's explicit sovereignty. Covenants alone are lawfully established by a *self-maledictory oath* under God. The oath-taker calls down God's wrath upon himself if he ever violates the stipulations (laws) of the covenant document. All other relationships are either personal (e.g., friendship) or contractual (e.g., a legal business arrangement). God is the final Judge because He is the Creator, and He brings His judgments, in time and eternity, in terms of His permanent ethical standards (i.e., biblical law).

Covenantalism has developed no separate philosophical tradition in Western history, for Christian philosophers, including those interested in society, prior to Cornelius Van Til (1885-1988) virtually always adopted in the name of Christ some version of either realism or nominalism.[13] The biblical covenant model is based on *creationism*, not realism or nominalism. This philosophy asserts an absolute separation of being between God and any aspect of the creation: *the Creator-creature distinction*. This concept, so fundamental to Van Til's philosophy, categorically denies the existence of a chain of being linking God to the cosmos (realism). Creationism leads to providentialism, which affirms the absolute authority of God and His sovereign control over all things in history (i.e., His decree), thereby denying the

11. For example, John Locke, Adam Smith, Edmund Burke.

12. For example, Jean Jacques Rousseau, Karl Marx, V. I. Lenin.

13. There is really only one major figure in the history of modern political theory who affirmed the covenantal position: Johannes Althusius. See *The Politics of Johannes Althusius*, translated and edited by Frederick S. Carney (London: Eyre & Spottiswoode, [1603] 1964). John of Salisbury (12th century) was to some extent a covenantalist.

autonomous power of man to name any aspect of the cosmos authoritatively (nominalism). Covenantalism is a separate philosophical system.

Historical Sanctions and Millennial Eschatology

As I hope to show in this book, there is more to social theory than eschatology. There are all five aspects of the social bond. A comprehensive study of social theory would have to include all five. I have decided, however, to limit my discussion primarily to millennial eschatology and sanctions, meaning the idea of sanctions *in history* – sanctions imposed by God and governed by specific moral and legal standards. I could also have discussed sovereignty, hierarchy (authority), and law, but the great dividing lines within Christianity today are associated with sanctions and the historical result of these sanctions: millennialism. Here is where the great debate occurs. Christians generally agree with each other on the idea of the sovereignty of God, although the Calvinists are the "hard-liners" on this subject: the absolute sovereignty of God and the non-autonomy of man. Christians also agree that there must be hierarchies in life, although they tend to adopt the family as their model rather than the Church, since there is more agreement today regarding the proper structure of the family. (This structure of the Christian family has changed many times in the past, but each era seems to think that the present structure is *the* biblical model.) The churches do verbally agree that Christians must obey God's moral law, a concept left judiciously and judicially undefined.

But why single out ("double out"?) historical sanctions and millennialism? Because the debate over law would be too complex. Which laws? Natural laws? Old Testament laws? Which natural or Old Testament laws? How interpreted? How applied today? Few Christians have seriously thought about law and society in our era, and the seventeenth-century debates over law (casuistry) have faded from most Christians' consciousness.[14]

---

14. On the history of casuistry in general, see Kenneth E. Kirk, *Conscience and Its Problems: An Introduction to Casuistry* (rev. ed.; London: Longmans, Green, 1948). See also Thomas Wood, *English Casuistical Divinity in the Seventeenth Century* (London: S.P.C.K.,

They have no strong opinions regarding the proper legal (i.e., covenantal) foundation of society. They do have very strong opinions on God's historical sanctions and the millennium, and this has deeply affected their intuitively held views of society. Before exploring the question of sanctions and eschatology, however, we must first consider very briefly the question of law.

A Question of Law

Prior to the Newtonian intellectual revolution, all but a handful of Christians had adopted some version of medieval natural law theory, what we can call *organic natural law theory* (realism).[15] This version of natural law was based on the medieval Roman Catholic concept of a chain of being linking God and man. This medieval theory's roots were in Stoic natural law theory, in turn derived from Greek speculative thought.[16] The mind of man was seen as autonomous to some degree from God, the Bible, and the Church. Baptism, the celebration of the mass, and Church law were needed to make fallen man whole again, but man's intellectual autonomy in rational affairs (e.g., geometry) was asserted. The laws of nature were seen as autonomous and open to accurate investigation by all mankind. Natural law in society was seen as essentially metaphysical, i.e., underlying all human relationships. The key philosophical assumption was the idea of *shared being*, meaning a *real*, metaphysical link in a living, organic cosmos.

The mathematical-mechanical rationality of Cartesianism and Newtonianism destroyed this organic worldview in the Protestant West. After Newton, Christians and non-Christians alike adopted a new version of natural law theory, what we can call *mechanical natural law theory* (nominalism). It rested on the hypothesis of a distant creator God so far removed from the creation that He intervenes only occasionally, in order solely to

---

1952). On the history of Roman Catholic casuistry, see Albert J. Jonsen and Stephen Toulmin, *The Abuse of Casuistry: A History of Moral Reasoning* (Berkeley: University of California Press, 1988).

15. The exceptions historically were nominalists. The Franciscans, following Franciscan William of Occam, linked the Spiritualist tradition with philosophical nominalism.

16. On this point, see the writings of Herman Dooyeweerd and Cornelius Van Til.

keep the mechanical "clock" of creation operating smoothly. The mind of man was seen as autonomous from both biblical law and Church law. What is crucial to man's scientific understanding is his knowledge of the mathematical structure of the universe. Steadily, social philosophers sought analogously rigorous relationships in human society.[17] Natural law in society was seen as exclusively contractual; hence, the conclusion: "no social contract, no legitimacy." The underlying assumptions of this worldview did not survive Darwinism (a new, impersonal organicism) in the late nineteenth century and quantum physics (a new, impersonal irrationalism) in the early twentieth.[18]

Natural law theory in both forms prevented the development of a uniquely biblical social theory. The doctrine of the biblical covenant was missing, since one or more of its five points were denied: (1) the absolute personal sovereignty of God over both nature and human history; (2) the hierarchical authority of all human institutions under God's limited, delegated sovereignty; (3) biblical law as authoritative in all civilizations; (4) God's historical sanctions (blessing and cursing), imposed in terms of His Bible-revealed law; and (5) the development of history in response to the imposition of God's sanctions, though mitigated temporarily by His mercy.[19] Point one is called Calvinism; point two is called representative government; points three and four are called theonomy; and point five is called postmillennialism. They are a package deal. Without all five, it is impossible to construct an exclusively and covenantally faithful biblical social theory.

What I argue in this book is that law, historical sanctions, and eschatology are uniquely linked together in ways denied by virtually the whole of the modern Church. God's stipulations (laws), God's historical sanctions, and God's kingdom triumph in

---

17. Louis I. Bredvold, *The Brave New World of the Enlightenment* (Ann Arbor: University of Michigan Press, 1961).

18. Gary North, *The Dominion Covenant: Genesis* (2nd ed; Tyler, Texas: Institute for Christian Economics, 1987), Appendix A: "From Cosmic Purposelessness to Humanistic Sovereignty."

19. Ray R. Sutton, *That You May Prosper: Dominion By Covenant* (Tyler, Texas: Institute for Christian Economics, 1987).

history are a unit. This is not to deny that God's absolute predestinating sovereignty is what guarantees His kingdom's historical triumph, or that Christians, as members of God's Church, are not God's kingdom representatives in history. But the great debate has come over the inextricable relationship between biblical law, God's historical sanctions, and cultural progress over time. Yet most modern covenant theologians expressly deny this connection.[20] They also refuse to define *covenant*. This has been going on for four centuries.

A Question of Sanctions

"The history of all hitherto existing society is the history of class struggles." This is the opening paragraph of Part I of the *Communist Manifesto* (1848).[21] The fact that Marx never did define "class" (i.e., hierarchy) in terms of his theoretical system did not in the least hinder the growth of the Communist movement.[22] He clearly had a unified concept of sanctions and eschatology, and it was this belief, above all, that motivated his disciples: "Centralisation of the means of production and socialisation of labour at last reach a point where they become incompatible with their capitalist integument [covering]. This integument is burst asunder. The knell of capitalist private property sounds. The expropriators are expropriated."[23]

Marx was wrong. In 1989, the death knell of Marxist Communism sounded, except in Red China, and even in this case, it was only the application of military sanctions against unarmed students that gave Chinese Communism a stay of execution. This was viewed by the whole non-Communist world on satellite television, and Red China lost any claim to moral legitimacy. Lost legitimacy is very difficult to regain. Non-Chinese Communism lost its moral legitimacy in a much less spectacular way.

---

20. See Chapter 7, below.

21. Karl Marx and Frederick Engels, "Manifesto of the Communist Party," in Marx and Engels, *Collected Works* (New York: International Publishers, 1976), VI, p. 482.

22. He began to define "class" in the last few paragraphs of his posthumously published third volume of *Capital*. The manuscript then breaks off. He lived for another fifteen years after he ceased working on it.

23. Karl Marx, *Capital* (New York: Modern Library, [1867]), p. 837.

Communist producers of goods and services, held legally unaccountable to enslaved consumers for over seventy years, finally failed to deliver the goods. Communist economies all went bankrupt economically, but far more significantly, went theoretically bankrupt. They lost their legitimacy because it had been based on a promise of a better economic world to come. So utterly hopeless is Communism as an economic system, *The Economist* commented with characteristic English wit, that not even Germans could make it work.[24] While the implements of Russian nuclear sanctions are still growing in number, those sanctions, if ever applied, will not be Marxist, merely Russian. Marxism is dead. Its few remaining defenders are Western college professors: tenured upholders of lost causes. Any social philosophy that is dependent on college professors to keep it alive is already suffering from rigor mortis.

This is not to say that Leninism is dead. Leninism is a theory of power, not a theory of economics.[25] Its strategy, in Lenin's own words, is two steps forward and one step back.[26] Mikhail Gorbachev is a Leninist, and a declared one at that. What he is throwing out is Marxian socialism, just as Lenin did with his New Economic Policy in 1921. For the sake of the Leninist cause, Gorbachev is abandoning Marxism. But he is not abandoning Leninism's power religion. What he now appears to be doing is substituting the strategy of the founder of the Italian Communist Party, Antonio Gramsci, who was Lenin's contemporary. Gramsci rejected the Marxist-Leninist ideal of a workers' revolution as a strategy for conquering the West. He designed a propaganda campaign promoting atheism and relativism as a means of subverting the then-marginally Christian West.[27]

The question is: Can Leninism as an ideology exist apart from socialism? Can it exist apart from Marx's goal of destroying the

---

24. "D-mark day dawns," *The Economist* (June 30, 1990), p. 3.

25. John P. Roche, *The History and Impact of Marxist-Leninist Organizational Theory* (Cambridge, Massachusetts: Institute for Foreign Policy Analysis, 1984).

26. V. I. Lenin, *One Step Forward, Two Steps Back (The Crisis of Our Party)* (Moscow: Progress Publishers, [1904] 1978).

27. Malachi Martin, *The Keys of This Blood* (New York: Simon & Schuster, 1990), ch. 13.

bourgeoisie? My answer: *no*. Marxism is a theory of final sanctions in history, of class revenge, of envy. It is a deeply religious worldview that proclaims both personal and corporate salvation through revolution followed by the application of ruthless centralized power. It cannot co-exist with a free market capitalist order. Thus, Gorbachev's *tactic* of abandoning Marx's socialism is in fact a *strategy* leading to the self-destruction of Communism. Marxism is officially dead. Gorbachev has publicly buried it. Leninism, though well-armed militarily, is now dying.

Power is not enough. Marxism-Leninism is far more than a philosophy of power. It is, in the words of Peter Drucker, "the promise of an everlasting society that achieves both social perfection and individual perfection, a society that establishes the earthly paradise. It was this belief in salvation by society that gave Marxism its tremendous appeal."[28] Marxism is a *power religion*, but religion is supposed to heal man's wounds. Marxism has failed as a religion, and now it will be replaced as a worldwide ideological movement. It no longer fulfills its original role. The most successful secular religion in history has failed.

Gramsci's Marxism is really not Marxism. It is merely socialist humanism, and socialist humanism is now out of favor, East and West. Fascism is alive and well – the "government-business partnership" – but Marxian socialism is dead. Gramsci left Soviet Russia, preferring a jail sentence in Fascist Italy to a death sentence from Stalin.[29] In this sense, Gorbachev is a true disciple of Gramsci: he prefers Fascism to Stalinism. But unlike Gramsci, Gorbachev thinks he will run the prison, which is now under construction. This prison is the transnational New World Order.

Covenantal Struggles

Marx and Engels were close to the truth – close enough to create the most powerful secular religion in man's history. Society is indeed a history of struggles. Paraphrasing Marx and Engels, we can say: "The history of all hitherto existing society is the history of covenantal struggles." This conflict began with

28. Peter F. Drucker, *The New Realities* (New York: Harper & Row, 1989), p. 10.
29. Martin, *Keys*, p. 246.

the serpent's tempting of Eve in the garden. It continues in our day. It will continue until the final judgment. *There is a gigantic struggle in history between covenant-keepers and covenant-breakers.* We know where this struggle is headed: toward the total defeat of covenant-breakers at the end of time.

Covenant-breakers want one thing above all: *to escape the negative sanctions of the final judgment.* Modern humanism has denied the existence of such a final judgment. It has sought to transfer the very concept of final judgment into history. Social theories that are built on the second law of thermodynamics (entropy) are examples of this outlook.[30] There are only historical sanctions, we are told, and these sanctions are imposed by either man or nature. Eschatology becomes immanentized: dragged out of heaven and into history exclusively. It is stripped of every trace of the transcendent.

Covenant-keepers, in contrast, assert the existence of sanctions beyond history, both personal (after death) and cosmic (end of time). But Christian thinking for the most part over many centuries has concentrated only on these final sanctions. God's sanctions in history, both positive and negative, have been explained in terms of God's inscrutable will. They have been seen as essentially random from man's perspective. Amillennial theologian Meredith Kline writes: "And meanwhile it [the common grace order] must run its course within the uncertainties of the mutually conditioning principles of common grace and common curse, prosperity and adversity being experienced in a manner largely unpredictable because of the inscrutable sovereignty of the divine will that dispenses them in mysterious ways."[31]

This view of God's historical sanctions (random) has produced *an operational alliance between covenant-breakers and covenant-keepers.* Covenant-breakers have sought to make all the meaningful sanctions exclusively historical and exclusively natural. This is an aspect of worshipping what Herbert Schlossberg calls the

---

30. Gary North, *Is the World Running Down? Crisis in the Christian Worldview* (Tyler, Texas: Institute for Christian Economics, 1988).

31. Meredith G. Kline, "Comments on an Old-New Error," *Westminster Theological Journal,* XLI (Fall 1978), p. 184.

twin idols of mankind: idols of history and idols of nature.[32] Covenant-keepers have not accepted this worldview in theory, but most have accepted it in practice. *Random historical sanctions* become the operational equivalent of *no historical sanctions*. This leaves humanism's sanctions as an effective monopoly in history. Furthermore, throughout most of man's history, these sanctions have been closely associated with the exercise of State power. Those who have affirmed meaningful sanctions only in history have sought and gained political power. Modern Christians, in contrast, have denied that God's predictable, covenantal sanctions apply to history, and have also denied their legitimate enforcement by the covenant-keeping representatives of God. They have sought, first, to shun all political power and, second, to escape its effects. This leaves covenant-breakers in control of society by default. This covert alliance between humanists and pietists has led to the visible triumph of the power religion over the escape religion.

The power religion and the escape religion are united in their determined opposition to the idea of God's covenant sanctions in history.[33] Understandably, the defenders of humanist theocracy – the religion of autonomous man – are outraged by the message of biblical theocracy. Man, they insist, must rule in history whenever nature departs from her throne (or is pushed off by man). Less recognized is the fact that the defenders of God's random historical sanctions have by default accepted the moral legitimacy of this humanist theocracy, at least in the form known as political pluralism – what I have called right-wing Enlightenment political theory.[34]

There is no neutral cultural and social vacuum. Either covenant-keepers will make and enforce the laws of society, or else covenant-breakers will. There is no third alternative, long-term.

---

32. Herbert Schlossberg, *Idols of Destruction: Christian Faith and Its Confrontation with American Society* (Washington, D.C.: Regnery Gateway, [1983] 1990), p. 11.

33. Gary North, *Moses and Pharaoh: Dominion Religion vs. Power Religion* (Tyler, Texas: Institute for Christian Economics, 1985), pp. 2-5.

34. Gary North, *Political Polytheism: The Myth of Pluralism* (Tyler, Texas: Institute for Christian Economics, 1989), pp. 398, 540.

Modern political pluralism is merely a temporary cease-fire.[35] One side or the other must eventually gain control. This will be the humanist side if covenant-keepers retain their faith in the randomness of God's sanctions in history, for humanism is a consistent theology of man's sovereignty. *Consistency wins, for it can mobilize the hearts and minds of men.* The inconsistency and philosophy of despair of the classical civilization of antiquity could not withstand the consistency and eschatological vision of Christianity.[36] For the past three centuries, however, the consistency and vision of humanism has overcome the inconsistency and lack of historical vision of Christianity. Today, with humanism in disarray and Christianity in seemingly equal disarray, it is not clear from the available evidence which side will win. But one or the other will, unless a third contender appears.[37]

Christianity's problem is this: *you cannot beat something with nothing.* If we seek to persuade people to embrace our religion, we need to offer good reasons why. Guaranteed historical defeat is not one of them. A positive eschatology is important.

A Question of Eschatology

Communism has served as the ultimate model of all humanistic social theories: consistent, comprehensive, life-changing, and life-absorbing. In its early days, it demanded the whole of men's lives.[38] Communism has been able to demand this degree of sacrifice because it is a religion.[39] Like all religions, it possesses an explicit eschatology. This millennial eschatology is optimistic,

---

35. *Ibid.*, pp. xix, 2, 4, 227-28, 250, 265, 294, 630-31.

36. Charles Norris Cochrane, *Christianity and Classical Culture: A Study of Thought and Action from Augustus to Augustine* (New York: Oxford University Press, [1944] 1957).

37. One contender today is Islam.

38. Benjamin Gitlow, *The Whole of Their Lives* (New York: Scribner's, 1948). Gitlow became the head of the American Communist Party in 1929. Gitlow's autobiography is one of many by former Communists who gave everything to the Party and then grew disillusioned and defected. The most eloquent of these is *Witness* by Whittaker Chambers (New York: Random House, 1952). See also Freda Utley, *Lost Illusion* (Philadelphia: Fireside Press, 1948); Bella V. Dodd, *School of Darkness* (New York: Devin-Adair, 1954); Louis Francis Budenz, *This Is My Story* (New York: McGraw-Hill, 1947); and Maurice L. Malkin, *Return to My Father's House* (New Rochelle, New York: Arlington House, 1972).

39. Gary North, *Marx's Religion of Revolution: Regeneration Through Chaos* (Tyler, Texas: Institute for Christian Economics, [1968] 1989).

world-embracing, world-transforming, and exclusively this-worldly. It is a vision of victory.[40] The Soviet Union remains militarily the best-armed nation on earth, but the nation's theoretical fundamentals are no longer seriously believed by its people or its intellectuals, as Solzhenitsyn has been telling the West ever since his deportation from the Soviet Union in 1974. Now this moral bankruptcy is visible to all. But Communism's rulers have held unprecedented power. Communism is the incarnation of the power religion.

Few scholars would deny the close relationship between Communist eschatology and Communist social theory. Few would deny the importance of Communist eschatology in the rapid rise and then the geographical triumph of Communism after 1917 – a victory that only came to a halt, at least for the moment, in late 1989. Communist eschatology helped not only Communism; it helped socialism in general. As Ludwig von Mises wrote in 1922, "Nothing has helped the spread of socialist ideas more than this belief that Socialism is inevitable. Even the opponents of socialism are for the most part bewitched by it: it takes the heart out of their resistance."[41] What should also be recognized is the close connection between Communist eschatology and the Communist theory of historical sanctions. Again, citing Mises: "From the theory of the class-war, Marxians argue that the socialist order of society is the inevitable future of the human race."[42] *Eschatology and historical sanctions*: the diabolical genius of Marx and Engels linked them together self-consciously. The religion of Marxism, in this sense (as in others), is a perverse imitation of biblical covenantalism.

Christianity

The three major Christian eschatological systems – premillennialism, amillennialism, and postmillennialism[43] – have ines-

---

40. Francis Nigel Lee, *Communist Eschatology* (Nutley, New Jersey: Craig Press, 1974).

41. Ludwig von Mises, *Socialism: An Economic and Sociological Analysis* (New Haven, Connecticut: Yale University Press, [1922] 1951), p. 282. Reprinted by Liberty Classics, Indianapolis, Indiana.

42. *Ibid.*, p. 344.

43. Pre-, a-, and post- refer to the timing of the bodily return of Jesus Christ: before

able implications for the development of social theory. This fact was ignored for centuries by Christian theologians generally and by the tiny handful of Christians who over the centuries have dealt at least peripherally with the question of social theory.[44] The relationship between millennialism and social theory was not even discussed, let alone studied in depth. The topic in recent years has been considered sporadically and peripherally by a few Christian theologians only because of the appearance of the Christian Reconstruction movement, which is self-consciously postmillennial and which has specialized in the study of social theory.[45]

Ironically, secular historians have in recent decades begun to understand that such relationships have existed in Western history.[46] Why have Christian scholars paid little or no attention to this growing body of scholarly literature? First, they seldom keep up with academic literature outside their own narrow theological specialties. Second, the existence of such a relationship between eschatology and social theory raises many difficult personal questions regarding church membership, continued employment by Christian organizations, and relationships within Christian organizations. If a particular eschatology is true, and if it seems to lead to a particular theory about how society is required by God to be governed, then what should the local church do when its members or officers affirm the particu-

---

the millennial kingdom on earth, in the absence of a millennial kingdom on earth, or after a millennial kingdom on earth.

44. This concern was usually a subordinate part of the discipline of casuistry: the application of (hopefully) Christian ethical principles to historical circumstances.

45. The critics of Christian Reconstruction have mislabeled the Reconstructionists' intellectual specialization with a supposed downplaying of traditional theology. First, it is the repeated and almost universal error of the critics to imagine that Christian Reconstructionists believe that society is transformed first and foremost through politics. This view of social change is the myth of humanism, not Christian Reconstruction. Second, society is far wider than politics, so the Christian Reconstructionists are concerned with far more than mere political transformation. Third, the Reconstructionists are convinced that the regeneration of a majority of people by the irresistible grace of the Holy Spirit is the sole basis of long-term social reconstruction using a biblical model. See Gary North and Gary DeMar, *Christian Reconstruction: What It Is, What It Isn't* (Tyler, Texas: Institute for Christian Economics, 1991). See also Gary North, *Dominion and Common Grace: The Biblical Basis of Progress* (Tyler, Texas: Institute for Christian Economics, 1987), ch. 6.

46. See Chapter 1, footnote #11.

lar eschatology but then deny its social implications? Even more painfully, what if the denomination specifically insists on eschatological neutrality in the ordination of its officers? Third, it raises psychological questions: "I believe in *this* eschatology. Must I also believe in *that* social theory if I am to remain theologically consistent? Can I even develop a Bible-based social theory that is consistent with my eschatology?"[47] These questions disturb amillennialists and premillennialists alike, for both groups systematically shun social theory. Above all, these questions disturb that handful of dispensational premillennialists who are also social activists: the problem of consistency.[48]

Christian responses have been mixed to Christian Reconstructionism's claims in favor of an explicitly biblical social theory. Some of these critics insist that the traditional categories of Stoic and medieval natural law theory are universally valid, and therefore constitute the only legitimate foundation of social theory in a post-Resurrection world – a pluralist, humanist-dominated world. Others take the seemingly less controversial approach, professing ignorance, but implicitly proclaiming ignorance as universally binding. They proclaim a kind of spiritual agnosticism. They thereby deny the possibility of Christian social theory, let alone its necessity. For example, English Calvinist Baptist Errol Hulse writes: "Who among us is adequately equipped to know which political philosophy most accords with biblical principles?"[49] (Implication: certainly not the theonom-

47. For a discussion of these sorts of problems, see D. Clair Davis, "A Challenge to Theonomy," in William S. Barker and W. Robert Godfrey (eds.), *Theonomy: A Reformed Critique* (Grand Rapids, Michigan: Zondervan Academie, 1990), ch. 16.

48. A classic example is Professor H. Wayne House, who in 1990 left Dallas Theological Seminary for Western Baptist College in Oregon. He is both a social activist and a dispensationalist. See Richard A. Fowler and H. Wayne House, *The Christian Confronts His Culture* (Chicago: Moody Press, 1983). His failure to respond in print to Bahnsen and Gentry's detailed refutation of House and Ice's *Dominion Theology: Blessing or Curse?* (Portland, Oregon: Multnomah Press, 1988), is indicative of his problem. His silence gives the appearance of the short-circuiting of his worldview, especially since he has now resigned from seminary teaching. See Greg L. Bahnsen and Kenneth L. Gentry, *House Divided: The Break-Up of Dispensational Theology* (Tyler, Texas: Institute for Christian Economics, 1989). For a truly pathetic attempt by a dispensational theologian to respond to *House Divided*, see John Walvoord's review in *Bibliotheca Sacra* (July-Sept. 1990). For my response, see "First, the Brain Goes Soft," *Dispensationalism in Transition*, III (August 1990).

49. Errol Hulse, "Reconstructionism, Restorationism or Puritanism," *Reformation*

ists!) That this same agnosticism can easily be applied to the doctrines of the Trinity, baptism, and Church government never seems to occur to these "agnostic" critics. There is an implicit syllogism lurking here: "Ignorance is bliss. Knowledge is power. Power is responsibility. Responsibility is terrifying. Let's stick with ignorance." This is the worldview of pietistic Anabaptism, but it is no longer restricted to Anabaptists. It is nearly universal in Christian circles, except when offset or heavily qualified by "neutral" natural law theory. It has produced an attitude hostile to all systematic discussions of a uniquely biblical social theory.

Conclusion

The three views of social theory – organicism, contractualism, and covenantalism – establish the limits of social theory. There is no fourth alternative. Christians must adopt one of these three approaches, either unconsciously or self-consciously. But there are many Christians who prefer not to make this decision. Let me remind them: "no decision" is still a decision. There is no neutrality.

The possibility of devising a uniquely biblical social theory is denied by those who reject the continuing validity of the Old Testament case laws in New Testament times. At best, by adopting a Stoic-medieval view of natural law theory, the Christian can make some contributions, based on his knowledge of the Bible. But the resulting hybrid social theory will not be uniquely Christian. Natural law theory is judicially and morally unstable, even without Christianity's appended contributions. Instability has been the fate of natural law theory from the days of the Stoics. The mind of autonomous man is in rebellion against God, the truth, and morality. It cannot be trusted to formulate first principles or to remain logically consistent to them. It is not that natural law is in need of revision by Christian principles. It is that Christian principles are reliable, whereas natural law

---

Today, No. 116 (July-Aug. 1990), p. 25. By Puritanism, he means the pietistic wing of seventeenth-century English Puritanism, not Cromwell's New Model Army or the New England Puritans. He means the Puritanism of the cloister, best represented by William Gurnall's *Christian in Complete Armour*, 2 vols. (London: Banner of Truth, [1655-62] 1964).

theory is a myth of Hellenistic Greek scholars who were seeking to invent universal moral principles in the midst of a collapsing social and political order in late Greek antiquity. It was a system of elitist logic designed for men willing to abandon politics altogether in order to submit to a universal empire.[50] Natural law theory was a makeshift affair from the beginning: a substitute for the defunct moral order of the defeated Greek *polis*. It is just one more example of secular humanism in action.

Its only major victory was achieved when late-medieval Christian philosophers breathed new life into it by arguing that it was consistent with Christianity. It suffered a major defeat by Kant in the late eighteenth century. Darwin then proclaimed autonomous nature's randomly changing responses to randomly changing environmental forces as the sole necessary explanation for nature's apparent orderliness. No designing God was necessary to explain this order. Society and personal morality evolve: no fixed species means no fixed morality. Natural law theory therefore could no longer be taken seriously by the vast majority of humanists.

A few Christians – Roman Catholic neo-scholastics and fundamentalist Norman Geisler (trained in a Jesuit university) – still try to defend a hybrid version of Christianity and natural law theory, always carefully undefined as "right reason." No one in the academic world pays much attention. Natural law theory, a hybrid intellectual mule from the beginning, is now regarded as sterile. Only a few Christians vainly hope that it will eventually produce offspring. It is an ancient hope, one yet to be rewarded.

Even among those who accept the validity of biblical law as a moral and legal standard – and there are few who do – the incentive to construct a biblical social theory fades if the view of biblical law does not include the historical sanctions that God has said are attached to cosmic His law-order. If these sanctions are denied, then eschatology is cut off from biblical ethics. Conversely, if an eschatology is adopted that denies the reality of an expanding Christian civilization over time, then the predictable

50. Sheldon S. Wolin, *Politics and Vision: Continuity and Innovation in Western Political Thought* (Boston: Little, Brown, 1960), pp. 80-82.

historical sanctions of God's law-order are implicitly or explicitly being denied. God's law, His predictable historical sanctions, and millennialism are intertwined in God's three institutional covenants: Church, family, and State. Deny these covenantal connections, and you thereby deny the possibility of constructing a uniquely biblical social theory.

There is no neutrality in life. He who denies the possibility of a uniquely biblical social theory must adopt a non-Christian social theory. He may do so either consciously or unconsciously, but he will choose something. There are no theoretical vacuums. There are no social vacuums. Jesus taught: "No man can serve two masters: for either he will hate the one, and love the other; or else he will hold to the one, and despise the other. Ye cannot serve God and mammon" (Matt. 6:24). "He that is not with me is against me; and he that gathereth not with me scattereth abroad" (Matt. 12:30). This applies to social theory, too.

3

COVENANTAL PROGRESS

Therefore thou shalt keep the commandments of the L*ORD thy God, to walk in his ways, and to fear him. For the* L*ORD thy God bringeth thee into a good land, a land of brooks of water, of fountains and depths that spring out of valleys and hills; A land of wheat, and barley, and vines, and fig trees, and pomegranates; a land of oil olive, and honey; A land wherein thou shalt eat bread without scarceness, thou shalt not lack any thing in it; a land whose stones are iron, and out of whose hills thou mayest dig brass. When thou hast eaten and art full, then thou shalt bless the* L*ORD thy God for the good land which he hath given thee.* ***Beware that thou forget not the*** **L*ORD*** ***thy God, in not keeping his commandments, and his judgments, and his statutes, which I command thee this day****: Lest when thou hast eaten and art full, and hast built goodly houses, and dwelt therein; And when thy herds and thy flocks multiply, and thy silver and thy gold is multiplied, and all that thou hast is multiplied; Then thine heart be lifted up, and thou forget the* L*ORD thy God. . . . And thou say in thine heart, My power and the might of mine hand hath gotten me this wealth. But thou shalt remember the* L*ORD thy God: for* ***it is he that giveth thee power to get wealth, that he may establish his covenant*** *which he sware unto thy fathers, as it is this day. And it shall be, if thou do at all forget the* L*ORD thy God, and walk after other gods, and serve them, and worship them, I testify against you this day that ye shall surely perish (Deut. 8:6-14a, 17-19).* (emphasis added)

This passage in Deuteronomy presents the biblical basis of progress in history. Without this vision of God's covenantal judgments in history, there can be no legitimate Christian basis for belief in God-honoring cultural advancement over long periods of time. It establishes the concept of God's sanctions in history, both positive and negative. The passage teaches that in history, there will be both "positive feedback" and "negative feedback." *Any attempt to renounce this passage as no longer judicially binding in the New Covenant era is inescapably a denial of any biblical basis for God-honoring cultural progress in history.*

The passage begins with an imperative: "Therefore thou shalt keep the commandments of the LORD thy God, to walk in his ways, and to fear him." It immediately offers a reason: "For the LORD thy God bringeth thee into a good land, a land of brooks of water, of fountains and depths that spring out of valleys and hills." God was about to give to this people an unmerited gift in the midst of history: control over the Promised Land. Here is a fundamental principle of both theology and history: *God's grace precedes man's response.* The proper response is obedience to God's revealed law.

The Paradox of Deuteronomy 8

It is God who "giveth thee power to get wealth, that he may establish his covenant which he sware unto thy fathers, as it is this day." It could not be any clearer: the economic success that God was promising to His covenant people in the future was based on the original promise given to Abraham, Isaac, and Jacob. There is no autonomous power in man's possession that enables him to become productive. As James put it, "Every good gift and every perfect gift is from above, and cometh down from the Father of lights, with whom is no variableness, neither shadow of turning" (James 1:17). The power to get wealth was God's *re-confirmation* of the Sinai covenant with Israel, which was in turn a *renewal* of His original covenant with the Patriarchs.

Another sign of the covenantal nature of these promises was God's promise of future negative sanctions. "And it shall be, if thou do at all forget the LORD thy God, and walk after other gods, and serve them, and worship them, I testify against you this day that ye shall surely perish." This is the sanction of *covenantal death and corporate disinheritance.*

The biblical covenant establishes the possibility of long-term economic growth, a promise that was unique in the ancient world. It established the possibility of *compounding*. If His covenant people remain faithful, He promised them, they would greatly expand their possessions. The capital and resources needed to extend God's kingdom across the face of the earth are assured, all in good, covenant-keeping time. But if men misinterpret the source of their wealth and attribute it humanistically to the work of their own hands, they become guilty of idolatry. God will come to judge them in the midst of history.

This is the paradox of Deuteronomy 8: *wealth is both a positive and negative sanction*. The Israelites began their fulfillment of the dominion covenant with wealth that they did not produce. They were given the law of God, the ultimate tool of dominion.[1] They were told to obey it. The reason given is intensely practical: because God is going to deliver a rich land into their hands. This in turn will call for continued thankfulness: "When thou hast eaten and art full, then thou shalt bless the LORD thy God for the good land which he hath given thee." This thankfulness will be a sign to God of their continued covenantal faithfulness.

The wealth of the land could become a snare to them. Here is the paradox of wealth. "Beware that thou forget not the LORD thy God, in not keeping his commandments, and his judgments, and his statutes, which I command thee this day." God then lists the many economic blessings that can serve as a snare: ". . . thou hast eaten and art full, and hast built goodly houses, and dwelt therein; And when thy herds and thy flocks multiply, and thy silver and thy gold is multiplied, and all that thou hast is multiplied." The language points back to the original covenant with Adam: "And God blessed them, and God said unto them, Be fruitful, and multiply, and replenish the earth, and subdue it: and have dominion over the fish of the sea, and over the fowl of the air, and over every living thing that moveth upon the earth" (Gen. 1:28). The two tables of the law become covenant-keeping man's multiplication tables.

So, the external blessings can become the means of man's public display of his covenantal rebellion, which is followed by God's covenantal wrath. The positive feedback of obedience, thankfulness, and further blessings can become the negative

---

1. Gary North, *Tools of Dominion: The Case Laws of Exodus* (Tyler, Texas: Institute for Christian Economics, 1990).

feedback of disobedience, humanism, and destruction. *All of this is historical.* This is because God's covenant is historical. History has eternal consequences.

Some critic might conclude that because wealth and visible success can be snares as well as blessings, the sanction of success is neutral. It does not allow us to distinguish between good and evil men. If wealth were both compounding and unbounded in time, this criticism would carry considerable weight. It would then be true that in history the sanction would *appear* to be neutral. But the sanction would not be neutral; it would be perverse. *It would subsidize evil.* The covenant-breaker would have no external reason to repent. But the point is that all the positive sanctions for a covenant-breaking society are limited by time. Like the trap that eventually gets sprung, so is God's negative sanction of wealth to covenant-breakers.

The covenant-keeper has more than the external sanction of wealth itself to inform him regarding the positive or negative impact of the sanction. He has God's revelation of Himself in the Bible. The covenant-keeper is capable of making accurate moral judgments apart from mere visible sanctions. He knows what God did to Israel in the wilderness when they complained against Him, demanding more blessings. "And he gave them their request; but sent leanness into their soul" (Psa. 106:15). Men recognize the truth of this. A lyric by Steve Gillette and David MacKechnie has summarized quite well this condition of emptiness in the midst of wealth: "We've got all of the nice things we wanted, but we lost the good thing we had." The covenantal question is not simply this: "How much success does covenant-breaking society enjoy?" It is this: "How much longer will God continue to lure His enemies into His trap?"

Exponential Growth

Nothing physical grows forever. At some point, the growing thing, whether individual or social, confronts inescapable environmental limits. This is as true of material goods as it is of populations. Anything that grows eventually runs out of space and material resources to sustain its growth. Anything that could grow indefinitely, no matter how slowly, would in time approach infinity as a limit. As time went on, the upward growth curve would become exponential. But there are limits to growth. The creation is not infinite.[2] This includes time: the only irreplaceable resource.

This finitude is not simply an aspect of the curse of the ground in Genesis 3:17-18. The material realm had curse-free limits even in the pre-fall era. The earth was only so big; so was the universe. So, the command to be fruitful and multiply contained an unstated assumption: *there are limits on mankind's time for dominion-testing*. At some point, the species known as man would have become a host, like the angels: no more multiplication. Mankind would eventually have reached its numerical limits. This would have been the case even in a sin-free world.

The very possibility of sustained growth points to the ultimate limit: *time*. Either growth must cease or time runs out. This is why modern man, while dedicated to the pursuit of economic growth, knows that this quest is ultimately doomed. His universe is finite. Growth points to his finitude, and more important, to the end of time. This thought is repugnant to covenant-breaking man, for it points to God's final judgment. Modern man then invents alternatives to God's final judgment and the end of time, the main one being nature's impersonal final judgment, the heat death of the universe.[3] In the meantime, a few economists[4] and a lot of political activists (the "greens") have become defenders of State-imposed limits to growth, for the sake of the environment and mankind's "quality of life." (Who will define and police this high quality?)

Man's problem is not economic growth. His problem is sin. But he does not want to face this covenantal fact, so he seeks alternative explanations for his condition, as well as alternative solutions to it.

---

2. Gary North, "The Theology of the Exponential Curve," *The Freeman* (May 1970); reprinted in North, *Introduction to Christian Economics* (Nutley, New Jersey: Craig Press, 1973), ch. 8.

3. Gary North, *Is the World Running Down? Crisis in the Christian Worldview* (Tyler, Texas: Institute for Christian Economics, 1988), ch. 2.

4. Most notably, E. J. Mishan.

Solutions and Trade-Offs

This view of the limits of growth has consequences for social theory. Biologist Garrett Hardin, an articulate spokesman for the humanist worldview (and a dedicated pro-abortionist), has put it this way: "If a system that includes positive feedback is to possess stability, it must also include 'negative feedback.' " He uses the thermostat as his model: when a room gets too hot, the thermostat cuts off the heat. When it gets too cold, it turns the heat back on. This stability cannot be perfect: a thermostat needs a fixed range of temperature in which to function. But the goal is stability.[5] If applied to society, this outlook becomes the justification of a steady-state theory, *if time is seen as essentially unbounded*.[6] The Bible, however, teaches that time is bounded.

There are two approaches to the "thermostat society." First is the approach of the free market: automatic social controls are built into the economic system by mankind's evolving social institutions. They keep society stable. The second approach is that of the French Revolution, socialism, and Communism: a scientifically planned and technocratically administered controls system. In order to maintain stability, society needs central planning. Neither approach acknowledges God's covenants.

There are many names for these rival approaches to social theory. Thomas Sowell's choice is as good as any: the *constrained* vision and the *unconstrained* vision. The first sees mankind as under naturally and historically imposed constraints or limits, which include constraints on our knowledge.[7] The second sees the existing constraints as primarily the result of faulty human institutions that are based on ignorance and superstition.[8] Better knowledge is the goal of both approaches. The first sees

---

5. Garrett Hardin, "The Cybernetics of Competition: A Biologist's View of Society," in Helmut Schoeck and James W. Wiggins (eds.), *Central Planning and Neo-Mercantilism* (Princeton, New Jersey: Van Nostrand, 1964), p. 66.

6. This is the position of Jeremy Rifkin in his book, *Entropy: A New World View* (1980). For a critique of Rifkin, see North, *Is the World Running Down?*

7. F. A. Hayek, "The Use of Knowledge in Society" (1945); reprinted in Hayek, *Individualism and Economic Order* (University of Chicago Press, 1948), ch. 4.

8. F. A. Hayek, *The Counter-Revolution of Science: Studies on the Abuse of Reason* (2nd. ed.; Indianapolis, Indiana: Liberty Press, [1952] 1979).

knowledge as social and traditional, growing slowly over time, being tested in the real world. The second sees knowledge as the product of an elite corps of neutral, objective philosophers and scientists. Social progress is the goal of both. The first sees it as the result of slow social evolution, including free market competition. The second sees it as the product of central planning and political power. The first viewpoint is essentially evolutionary and politically decentralist; the second is essentially revolutionary and politically centralist.[9]

Each of these social visions, however, presumes *the autonomy of man and man's institutions*. Both views deny the existence of a God who intervenes directly into history, bringing His sanctions in terms of His permanent ethical standards. Each vision is thoroughly humanistic. Both are the product of Enlightenment speculation. Economists in both camps begin with the presupposition of agnosticism regarding the supernatural.

Sowell describes the constraints school as holding to a world of scarcity and inescapable *trade-offs* in life. We must give up *this* in order to gain *that*. The second school is far more perfectionist. It searches for *solutions*, irrespective of trade-offs. It tends not to count the costs of action, especially costs of human suffering. Sowell quotes Thomas Jefferson on the bloodbath of the French Revolution: "My own affections have been deeply wounded by some of the martyrs to this cause, but rather than it should have failed, I would have seen half the earth desolated."[10]

Sowell uses another pair of adjectives to describe the conflict of visions: *prudent* vs. *perfectionist*. The "constraints visionary" wants change, but prudent change. The "unconstraints visionary" believes in the perfectibility of man. The first thinks that human nature is fixed; the second believes that human nature is plastic or flexible.[11]

It is clear that the conservative social tradition and the free market economic tradition are both constraints-oriented in their

---

9. Thomas Sowell, *A Conflict of Visions: Ideological Origins of Political Struggles* (New York: William Morrow, 1987), ch. 2.

10. *Ibid.*, p. 34. Jefferson, letter of Jan. 3, 1793. *The Portable Thomas Jefferson*, edited by Merrill D. Peterson (New York: Penguin, 1975), p. 465.

11. *Ibid.*, pp. 25-26.

view of how society operates, even when the specific intellectual defenses of free market economic policies are made in terms of rigorous logic and a deep faith in logic.[12] It is equally clear that the socialist tradition until very recently has been grounded on the denial of permanent environmental limits on man. The socialist always blamed man's poverty on defective social institutions based on private property. Apart from these corrupt institutions, nature would bestow her bounty on all men. Consider the estimate made by Marxist economist Howard J. Sherman (my former professor), probably the most widely published academic American Marxist economist. In 1972, he estimated that the United States had achieved such productivity that over a period of years, given proper central planning, price tags could be removed from 80% of the available goods. The remaining 20% would be luxury goods.[13]

For almost two centuries, each school of thought claimed that its system could "deliver the goods," but socialists after 1980 were forced to admit that socialism does not deliver so many goods and services as capitalism does. They hid until 1989 behind the "quality of life" argument: socialist countries supposedly had a better quality of life, despite their lower per capita wealth. Then Red China and Eastern Europe exploded (and Red China then contracted back into tyranny). In the aftermath, the West learned what only specialists had argued before the Chernobyl accident in 1986: the Communist world had been far more polluted than societies in the free world.[14] Tyranny, central planning, and poverty turn out to be bad for the quality of life. This was a shock to the socialists from which they will have difficulty recovering.

Shifting Arguments

Today, the unconstraints argument has shifted again: the

12. I have in mind the *a priorism* of Ludwig von Mises and Murray Rothbard.

13. Cited in "The Unorthodox Ideas Of Radical Economists Win a Wider Hearing," *Wall Street Journal* (Feb. 11, 1972), p. 1.

14. Marshall Goldman, *The Spoils of Progress* (Cambridge, Massachusetts: MIT Press, 1972).

great evil of capitalism is seen in its commitment to material economic growth. The world *is* limited, socialists now insist. What is needed now, they say, is a system of international, centrally imposed restraints on all polluting production, yet which also allows freedom to consumers and decentralized "networking." They do not show how this fusion of central planning and local initiative is possible. In short, they have no economic theory, a point Mises made in 1920.[15]

Some defenders of the free market also shifted their focus: from material output to information. Previously, they had seen the economy as materially unlimited (open-ended) in the longer run, even though constrained by scarcity in the short run. After 1980, they began to talk about man's own mind as the primary source of wealth. As a progressing society shifts from manufacturing to services and information, it progressively escapes the fetters of material limits. There has been a near apotheosis of autonomous man, the entrepreneur.[16] The power of man's mind is viewed as bordering on alchemy: *from the self-transcendence of man's mind to a transcended environment.*[17]

The Christian View of Progress: Personal and Social

The biblical view, being covenantal, is radically different from both the constraints and unconstraints view, for it begins with a different view of God, man, and history. But because social theory has been ignored by Christians for centuries, and because they have tended to absorb the reigning opinions from the intellectual world around them, Christians have not articu-

---

15. Ludwig von Mises, *Economic Calculation in the Socialist Commonwealth* (Auburn, Alabama: Mises Institute, [1920] 1990).

16. Warren T. Brookes, *The Economy in Mind* (New York: Universe Books, 1982). Universe Books became briefly famous a decade earlier for publishing *The Limits to Growth*, the doomsday book on the rapid depletion of material resources. Brookes is a Christian Scientist, and his book reflects the view of man as not being under the constraints of sin or God's curse. Julian Simon, *the Ultimate Resource* (Princeton, New Jersey: Princeton University Press, 1981); Herman Kahn, *The Coming Boom: Economic, Political, Social* (New York: Simon & Schuster, 1982); George Gilder, *The Spirit of Enterprise* (New York: Simon & Schuster, 1984).

17. George Gilder, *Microcosm: Introduction to the Quantum Era of Economics and Technology* (New York: Simon & Schuster, 1989).

lated this alternative. It is time to begin.

The fundamental objection that Christianity has with the *constraints view* is that the constraints view has no doctrine of regeneration. It does not acknowledge that Jesus Christ, as perfect humanity, entered history to become a model for the world. It also does not acknowledge that in the death, resurrection, and ascension of Jesus in history, a new world order was inaugurated. This new order begins with the interior life of the individual: "Therefore if any man be in Christ, he is a new creature: old things are passed away; behold, all things are become new" (II Cor. 5:17). Man's nature is not fixed. It can be changed in an instant through conversion: the doctrine of regeneration. This personal transformation extends to man's social institutions, beginning with the Church. It will ultimately affect man's physical existence: "There shall be no more thence an infant of days, nor an old man that hath not filled his days: for the child shall die an hundred years old; but the sinner being an hundred years old shall be accursed" (Isa. 65:20).

Christianity's fundamental objection to the *unconstraints view* is that this transformation of human nature, although it takes place in history, does not originate in this world. "For by grace are ye saved through faith; and that not of yourselves: it is the gift of God: Not of works, lest any man should boast" (Eph. 2:8-9). This change is not a product of social engineering. Man's earthly environment has nothing to do with the change, except as the arena in which the change takes place. "So then faith cometh by hearing, and hearing by the word of God" (Rom. 10:17). Hearing the gospel is a necessary but not sufficient cause of the transformation of human nature. "But the natural man receiveth not the things of the Spirit of God: for they are foolishness unto him: neither can he know them, because they are spiritually discerned" (I Cor. 2:14).

Perfection: Past, Present, and Future

Christianity has what the constraints view needs but cannot attain: a concept of perfection in history. Jesus Christ was perfect. He lived in perfect conformity to God the Father's perfect standards of righteousness. "And the Holy Ghost descended in a bodily shape like a dove upon him, and a voice came from heaven, which said, Thou art my beloved Son; in thee I am well pleased" (Luke 3:22). "For he received from God the Father honour and glory, when there came such a voice to him from the excellent glory, This is my beloved Son, in whom I am well pleased" (II Pet. 1:17). "For he hath made him to be sin for us, who knew no sin; that we might be made the righteousness of God in him" (II Cor. 5:21).

At the time of a person's salvation, the legal status of Jesus is *imputed* to him. This means that God's judicial declaration to Jesus, "Not guilty!", is judicially transferred to the sinner in question. This is the doctrine of *justification*. Paul wrote of Abraham's faith in God's promise to him:

> (As it is written, I have made thee a father of many nations,) before him whom he believed, even God, who quickeneth the dead, and calleth those things which be not as though they were. Who against hope believed in hope, that he might become the father of many nations, according to that which was spoken, So shall thy seed be. And being not weak in faith, he considered not his own body now dead, when he was about an hundred years old, neither yet the deadness of Sarah's womb: He staggered not at the promise of God through unbelief; but was strong in faith, giving glory to God; And being fully persuaded that, what he had promised, he was able also to perform. *And therefore it was imputed to him for righteousness*. Now it was not written for his sake alone, that it was imputed to him; But for us also, to whom it shall be imputed, if we believe on him that raised up Jesus our Lord from the dead; Who was delivered for our offences, and was raised again for our justification (Rom. 4:17-25). (emphasis added)

Jesus Christ's legal status ("not guilty") is transferred to the redeemed (bought-back) person for a purpose: to enable the person to begin a life-long walk with God. Paul moved from Abraham's example to our tribulations in this life:

> Therefore being justified by faith, we have peace with God through our Lord Jesus Christ: By whom also we have access by faith into this grace wherein we stand, and rejoice in hope of the glory of God. And not only so, but we glory in tribulations also: knowing that tribulation worketh patience; And patience, experi-

ence; and experience, hope: And hope maketh not ashamed; because the love of God is shed abroad in our hearts by the Holy Ghost which is given unto us. For when we were yet without strength, in due time Christ died for the ungodly. For scarcely for a righteous man will one die: yet peradventure for a good man some would even dare to die. But God commendeth his love toward us, in that, while we were yet sinners, Christ died for us. Much more then, being now justified by his blood, we shall be saved from wrath through him (Rom. 5:1-9).

But there is more to salvation than justification. There is also *sanctification*. The moral perfection of Jesus is transferred to the redeemed person. This transfer is *definitive*: a once-only lifetime event. It is also *progressive*: working out its implications in the life of every saint (set-apart person).[18] He is to fight the good fight of faith:

> But godliness with contentment is great gain. For we brought nothing into this world, and it is certain we can carry nothing out. And having food and raiment let us be therewith content. But they that will be rich fall into temptation and a snare, and into many foolish and hurtful lusts, which drown men in destruction and perdition. For the love of money is the root of all evil: which while some coveted after, they have erred from the faith, and pierced themselves through with many sorrows. But thou, O man of God, flee these things; and follow after righteousness, godliness, faith, love, patience, meekness. Fight the good fight of faith, lay hold on eternal life, whereunto thou art also called, and hast professed a good profession before many witnesses (I Tim. 6:6-12)

He is to run the good race:

> Know ye not that they which run in a race run all, but one receiveth the prize? So run, that ye may obtain. And every man that striveth for the mastery is temperate in all things. Now they do it to obtain a corruptible crown; but we an incorruptible. I therefore so run, not as uncertainly; so fight I, not as one that beateth the air: But I keep under my body, and bring it into subjection: lest that by

18. Gary North, *Unconditional Surrender: God's Program for Victory* (3rd ed.; Tyler, Texas: Institute for Christian Economics, 1988), pp. 66-72.

any means, when I have preached to others, I myself should be a castaway (I Cor. 9:24-27).

So, the biblical view of man has a *concrete universal*: Jesus Christ, the Incarnate Son of God. He came in history specifically to meet God's standards. This is a categorical denial of the theology of the "inevitable trade-offs" view of life. Jesus did not sacrifice the good for the best. He did not choose the lesser of two evils. He did exactly what God wanted Him to do. *Jesus Christ is history's solution*. He did not compromise with evil. He is therefore not a trade-off in the usual sense of the word, unless redeemed men worry about losing hell as the price of gaining heaven. This significantly qualifies the constraints view of man.

We are to walk in life by imitating Christ. "Be ye followers of me, even as I also am of Christ" (I Cor. 11:1). "Be ye therefore followers of God, as dear children" (Eph. 5:1). "Let this mind be in you, which was also in Christ Jesus" (Phil. 2:5). The requirement is rigorous: "Be ye therefore perfect, even as your Father which is in heaven is perfect" (Matt. 5:48). This sounds very much like the unconstrained view of man. It seems like a denial of the constrained view's trade-offs of life. Yet if man is a sinner, he is constrained. How can this paradox be resolved?

Trade-Offs vs. Perfection

The requirement of pursuing perfect moral standards is not to say that we, in our sin (primary) and ignorance (secondary), do not make trade-offs in life. Jesus was clear: there are always costs and benefits in life, and we must count them carefully:

> For which of you, intending to build a tower, sitteth not down first, and counteth the cost, whether he have sufficient to finish it? Lest haply [it happen], after he hath laid the foundation, and is not able to finish it, all that behold it begin to mock him, Saying, This man began to build, and was not able to finish. Or what king, going to make war against another king, sitteth not down first, and consulteth whether he be able with ten thousand to meet him that cometh against him with twenty thousand? Or else, while the other is yet a great way off, he sendeth an ambassage, and desireth conditions of peace. So likewise, whosoever he be of you that forsaketh

not all that he hath, he cannot be my disciple (Luke 14:28-33).

The point is, as we mature in the faith, these trade-offs between sin and righteousness become less burdensome, i.e., less costly. When we walk on God's path, the "alternative income" potentially derived from walking on Satan's path becomes progressively lower. "For what is a man profited, if he shall gain the whole world, and lose his own soul? or what shall a man give in exchange for his soul?" (Matt. 16:26). Let us consider a concrete example. I could murder my wife and collect the insurance money. I might even get away with the crime in this life. She could do the same to me. The point is, the "forfeited income" of the face value of each of our insurance policies is of zero value to us with respect to the act of murder. The trade-off – "not murdering my spouse vs. the forfeited income" – does not enter our calculations. It is therefore not a cost to either of us, economically speaking, for the only valid cost (at least some economists assure us) is individual psychic cost.[19] Furthermore, if this "non-calculation" were not nearly universal among married people (common grace), insurance companies could not afford to write life insurance policies, and certainly not large ones. So, the paradox is resolved by progressive sanctification.

The possibility of personal moral progress is always before each person. But the Bible is specific: *widespread moral progress will produce widespread economic growth.* The biblical covenant links obedience to God's law with God's blessings, which include prosperity (Deut. 28:1-14).

Christianity asserts that there has been perfection in history. It also teaches that, by the power of God's regeneration of individuals and their progressive sanctification, people can approach perfection as a limit. We cannot achieve perfection in history. "If we say that we have no sin, we deceive ourselves, and the truth is not in us" (I John 1:8). Nevertheless, we are required by God to work toward perfection. This is why we

---

19. See James Buchanan, *Costs and Choice: An Inquiry on Economic Theory* (University of Chicago Press, 1969). See my discussion of value theory in North, *The Dominion Covenant: Genesis* (2nd ed; Tyler, Texas: Institute for Christian Economics, 1987), ch. 4; North, *Tools of Dominion*, pp. 1087-1100.

were granted salvation: to walk on God's righteous path.

> For by grace are ye saved through faith; and that not of yourselves: it is the gift of God: Not of works, lest any man should boast. For we are his workmanship, created in Christ Jesus unto good works, which God hath before ordained that we should walk in them (Eph. 2:8-10).

The Covenantal Necessity of a Personal Revolution

The Christian view of man is that man is born in sin and corruption. He is not born free, contrary to Rousseau.[20] If man is in cultural and political chains, then this is because of his sin. His sin is not merely institutional; it is innately personal. In this sense, Christianity agrees with the older conservatism's view of man (though not the newer, "economy in mind" doctrine of humanity): man is inherently limited. Yet Christianity also teaches that a definitive transformation of the individual can take place in history. An individual can be judicially and morally transformed in a moment. This is the ultimate revolution in life. It cannot be imposed by other men; it is an act of coercion by God: irresistible grace.

> Not by works of righteousness which we have done, but according to his mercy he saved us, by the washing of regeneration, and renewing of the Holy Ghost (Titus 3:5).

> For as the Father raiseth up the dead, and quickeneth them; even so the Son quickeneth whom he will (John 5:21).

> That the God of our Lord Jesus Christ, the Father of glory, may give unto you the spirit of wisdom and revelation in the knowledge of him: The eyes of your understanding being enlightened; that ye may know what is the hope of his calling, and what the riches of the glory of his inheritance in the saints (Eph. 1:17-18).

> And when the Gentiles heard this, they were glad, and glorified the word of the Lord: and as many as were ordained to eternal life

---

20. "Man is born free; and everywhere he is in chains." Jean Jacques Rousseau, *The Social Contract* (1762); *The Social Contract and Discourses* (New York: Dutton, 1913), p. 3.

believed (Acts 13:48).

John answered and said, A man can receive nothing, except it be given him from heaven (John 3:27).

For he saith to Moses, I will have mercy on whom I will have mercy, and I will have compassion on whom I will have compassion. So then it is not of him that willeth, nor of him that runneth, but of God that sheweth mercy (Rom. 9:15-16).

For who maketh thee to differ from another? and what hast thou that thou didst not receive? now if thou didst receive it, why dost thou glory, as if thou hadst not received it? (I Cor. 4:7).

Of his own will begat he us with the word of truth, that we should be a kind of firstfruits of his creatures (James 1:18).

Wherefore I give you to understand, that no man speaking by the Spirit of God calleth Jesus accursed: and that no man can say that Jesus is the Lord, but by the Holy Ghost (I Cor. 12:3).

And a certain woman named Lydia, a seller of purple, of the city of Thyatira, which worshipped God, heard us: whose heart the Lord opened, that she attended unto the things which were spoken of Paul (Acts 16:14).

This instant transformation needs time and self-government to work itself out in history. The *discontinuous event of salvation* subsequently requires the *continuous battle with sin* in history. There is a spiritual war going on in each man's inward parts.

For we know that the law is spiritual: but I am carnal, sold under sin. For that which I do I allow not: for what I would, that do I not; but what I hate, that do I. If then I do that which I would not, I consent unto the law that it is good. Now then it is no more I that do it, but sin that dwelleth in me. For I know that in me (that is, in my flesh,) dwelleth no good thing: for to will is present with me; but how to perform that which is good I find not. For the good that I would I do not: but the evil which I would not, that I do. Now if I do that I would not, it is no more I that do it, but sin that dwelleth in me. I find then a law, that, when I would do good, evil is present with me. For I delight in the law of God after the inward man: But I see another law in my members, warring against the

> law of my mind, and bringing me into captivity to the law of sin which is in my members. O wretched man that I am! who shall deliver me from the body of this death? I thank God through Jesus Christ our Lord. So then with the mind I myself serve the law of God; but with the flesh the law of sin (Rom. 7:14-25).

Civil Government

Civil law plays a role in this war: the public suppression of evil. The State imposes negative sanctions against evil public acts. The civil magistrate is in fact a minister of God.

> Let every soul be subject unto the higher powers. For there is no power but of God: the powers that be are ordained of God. Whosoever therefore resisteth the power, resisteth the ordinance of God: and they that resist shall receive to themselves damnation. For rulers are not a terror to good works, but to the evil. Wilt thou then not be afraid of the power? do that which is good, and thou shalt have praise of the same: *For he is the minister of God to thee for good.* But if thou do that which is evil, be afraid; for he beareth not the sword in vain: *for he is the minister of God*, a revenger to execute wrath upon him that doeth evil. Wherefore ye must needs be subject, not only for wrath, but also for conscience sake. For this cause pay ye tribute also: for they are God's ministers, attending continually upon this very thing. Render therefore to all their dues: tribute to whom tribute is due; custom to whom custom; fear to whom fear; honour to whom honour (Rom. 13:1-7). (emphasis added)

But the State is not an agency of salvation. It does not save man by making him positively good. It merely suppresses certain evil public acts of men. Thus, the Christian view of civil government is far closer to the constrained view of man. It is totally opposed to the messianic State of the unconstrained view. Christianity teaches that the reform of society must begin with the reform of the individual. To sustain a positive reform of society, God must initiate His transforming grace among many people.[21] He is the agent of positive transformation, not the State. All that the State can lawfully do is to suppress public

21. Gary North, *Dominion and Common Grace: The Biblical Basis of Progress* (Tyler, Texas: Institute for Christian Economics, 1987), ch. 6.

evil. It imposes negative sanctions, rarely positive ones (e.g., roads). This is clearly an anti-socialist view of civil authority.

Perfect Standards, Imperfect Applications

Moral-social standards are fixed. On this point, Christianity opposes both the social evolution of the constrained view[22] and the social revolution of the unconstrained view. God's revealed law is permanent. It cannot be improved on.

There is no doubt, however, that the application of these perfect standards to historical cases – the art of *casuistry* – is a trial-and-error process. It takes generations of experimentation and evaluation for a society to work out the implications of God's laws in history. History is always moving forward. Thus, the task of Christian reconstruction never ends. Even in the world beyond the final judgment, there will be trial and error and progress. Man cannot *comprehend* God. Man can never *surround* God's being or His mind. Man is a creature. Thus, life in this world is at best a never-ceasing striving toward perfection. In this sense, Christian social theory is closer to the constrained view than the unconstrained. Redemptive history is a continuous process. Step by step, we are required by God to learn from our mistakes and improve ourselves. Basic to this learning process in history is a system of sanctions: positive and negative. We call God's negative sanctions against His people *chastening*.

> Wherefore seeing we also are compassed about with so great a cloud of witnesses, let us lay aside every weight, and the sin which doth so easily beset us, and let us run with patience the race that is set before us, Looking unto Jesus the author and finisher of our faith; who for the joy that was set before him endured the cross, despising the shame, and is set down at the right hand of the throne of God. For consider him that endured such contradiction of sinners against himself, lest ye be wearied and faint in your minds. Ye have not yet resisted unto blood, striving against sin. And ye have forgotten the exhortation which speaketh unto you as unto children, *My*

---

22. I have in mind here the moral vision of those conservatives and economists who reject natural law theory and natural rights theory, meaning the vast majority of them since Darwin.

> *son, despise not thou the chastening of the Lord, nor faint when thou art rebuked of him: For whom the Lord loveth he chasteneth, and scourgeth every son whom he receiveth.* If ye endure chastening, God dealeth with you as with sons; for what son is he whom the father chasteneth not? But if ye be without chastisement, whereof all are partakers, then are ye bastards, and not sons. Furthermore we have had fathers of our flesh which corrected us, and we gave them reverence: shall we not much rather be in subjection unto the Father of spirits, and live? For they verily for a few days chastened us after their own pleasure; but he for our profit, that we might be partakers of his holiness (Heb. 12:1-10). (emphasis added)

Conclusion

Basic to biblical social theory is the idea of cultural progress. God brings His positive and negative sanctions in history in terms of His fixed moral standards, which are revealed clearly *only* in the Bible. There is a concrete universal in history who has met these moral and judicial standards: Jesus Christ. Perfection has been attained once (and only once) in history. This perfection is imputed to redeemed people at the point of their salvation (definitive sanctification). Nevertheless, perfection is not reached in history. It is a lifelong process (progressive sanctification).

What is true of the individual is also true of covenantal and non-covenantal corporate units. Their members are required to strive all through history to reach perfection as a corporate limit, by means of self-government, Church government, family government, and civil government. Each form of government involves the application of appropriate sanctions. When their representatives refuse to apply them, God will apply His appropriate negative corporate sanctions in history.

This only states what the social ideal is. The question then arises: *Can social progress be realized in history?* Is it like individual sanctification: attainable progressively in history? On the answer to this question, the Church has long been divided. Generally, the answer has been that there is no covenantally meaningful social progress. This has had crucial implications for Christian social theory, or the absence thereof.

4

PESSIMILLENNIALISM

In history and time on earth, God is preparing a people to whom He can make known, and who will be able to appreciate, the boundless riches of the glory of His grace, and from whom He will receive an appropriate measure of response. Such a response can come only from those who, having ceased to consider their own personal salvation as the chief end of life, pass their time here on earth as the willing bond-servants of Christ, with their eyes fixed upon the stupendous consummation towards which all history moves, and in the achievement of which they must play their own humble but necessary part. This part can be effectively performed only by those who have attained some intellectual maturity and have made earnest efforts to understand the revealed will and purposes of God, much of which is couched in the form of predictive prophecy.

Roderick Campbell (1954)[1]

Christian Reconstructionists, as both postmillennial and theonomic,[2] have from the beginning challenged the two rival dominant eschatological theories, premillennialism and amillennialism ("pessimillennialism" as Nigel Lee has identified them), both of which deny that Christianity will be dominant culturally or any other way when Jesus Christ returns physically to bring His judgment. The Church supposedly will not succeed in fulfilling Christ's Great Commission during Church history: baptizing and discipling the nations (Matt. 28:18-20).[3] Both of these

1. Roderick Campbell, *Israel and the New Covenant* (Tyler, Texas: Geneva Divinity School Press, [1954] 1981), p. 182.

2. Greg L. Bahnsen, *Theonomy in Christian Ethics* (Phillipsburg, New Jersey: Presbyterian and Reformed, [1977] 1984).

3. Kenneth L. Gentry, Jr., *The Greatness of the Great Commission: The Christian Enterprise*

millennial views are also intensely antinomian in their modern formulations, and, as I argue in this book, also antinomian in principle. I mean by "antinomian" that the defenders of each pessimillennial system deny the continuing authority of the Old Testament case laws in the New Testament era.[4]

The fundamentalist tradition has been dominant culturally in American evangelical circles.[5] The Calvinist-Reformed tradition has until recently dominated the realm of scholarship in evangelical circles, with Lutheranism contributing some material in Bible exegesis. Lutheranism has always been amillennialist, while twentieth-century Calvinism, heavily influenced by the Dutch, has also been amillennialist. In recent years, neo-evangelicalism has combined Arminianism, mild theological liberalism, mild theological conservatism, pluralism, and a narrowly ecclesiastical Calvinism into a curious but unstable mixture of social concern coupled with an explicit denial of the possibility or desirability of biblical law-based solutions.

Because Christian Reconstructionism is a philosophy of social activism,[6] it has had to confront the fundamentalists, whose dominance in twentieth-century American evangelicalism has crippled most attempts at Christian social reform.[7] The only major exception to this rule was the post-World War I passage of the Eighteenth Amendment to the Constitution, which outlawed the manufacture or sale of alcoholic beverages, and which

---

in a Fallen World (Tyler, Texas: Institute for Christian Economics, 1990),

4. Gary North, *Tools of Dominion: The Case Laws of Exodus* (Tyler, Texas: Institute for Christian Economics, 1990), ch. 2. It is conceivable that a few dispensational theologians might admit privately that the Old Testament's case laws will be used by Jesus to judge the nations during the future millennial age. They do not admit this possibility in public, however. In any case, they would regard this as judicially and culturally irrelevant for the "Church Age."

5. Symposium on the Failure of the American Baptist Culture, *Christianity and Civilization*, I (1983).

6. Gary North, *Is the World Running Down? Crisis in the Christian Worldview* (Tyler, Texas: Institute for Christian Economics, 1988), Appendix C: "Comprehensive Redemption: A Theology for Social Action"; reprinted from *The Journal of Christian Reconstruction*, VIII (1981); North, *Backward Christian Soldiers? An Action Manual for Christian Reconstruction* (Tyler, Texas: Institute for Christian Economics, 1984); Gentry, *Greatness of the Great Commission*.

7. George M. Marsden, *Fundamentalism and American Culture: The Shaping of Twentieth-Century Evangelicalism, 1870-1925* (New York: Oxford University Press, 1980).

was repealed in 1933. Prohibition is almost universally acknowledged to have been a social and political disaster.[8] This was the last politically successful crusade by American fundamentalists. They had considerable support from humanistic Progressives and statist power-seekers; they did not achieve this alone. It is the premier twentieth-century American example of the alliance between the escape religionists and the power religionists.[9]

Simultaneously, because Christian Reconstructionism is also an intellectual movement, it has had to challenge the amillennialists and the neo-evangelicals. In short, Christian Reconstructionists have had to fight a "two-front" war. This theological war is not merely a two-front war eschatologically (against two rival millennial views); it is also a two-front war judicially (against two rival views of God's law and His historical sanctions).[10] Theonomy and postmillennial eschatology cannot be separated theologically. Covenant theology necessarily involves a specific theory of God's law and God's sanctions in history.[11] The biblical covenant model is an unbreakable, self-consistent unit. But to accept this statement as fact is to adopt a uniquely biblical view of history, society, and progress, a step that few Bible-affirming theologians are willing to take. When even Greg Bahnsen denies this unity,[12] it is not surprising that the histori-

---

8. John Kobler, *Ardent Spirits: The Rise and Fall of Prohibitionism* (New York: Putnam's, 1973).

9. James H. Timberlake, *Prohibition and the Progressive Movement, 1900-1920* (New York: Atheneum, 1970); Murray N. Rothbard, "World War I as Fulfillment: Power and the Intellectuals," *Journal of Libertarian Studies*, IX (Winter 1989), pp. 83-87. It is worth noting that conservative Presbyterian spokesman J. Gresham Machen opposed the Presbyterian Church's support of the Volstead Act, for which he was publicly attacked by the general Christian public. Ned B. Stonehouse, *J. Gresham Machen: A Biography* (2nd ed.; Philadelphia: Westminster Theological Seminary, [1955] 1978), pp. 387-88.

10. On the one side, a hybrid of natural law theory and the Bible. On the other, a vague moral law position that is never defined or applied to specific cases.

11. Ray R. Sutton, *That You May Prosper: Dominion By Covenant* (Tyler, Texas: Institute for Christian Economics, 1987), ch. 4.

12. Greg L. Bahnsen, *By This Standard: The Authority of God's Law Today* (Tyler, Texas: Institute for Christian Economics, 1985), p. 8. It is my opinion that Rev. Bahnsen's denial that theonomy inherently implies postmillennialism – the question of God's covenantal sanctions in history – is motivated in part by his attempt to adopt a strategy of fighting two separate theological wars rather than an interlinked two-front war. He faces an institutional dilemma. He insists that theonomy is alone biblical and therefore is consis-

cal sanctions section of the biblical civil covenant (point four) is rarely discussed and never affirmed as continuing in New Testament times by the vast majority of those who call themselves covenant theologians.

Premillennialism

Historic premillennialists, meaning non-dispensationalists, are few in number. A comparative handful of these few premillennial scholars have sought to produce works demonstrating their social concern ever since the publication of Carl F. H. Henry's book, *The Uneasy Conscience of Modern Fundamentalism* (1947), which can be said to have launched the neo-evangelical movement.[13] Yet not one published book outlining a comprehensive and explicitly biblical social theory has come from any historic premillennialist in the post-World War II era. (As far as I can determine, none has come from any premillennialist,

---

tent with the Westminster Confession of Faith, Chapter XIX. He is also an ordained minister in the Orthodox Presbyterian Church, which, like all modern Bible-believing Presbyterian churches except the tiny Bible Presbyterian Church, is officially neutral eschatologically and is dominated by amillennialists. To argue that theonomy necessarily implies postmillennialism is necessarily to affirm the institutional strategy – extremely long term, paralleling the coming of the promised millennial blessings – of tightening up the Church's confessional standards on both eschatology and law, and then screening out all premillennial and amillennial church officers, which is what both Rushdoony and I recommend. Bahnsen is publicly content with the existing 1789 American revision of the original 1646 Westminster Standards, a revision imposed in order to make them conform with the political pluralism of the anti-Trinitarian U.S. Constitution. See Gary North, *Political Polytheism: The Myth of Pluralism* (Tyler, Texas: Institute for Christian Economics, 1989), pp. 543-50. Nevertheless, I have not gone so far as Rushdoony has, i.e., to assert that amillennialism and premillennialism are literally blasphemy. "Amillennialism and premillennialism are in retreat from the world and blasphemously surrender it to the devil. . . . To turn the world-conquering word of the sovereign, omnipotent, and triune God into a symbol of impotence is not a mark of faith. It is blasphemy." R. J. Rushdoony, "Postmillennialism vs. Impotent Religion," *Journal of Christian Reconstruction*, III (Winter 1976-77), pp. 125-26.

13. The bankruptcy of the neo-evangelical movement today can be seen in *Evangelical Affirmations*, edited by Kenneth S. Kantzer and Carl F. H. Henry (Grand Rapids, Michigan: Zondervan Academie, 1990). See especially Chapter 7: "Social Ethics." These essays were presented at a 1989 conference of the National Association of Evangelicals. The 385 theologians in attendance could not agree that the Bible teaches the doctrine of eternal punishment as against the Seventh-Day Adventist doctrine of annihilationism. The vote to affirm the existence of hell was split, but the chairman announced that the vote had failed to gain a majority. See *World* (June 3, 1989), p. 9.

ever.) Rev. Francis Schaeffer is the best example. His works are intellectual in tone, but he never attempted to offer a positive alternative to the prevailing humanist culture that he so eloquently dissected.[14] He wrote intellectual history, literary and art criticism, and apologetics, but not social theory.

Rev. Schaeffer was politically conservative, although this was seldom made clear in his books, and he never defended this conservatism biblically. In this sense, he was like amillennialist philosopher-apologist Cornelius Van Til, who taught Schaeffer apologetics at Westminster Theological Seminary, 1935-37. Unlike Schaeffer, most of the other contemporary premillennial authors who have been concerned with social action have been political liberals of the Wheaton College-*Christianity Today*-Inter-Varsity perspective: "trendier than thou" Christianity. They have not been willing to admit publicly what dispensational premillennialist Tommy Ice freely admitted in a debate with Gary DeMar and me: "Premillennialists have always been involved in the present world. And basically, they have picked up on the ethical position of their contemporaries."[15] This is what R. J. Rushdoony and I had been saying about premillennialists for a quarter century before that debate took place.

Dispensational premillennialists have tended to be politically conservative. They usually agree with the social, political, and economic views of the Christian Reconstructionists. They object only to our Bible-based, Old Testament law-based methodology. They prefer not to discuss why they agree with our conclusions, for then they would have to show how they arrived at their conclusions, which they cannot support without appealing to either to secular humanist conservative thinkers or Roman Catholic conservative thinkers. The neo-evangelical premillennialists (mostly liberals) have generally regarded as their ideological colleagues not the "red neck fundamentalists" and political conservatives, but rather the politically liberal professors who taught them in state universities and other humanist insti-

---

14. North, *Political Polytheism*, ch. 4.

15. Gary DeMar, *The Debate Over Christian Reconstruction* (Ft. Worth, Texas: Dominion Press, 1988), p. 185.

tutions of higher academic certification.[16] Neither group has shown that the Bible supports its position.

Is Christian social theory relevant? Second, is it possible? The premillennialists make social theory *irrelevant* by asserting the progressive impotence and external defeat of the Church and Christian institutions prior to the Second Coming of Jesus Christ to set up an earthly millennial kingdom. But far more important for the development of Christian social theory, this perspective, being antinomian with respect to God's covenant law, denies the existence of God's culture-wide sanctions in history, at least prior to Jesus' millennial kingdom on earth. As I argue in this book, this anti-sanctions perspective makes *impossible* the development of a specifically biblical social theory.

Because the modern premillennial, dispensational tradition has not been interested in scholarship in general, its spokesmen have not been expected by the movement's own members to provide a biblical social theory. All they have had to do is voice their approval of the U.S. Constitution, free enterprise, the nuclear family, and the American civil religion. But the amillennial tradition is different. For one thing, it has been more oriented toward European thought and culture, in which it has its historical roots. For another, it has been far more interested in scholarship. This has been especially true of the Dutch Calvinist wing, which sometimes imitates German scholarship in its rigor and prolixity (e.g., Herman Ridderbos). The question arises: What about amillennial social theory? Does such a thing exist?

Amillennialism

The amillennialists share two key viewpoints with the premillennialists: *antinomianism* with respect to the authority of the Old Testament case laws and *historical pessimism* regarding the cultural efforts of Christians in history. Historically, the Lutherans have admitted as much. They are amillennial.[17] Luther was an

16. In this sense, Carl F. H. Henry is an anomaly; he, too, is generally conservative politically, but he does not write much about politics. Henry was educated before the post-War expansion of higher education in America, i.e., before liberalism took over.

17. *The "End Times": A Study on Eschatology and the Millennium*, Report of the Commis-

amillennialist and self-consciously an ethical dualist, asserting a radical dichotomy between Christians and pagans with respect to their need for civil law.[18] Christians do not need civil law, Luther insisted, let alone Old Testament civil law; only pagans need civil law. "Now observe," he wrote of Christians, "these people need no temporal law or sword. If all the world were composed of real Christians, that is, true believers, there would be no need for or benefits from prince, king, sword, or law. They would serve no purpose, since Christians have in their heart the Holy Spirit, who both teaches and makes them to do injustice to no one, to love everyone, and to suffer injustice and even death willingly and cheerfully at the hands of everyone."[19] Given such a view of civil law,[20] it is understandable why there has never been any attempt by Lutheran scholars to develop a uniquely biblical social theory. From Luther's colleague Philip Melanchthon[21] until today, Bible-believing Lutheran social commentators have relied on some variant of Stoic and Roman Catholic natural law theory in all discussions social and political. The Calvinists have adopted other approaches.

Grammar, Structure, Symbol

A contemporary example of this systematic denial of God's historic sanctions, especially in the realm of civil government, is a book by a professor at Reformed Theological Seminary, Richard L. Pratt, Jr., *He Gave Us Stories: The Bible Student's Guide to Interpreting the Old Testament Narratives*.[22] Professor Pratt does not even mention the word "covenant" until page 285 of this

---

sion on Theology and Church Relations of the Lutheran Church – Missouri Synod (Sept. 1989).

18. Charles Trinkaus, "The Religious Foundations of Luther's Social Views," in John H. Mundy, et al, *Essays in Medieval Life* (Cheshire, Connecticut: Biblo & Tannen, 1955), pp. 71-87. See also Gary North, "The Economic Thought of Luther and Calvin," *Journal of Christian Reconstruction*, II (Summer 1975), pp. 76-89.

19. Martin Luther, "Temporal Authority: To What Extent It Should Be Obeyed" (1523), *Luther's Works* (Philadelphia: Fortress Press, 1962), XLV, p. 89.

20. See also the Augsburg Confession, XVI:3.

21. Clyde Leonard Manschreck, *Melanchthon: The Quiet Reformer* (New York: Abingdon, 1958), ch. 22.

22. Brentwood, Tennessee: Wolgemuth & Hyatt, 1990.

nearly 500-page book on the Old Covenant. He outlines the five-point covenant structure on page 286, but does nothing with it. He does not offer a single example of how this model was used in any Old Covenant narrative, nor does he mention the prophets' use of it. He suggests no application of the covenant model in society, either in the Old Testament or the New Testament. His only other reference to the covenant – but not its five points – is a brief mention of "major covenant events in the days of Adam, Noah, Abraham, Moses, and David."[23] He does not say what these events were. He then implicitly abandons covenant theology for what he calls the "organic model"[24] and "organic developments."[25] But when stripped of its judicial (i.e., covenantal) foundations, as Pratt clearly insists that it should be,[26] social organicism becomes the worldview of Roman Catholicism, philosophical realism, and traditional secular conservatism. Organicism is an alternative to covenant theology, not an application of it.[27] Yet all of this is presented to the reader as an exercise in biblical hermeneutics by a Calvinist covenant theologian. Calvinistic, yes; covenantal, no.

Yes, God did give us many stories. The questions are: What kind of stories? With what moral? With what structure? Leading to what action, both personal and corporate? Pratt does not say. He is subtly attempting to substitute a symbolic-literary interpretation of the Bible for the traditional grammatical-historical approach. The problem is, neither of these approaches alone tells us what the theology of the Bible is. The war between the two camps goes on, when it could be resolved by settling the neglected issue: the *theological structure* governing the narratives. What is this structure? The biblical covenant model.[28]

The medieval trivium reflected the tripartite division of

23. *Ibid.*, p. 337.
24. *Ibid.*, p. 341.
25. *Ibid.*, p. 344.
26. *Ibid.*, pp. 343-44.
27. On the misuse of the organic model, see Gary North, *Moses and Pharaoh: Dominion Religion vs. Power Religion* (Tyler, Texas: Institute for Christian Economics, 1985), ch. 17: "The Metaphor of Growth: Ethics."
28. Sutton, *That You May Prosper*.

Scriptural interpretation. The trivium was grammar, logic, and rhetoric. There is good evidence that the very development of the child's mind as he becomes an adult is tied closely to this structure.[29] The Bible expositor must carefully deal with the grammar of each text, but not to the exlusion of the underlying theological structure or its symbolism (literary framework). Similarly, the examination of the subtle symbols and allegories of the Scripture – the rhetorical component of the texts – must not be attempted apart from both grammar and theology. To ignore both grammar and theological structure leads directly to the allegorical methodology of the Roman Catholic Church that the Reformation challenged. What both the grammatical-historical school and the "wild blue yonder" symbolic interpretation school reject is the idea that the Pentateuch and the Book of Deuteronomy provide us with God's master plan, a five-point theological structure. They resent the "procrustian bed" of the covenant model, preferring instead other text-stretching beds, such as the six loci of seventeenth-century Protestant Scholasticism[30] or the five points of Calvinism.[31] While these can be derived theologically from the whole of Scripture, they are not found in the actual structure of any biblical text. The five-point covenant model is.

Common Grace

Cornelius Van Til, the Dutch-American Calvinist philosopher, was a defender of what I have called common grace amillennialism. There are two general schools of thought within this movement: Van Til's and Meredith G. Kline's, Van Til's colleague at Westminster Theological Seminary. Van Til's view is self-consciously pessimistic. Kline's is officially neutral with respect to progress in history. I categorize these rival views as (1) Bad News for Future Christian Man and (2) Random News

---

29. Dorothy L. Sayers, "The Lost Tools of Learnning" (1947); reprinted in *Journal of Christian Reconstruction*, IV (Summer 1977).

30. Theology proper (God), hamartiology (sin), Christology, soteriology (redemption), ecclesiology (Church), and eschatology (last things).

31. Total depravity of man, God's unconditional election, limited (specific) atonement, irresistible grace, and the perseverance of the saints.

for Future Christian Man. The Bad News school tends to be more politically conservative ("Hold the fort, boys!"), though generally non-committal in public; the Random News school tends to be politically liberal ("Let's shoot over the attackers' heads!"), and more likely to be outspoken. First, the bad news:

> But when all the reprobate are epistemologically self-conscious, the crack of doom has come. The fully self-conscious reprobate will do all he can in every dimension to destroy the people of God. So while we seek with all our power to hasten the process of differentiation in every dimension we are yet thankful, on the other hand, for "the day of grace," the day of undeveloped differentiation. Such tolerance as we receive on the part of the world is due to this fact that we live in the earlier, rather than in the later, stage of history. And such influence on the public situation as we can effect, whether in society or in state, presupposes this undifferentiated stage of development.[32]

Van Til's position is clear: as history develops, the persecution of Christians by the reprobates increases. The good get better, while the bad get worse; the good get less influential, while the bad get increasingly dominant. Everyone becomes more self-conscious, and spiritual darkness spreads. Christians should therefore be thankful that they live today rather than later. We are tolerated today, he says; later, we shall be persecuted. This is the traditional amillennial view of the future.

The amillennialists of the Dutch Calvinist common grace school of thought are different from the Lutherans. Unlike the Lutherans, who are ethical dualists, the Dutch common grace amillennialists have repeatedly asserted both the moral necessity and the intellectual possibility of developing explicitly Christian alternatives to humanist thought in every area of life.[33] This is the "world and life" Calvinism of Abraham Kuyper.[34] Their

---

32. Cornelius Van Til, *Common Grace* (1947), reprinted in *Common Grace and the Gospel* (Nutley, New Jersey: Presbyterian & Reformed, 1972), p. 85.

33. Henry R. Van Til, *The Calvinistic Concept of Culture* (Philadelphia: Presbyterian & Reformed, 1959). Henry Van Til was Cornelius' nephew.

34. Abraham Kuyper, *Lectures on Calvinism* (Grand Rapids, Michigan: Eerdmans, [1898] 1931). Kuyper was the Prime Minister of the Netherlands at the turn of the century. He also founded the Free University of Amsterdam. Frank Vanden Berg,

problem is this: they have yet to describe in detail just what this uniquely Christian social theory is. Also, they have not identified those biblical passages from which such a comprehensive social theory might be developed. Theirs has been a strictly negative intellectual and social apologetic.[35] They have tried to beat something – modern humanism – with nothing specific.

This movement is subdivided between political conservatives and political liberals, with the liberals dominant, especially in print. The political conservatives, like premillennialist Francis Schaeffer, have contented themselves with writing books on the evils and threats to freedom from modern humanism (e.g., H. Evan Runner, H. Van Riessen).[36] The liberals, like the politically liberal neo-evangelical premillennialists, have recommended the bankrupt solutions – bankrupt economically, intellectually, and politically – of modern Keynesian economics,[37] as well as modern political pluralism[38] (e.g., the Toronto-based Institute for Christian Studies and Wedge Publishing).

Neither side has been able to show precisely what the Bible

Abraham Kuyper: A Biography (St. Catherines, Ontario: Paideia Press, [1960] 1978).

35. See especially the works of Herman Dooyeweerd, most notably *A New Critique of Theoretical Thought*, 4 vols. (Philadelphia: Presbyterian & Reformed, 1954).

36. On Van Riessen, see Chapter 5, below. Runner and Van Riessen wrote for an annual publication in the early 1960's, *Christian Perspectives*.

37. Sometimes this is disguised in the language of medieval guild socialism. Sometimes, however, they have adopted the language of Marxism. Hendrik Hart wrote in 1972: "Today we still have to learn to listen to the words of Marx." Hart, "Alienation," in John H. Redekop (ed.), *Labor Problems in Christian Perspective* (Grand Rapids, Michigan: Eerdmans, 1972), p. 293. He also referred to Marx's "just and courageous protest" (pp. 293-94). Furthermore, speaking of modern revolutionary movements, "If the Church is not strong enough to listen to these movements and learn from them, it does not have the strength to live anymore" (p. 294). This was the standard fare of the "we, too, are academically relevant" neo-Dooyeweerdian radicals in the 1970's. Thankfully, they faded away in the 1980's. The visible collapse of the European Marxist regimes – though not the Soviet Union's military might – in late 1989 should permanently bury the yellowing pages of such 1970's propaganda.

38. An example of such writing is "principled pluralist" James Skillen's early effort, "The Governor and the Chef," *Vanguard* (May/June 1971). *Vanguard* was published by the Institute for Christian Studies. These men appeal endlessly to unspecified "creation principles," yet they also deny that the Bible provides explicit blueprints (or "cookbook recipes," to use Skillen's analogy) for specific political or economic action. The heart and soul of their social theory is this: "The creation, you see, is open-ended." Skillen, p. 20. Cf. North, *Political Polytheism*, pp. 15-17, 121-25.

specifically requires of society, since this would require an appeal to the Old Testament case laws, which both sides reject as no longer judicially binding in the New Testament era. Therefore, they have no plan of action or social reform. A representative statement of the social theory of common grace amillennialism is Bob Goudzwaard's: "A program of action drawn up to carry out a blueprint evokes the impression of a short-term realization of objectives. . . . What follows, therefore, presents no program of action."[39] This statement appears on page 188 of a book with only 249 pages of text, and follows a lengthy attack on both capitalism and Western civilization's idea of progress. This is typical of the Dooyeweerdian movement: all dynamite and no cement.[40] It disappeared from the Christian intellectual scene in the early 1980's. It had never enjoyed very much influence outside of Christian Reformed circles.[41]

The Problem of Two Leavens

These common grace Dutch scholars and their North American academic disciples have all been amillennialists. As amillennialists, they believe that Satan's earthly kingdom and influence will expand over time until Jesus Christ comes with His angels in final judgment. This assertion of the cumulative, visible triumph of Satan's kingdom in history is inherent in all amillennialism. This view of New Testament era history *defines* amillennialism. Amillennialism, as with premillennialism's view of everything that takes place prior to the millennium, is essentially a reversed form of postmillennialism: *postmillennialism for Satan's kingdom.*[42] The idea that there can be an "optimistic amillennialism" is difficult to take seriously. Even the barest

39. Bob Goudzwaard, *Capitalism and Progress: A Diagnosis of Western Society* (co-published by Wedge and Eerdmans, 1979), p. 188. He nevertheless calls for a no-growth, steady-state economy for Western Europe and North America: p. 194. Behind every denial of a blueprint there lurks a hidden agenda and a secret blueprint.

40. North, *Political Pluralism*, ch. 3. See also North, *The Sinai Strategy: Economics and the Ten Commandments* (Tyler, Texas: Institute for Christian Economics, 1986), Appendix C: "Social Antinomianism."

41. I include here Westminster Theological Seminary.

42. North, *Political Polytheism*, p. 139.

outline of such a theology has never been offered. Any amillennial scheme must proclaim one of two positions: either linear history downward into public evil (Van Til's view) or ethically random historical change in a world presently controlled by covenant-breakers (Kline's view).[43] Perhaps some energetic and creative amillennialist will make the exegetical attempt someday, but so far, optimistic amillennialism is simply soft-core postmillennialism for amillennialists still in transition.[44]

Despite the structural cultural pessimism built into all amillennialism, common grace amillennialists often insist that God's kingdom also develops and even expands in history. But how can both kingdoms expand simultaneously? It is covenantally inconsistent to argue, as these amillennialists do argue, either implicitly or explicitly, that Satan's *visible* kingdom expands in history, while only God's *invisible* kingdom expands. The biblical concept of these rival kingdoms is this: rival *civilizations*. Each is both natural and supernatural. Each is a covenantal unit. If Satan's kingdom has both a spiritual and an institutional side, then so must God's. How can one kingdom (civilization) expand if it does not progressively push the other out of history's cultural loaf? Yet common grace amillennialists insist that each kingdom expands. Evil "leaven" wins, despite Matthew 13:33.

They can defend this two-leavens perspective only by playing games with language. They belatedly admit in the back pages of their books that Satan's earthly covenantal representatives will progressively impose their negative sanctions against Christians as history advances. This admission makes ludicrous the idea of God's kingdom in history. Amillennialism proclaims *a kingdom whose designated representatives cannot bring the King's sanctions in history*, which is a denial of any judicial connection between God's kingdom-civilization and history. Yet it is precisely this that amillennialists proclaim: a kingdom whose only predictable, institutional, covenantal sanctions in history are ecclesiastical and familial, never civil. This makes God the Lord of a declining percentage of churches and families, but not of history. As

43. See Chapter 7, below.

44. I have never heard of anyone who claims to be an optimistic premillennialist.

Bahnsen says, "what they object to in postmillennial writers is the inclusion of external, visible, this-earthly aspects within the scope of the kingdom of God in this age."[45]

Calvinistic amillennialists cannot easily avoid the covenantal language of continuity, victory, and lordship. Such language is basic to the heritage of Calvinism, since Calvinism in the formative sixteenth and seventeenth centuries was generally postmillennial.[46] Amillennial Calvinists still use this optimistic language, yet they deny the kingdom's progressive visible manifestation in history. They make their position clear: "There is no room for optimism: towards the end, in the camps of the satanic and the anti-Christ, culture will sicken, and the Church will yearn to be delivered from its distress."[47] They proclaim God's victory in one passage, yet they deny almost all cultural traces of it in another. They sound a battle cry for historical defeat. This is schizophrenic.

"Things Are Not What They Seem"

Consider Revelation 5. This passage pictures the resurrected Christ in heaven:

> And when he had taken the book, the four beasts and four and twenty elders fell down before the Lamb, having every one of them harps, and golden vials full of odours, which are the prayers of saints. And they sung a new song, saying, Thou art worthy to take the book, and to open the seals thereof: for thou wast slain, and hast redeemed us to God by thy blood out of every kindred, and tongue, and people, and nation; And hast made us unto our God kings and priests: and we shall reign on the earth (Rev. 5:8-10).

---

45. Greg L. Bahnsen, "This World and the Kingdom of God," in Gary DeMar and Peter J. Leithart, *The Reduction of Christianity: A Biblical Response to Dave Hunt* (Ft. Worth, Texas: Dominion Press, 1988), p. 352.

46. Iain Murray, *The Puritan Hope: A Study in Revival and the Interpretation of Prophecy* (London: Banner of Truth Trust, 1971); J. A. De Jong, *As the Waters Cover the Sea: Millennial Expectations in the Rise of Anglo-American Missions, 1640-1810* (Kampen, Netherlands: Kok, 1970); Greg L. Bahnsen, "The *Prima Facie* Acceptability of Postmillennialism," *Journal of Christian Reconstruction*, III (Winter 1976-77), pp. 76-88.

47. H. de Jongste and J. M. van Krimpen, *The Bible and the Life of the Christian* (Philadelphia: Presbyterian & Reformed, 1968), p. 85.

The text is specific: *the elders in heaven will reign upon the earth.* Because they were in a disembodied spiritual state at the time of John's revelation, they can be said to reign on earth in the future in one of four ways: (1) physically (during pop-dispensationalism's future millennium);[48] (2) representatively (during postmillennialism's progressive judicial millennium); (3) post-historically (after the final judgment), thereby making the whole passage irrelevant for history; or (4) symbolically.

This passage presents a major dilemma for the amillennialist expositor. He cannot appeal to either of the first two exegetical options and still remain amillennial, yet he does not want to adopt the third, since this section of the Book of Revelation is generally believed by commentators to apply to history, not to the post-resurrection state. His only other choice is to interpret the Revelation 5:10 symbolically. Such an appeal to symbolism also destroys the passage's relevance for history.

William Hendriksen, one of the premier amillennial expositors in the twentieth century, cannot gracefully avoid this problem in his commentary on the Book of Revelation. He barely tries to escape. He begins with this presupposition: "The theme of this book is: *the Victory of Christ and of his Church over the Dragon (satan) and his Helpers*. The Apocalypse intends to show you, dear believer, that things are not what they *seem!*"[49] Things must be very different from what they seem to Mr. Hendriksen,

48. The possibility of mixing resurrected saints and fallen humanity during the coming millennium has not been taken seriously by professionally trained dispensational theologians (e.g., John Walvoord, J. Dwight Pentecost), but popularizers of the dispensational position (e.g., Dave Hunt) have asserted that this will take place. See John Walvoord, *The Rapture Question* (rev. ed.; Grand Rapids, Michigan: Zondervan, 1979), p. 86; J. Dwight Pentecost, "The Relation between Living and Resurrected Saints in The Millennium," *Bibliotheca Sacra*, vol. 117 (Oct. 1960), pp. 337, 341. Hunt offers his contrary opinion: "After the Antichrist's kingdom has ended in doom, Jesus will reign over this earth at last. Which of these kingdoms we will be in depends upon the choice we make now – for God's truth or for the Lie." Dave Hunt, *Peace Prosperity and the Coming Holocaust* (Eugene, Oregon: Harvest House, 1983), p. 263; see also below, p. 256. In 1988, during his debate with me and Gary DeMar in Dallas, he re-stated his view that resurrected saints will rule on earth during the millennium. A set of audiotapes or a videotape of that debate can be ordered from the Institute for Christian Economics.

49. W. Hendriksen, *More Than Conquerors: An Interpretation of the Book of Revelation* (Grand Rapids, Michigan: Baker, [1939] 1965), p. 12.

since he is an amillennialist, and therefore he sees the history of the Church as a progressive defeat for the gospel's social and cultural influence. He recognizes that Revelation 5:10 really refers to Christians on earth, and not simply to the 24 elders and the four angelic beings in heaven. Obviously, Christians and angels in heaven cannot be defeated, yet Christians on earth do appear to be defeated. He asks: "Do they *seem* to be defeated? In *reality* they *reign!* Yes, they reign *upon the earth*, 5:10; in *heaven with Christ a thousand years*, 20:4; *in the new heaven and earth for ever and ever*, 22:5."[50]

This is theological mumbo-jumbo. Departed Christians can be said to reign literally in heaven; fine. They will reign literally after the final resurrection; also fine. But how in the name of grammar and consistent usage can they be said in the same verse to reign on the earth *in history* – "we shall reign on the earth"? Surely not literally; Hendriksen is an amillennialist, not a dispensationalist.

The answer is found in point two of the biblical covenant model: *representation*. This can be of two kinds: symbolic (non-historical) and judicial.[51] The postmillennialist says that the earthly Church Militant represents *in history* the rule of the heavenly Church Triumphant. The Church Triumphant prays for the historic success of the Church Militant: "How Long, O Lord?" (Rev. 6:10a). The Church Militant progressively becomes victorious in history, so the saints in heaven can be said to rule on earth. But the amillennialist cannot admit this. He adopts instead the language of *symbolic representation* (non-historical). He identifies those spoken of in the passage as appearing to be defeated, which is not in the actual text. Christians in heaven surely are not defeated. Because the elders in heaven reign, the Christians on earth are said to reign, too. Heaven's victory cannot serve as a meaningful guide to history. The victory is merely symbolic; history is institutionally irrelevant. The Book

50. *Ibid.*, pp. 13-14.

51. Unless premillennialists adopt Dave Hunt's pop-dispensationalism, with its doctrine of resurrected saints and mortals living side by side during the millennium, they too are forced to adopt the language of representation.

of Revelation becomes an enigma: "The Apocalypse intends to show you, dear believer, that things are not what they *seem!*" If this seems confusing, it is because amillennialism is confusing.

Either Christians will reign on earth and in history (i.e., pre-Second Coming) or they will not. If neither we nor our covenantal successors will ever be able in history to apply the Bible-specified sanctions of the heavenly King whom we represent on earth, then Christians cannot be said ever to reign in history. The language of "reigning" would then be both misleading and inappropriate. The issue here is simple: *Christians' possession of the judicial authority to impose negative civil sanctions or the private economic power to impose both positive and negative cultural sanctions.* Amillennialists categorically deny that Christians will ever exercise such widespread authority or influence. Thus, amillennialists have yet to explain this eschatologically crucial biblical text from Revelation. It speaks of Christians who reign on earth.

Utopianism Without Earthly Hope

It does even less good to encourage the optimism of your readers by proclaiming, as Raymond Zorn does, that "to the extent that the world is christianized by the Church's efforts, it exhibits to that degree at least, the all-inclusive power of Christ by which His victory since Calvary is brought to actualization,"[52] if you do not really believe that the Church ever can achieve the Christianization of the world in history. Yet this is standard theological fare among amillennialists. A few pages after the ingeniously qualified phrase "to the extent that" was added by the author to a sentence displaying considerable verbal optimism, he added: ". . . Jesus came to found a kingdom that was not of this world."[53] (The implicit move toward an inner, "higher," "victorious" mysticism here should be obvious, although it has never been obvious to Calvinistic amillennialists, unlike medieval Catholic amillennialists.) Zorn then tells us

52. Raymond O. Zorn, *Church and Kingdom* (Philadelphia: Presbyterian & Reformed, 1962), p. 146.

53. *Ibid.*, p. 180.

that a tyrannical one-world State appears to be imminent.[54] This State will be overcome by Christ only at His return in final judgment.[55] That is, only with the end of history (a cosmic discontinuity) can Christians expect deliverance from political tyranny. Some victory!

Then what is the Christian's task in history? Zorn is straightforward: to submit to the powers of political evil, since they have won the political battle and possesses lawful authority. The Church "must loyally give to the State whatever is necessary for its existence."[56] The Church is simply a watchman, testifying to the evils of the day.[57] Its grim historical task is to bear witness to a kingdom which will contract throughout history, but which will then triumph in the discontinuity of final judgment. Zorn therefore calls Christians to the utopian task of calling other men to participate in building a universal kingdom that will not in fact become established in history, i.e., *kingdom-building in a world of continual, external, visible defeat*. He calls this task, "Bearing witness to and directing toward the true utopian goal."[58] (And the critics call postmillennialists "utopian"!) The Church's continuity of progressive visible defeat in history is called victorious only because of a final, divinely imposed discontinuity that ends history. The kingdom triumphs no place (utopia) on earth.

Such a view of history is not congenial to the development of social theory. But is it utopian? Utopian causes have always attracted followers by promising the possibility of achieving the seemingly impossible sometime in the future. A utopian movement has at least implicitly promised a future cultural transition to a better world, despite the seeming discontinuity involved in getting from "here" to "there." Utopian movements present a description, however theoretical and however historically remote, of a better world to come *in history*. They are utopian in the sense that there is no clear-cut systematic program to get

54. *Ibid.*, p. 182.
55. *Ibid.*, p. 184.
56. *Ibid.*, pp. 185-86.
57. *Ibid.*, p. 187
58. *Ibid.*, p. 214. Why Rushdoony wrote the Foreword to this amillennial book escapes me.

from this world to the promised world. There is no program of continuity, i.e., cultural or political reform. Utopian causes tend to become *apocalyptic*: waiting for a history-transforming, society-transforming, discontinuous event.

Compare this with the amillennialists' attempt to recruit and motivate dedicated followers on their uniquely *anti-historical* premise that the Bible's promised better world can be achieved only at the end of history, after the great discontinuity of final judgment and the abolition of history. They make no attempt to describe the daily operations of this future, post-resurrection world. This is reasonable; the Bible doesn't. What can we say about a sin-free, curse-free future society? Not much. Until the post-resurrection world comes, they teach, this world will get worse for Christians. Nevertheless, Christians are told to be salt and light to the doomed world, laboring mightily to bring in the kingdom of God on earth, even though God supposedly has not given judicial guidelines to His people in the New Testament era. This is utopianism without historic fulfilment, apocalypticism without earthly hope. Only a future apocalyptic event can bring the new world order its visible incarnation. Such a view destroys any legitimate confidence in the earthly fruits of covenant-keeping man's labor.

Common grace amillennialists affirm the expansion of Satan's kingdom in history. They also affirm the simultaneous expansion of Christ's kingdom in history. To make way for the leavening process of both kingdoms, they define Satan's kingdom as relating to civilization and Christ's kingdom as relating to the human heart, the Church, and the family. The leavening process of Satan steadily displaces the traces of Christian culture until, at the very end, the Christians are facing complete destruction. Then Jesus will return to judge the world and put an end to Church-engulfing (or Church-stalemating) history.

The Ambiguity of Amillennial History

Calvin Seminary professor Anthony Hoekema, in his chapter, "The Meaning of History," favorably cites Hendrikus Berkhof's 1966 book, *Christ the Meaning of History*. Berkhof writes: "There is no equilibrium between cross and resurrection. The shadows created by Christ's reign are completely a part of this dispensation, while the light of his reign will remain dim to the end."[59] Christ, the shadow in history! Then what does this make Satan? Berkhof and Hoekema are far too astute to raise this thorny but obvious question. Hoekema then goes on to defend a fundamental assertion of amillennialism: the ambiguity of history.

> Here again we see the ambiguity of history. History does not reveal a simple triumph of good over evil, nor a total victory of evil over good. Evil and good continue to exist side by side. Conflict between the two continues during the present age, but since Christ has won the victory, the ultimate outcome of the conflict is never in doubt. The enemy is fighting a losing battle.[60]

Notice the ambiguity of his phrasing of the issue. The good does not "simply" triumph over evil. Why *simply*? Evil does not "totally" triumph over good. Why *totally*? This is not clear. There is some kind of hidden eschatological agenda underlying such peculiar phrasing. What is very clear, however, is that his final sentence is misleading. The enemy, given the amillennial outlook, is indeed fighting a *lost cause*, but he is surely *not* fighting a *losing battle*. He is fighting at the very least a long-term historical stalemate, and probably an overall cultural victory. Under the most favorable possible interpretation, Hoekema is promoting a version of the stalemate religion.[61] This is the religion of cultural cease-fires rather than Christian victory.

Hoekema understands what this means for history: the absence of meaningful progress. "Can we say that history reveals genuine progress? Again we face the problem of the ambiguity of history. For every advance, it would seem, there is a corresponding retreat. The invention of the automobile has brought with it air pollution and a frightful increase in highway acci-

59. Anthony A. Hoekema, *The Bible and the Future* (Grand Rapids, Michigan: Eerdmans, 1979), p. 35.

60. *Idem.*

61. Gary North, *Backward, Christian Soldiers? An Action Manual for Christian Reconstruction* (Tyler, Texas: Institute for Christian Economics, 1984), ch. 11: "The Stalemate Mentality."

dents. . . . Progression is paired with retrogression."[62]

Let us not mince words. This view of history is *Manichean.* While the Manicheans profess faith in an endless struggle between good and evil, the amillennialists modify this view only slightly with respect to history. This view leads either to an acceptance of ethical dualism or permanent frustration: (1) the acceptance of common ground, "natural" ethics for the world, with a different personal ethics for Christians (dualism); or else (2) the assertion of a unified Christian ethical system that will never gain widespread public acceptance in history (frustration).

What is nothing short of astounding is that Hoekema, after having presented Manicheanism in the name of Christianity, then declares: "*The Christian understanding of history is basically optimistic.*"[63] How can he defend such a statement? Simple: by adopting deliberately misleading terminology. "The Christian believes that God is in control of history and that Christ has won the victory over the powers of evil. This means that the ultimate outcome of things is bound to be not bad but good, that God's redemptive purpose with the universe will eventually be realized, and that 'though the wrong seems oft so strong, God is the ruler yet.' " The key word here is *ultimate*. This is a crucial amillennial weasel word. It means *not in history*. Previous example: ". . . the ultimate outcome of the conflict is never in doubt." But he began his introductory statement by defending Christian optimism regarding history. All his defense proves is that Christians do have legitimate optimism regarding the final judgment. This is hardly the basis of a successful challenge to modern humanism. It surrenders history to covenant-breakers.

I will say this as plainly as I can: if anything like this were done by a profit-seeking business in the United States, it would be illegal. Under federal law, there is a *truth in advertising* rule. Specifically, this prohibited tactic is known as *bait and switch.* A firm advertises a product at a low price, but it does not actually have this advertised product. Once the customer is lured into the showroom, he is pressured to buy a different product at a

62. Hoekema, *The Bible and the Future*, pp. 35-36.
63. *Ibid.*, p. 38.

higher price. *Bait and switch has been the most commonly used tactic in selling common grace amillennialism to Christians in the twentieth century*. This practice is unconscionable, but it is so familiar to its academic defenders that it is not given a second thought.

Common grace amillennialists call Christians to a cultural battle, yet they also assure these potential recruits that there is no hope in history. The efforts of Christians to make the world a better, covenant-honoring place are inescapably going to be thwarted as time goes on. This, Zorn says, is "bearing witness to and directing toward the true utopian goal." But this utopianism is a utopianism without any possibility of fulfilment. It is therefore not truly utopian; it is at bottom apocalyptic. It waits on God to end history, not for Christians to transform history through their covenantal obedience. It calls for activism and encourages passivity. It is at bottom schizophrenic.

Shared Perspective: Historical Discontinuity

Norman Geisler, a dispensationalist and a defender of Thomistic natural law theory, has pointed to the shared perspective of premillennialism and amillennialism with respect to time. The issue, he says, is their common assertion of a fundamental discontinuity between the present order and the coming kingdom of God. He correctly observes that "most amillenarians look to the future return of Christ and to His eternal Reign as discontinuous with the present. Hence they do not view their present social involvement as directly related to the emergence of the future kingdom of God. In this respect amillenarians are more like premillenarians and have thereby often escaped some of the extremes of postmillennialism."[64] The central shared doctrine, then, is the doctrine of *the Church's historical discontinuity with the world beyond Christ's Second Coming*. On this point, Geisler is correct. Pessimillennialism denies any meaningful continuity.

There is no question that Geisler is reacting to Christian Reconstruction in raising this issue. He clearly recognizes the

64. Norman L. Geisler, "A Premillennial View of Law and Government," in *The Best in Theology*, edited by J. I. Packer (Carol Stream, Illinois: Christianity Today, Inc., 1987), I, p. 256.

inescapable connections linking biblical law, God's historical sanctions, millennialism, and social theory. Having affirmed premillennial dispensationalism, and therefore having denied the New Testament continuity of Old Testament law, he sought a means of affirming even the possibility of social theory. He adopted natural law theory. This is consistent. Having denied the only means of developing Christian social theory (biblical law and God's historical sanctions in enforcing this law), he adopted an officially intellectually and ethically neutral social theory. Here is his theoretical problem: *there is no neutrality.*

Very few Christian social commentators or theologians have been willing to follow Geisler's lead. Those who are professionally trained philosophers know that nothing remains of natural law theory in a post-Kantian world. Most Christians have not been trained in philosophy, but they have at least picked up from popularizers like Francis Schaeffer the idea that there can be no neutrality. The problem they face is the same one that both Schaeffer and Van Til faced: once we scrap natural law theory, what is left?[65] Kantianism? But this leads to Barthianism and neo-orthodoxy. Existentialism? This is clearly a dead end. There is only one consistent worldview that is based solely and self-consciously on the Bible: theonomy. They would rather die than accept this answer. So, they wind up promoting some rejected humanist fad that is based on modernism (what else?) but which does not initially appear to be. The few dispensationalists who read such things may prefer *National Review* or possibly *The American Spectator*, while the neo-evangelicals may read *New Republic*, but it makes no fundamental difference. All sides indirectly adopt humanism as the basis of their social philosophy. They cannot defend their social and political preferences by an appeal to the Bible. So, they cease making systematic appeals to the texts of the Bible. It is just too embarrassing.

The result is painfully obvious even to them: nobody takes them very seriously. Quite frankly, nobody should. They have neither the political clout to scare anyone holding office nor the philosophical clout to propose an consistent, viable, *biblical*

65. North, *Political Polytheism*, chapters 3, 4.

alternative. It is not that they are short on brains. They are, however, woefully short on biblical presuppositions. They do not command much respect, even within their own circles, when they announce: "Thus sayeth *The Wall Street Journal*," or "Thus sayeth *The New York Times*."

Conclusion

When Christians do not view their present social involvement as possessing a fundamental continuity with the emergence (i.e., development or extension) of the kingdom of God in history, they have little incentive to develop a specifically Christian social theory. If they also deny the fundamental continuity of Old Testament law and God's sanctions throughout history,[66] they will be sorely tempted to revert to the supposedly universal and common logical categories of Stoic and Scholastic natural law theory, as Geisler has done. Lacking both the temporal incentive for dominion (God's positive sanctions in history) and the judicial tools of dominion (biblical law),[67] they deny the legitimacy of Christians' dominion in history by means of the biblical covenant, through the empowering of the Holy Spirit.

Both premillennialism and amillennialism deny that there will ever be a Christian civilization prior to Christ's Second Coming. In saying this, both viewpoints promote an antinomian outlook. Their defenders usually deny the continuing validity of the Old Testament case laws, but even when the case laws are not denied, these theologians deny the continuing presence of God's historical sanctions – sanctions that they freely admit were attached to His law-order in the Old Covenant era, at least in the case of national Israel. But God's covenant law without God's predictable, historic, corporate sanctions is like a nail without a hammer. It is useless for constructing anything.

A few premillennialists and amillennialists have offered very cogent criticisms of modern humanist culture, but these critics have never offered a uniquely Christian alternative to the humanism they reject. This exclusive negativism has the effect of

---

66. Pratt, *He Gave Us Stories*, pp. 343-44.
67. North, *Tools of Dominion*, *op. cit.*

discouraging their followers. This lack of a legitimate cultural alternative has persuaded most Christians to shorten their time horizons. They lose hope in the future: *present-orientation*.

If there is no cultural alternative to humanism available in history, then the only reasonable Christian response is to pray for either the Rapture (dispensationalism) or the end of history (amillennialism). (Historic premillennialists and post-tribulational dispensationalists believe that the millennium will come only after Christians have gone through Armageddon and the Great Tribulation. I have no idea what they pray for.)

Premillennialists and amillennialists share a commitment to a coming *cosmic* discontinuity as the Church's great hope in *history*: deliverance from on high (and in the case of premillennial dispensationalism, deliverance *to* on high). Again, citing Norman Geisler: "Hence they do not view their present social involvement as directly related to the emergence of the future kingdom of God. In this respect amillenarians are more like premillenarians and have thereby often escaped some of the extremes of postmillennialism." This affirmation of a coming cosmic discontinuity cuts the ground from under the Christian who would seek to discover a uniquely biblical social theory. It also undercuts the incentive for social action. Social action becomes a holding action at best and a kamikaze action at worst.

The Church is believed to be incapable of changing history's downward move into cultural evil. Social action is therefore adopted on an *ad hoc* basis: solving this or that immediate local problem. Effective Christian social action supposedly can accomplish little; therefore, it requires neither a long-term strategy nor a systematic concept of ethical cause and effect. Political power, not ethics, is viewed as historically determinative. Power is seen as a necessary evil today. Christians are supposedly never to exercise political power in the "Church Age." Either they cannot or should not exercise it (possibly both).

The result is predictable: the absence of Christian social theory.

5

THE SOCIETY OF THE FUTURE

For, behold, I create ***new heavens and a new earth****: and the former shall not be remembered, nor come into mind. But be ye glad and rejoice for ever in that which I create: for, behold, I create Jerusalem a rejoicing, and her people a joy. And I will rejoice in Jerusalem, and joy in my people: and the voice of weeping shall be no more heard in her, nor the voice of crying.* ***There shall be no more thence an infant of days, nor an old man that hath not filled his days: for the child shall die an hundred years old; but the sinner being an hundred years old shall be accursed.*** *And they shall build houses, and inhabit them; and they shall plant vineyards, and eat the fruit of them. They shall not build, and another inhabit; they shall not plant, and another eat: for as the days of a tree are the days of my people, and mine elect shall long enjoy the work of their hands. They shall not labour in vain, nor bring forth for trouble; for they are the seed of the blessed of the LORD, and their offspring with them (Isa. 65:17-23).* (emphasis added)

Isaiah introduces this prophecy by saying that it refers to the New Heaven and the New Earth. The key question is this: Is this coming era historical or post-resurrection? The language of Isaiah is straightforward: an era is coming, *in history*, when the person who dies at age one hundred will be considered as a child, an indication of a major extension of men's lifespans. Also, sinners will be accounted accursed. This appears to be an application of Isaiah's prophecy of the millennial era's improved moral self-consciousness, when vile people will not be called liberal,[1] and churls will not be called bountiful (Isa. 32:5). In

1. Consider the United States' federally financed "art," with its religious and moral perversion. Any attempt to de-fund it by removing tax money until the National Endow-

short, there will be a coming age in which covenantal wisdom is paralleled by long life. But it will still be an age of death and sin. This is the reason why the exercise of covenantal wisdom will be possible. It will still be possible to distinguish good from evil, long life from short life, cursings from blessings.

No verse in the Bible makes it plainer that amillennial eschatology cannot possibly be true. Even if we take these words symbolically (i.e., as rhetoric), they still have to apply to history, for sinners will not be present in the post-resurrection world. They will not participate in the post-resurrection New Heaven and New Earth. Isaiah made it perfectly clear: *he was talking about history*. These words cannot possibly apply to the post-resurrection world. There will be a coming era of blessing in history. God's positive *historical* sanctions on covenant-keepers will bring victory to His earthly kingdom. It is quite understandable why Archibald Hughes, an amillennial theologian, mentioned this passage in only two brief sentences in his book, *A New Heaven and a New Earth*.[2] This passage refutes his eschatology. (So much the worse for Isaiah, apparently!) Herman Ridderbos is wiser still: he never even mentioned the verse in a book on the kingdom of God that is over 500 pages long.[3] (He compensates for this omission by citing hundreds of German liberal theologians, most of whom outlived their theories.)[4] One man, however, has accepted the challenge. We therefore need to examine his exegesis in detail to see whether the amillennial interpretation of Isaiah 65:20 can be sustained.

---

ment of the Arts draws up artistic guidelines is attacked as illiberal.

2. Archibald Hughes, *A New Heaven and a New Earth* (Philadelphia: Presbyterian & Reformed, 1958). The book's subtitle defines away the problem: *An Introductory Study of the Coming of the Lord Jesus Christ and the Eternal Inheritance*. But what of the Church's historical inheritance? For amillennialists, there is none except, possibly, escalating persecution.

3. Herman Ridderbos, *The Coming of the Kingdom* (Philadelphia: Presbyterian & Reformed, 1963).

4. It is one of the tragic wastes of sharp theological minds that they feel compelled to shadow box with dead German theologians all of their lives. It makes them nearly as incoherent as their opponents, and nearly as impotent. Ridderbos followed *The Coming of the Kingdom* with a somewhat less turgid book, *Paul: An Outline of His Theology* (1975), a 562-page outline in small print. He smote dead Germans, hip and thigh, throughout his career. No one noticed. No one ever does, especially living German theologians.

Dr. Hoekema's Heroic Failure

Calvin Theological Seminary professor Anthony A. Hoekema (now deceased) was honest about this passage's importance. Referring to Isaiah 65:20, he announced: "We must admit that this is a difficult text to interpret." Not impossible; merely difficult. Then he attempts to escape the dilemma by denying that the text is to be taken literally.

> Is Isaiah telling us here that there will be death on the new earth? In my judgment this cannot be his meaning, in the light of what he has just said in verse 19: "No more shall be heard in it [the Jerusalem being described – A.A.H.] the sound of weeping and the cry of distress." Can one imagine a death not accompanied by weeping?[5]

Well, quite frankly, yes, I can imagine it. There is a biblical text relating to this very problem, Leviticus 21:10-13. The high priest was forbidden to mourn publicly after the death of a close relative. As a kingdom of priests, we should begin to strive to match this self-restraint. I think this could well become biblical etiquette in an era of millennial blessings, for three reasons. First, the sting of death will be progressively reduced. People will not fear death so greatly as they do now. The transition from physical life to physical death will not be so familiar a threat during an era in which people live very long lives. Second, the cry of distress (v. 19) refers to personal spiritual pain (II Sam. 22:7; Psa. 18:6). This degree of pain need not be prevalent in an era of millennial blessings. Third, the covenantal passage from death to life in history will be made by a majority of those dwelling in "Jerusalem," meaning God's Church. The close relatives of those deceased who have made the transition into eternity will not be so devastated as they are today.

This is already true today to some extent, Paul says, indicating that Christians have begun the transition in history to that coming millennial era of blessings, and then on to the post-resurrection world beyond: "But I would not have you to be ignorant,

---

5. Anthony Hoekema, *The Bible and the Future* (Grand Rapids, Michigan: Eerdmans, 1979), p. 202.

brethren, concerning them which are asleep, that ye sorrow not, even as others which have no hope" (I Thess. 4:13). Paul also writes: "But this I say, brethren, the time is short: it remaineth, that both they that have wives be as though they had none; And they that weep, as though they wept not; and they that rejoice, as though they rejoiced not; and they that buy, as though they possessed not; And they that use this world, as not abusing it: for the fashion of this world passeth away" (I Cor. 7:29-31). As we move in history toward a tears-free eternity, our behavior should reflect both our faith and our historical experience as victors. There will be a progressive drying up of tears as covenant history unfolds.

Hoekema raises a legitimate question: *What about weeping?* He notes its absence (v. 19). But because he is defending a particular eschatology, he wipes away the tears exegetically by *wiping away history*. This is strictly a tactical ploy; his view of a tears-free future beyond the grave does not come from the text or from normal principles of Old Testament interpretation. It comes from his amillennial interpretive scheme. He argues in effect that history and tears are ontologically inseparable. Any absence of tears absolutely has to mean the absence of history, with no exceptions. This is strict amillennial exegesis.

The Prophets' Use of Language

The question I raise in response is this: Would those who heard Isaiah's message have grasped this hypothetical ontological relationship: tears and history? Would they have had even the slightest inkling that Isaiah was talking exclusively about a death-free eternal state rather than history? Not if they had heard his previous reference to a world without tears. The context was historical and earthly:

> For thou hast made of a city an heap; of a defenced city a ruin: a palace of strangers to be no city; it shall never be built. Therefore shall the strong people glorify thee, *the city of the terrible nations shall fear thee*. For thou hast been a strength to the poor, a strength to the needy in his distress, a refuge from the storm, a shadow from the heat, when the blast of the terrible ones is as a storm against the wall.

> Thou shalt bring down the noise of strangers, as the heat in a dry place; even the heat with the shadow of a cloud: the branch of the terrible ones shall be brought low. And in this mountain shall the LORD of hosts make unto all people a feast of fat things, a feast of wines on the lees [aged wine], of fat things full of marrow, of wines on the lees well refined. And he will destroy in this mountain the face of the covering cast over all people, and the veil that is spread over all nations. *He will swallow up death in victory; and the Lord GOD will wipe away tears from off all faces; and the rebuke of his people shall he take away from off all the earth*: for the LORD hath spoken it. And it shall be said in that day, Lo, this is our God; we have waited for him, and he will save us: this is the LORD; we have waited for him, we will be glad and rejoice in his salvation. For in this mountain shall the hand of the LORD rest, and Moab shall be trodden down under him, even as straw is trodden down for the dunghill (Isa. 25:2-10). (emphasis added)

That this message is filled with symbolic language ought to be admitted by all expositors. Marrow, wines, and fat sound like the ultimate nightmare of modern dieticians. Modern, sedentary, urban man, who consumes far too many of these gastronomic delights, would no doubt be wise to eat more skinless chicken and leafy green vegetables.[6] Our positive blessings have become a potential curse to us, if we lack will-power. Ours is a prosperous era in which it is far more affordable for gluttons and drunkards to indulge their sins. But Isaiah's vision was magnificent to a people who did not eat meat very often because of its great expense and the absence of refrigeration. Yes, the prophets did use symbolic language. They even mixed in the language of post-judgment victory with their historical visions.

But so does the New Testament. Jesus announced this to His followers: "In the last day, that great day of the feast, Jesus stood and cried, saying, If any man thirst, let him come unto me, and drink" (John 7:37). This language is symbolic, yet it is a fulfillment of the prophecy of Isaiah 49:8-13.[7] Revelation 7:16-17 is a passage dealing with Church history, and it uses

---

6. Perhaps in the millennial era to come, scientists will find ways to overcome these fatty negatives, and it will be back to well-marbled steaks and pork roasts!

7. David Chilton, *The Days of Vengeance: An Exposition of the Book of Revelation* (Ft. Worth, Texas: Dominion Press, 1987), p. 223.

language similar to Jesus' announcement at the feast, but then adds hope regarding tears. "They shall hunger no more, neither thirst any more; neither shall the sun light on them, nor any heat. For the Lamb which is in the midst of the throne shall feed them, and shall lead them unto living fountains of waters: and God shall wipe away all tears from their eyes." Total fulfillment will come, of course, only after final judgment, but partial fulfillment comes in history. (Or are we to deny the positive cultural blessings of Jesus' living water in history?) Revelation 21:4 seems to refer exclusively to the post-resurrection world: "And God shall wipe away all tears from their eyes; and there shall be no more death, neither sorrow, nor crying, neither shall there be any more pain: for the former things are passed away." Yet even here, these is some degree of fulfillment in history.[8] What amillennialist expositors refuse to acknowledge is this: the transition from today's world to the post-resurrection world does not take place overnight. It takes place historically. So they remove all traces of history from prophetic messages of comprehensive victory and visible blessings.

Expositors recognize that *the Old Covenant's message was geared primarily to history, not to a world beyond the grave*. When a prophet spoke of wiping away tears, his audience would not have imagined that he was talking exclusively about the post-resurrection world, where the problem of tears obviously will not be an issue. Isaiah's message was one of *judgment in history* (Babylon invaded Judah about 175 years later), but the prophet also promised Israel's post-judgment restoration. Who in Isaiah's day would have imagined that this restoration would be exclusively post-*final* judgment? Who, for that matter, in Nehemiah's day of restoration would have imagined it?

The amillennial interpretation of the prophets is to assert that the texts dealing with negative sanctions refer to *historical* judgments on the nation of Israel (e.g., the Babylonian captivity), but the texts dealing with God's miraculous positive sanctions deal only with the *discontinuous post-final judgment era*. There is no continuity in history linking (1) the restoration of Israel, (2) the

8. *Ibid*., p. 547.

Church, and (3) the coming era of millennial blessings. In short, God's corporate cursings are continuous in history, but *His world-transforming blessings will be cosmic and discontinuous*: beyond history. Those who heard the prophets' bad news were to fear God, but when they heard the message of miraculous social transformation, they were to pay no attention, except in a symbolic sense: a world beyond history. Nebuchadnezzar was real; tears were real; but the possibility of future cultural transformation is merely symbolic. If this is true, then this theological conclusion is inescapable: *biblical social theory is also symbolic*.

Here is my point: *amillennialism cannot deal exegetically with God's positive corporate sanctions in New Covenant history*. This is one of my major contentions in this book. God's positive corporate sanctions are said to relate *primarily* to "sacred history," meaning the biblical narratives in the Old Covenant.[9] They are past events, aorist tense: completed. (This could be called "preterism for eschatological pessimists": the good news for society is past.) But what about the possibility of a secondary application in New Covenant history of the good news of future corporate cultural transformation? For the amillennialist, there is no "secondarily"; there is only "primarily." This presents a major problem for the development of amillennial social theory: explicitly biblical, no humanism, and no "neutral" natural law. It makes it impossible.

"Why 'Death' Simply Cannot Mean Death"

Hoekema does not stop with his assertion that the tears of Isaiah 65:19 will be wiped away only in the post-resurrection world. He goes on. (There is an old slogan, "When you're in a hole, stop digging.") "In the light of the foregoing I conclude that Isaiah in verse 20 of chapter 65 is picturing in figurative terms the fact that the inhabitants of the new earth will live incalculably long lives." Notice what he is doing. First, he denies that *death* actually refers to death. Second, he speaks of incalculably long lives in the New Heaven and New Earth, an odd prophetic way of saying "eternal, death-free living." Professor

9. On sacred history, see Hoekema, *Future*, pp. 25-26.

Hoekema is about to make a very slick interpretive move: out of history and into eternity.

His major problem is to get rid of the word *sinner*. There will not be any sinners dwelling in the eternal New Heaven and New Earth. If the New Heaven and New Earth refer exclusively to the post-judgment age, then sinners must be eliminated from the text. Dr. Hoekema rises to the occasion. Unfortunately, his common sense does not rise with him.

> Since the word translated *sinner* in the last clause means someone who has missed the mark, I would again prefer the NIV rendering, "he who fails to reach a hundred will be considered accursed." It is not implied that there will be anyone on the new earth who will fail to attain a hundred years.[10]

How, pray tell, does someone *not* reach age one hundred? I would have thought there could only be one way: *he dies first.* But, Hoekema assures us, this text in no way implies that anyone will fail to reach age one hundred. So, there will be no weeping in Jerusalem, because sinners, who are not in fact sinners, but merely people who miss the mark, will not be dying before age one hundred, because the text in no way implies that anyone will die. "For the child shall die" means that no one will die. If this sounds suspiciously like a Christian Science lay reader's explanation of John 11:14, "Then said Jesus unto them plainly, Lazarus is dead," this is because the goal is the same: *escaping the plain (and also figurative) meaning of the text.*

If death in this passage does not actually refer to death, then what was Isaiah's point? What message was he trying to convey? Why did he bring up the possibility of the death of people "who miss the mark," if there will be neither death nor sin in that exclusively future, exclusively post-historical era? What has the language of death got to do with a sin-free "missing of the mark"? What has the verse got to do with anything, if sin, death, and history are all spirited away?

---

10. *Ibid.*, p. 203.

Denying a Future Covenantal Discontinuity

None of his exegetical dancing does Dr. Hoekema any good. He can of course interpret the text figuratively, but he cannot remove it from history. Isaiah's prophesied judgments against the nation of Israel took place in history. *The amillennialist's exegetical problem with Isaiah 65 is history*, not the prophet's possibly figurative use of language. "*I create*," God said. The New Heaven and New Earth are begun in history. Yes, this text can conceivably be translated *will create*, since Hebrew does not distinguish between the present and future tenses, and the NIV translators, with an eye on the amillennial book buying public, did so. No other major Bible translation does. When your eschatology rests heavily on a peculiar translation found only in the NIV, you are skating on thin ice. In any case, even if we accept the future tense, this could (and does) mean "create in history": at the nation's return from Babylon, at the ascension of Jesus Christ, at the sending of the Holy Spirit at Pentecost, and at the fall of Jerusalem. (I should add: in the millennium of blessings.) It is a multi-stage process that culminates at the final judgment. But amillennialists insist that the New Heaven and New Earth begin only at the final judgment.

Hoekema makes it clear in his discussion of the New Earth – which is exclusively post-resurrection – that the key issue is the denial of history, not the denial of hermeneutical literalism. "Prophecies of this nature should be understood as descriptions – in figurative language, to be sure – of the new earth which God will bring into existence after Christ comes again – a new earth which will last, not just for a thousand years, but forever."[11] The issue is *post-historical fulfillment*, not literalism: "There will be a future fulfillment of these prophecies, not in the millennium, but on the new earth. Whether they are all to be *literally* fulfilled is an open question; . . ."[12] What is a closed question is the question of historical fulfillment. There will be none.

The issue under discussion is the possibility of a future historical discontinuity, worldwide, in which the Holy Spirit con-

11. *Ibid.*, p. 276.
12. *Idem.*

verts large numbers of people to saving faith. The issue is not extended lifespans as such. If modern science were to find a chemical or biological way to change the supposed internal time clock that governs the aging process in humans, and thereby extend the life expectancy of mankind, Dr. Hoekema would not regard this as the advent of the New Earth. Neither would I. The issue is *God's historical sanctions*: the differentiation made by the general public between the moral quality of long lives lived by covenant-keepers and covenant-breakers. What he is rejecting is what postmillennialism affirms: a coming *spiritual discontinuity* in history that accompanies a *cultural and even biological discontinuity*. He predicts spiritual, covenantal continuity in history – churls will continue to be called bountiful – no matter what covenant-breaking science may invent. I predict a spiritual, covenantal discontinuity in history – increasingly bad times for churls – no matter what covenant-breaking science invents. The two views cannot be reconciled. They cannot both be correct.

Anthony Hoekema has written the most comprehensive presentation of the Calvinist amillennial case. His book is the only full-scale, English-language presentation of the amillennial position, certainly from the Dutch tradition, but probably in the history of the position. He grapples with Isaiah 65:20. A difficult passage to interpret from an amillennial viewpoint? Not just difficult; *impossible*, unless you intend to embarrass yourself in public. No better proof exists of the impossibility of this task than Dr. Hoekema's valiant attempt. It was a theologically necessary but thankless task that his amillennial predecessors had preferred to skate around rather than across. Dr. Hoekema, a courageous man, skated as fast as he could, but fell through the ice anyway. He gets an A for effort, but a D- for performance.

I have done my best to expose Dr. Hoekema's exegesis of Isaiah 65:20 as little short of preposterous. If I have done my work well, his interpretation appears foolish. This is because it really *is* foolish. But Dr. Hoekema was no fool. Early in his career, he wrote the most tightly argued, theologically rigorous, fully documented study of the theologies of the four major cults that we have available.[13] So, his problem was not that he was an incompetent theologian; his problem was that his millennial view cannot be defended without the manufacture of silly interpretations of those passages that predict Christian victory in history. The reader needs to understand: his book is virtually the only recent common grace amillennial study that devotes even one chapter to the question of the meaning of history in relation to amillennial eschatology. The others steadfastly ignore it, with only one exception: H. van Riessen's *Society of the Future*. But van Riessen was neither an historian nor a theologian.

Van Riessen's Vision

This coming era of blessings will be marked by economic freedom. Men will keep the fruits of their labor. They will leave an inheritance to their children. "And they shall build houses, and inhabit them; and they shall plant vineyards, and eat the fruit of them. They shall not build, and another inhabit; they shall not plant, and another eat: for as the days of a tree are the days of my people, and mine elect shall long enjoy the work of their hands. They shall not labour in vain, nor bring forth for trouble; for they are the seed of the blessed of the LORD, and their offspring with them" (Isa. 65:21-23). There is a blessed earthly inheritance ahead *in history* for God's covenant people. All this is denied by amillennial theologians, especially in the twentieth-century Dutch tradition. We can see this message of *disinheritance in history* in the writings of H. Van Riessen.

Van Riessen was a professor of philosophy at the University of Technology at Delft in the Netherlands. His book, *The Society of the Future* (1957), serves as a coherent introduction to amillennial social criticism. He was critical of the bureaucratic, planned society of socialism. He understood the depersonalization of modern industrial life. He saw the breakdown of modern humanist ethics, philosophy, and confidence about the future. He saw that ethical neutrality leads to nihilism. But like premillennialist Francis Schaeffer, who also offered cogent criticisms

---

13. Anthony A. Hoekema, *The Four Major Cults* (Grand Rapids, Michigan: Eerdmans, [1963] 1986).

without biblical alternatives,[14] Van Riessen saw no hope. Why no hope? "For Babylon will be the city of the end."[15]

How should we then live? On the one hand, aggressively. "We should not try to escape from the world, but to work in it as a Christian should."[16] But to do this, we theonomists hasten to add, Christians need more data on the *should* aspect of Christian living. We need specifics. He offers none. Biblical law is not even mentioned in his book. What he offers is a counsel of Stoic despair: "The normal situation for the community of Jesus is not to be influential and prosperous but poor and oppressed."[17] When he says "normal," he means *normative throughout history*. In constructing this view of history, amillennialists see the sufferings of Job as normative, not the restoration and multiplication of Job's blessings after his time of suffering. "So the LORD blessed the latter end of Job more than his beginning" (Job. 42:12a). His post-suffering blessings were apparently random, having nothing fundamental to do with the overall spiritual message of the Book of Job. In short, amillennialists imply, the story of Job is not essentially covenantal: *the blessings and cursings of history are not related to one's ethical behavior in history*. At best, they were not very closely related in Job's day, and in the New Testament, they are not related in history in any predictable fashion.[18] This view of Job is a denial of the biblical covenant's continuing authority in the New Testament era.[19] Nevertheless, it has long been presented in the name of covenant theology.

---

14. Gary North, *Political Polytheism: The Myth of Pluralism* (Tyler, Texas: Institute for Christian Economics, 1989), ch. 4.

15. H. van Riessen, *The Society of the Future* (Philadelphia: Presbyterian & Reformed, 1957), p. 233.

16. *Ibid.*, p. 234.

17. *Idem.*

18. Van Til explicitly says this. Regarding the New Testament application of the story of Job, he writes: "Between the time of paradise lost and paradise regained the balance will not always be maintained. More than that, it may even be said that it seems as though it is often true that those who are righteous are not as prosperous as those who are not righteous. At any rate, there is great unevenness throughout the course of history." Cornelius Van Til, *Christian Theistic Ethics*, vol. III of *In Defense of Biblical Christianity* (Phillipsburg, New Jersey: Presbyterian & Reformed, [1958] 1980), p. 104.

19. Ray R. Sutton, *That You May Prosper: Dominion By Covenant* (Tyler, Texas: Institute for Christian Economics, 1987), p. 68.

Today's Prosperity

The second half of the twentieth century has been a time of great prosperity for the West. This raises the old question of God's historical sanctions. How is it that spiritual rebellion seems to bring economic prosperity? Van Riessen's answer is much the same as best-selling dispensational author Dave Hunt in his *Peace Prosperity and the Coming Holocaust* (1983): modern prosperity is all a gigantic spiritual deception. Hunt says that this deception is being engineered by Satan through the New Age movement.[20]

(I argue in Chapter 7 that unless Christians accept biblical covenantal standards of wealth and progress, there is a very real possibility that they could be deceived in this way. This is why it is so important for Christians to understand and accept the biblical covenant model. But Hunt, as a dispensationalist and an extreme pietist theologically, rejects biblical law. Thus, he also rejects the legitimacy of wealth, at least for those who do not live on paperback book royalties. The rejection of the legitimacy of wealth is an odd theological position for a man whose only formal training is accounting, which is perhaps the most crucial technical pillar of modern capitalism. Perhaps he had originally planned to specialize only in Christians' bankruptcy cases.)

Van Riessen, a more scholarly analyst than Mr. Hunt, says that this deception is a product of secularization. He warns: "While living in an oasis, we must guard against looking upon the oasis as a general condition, forgetting the desert. . . . The danger lurking in a long period of prosperity for Christians is that they are apt to get secularized gradually without being aware of it, and even that they are carried away by the spirit of the age. We are perhaps not oppressed because we no longer take offense."[21] There is darkness coming: "We should know

---

20. *Everything* defined as evil in Hunt's worldview seems to have been engineered or captured by the New Age movement, which he calls sorcery. (This apparently includes commas in book titles, not to mention indexes, which he carefully avoids.) Cf. Dave Hunt and T. A. McMahon, *The Seduction of Christianity: Spiritual Discernment in the Last Days* (Eugene, Oregon: Harvest House, 1985). For a critique of this whole approach, see Bob and Gretchen Passantino, *Witch Hunt* (Nashville, Tennessee: Nelson, 1990).

21. Van Riessen, *Society of the Future*, p. 234.

that the time will come when our position will be entirely lost, but Christ shall nevertheless rule the world."[22] The process is irreversible, he insists: "The history of Western culture is in the main a history of a Christian culture followed by a secularization, increasing in extent and intensity. It is moving to a final catastrophe."[23]

Prosperity is said to be a spiritual oasis. It surely can be. This is the paradox of Deuteronomy 8: wealth is both a positive and a negative sanction in history. But for van Riessen, *wealth is exclusively a negative corporate sanction*. It is a spiritual desert. The Christian, in whose hands wealth can be a positive sanction, must regard the wealth around him as a sign of God's cultural disinheritance of the Church's healing work in history.

Then what of this Proverb? "The wealth of the sinner is laid up for the just" (Prov. 13:22b). "It applies only to individuals, not to societies," says the amillennialist. But God delivered the land of Canaan into the hands of the Israelites, disinheriting the Canaanites, but providing an inheritance to His people. "Old Testament, Old Testament!" shouts the amillennialist. This is supposed to end the argument. It is the major offense of Christian Reconstructionism that its view of Old Testament law and God's historical sanctions keeps the argument alive. This offers hope to society: the hope of God's inheritance to His people in history. The amillennialist deeply resents this offer of hope.

A Society Without Legitimate Hope

Van Riessen offered no alternative, no plan of action, and no hope. He ended with this call to . . . to . . . a stiff upper lip: "Defeatism or passive resignation to our situation with all the risks attached to the latter only mean the neglect of our vocation. On the other hand superficial optimism based on some favorable phenomena or on a distorted global picture of our situation would be dangerous. In this difficult time it is essential for us to have a correct insight into our condition, an ardent faith in our calling irrespective of the results of our work, quiet

---

22. *Ibid.*, p. 235.
23. *Idem.*

determination on the right course towards the future and critical reflection on anything presenting itself to us in this course."[24]

Having presented his chilling forecast of bad things to come, van Riessen came back in 1960 to assure his Dutch-American readers that "Christians are going to change the world. They have to urge mankind to follow God's will. But knowledge changes nothing. It is the believing heart that alters the world."[25] Unfortunately for the Church, there will never be many of these believing hearts in history, according to what amillennialism teaches. So, precisely *how* will Christians change the world? Van Til said this Christian influence will only make non-Christians more aware of their own intellectual inconsistency, thereby bringing increasingly severe persecution against the Church. Van Riessen did not say how Christianity will change the world. He did not need to. *The Society of the Future* had said enough.

When I was a teenager in a public high school, the boys' athletic dressing room had this motto painted on the wall: "When the going gets tough, the tough get going." Van Riessen adopted something like this schoolboy's motto as a substitute for Christian social philosophy. This, quite frankly, has been amillennialism's tactic for at least half a millennium.

Question: Wouldn't the wise person adopt a different version of the motto? "When the going gets tough, the tough may get going, but the weak get out of the way." This has been the operational motto of Christians for well over a century. They have read and fully understood four generations of premillennial and amillennial dissertations and tracts, and they have acted accordingly. Whenever possible, they have bought themselves a hoped-for oasis, usually with a lot of debt, and they have then prayed to God to keep the desert sands outside its boundaries until they die. Nothing has shortened Christianity's time perspective more effectively than eschatological pessimism. Christian laymen are not fools. They have read the pessimillennialists'

24. *Ibid.*, p. 308.

25. Hendrik van Riessen, "The Christian Approach to Science," *Christian Perspectives* (1960), p. 3.

version of David and Goliath – Goliath defeats David – and they have concluded: "Don't get into an unnecessary confrontation with Goliath." They are not naive. The pessimillennial theologians are naive, however. In their tenured academic security,[26] they call Christian laymen to get into the battle. "Let's you and Goliath fight," they call out to the potential Davids of the world. But all the Davids are at home, tending sheep; only Sauls are in the battlefield. So the Sauls of the world put down the theologian's book, turn on the T.V., and put a bag of popcorn into the microwave. They are a lot wiser than their spiritual counsellors are. They are not interested in kamikaze tactics. The personal price is too high, and the cultural payoff is too low.

Trans-Historical Victory

Chapter 42 of R. B. Kuiper's *The Glorious Body of Christ*, "Conqueror of the World," is filled with the language of victory. He writes: "Amazing as it may seem, the insignificant church is out to conquer the world. Not only is it striving to do this; it is succeeding. And surpassing strange to say, not only is victory in sight for the church; it is a present reality."[27] Surpassing strange, indeed! The word "succeeding" indicates progress, but the words "present reality" give away the game. Only in the post-historical world will we see in retrospect the nature of this victory: a victory in disguise.

He includes a subsection, "The Duty of Conquest." He calls Christians to an earthly battle that his millennial view denies they can win, but he refuses to state this explicitly. He fools them with misleading language. He also includes another subsection, "The Reality of Victory." He writes: "That the church will in the end overcome the world is a foregone conclusion, for it will share in the ultimate and complete triumph of Christ, its Head."[28] (Notice the presence of the familiar amillennial weasel word: *ultimate*, meaning *not in history*.) This is a devious way of

---

26. "When the going gets tough, the professors seek tenure."

27. R. B. Kuiper, *The Glorious Body of Christ* (Grand Rapids, Michigan: Eerdmans, 1958), p. 274.

28. *Ibid.*, p. 277.

admitting that the Church in history will *not* overcome the world, and that any victory it will enjoy will be post-history, when the direct intervention of God interrupts history at the final judgment.

The Church in the amillennial framework has about as much to do with this final victory of Christ over the world of sin and corruption as a little old lady has in arresting a large gang of muggers, while she is being beaten to a pulp, at the moment when the police finally arrive. According to amillennialism, the Church's role in Christ's victory is that of a helpless, impotent victim, whose only earthly hope is that a Deliverer might arrive in the nick of time, meaning at the *end* of time. Her only hope is to be unexpectedly delivered overnight from the burdens of history, not delivered by means of a gospel-transformed history.

The Deliberate Misuse of Language

Kuiper's next sentence is even more telling: "But Scripture also teaches that the Church's victory over the world is a present reality." Victory? Should we call amillennialism's vision of the Church's future a vision of victory? Only if our task is to misuse language and confuse our readers.

Kuiper, like all amillennialists, refused to offer a biblical theory of *historical continuity*: an explanation of how the Church gets from its visible impotence in the present to the glorious victory of the future. The Church's "victory" is non-historical in the present, and it will be post-historical in the future.

Kuiper warned against the theology of Karl Barth,[29] but his own view of Church history – especially its future history – was essentially Barthian. Barth proclaimed two forms of history, a history of real-world events, which he called *Historie*, and Christ's world of "hidden history" (*Geschichte*, pronounced "gu-SHIKtuh") – a trans-historical, non-rational encounter – that cannot be revealed by, *or judged by*, the factual records and documents of history.[30] For Barthians, the non-Christian reality of

---

29. R. B. Kuiper, *To Be or Not to Be Reformed: Whither the Christian Reformed Church?* (Grand Rapids, Michigan: Zondervan, 1959), pp. 39, 157.

30. Van Til, *Christianity and Barthianism* (Philadelphia: Presbyterian & Reformed,

history does not call into question the meaning of man's "encounter" with "Christ." Van Til recognized that Barth's view of history was the product of his Kantian, apostate presuppositions. He recognized that Barth used the language of the Bible and Christian orthodoxy to confuse his Christian readers.[31]

Yet Kuiper did something analogous. He used the language of victory when discussing history. Like Barth, he did not mean "history" in the normal sense: cause and effect in temporal succession. Like Barth, he adopted a dialectical view of history. He differentiated between: (1) the real historical world, where, as time goes by, you will get your Christian head kicked in by the reprobates; and (2) a trans-historical world of your "realized victory," which cannot be revealed by, *or judged by*, the factual historical reality of the Church's increasingly visible defeat. Kuiper hid the spiritual victory of the Church safely outside of the grim reality of reprobate-dominated history, just as Barth hid each man's non-rational encounter with his Kantian "Christ" outside of fact-based and fact-judged history. Kuiper proclaimed a symbolic world of non-historical *Victoriegeshichte* as a substitute for Barth's equally non-historical *Geschichte*.

Understandably, this misuse of the language of victory is annoying to those of us who are really serious about developing a theory of Christian victory in history. Better Van Til's forthrightness: a theory of history that openly admits that Christians, like that little old lady, are going to get mugged, and mugged ever more frequently and ever more viciously.[32] He did not sugar-coat his eschatological poison pill.

False Packaging

What I resent is that these Calvinistic amillennial theologians use the language of victory to describe the agony of defeat. This is misleading; I contend that it is also deliberate. They should

---

1962), ch. 1.

31. "It is at this point that the question of 'traditional phraseology' has its significance. The 'simple believer' is all too often given new wine in old bottles. It is our solemn duty to point this out to him." *Ibid.*, p. 2.

32. Cf. North, *Political Polytheism*, ch. 3.

openly proclaim in Chapter 1 of their books the *inevitable, God-predestined defeat of Christianity in history*. They should hasten to remind their readers that the gospel of Christ will fail to redeem this visible world of temporal cause and effect, or significantly restrain its evil, or protect Christians and especially their heirs from an inevitably triumphant tyranny. They should tell their readers well in advance: "I am calling you to a life of frustration, of shattered hopes and visible defeat; and your children will have it even worse." Most important of all, they should then present the exegetical case for amillennialism.

They categorically refuse to do this. Instead, they adopt the optimistic language of victory that only postmillennialists can legitimately use, and then they shave all historical meaning away from it. Amillennialists know that eschatological pessimism can be sold successfully in the Protestant West (as distinguished from the mystical Eastern Orthodox tradition of submission to defeat and suffering in history) only when it can be tied to a death-free escape hatch out of history, i.e., the pre-tribulation Rapture of the saints, which they reject.[33] So they announce victory in the large print and then incrementally substitute historical defeat in the fine print.

This is why Calvinistic amillennialism is fraudulent. No softer word will do. It is fraudulent, not because this eschatology is incorrect, which would simply be a matter of intellectual error, but because *its packaging is stolen*. Amillennialists too often wrap their psychological poison pill of historical and cultural pessimism in the bright colors of postmillennial optimism. They use bright wrapping paper for their culturally empty boxes. If they were to adopt a similar tactic on Christmas morning with their children, they would destroy their children's trust in them and their bright promises about the future. Yet they feel no compunction against doing this to trusting laymen, who do not

---

33. Dave Hunt, the best-selling pop-dispensationalist author, announces at the end of his book, under the section "A Positive Note," this exclusively pre-tribulational, premillennial hope: "Yes, Jesus left His disciples with a positive note. He promises to return. The fulfilment of that promise is going to take those people who have believed it and are looking for Him out of this world before the holocaust." Hunt, *Peace Prosperity and the Holocaust*, p. 262.

recognize the rhetorical impulse of this deception. This practice is a great disservice to faithful, trusting Christian laymen.

Reaping What You Sow

Fortunately, this strategy of deception is self-defeating. The readers eventually learn to ignore the language of victory. Proclaiming historical defeat in the fine print, amillennialists reap the inevitable institutional fruits. They struggle all their lives to keep their shrinking, ghetto churches afloat, silently sending their children off to their Christian day schools (maybe) and then to their little denominational colleges, which are increasingly liberal, both theologically and politically. After all, the laymen know that such grim developments are inevitable. Why waste resources fighting the eschatologically inevitable? *Hunker down!* Laymen are permitted by the churches' authorities only to watch silently from the institutional sidelines while their own children reject everything they themselves hold dear. And if their children do return to the church, it is all too often because they know that the next generation of pastors – their collegiate peers – will soon begin to impose the familiar campus liberalism in the denomination's pulpits; and if not liberalism, then at least the worldview of Christianity's cultural irrelevance.

There is continuity in history. It will either be a continuity of victory or a continuity of defeat. It will end either with the return of Jesus to set up an earthly kingdom (premillennialism) or at the end of time (amillennialism and postmillennialism). Until the coming cosmic discontinuity, both the premillennialists and the amillennialists insist, Christians can expect progressively bad news, progressively tyrannical conditions, and progressively less influence. Premillennialists at least allow a thousand years of earthly kingdom relief; amillennialists do not. Amillennialists are, as Rushdoony once remarked, premillennialists without earthly hope. As I wrote in *Political Polytheism*: "Let us understand the nature of amillennialism. Insofar as eschatology refers to human history, *amillennialism is postmillennialism for covenant-breakers*. Covenant-breakers take dominion progressively in history. (Dispensational premillennialism is also postmillennialism for covenant-breakers, insofar as eschatology refers to the Christians who live and labor prior to Jesus' physical Second Coming, the so-called Church Age. All their good works will be swallowed up during the great tribulation period, either immediately before Jesus returns – the post-tribulation position – or in the seven-year period which follows the so-called 'secret Rapture': pre-tribulationism.) *Postmillennialism is an inescapable concept.* It is never a question of cultural triumph vs. no cultural triumph prior to Jesus' Second Coming; it is a question of *which kingdom's* cultural triumph."[34] The amillennialist has identified the victorious kingdom in history: Satan's. What, then, is the rational response of the Christian, if this amillennial vision is correct? What is to be done?

Defeatism: Active or Passive?

The optimistic vision of covenantal victory that is found in the Book of Isaiah is not taken seriously by common grace amillennialists. They see a continuous expansion of Satan's kingdom (i.e., civilization) in history. Amillennialism's view of history is clear: "Things are going to get a lot worse before they get worse." Van Riessen is consistent in this respect: he offers Christians no earthly hope for positive cultural transformation.

On the one hand, Dutch common grace amillennialists insist that there are uniquely Christian ways to explain the world and even to suggest to the lost as biblical alternatives. On the other hand, because they deny the continuing validity of Old Testament law, they never get around to describing precisely what these specific reforms are, or how these reforms are uniquely biblical, i.e., how the Bible compels us morally to accept them.

The implications of this outlook for the construction of a Christian social theory are devastating. The common grace amillennialists deny God's covenant-guaranteed sanctions in history. Worse; they offer a perverse view of these sanctions: God rewards covenant-breakers and penalizes covenant-keepers. There is no neutrality in history. Historical sanctions are an inescapable concept. The question is: Who imposes them, Christ

34. North, *Political Polytheism*, p. 139.

or Satan? But the common grace amillennialists steadfastly refuse to admit plainly what they are teaching. Instead, they frequently camouflage their discussion of God's kingdom with the language of postmillennial optimism. This is false packaging, and it has gone on throughout the twentieth century.

Despite this false packaging, the basic message of amillennial theology has penetrated the thinking of the laymen: they have retreated into their ecclesiastical and cultural ghettos. Again, I need to cite Christian Reformed Church minister (and president of Westminster Seminary) R. B. Kuiper, who warned his fellow Dutch-Americans: "By this time it has become trite to say that we must come out of our isolation. . . . Far too often, let it be said again, we hide our light under a bushel instead of placing it high on a candlestick. We seem not to realize fully that as the salt of the earth we can perform our functions of seasoning and preserving only through contact."[35] But nothing has changed, except that the leadership of the denomination has grown far more liberal than it was in Kuiper's day. The Christian Reformed Church still speaks with a Dutch accent. So does the Protestant Reformed Church. Despite their surface differences and old antagonisms over the common grace issue, they share a historically defeatist millennial outlook. Neither side has produced a distinctly, self-consciously Christian social theory. The Protestant Reformed Church never was interested in the project, while the Christian Reformed Church is now too liberal to care.

Flickering Lights Under a Bushel

Van Riessen writes: "Defeatism or passive resignation to our situation with all the risks attached to the latter only mean the neglect of our vocation."[36] He is correct. People who do not believe that Christian civilization will ever become a city on a hill, a light to the nations, and who recognize that there are extreme risks in trying to build such a city, are unlikely to accept those risks. Why bother? It is safer to keep your light under a bushel.

This is why pessimillennialism has inevitable consequences for

---

35. Kuiper, *To Be or Not to Be Reformed*, p. 186.
36. Van Riessen, *Society*, p. 308.

the development of Christian social theory. It lowers the perceived benefits of developing a distinctly Bible-based approach to social theory by denying that such a theory can ever be applied in culture. It preaches a system of historical continuity that proclaims the expansion of Satan's kingdom and the cultural defeat of Christ's. Understand: *a failure to expand is a defeat*; there is no neutrality. Satan's kingdom automatically triumphs in history if Christ's does not expand, since Satan is holding all of the yet-unconquered territory by Adam's default. Pessimillennialism argues implicitly that God brings positive sanctions to covenant-breakers and negative sanctions to covenant-keepers. And then, to ice the cake, it denies or ignores the case laws of the Old Testament. It rejects Christianity's tools of dominion.[37]

The best thing you can say about an outlook like this is that eventually it self-destructs. Attrition erodes the membership of any church that calls for commitment to developing a Christian worldview, yet also denies the very possibility of accomplishing this difficult task. Premillennialism at least baptizes its open philosophy of cultural retreat, and it ignores the whole question of social theory. Common grace amillennialism produces either guilt (no biblical answers) or liberalism (false answers).

Why has this come about? Because amillennialists do not understand biblical prophecy. They do not understand the ethically conditional character of biblical prophecy and the Holy Spirit's role in history. They have not seen that the Holy Spirit empowers God's covenant people progressively to meet the demands of God's law, and therefore enables them to gain the positive blessings of God in history.

The Ethically Conditional Character of Biblical Prophecy

Jonah was told by God to announce this prophetic message to the city of Nineveh: "Yet forty days, and Nineveh shall be overthrown" (Jonah 3:4b). The people believed him, and the result was Nineveh's national repentance:

---

37. Gary North, *Tools of Dominion: The Case Laws of Exodus* (Tyler, Texas: Institute for Christian Economics, 1990)

> So the people of Nineveh believed God, and proclaimed a fast, and put on sackcloth, from the greatest of them even to the least of them. For word came unto the king of Nineveh, and he arose from his throne, and he laid his robe from him, and covered him with sackcloth, and sat in ashes. And he caused it to be proclaimed and published through Nineveh by the decree of the king and his nobles, saying, Let neither man nor beast, herd nor flock, taste any thing: let them not feed, nor drink water: But let man and beast be covered with sackcloth, and cry mightily unto God: yea, let them turn every one from his evil way, and from the violence that is in their hands. Who can tell if God will turn and repent, and turn away from his fierce anger, that we perish not? And God saw their works, that they turned from their evil way; and God repented of the evil, that he had said that he would do unto them; and he did it not (Jonah 3:5-10).

The king of Nineveh understood biblical prophecy better than most modern Christians do. He recognized that God might be willing to reverse His judgment and not impose negative sanctions in history, even though He had said that He would. The king recognized that God's intent was ethical: to stop the sinning. God could do this either by bringing negative sanctions or by enabling the recipients of the message to reform their lives. Nineveh chose the latter approach. The city was spared.

Like pre-tribulational dispensationalists who are ready (if not willing) to see two-thirds of the Jews of Israel exterminated – see it safely from heaven, of course, after the Rapture[38] – and who rejoice at front-page headlines filled with bad news, because this tells us that "Jesus is coming soon," Jonah was depressed when the prophesied bad news turned into good news. "But it displeased Jonah exceedingly, and he was very angry" (Jonah 4:1). He had expected God to smash His enemies in forty days. But God *had* smashed them, in an ethically relevant sense. He had made them into something better: if not covenant-keepers, then at least covenant-observers.[39]

---

38. John F. Walvoord, *Israel in Prophecy* (Grand Rapids, Michigan: Zondervan Academie, [1962] 1988), p. 108.

39. A covenant-keeper is a regenerate person who obeys God's laws because of the ethical transformation within him. As a recipient of God's special, soul-saving grace, he is heir to God's covenant promises, including promises to his children. The biblical covenant offers continuity with the future (point five). Since Assyria subsequently became a ruthless

The "If" Clause

When God prophesies destruction against a person or nation, there is always an "if" clause in the prophecy. *If you do not repent,* God promises, negative sanctions in history will be brought against you. But always present is a way of escape: if you cease from your sins, you will avoid these negative sanctions. "There hath no temptation taken you but such as is common to man: but God is faithful, who will not suffer you to be tempted above that ye are able; but will with the temptation also make a way to escape, that ye may be able to bear it" (I Cor. 10:13).

It is this conditional nature of all prophecy that makes the outcome contingent on the ethical decisions of men. The offer of the gospel is always well-intentioned. God may choose not to enable men to accept it, and without this positive sanction, they will not accept it. "But the natural man receiveth not the things of the Spirit of God: for they are foolishness unto him: neither can he know them, because they are spiritually discerned" (I Cor. 2:14). But the offer is always legitimate. It is not a trick.[40]

Because neither the prophet nor the recipient of the threat knows in advance what the response of the recipient will be, neither knows for sure what God's response will be. The threat of negative sanctions is not the unconditional prediction of negative sanctions. Thus, whenever God prophesies external negative sanctions against a person or a corporate group, the interpreter of prophecy should have the "if" clause in the back of his mind. *The intent of the threat is to induce repentance.* God's prophecies are always ethical in intent.[41]

Because of this ethical character of biblical prophecy, there is no "sure thing" in prophetic matters when they relate to nega-

---

conqueror of Israel, showing no signs of saving faith, this element of continuity was absent. Thus, there was no full-scale repentance in Nineveh under Jonah's preaching. There was outward conformity to God's law: common-grace transformation. This was sufficient to delay the wrath of God for two centuries, until Assyria fell to Babylon.

40. Cornelius Van Til, *Common Grace and Witness-Bearing* (Phillipsburg, New Jersey: Lewis Grotenhuis, [1955]).

41. Sidney Greidanus, *The Modern Preacher and the Ancient Text: Interpreting and Preaching Biblical Literature* (Grand Rapids, Michigan: Eerdmans, 1988), pp. 232-34. He cites Jeremiah 18:7-8; 26:13-19; Isaiah 38:1-6; Joel 2:13-14.

tive sanctions in history. The presence of ethical conditionality removes from such prophecies the category of inevitability. The threatened sanctions are inevitable *if* the target of the threat persists in sin, but the target may repent. This is what God in principle always prefers. "The Lord is not slack concerning his promise, as some men count slackness; but is longsuffering to us-ward, not willing that any should perish, but that all should come to repentance" (II Pet. 3:9). In short, *biblical prophecy does not assume an inevitable continuation of existing ethical trends*. It only assumes a certain outcome *if* these existing trends continue.

Trend-Tending: The Illusion of Inevitability

Van Riessen's vision of the future is a grim one. It partakes of the same gloom as do modern humanism's pessimistic utopian novels, which he identifies as signs of the end of civilization.[42] He looks around him, and he does not like what he sees. He then extrapolates from 1957 into the future – a vision of the future governed by his unstated amillennial presuppositions. The question is: Are these trends inevitable (i.e., predestined)?

Robert Nisbet is a conservative sociologist and historian – more historian, by gift and choice, than sociologist. (How else could I have survived his graduate seminars?)[43] He has seen what has happened to many prophecies in history. He has also seen the character of modern social science prophecies today. There is not much difference, he concludes. They seldom come true. When they do, it is because the prophet has had a kind of brilliant insight into the present, not the future. The successes are based on imagination, not computer print-outs.

Commenting on a slew of "Year 2000" books published in the mid-1960's – a tradition going back to a communist pornogra-

---

42. Van Riessen, *Society*, ch. 2.

43. In case anyone is interested, I wrote two papers for him in 1967 and 1968, both of which are in print: "Max Weber: Rationalism, Irrationalism, and the Bureaucratic Cage," in Gary North (ed.), *Foundations of Christian Scholarship: Essays in the Van Til Perspective* (Vallecito, California: Ross House Books, 1976); and "The Cosmology of Chaos," Chapter 2 of *Marx's Religion of Revolution: Regeneration Through Chaos* (Tyler, Texas: Institute for Christian Economics, [1968] 1989). Never throw away an old term paper, I always say.

pher, Restif de la Bretonne, just prior to the French Revolution – he observed that these books were not really about changes in the future. They were about the writers' observations in the present. "But change is not, alas, what these books are predicting; they are only extrapolating present rates, many of which remind one of a mad psychologist predicting giants at age twenty on the basis of growth rates at age ten."[44]

> Only the unwary will be deluded into thinking that any of this is in fact the future. There have been statistician-soothsayers, I am certain, in all ages. In ancient Egypt there must have been such individuals to compute the number of pyramids there would be on earth two thousand years later; before that someone to compute the number of pterodactyls; after that, to compute the number of knights on horseback, wayfarer chapels, not to mention witches. It is a great game for the statistically-minded (like predictions year by year in the Pentagon of that infinitessimally small chunk of time represented by our engagement in Vietnam), and, as I say, I do not for the moment disparage it. It tells us about the present.[45]

Whenever we see such "prophecies" of the future, which are in fact observations about the present, we should beware. His warning should always be in the back of our minds: "Let us be clear on two points. (1) Events do not marry and have little events that grow into big events which in turn marry and have little events, etc.; (2) small social changes do not accumulate directionally and continuously to become big social changes."[46] Society must contend with such future factors as "the Random Event, the Maniac, the Prophet, and the Genius."

> We have absolutely no way of escaping them. The future-predicters don't suggest that we can avoid or escape them – or ever be able to predict or forecast them. What the future-predicters, the change-analysts, and trend-tenders say in effect is that with the aid of institute resources, computers, linear programming, etc. they will deal with the kinds of change that are *not* the consequence of the Random Event,

44. Robert A. Nisbet, "The Year 2000 and All That," *Commentary* (June 1968), p. 63.
45. *Idem.*
46. *Ibid.*, p. 66.

the Genius, the Maniac, and the Prophet. To which I can only say: there really aren't any; not any worth looking at anyhow.[47]

With respect to trend-tending, Van Riessen's *Society of the Future* bears a striking resemblance to Jacques Ellul's *The Technological Society*, which was published in France about five years after *The Society of the Future* appeared in the Netherlands. Ellul's book is more prolix, more eloquent, but essentially the same in terms of both message and content: we are heading toward the bureaucratic cage. This had been Max Weber's message a half century earlier. Ellul stressed the dark side of the technological imperative: "If it can be done, it will be done." Van Riessen emphasized the dark side of man's character. Neither of them offered a way out of mankind's supposed dilemma. The trends are irreversibly fixed.

But what of the discontinuous event? What of a Luther, a Calvin, a Wesley, or even an Abraham Kuyper? More important, what of a culture-transforming move by the Holy Spirit in the future? What of God's positive and negative sanctions in history? When His mercy runs out for covenant-breakers, what then? Will this somehow thwart the Church's Great Commission?

Amillennialism denies that such a culture-transforming positive work of the Holy Spirit will happen. This assertion is basic to amillennial eschatology. Similarly, the common grace amillennialist denies that God will bring comprehensive negative sanctions against the present humanist world order, even though He may from time to time smash a particular evil-doer, Hitler being the number-one example (especially for Dutchmen). Amillennialism is an *eschatology of downward continuity*, and the continuity it affirms is based on a denial of the significance of any meaningful historical discontinuity that might reverse the downward drift of civilization into the cultural void. (This is also true the Random News school, since there is no "kingdom neutrality" in history.) It denies a postmillennial *spiritual* discontinuity from outside of history that would reverse this present downward drift, as well as a premillennial *physical* discontinuity from out-

---

47. *Idem.*

side of history: the bodily return of Christ to set up a millennial kingdom. Amillennialism is inherently Bad News.

Conclusion

Amillennialism partakes of the "Jonah fallacy": a systematic ignoring of (1) the conditional, ethical character of all biblical prophecy and (2) the cultural work of the Holy Spirit. It therefore takes a particular approach to the "if" clause in all biblical prophecy. Whenever amillennial expositors see prophesies of Christianity's cultural victory (e.g., Psalm 2; 110; Isaiah 32; Jeremiah 32), they say to themselves, "These happy prophecies are ethically conditional. Men *will* fall into sin. The continuity of salvation cannot be maintained across generations. So, cultural victory cannot be maintained. Christians cannot hold conquered territory." Whenever they see prophecies of the afflictions of the Church in history, they think: "These are not conditional prophecies; the cultural triumph of Satan is sure."

The real question is this: Will the work of the Holy Spirit enable covenant-keepers to fulfill the bulk of the dominion covenant in history? In other words, *will He enable His covenant people progressively to meet the bulk of the covenant's ethical conditions?* The amillennialist categorically denies that He will, while the postmillennialist categorically insists that He will. There is no way to reconcile these rival views of covenantal history. One of these positions is wrong. This is why any assertion of an ideal of eschatological neutrality for the Church's creeds and standards is as naive as any other form of doctrinal neutrality. Over time, the Church will come to more rigorous standards. The postmillennialist is confident that these will be progressively accurate standards. In contrast, the amillennialist thinks that history is inherently ambiguous,[48] and therefore eschatology should be, too. If history is progressive, eschatology must reflect this. If it is ambiguous, then eschatology must reflect this. So, the amillennialist wants eschatological neutrality, which is another way of saying that he wants amillennialism dominant in the Church:

48. Hoekema, *The Bible and the Future*, pp. 35-36.

eschatological ambiguity. Eschatological ambiguity means, institutionally, the triumph of amillennialism. Eschatological liberty is *eschatological pluralism*. But there is no neutrality. Any assertion of neutrality is a cover for a hidden agenda (perhaps hidden even to those who promote neutrality).

The debate is over the Holy Spirit and what God has said that He will achieve in history. The amillennialist says that the Holy Spirit has been sent by the Father and the Son to achieve very little culturally in history through His people – the doctrine of *judicial representation*: point two of the biblical covenant model.[49] The postmillennialist says that God has a very broad definition of what constitutes salvation and restoration, and that His Spirit will achieve a great deal in history through His people. As an incentive for the development of biblical social theory, postmillennialism's vision of the comprehensive work of the Holy Spirit in history cannot be matched within Christian circles.

This assertion will be denied by pessimillennialists. A verbal denial is easy. Proving its accuracy will be more difficult. But the most important form of any such denial is to be able to point to an existing body of social theory that has been developed self-consciously in terms of one's eschatology. If this is missing, the public denials will be far less impressive. Denials are cheap; writing comprehensive social theory isn't.

Second, amillennialists indulge in the trend-tending fallacy of the humanist social scientists whom they challenge theologically. They see Satan's kingdom dominating today's world, and they extrapolate from the present. Any extrapolation from the present – whether *downward* or *random* – spells defeat for Christ's visible, institutional kingdom in history. ("Defeat" = *not victorious*; there is no neutrality.) Amillennial social commentators are spiritually blinded by the effects of their trend-tending. Their view of linear history is *linear downward toward the cultural void*. Therefore, they believe that the only thing that can save God's Church in history is either (1) an immediate and permanent cease-fire agreement with the enemy (cultural and political

---

49. Ray R. Sutton, *That You May Prosper: Dominion By Covenant* (Tyler, Texas: Institute for Christian Economics, 1987), ch. 2.

pluralism)[50] or else (2) Christ's Second Coming.

Amillennial theologians would do well to follow the example of the king of Nineveh. He believed in the ethical conditionality of God's prophecies, and responded accordingly. It can happen again in history. God is sovereign, not covenant-breaking man.

---

50. North, *Political Polytheism.*

6

TIME ENOUGH

They did eat, they drank, they married wives, they were given in marriage, until the day that Noe entered into the ark, and the flood came, and destroyed them all (Luke 17:27).

What is the nature of historical change? It is a combination of institutional continuity and discontinuity.[1] Long periods of normality are interspersed with revolutionary events that transform institutions and manners (Deut. 28:53-57). In the days of Noah, Jesus said, people married and were given in marriage. These familiar events went on for centuries. People assumed that these events were normal and normative. Then, in a period of forty days, everything ended. No one had suspected this except Noah and his family. This was historical discontinuity.

A Bible-based definition of *historical discontinuity* is this:

> An unprecedented period of God's culture-wide sanctions, in which the institutions of a covenant-breaking society are displaced through war, famine, or plague (negative), and/or voluntary reform (positive).

In the midst of such a major discontinuity, we always find the *continuity of God's covenant promises* to His people, embodied in all of those covenant-keepers who survive and then build society anew. They displace covenant-breakers and their ways.

Noah is the premier example of this covenantal process in

1. Gary North, *Moses and Pharaoh: Dominion Religion vs. Power Religion* (Tyler, Texas: Institute for Christian Economics, 1985), ch. 12: "Continuity and Revolution."

man's history. The Flood's *comprehensive discontinuity* was the potential basis of *comprehensive reconstruction* by covenant-keepers and their heirs. The Flood was a means of spiritual and cultural liberation for covenant-keepers. The Noachic Flood is the archetype of *physical* discontinuities in history, an event not to be matched again until the final judgment. It serves as the model for lesser physical and social events, as Jesus' statement reveals.

Babylon Is Fallen!

Another example from Scripture is the judgment against Babylon. On that last night, the king and his high officials had a feast. They brought out the gold and silver implements of the temple, stolen a generation earlier by Nebuchadnezzar. Then they ate from these holy implements in what was a satanic communion meal. That finished Babylon. God's negative corporate sanctions were imposed that night.

The discontinuity for Judah had been her captivity, and the sign of God's providential administration of that discontinuity was the sacking of His temple. But the time of involuntary captivity for Israel was about to end. The restoration of Israel was imminent. Babylon's total discontinuity was at hand, to be administered by Medo-Persia. The handwriting was on the wall for Babylon, literally.

In that final night's festivities, King Belshazzar had sought an explanation of the miracle of the hand's writing. He, like Nebuchadnezzar before him, called in Daniel to interpret. Daniel did, telling him it was the end of the road for Babylon in history. Rather than rejecting this negative news and punishing Daniel, the king initiated a covenantal transfer of civil authority to Daniel. Perhaps he did this hoping to gain the favor of God, but it was too late for halfway political measures. Something far more fundamental than politics was at stake.

> Then commanded Belshazzar, and they clothed Daniel with scarlet, and put a chain of gold about his neck, and made a proclamation concerning him, that he should be the third ruler in the kingdom. In that night was Belshazzar the king of the Chaldeans slain (Dan. 5:29, 6:1).

Daniel became the covenantal link between the Chaldean empire and the Medo-Persian empire. Once again, he became the counsellor of the king. Daniel, because he was God's man, provided the covenantal continuity between the two empires.

Under Darius and later under Cyrus, the Israelites were allowed to return to their land. The discontinuity of Babylon's fall became the historical foundation of restored geographical continuity for Israel. *It was a permanent discontinuity for Babylon, but a means of restoration for Israel.* The discontinuity of Babylon's fall was for the sake of covenant-keeping Israel. It furthered the continuity of God's earthly kingdom. This is true of every discontinuity in history.

This is how we are supposed to interpret the God-imposed discontinuities of history. *These discontinuities are not permanent in the expansion of God's earthly kingdom; instead, they are permanent in God's thwarting of each of the rival earthly kingdoms. God does not impose sanctions for the purpose of shortening the time-perspective of Christians; He imposes them to shorten the time-perspective of non-Christians.* God's historical sanctions are to remind covenant-keepers and covenant-breakers of Satan's short time frame: "Therefore rejoice, ye heavens, and ye that dwell in them. Woe to the inhabiters of the earth and of the sea! for the devil is come down unto you, having great wrath, because he knoweth that he hath but a short time" (Rev. 12:12).

This is the biblical view of historical discontinuities. But what of the promised future discontinuity of the bodily return of Jesus Christ? Here is where the debate begins.

The Sign of His Coming

> Now learn a parable of the fig tree; When his branch is yet tender, and putteth forth leaves, ye know that summer is nigh: So likewise ye, when ye shall see all these things, know that it is near, even at the doors. Verily I say unto you, *This generation shall not pass, till all these things be fulfilled.* Heaven and earth shall pass away, but my words shall not pass away. But of that day and hour knoweth no man, no, not the angels of heaven, but my Father only. But as the days of Noe were, so shall also the coming of the Son of man be. For as in the days that were before the flood they were eating and drinking, marrying and giving in marriage, until the day that Noe entered into the

ark, And knew not until the flood came, and took them all away; so shall also the coming of the Son of man be (Matt. 24:32-39). (emphasis added)

The premillennialist looks to the future for a literal fulfillment of this prophecy. He connects Jesus' words with the premillennial advent of Christ to set up His kingdom on earth. The postmillennial or amillennial[2] "preterist" ("past tense") interpretation looks backward to the fall of Jerusalem.[3] After all, Jesus' words were clear: "This generation shall not pass, till all these things be fulfilled" (v. 34). He was therefore using symbolic, apocalyptic language in order to describe the greatest *covenantally significant* physical discontinuity intervening between His ascension to heaven and the final judgment: the destruction of the old order, the Israelite kingdom. This, too, was a fulfillment of prophecy: "Therefore say I unto you, The kingdom of God shall be taken from you, and given to a nation bringing forth the fruits thereof" (Matt. 21:43).

Clearly, Jesus was drawing an analogy between the Flood and Israel's coming discontinuity. Before the Flood, things went on as always. Then the monumental change took place. There were similar discontinuities in biblical history. Pharaoh, for example, paid no attention to the shepherd from Midian and his resident alien brother. Then came nine plagues. These disturbed him briefly, but not permanently. Then came the tenth plague,

2. Most amillennialists see the dark prophecies of the Book of Revelation as still in the future. They share this belief with premillennialists. There are a few amillennialists who are preterists, notably C. Vanderwal (d. 1980), who noted the similarities between Hal Lindsey's view of the future Antichrist and Dutch Reformed commentators' view: Prof. S. Greijdanus (1908), Abraham Kuyper, Klaas Schilder, and Valentinus Hepp. C. Vanderwal, *Hal Lindsey and Biblical Prophecy* (St. Catherines, Ontario: Paideia Press, 1978), pp. 90-96. Both Luther and Calvin saw the popes as antichrists in their day, not exclusively in the future (p. 94).

3. David Chilton, *The Days of Vengeance: An Exposition of the Book of Revelation* (Ft. Worth, Texas: Dominion Press, 1987); Chilton, *The Great Tribulation* (Ft. Worth, Texas: Dominion Press, 1987); Kenneth L. Gentry, Jr., *The Beast of Revelation* (Tyler, Texas: Institute for Christian Economics, 1989); Gentry, *Before Jerusalem Fell: Dating the Book of Revelation* (Tyler, Texas: Institute for Christian Economics, 1989).

followed by the exodus and the destruction of Pharaoh and his army in the Red Sea. But Israel was delivered. The Red Sea was not an agency of discontinuity for Israel.

There is continuity, and there are also discontinuities. People usually expect the world around them to continue as before. This is especially true of those in rebellion against God. "Come ye, say they, I will fetch wine, and we will fill ourselves with strong drink; and to morrow shall be as this day, and much more abundant" (Isa. 56:12). Man's dream of perpetual moral rebellion coupled with ever expanding personal prosperity is not exclusively a modern vision. It was this same confidence in the future that kept Noah's generation from taking appropriate defensive moral measures.

Positive Sanctions

I have concentrated on God's negative sanctions in history. So does the Bible. It does not record any instances of God's positive corporate sanctions apart from parallel negative sanctions. (The case of Nineveh is unique: the mere threat of near-term sanctions produced a righteous public response.) The deliverance of Israel from Egypt cannot be understood apart from a discussion of God's judgments against Egypt. Similarly, the blessings given to Joshua's generation cannot be understood without reference to the Israelites' displacement of Canaan's cultures.

As I said in the Introduction, the Old Testament emphasizes institutional transformation in the presentation of the Bible's basic theme: *the transition from wrath to grace*. While there are a few Old Covenant instances of God's willingness to delay His negative sanctions because of the conversion of a king and his people's willingness to allow him to make some public institutional changes (Josiah is an example: II Kgs. 22-23), the hearts of the people never changed apart from God's imposition of culture-wide negative sanctions. The occasional, top-down, formal changes in Israel's institutional arrangements did not last long. Under Elijah, the representatives of the people slew the false priests, but their hearts had not changed, Jezebel still reigned, and Elijah had to flee to the wilderness again (II Kgs. 18). *The permanent cultural displacement of covenant-breakers under the Old*

Covenant was always violent.

In the New Testament, God's establishment of the Church changed the lives of those who were converted, but it did not change the social institutions of Israel. This did not happen until the fall of Jerusalem in A.D. 70, a generation later. The same can be said for the centuries-long conquest of Rome's culture by Christians. This did not take place until after a series of disasters had fallen on Rome: wars, confiscatory taxes, inflation, and Constantine's victory, followed by tribal invasions in the West that continued for centuries.

The New Testament's emphasis is on personal regeneration, not institutional. The emphasis is on *progressive sanctification over time*, not revolutionary displacement. The progressive sanctification of individuals is to produce the progressive sanctification of institutions. Christians are to be salt to the world. Still, this does not deny the life-and-death nature of the struggle. Jesus warned: "Ye are the salt of the earth: but if the salt have lost his savour, wherewith shall it be salted? it is thenceforth good for nothing, but to be cast out, and to be trodden under foot of men" (Matt. 5:13). It is either "them or us." Salt is used on God's fiery altar as a permanent sign of destruction: "For every one shall be salted with fire, and every sacrifice shall be salted with salt" (Mark 9:49). Salt was used in ancient world to pollute a newly defeated city's land, so that it would no longer grow crops. "And Abimelech fought against the city all that day; and he took the city, and slew the people that was therein, and beat down the city, and sowed it with salt" (Jud. 9:45). Salt is more than savor; salt is a means of destruction.

Christians are to destroy the enemy's city (civilization), though normally through voluntary conversions and progressive, long-term cultural displacement. Continuity, not discontinuity, is the institutional task of New Covenant social reform. On the one hand, it is not the task of the reformers to impose discontinuous corporate negative sanctions, except in the case of war or legitimate resistance by lower magistrates to domestic national tyranny: the Calvinist doctrine of interposition.[4] On the other hand,

4. John Calvin, *Institutes of the Christian Religion*, IV:20. See also "Junius Brutus,"

apart from God's widespread negative corporate sanctions, there have been few (if any) known cases of permanent Christian social transformation.

Christianity's positive sanctions in New Covenant history tend to be continuous rather than discontinuous. Even in the rare cases of mass revival – discontinuous positive moves by the Holy Spirit – these events have virtually never been followed by widespread cultural transformation (i.e., cultural continuity). God's enemies have inherited.[5] The reasons why: mass revivals have not been accompanied by (1) God's comprehensive negative sanctions or by (2) a comprehensive reform of civil law. (Note: I am speaking here of history, not prophesying.)

The Protestant Reformation is an example of institutional transformation, but one reason why it succeeded was that the Turks were almost at the gates of Vienna; the Pope and the Emperor had other pressing concerns besides Luther and Calvin. Also, it led to the Thirty Years War (1618-48), and the resolution of that war was the establishment of Erastianism: the king's religion became the religion of the people. This was hardly a long-term cultural solution. The humanists inherited.

Covenantal Displacement

The process of covenantal displacement is a war over cultural and judicial standards. It is a war over law. It is therefore a war to determine the god of the culture, for the source of law in any culture is its god.[6] The enemies of God very seldom surrender peacefully. They correctly perceive that they are fighting to the death covenantally, both personally and institutionally. This is what the Bible teaches: either the old Adam dies spiritually through the new birth in history or else God will publicly execute him eternally on judgment day. Covenant-breakers clearly perceive the life-and-death nature of the struggle for civilization; covenant-keepers seldom do. Christians prefer religious and

---

Vindiciae Contra Tyrannos (1579), the *Defense of Liberty Against Tyrants*.

5. See Chapter 11.

6. R. J. Rushdoony, *The Institutes of Biblical Law* (Nutley, New Jersey: Craig Press, 1973), p. 5.

political pluralism to covenantal Christian reconstruction. They almost always have.

Because Christians do not fully understand the covenantal implications of the faith, and also because churches drift into apostasy, Christianity steadily gives up ground to the enemy. It spreads westward, but as it moves forward, it surrenders its rear flanks. The history of Christianity can be seen on a globe of the world. It would appear on the globe as a shadow about 2,000 miles wide. As it moves north or west, it surrenders in the south and east. Arab Muslims took North Africa and Spain on Europe's southern flank while Irish missionaries were spreading the gospel in Northern Europe (632-732). Turkish Muslims took Byzantium (1453) just before Western Christianity crossed the Atlantic. Enlightenment paganism took Europe while Protestant Christianity was spreading westward in North America. The only major exceptions in history have been Catholicism's reconquest of Spain (732-1492) and the Greek revolt (1821-22).

We do not see God's positive historical discontinuities apart from His negative discontinuities against those being displaced. Nevertheless, the program of the Church is *peaceful positive displacement, soul by soul.* God wins, Satan loses: soul by soul. Who brings the necessary negative corporate sanctions? God does, not through the Church but through such means as pestilence, plague, and war. The Church is supposed to pray for God's negative discontinuities in history against entrenched corporate evil. This is why God gave us His imprecatory psalms to sing and pray publicly in the Church (e.g., Psalm 83).

Here is the biblical program for cultural transformation. *First,* the Church is to bring continuous positive sanctions into a covenant-breaking culture: preaching, the sacraments, charity, and the disciplining of its members (a negative sanction by the Church, but positive for society: it keeps other Christians more honest). *Second,* the Holy Spirit must also bring positive discontinuities into individual lives: conversion. This is at His discretion, not ours. *Third,* a sovereign God in heaven must bring His discontinuous, corporate, negative sanctions against covenant-breakers in history. Notice, above all, that it is God who brings negative corporate sanctions in society, not the Church. *The*

Church is an exclusively positive agent in society. I stress this because of the continuing misrepresentation of our position on social change by critics, both Christian and pagan. While these misrepresentations will continue, the reader has now been provided with an immunization shot.

This interpretive framework for biblical social transformation, if correct, *militates against ecclesiocracy*: the fusion of Church and State. If the Church is to bring exclusively positive sanctions in society rather than negative, and if the State is supposed to bring primarily negative sanctions,[7] then *Church and State are inherently separate institutions*. They have two separate functions covenantally, and therefore two separate systems of sanctions. (Again, the critics have systematically misrepresented our position on this point. I want to make our position clear.)

Another implication is *the denial of salvation by law*. Men cannot work their way into heaven. There can be no valid program of personal salvation that is based on the continuity of fallen man's labors. The Holy Spirit's discontinuous intervention into history alone can save men's souls. We are saved exclusively by grace. This means that *personal regeneration is initiated from outside of history into history*. This perspective is a denial of the messianic State and the social gospel movement. It is also a denial of liberation theology.[8] There can be no positive, continuity-based, institutional program that guarantees God's grant of salvation to fallen men. Special grace is discontinuous. Common grace, while continuous, is strictly a temporary grant of external healing to men and institutions. It is the equivalent of medical care in a hospice filled with terminal patients. It is a kindness unto death.

We have yet to see in history a case of the cultural displacement of covenant-breakers apart from the widespread imposition of God's corporate negative sanctions. Christians refuse to recognize this. They seek continuity: the temporary cease-fire of pluralism. Covenant-breakers then use their civil authority to

---

7. Gary North, *Tools of Dominion: The Case Laws of Exodus* (Tyler, Texas: Institute for Christian Economics, 1990), pp. 713, 856.

8. Gary North, *Liberating Planet Earth: An Introduction to Biblical Blueprints* (Ft. Worth, Texas: Dominion Press, 1987).

increase the persecution of Christians, who then conclude that Jesus is coming soon. The alliance continues: the power religion and the escape religion.

What is the nature of this alliance? The power religionists want to keep Christians gazing hopefully up at heaven, looking for their *physical* deliverance from beyond history, which the humanists regard as mythical but extremely useful for purposes of social control. The promotion of a similar "skyward" strategy of non-historical deliverance worked so well for the old South's slave owners in their control of their Christian slaves that the humanists have mimicked it. So have their targeted slaves. The leaders of modern Protestantism's pietistic escape religion, like the black "trustees" of the old South's plantation system, want to keep their subordinates firmly in place under their authority, not getting involved in areas of life unfamiliar to, or beyond the abilities of, those presently occupying the pulpits. They can use every invasion of liberty by the power religionists as proof of the imminent return of Christ. "Look up!" In the same way that sadists need masochists, and vice versa, so do humanists and pessimillennialists need and use each other.

While premillennialists are the primary offenders in this regard, we must not ignore Dutch amillennialists' contributions. Dr. W. H. Velema of Holland has certainly done his part to keep Christians looking skyward. He is reported by the Christian press of the Netherlands to have said: "The idea of the cultural mandate as a comprehensive system, is today, in view of the environmental crisis, no longer tenable." Because of the well-orchestrated, media-fanned, and barely scientifically defendable ecological crisis,[9] Dr. Velema is willing to scrap all plans for exercising a cultural mandate in history. His eschatological pessimism has overwhelmed his theology of culture. "With our cultural mandate we remain aliens in this world. That we must more often pray: 'Come, Lord Jesus, come.' "[10]

Christians were told to look skyward prior to the fall of Jerusalem (a covenantal, not a cosmic, discontinuity). "And when

---

9. Peter Sawyer, *Greenhoax Effect* (Wodonga, Victoria; Australia: Groupacumen, 1990).
10. John de Vos, "Gleanings," *Reformed Perspective* (May 1990), p. 16.

these things begin to come to pass, then look up, and lift up your heads; for your redemption draweth nigh" (Luke 21:28). But their deliverance came in history. Luke 21 is the chapter that predicts the surrounding of Jerusalem by the Roman army in A.D. 70: "And when ye shall see Jerusalem compassed with armies, then know that the desolation thereof is nigh. Then let them which are in Judaea flee to the mountains; and let them which are in the midst of it depart out; and let not them that are in the countries enter thereinto" (vv. 20-21). That one-time deliverance of the early Church is today long behind us. It is surely time for Christians to begin looking forward, in time and on earth, for their deliverance, not upward.

Why Continuity?

Men must look to the future and build for the future. They need to work out their vision of life over time (Phil. 2:12). If the world were a series of unpredictable events, we could not plan for the future. Without historical continuity, we would perish. So, God gives mankind (and even the devil and his angels) the common grace (i.e., an unearned, undeserved gift) of time.[11] For the covenant-keeper, time is one of his God-given means for building up his eternal treasure. God's common grace to him in history becomes a means of special grace in eternity.

> For we are labourers together with God: ye are God's husbandry, ye are God's building. According to the grace of God which is given unto me, as a wise masterbuilder, I have laid the foundation, and another buildeth thereon. But let every man take heed how he buildeth thereupon. For other foundation can no man lay than that is laid, which is Jesus Christ. Now if any man build upon this foundation gold, silver, precious stones, wood, hay, stubble; Every man's work shall be made manifest: for the day shall declare it, because it shall be revealed by fire; and the fire shall try every man's work of what sort it is. If any man's work abide which he hath built thereupon, he shall receive a reward. If any man's work shall be burned, he shall suffer loss: but he himself shall be saved; yet so as by fire (I Cor. 3:9-15).

---

11. Gary North, *Dominion and Common Grace: The Biblical Basis of Progress* (Tyler, Texas: Institute for Christian Economics, 1987), ch. 1.

For the covenant-breaker, in contrast, time is one of his God-given means for building up his eternal torment. God's common grace to him in history becomes a special curse in eternity.

> But and if that servant say in his heart, My lord delayeth his coming; and shall begin to beat the menservants and maidens, and to eat and drink, and to be drunken; The lord of that servant will come in a day when he looketh not for him, and at an hour when he is not aware, and will cut him in sunder, and will appoint him his portion with the unbelievers. And that servant, which knew his lord's will, and prepared not himself, neither did according to his will, shall be beaten with many stripes. But he that knew not, and did commit things worthy of stripes, shall be beaten with few stripes. For unto whomsoever much is given, of him shall be much required: and to whom men have committed much, of him they will ask the more. I am come to send fire on the earth; and what will I, if it be already kindled? (Luke 12:45-49).

Notice a very important fact, one that will become central in the next chapter: *there is continuity between this life and the afterlife.* Covenant-keepers and covenant-breakers will all receive their appropriate eternal rewards and punishments. This *covenantal* fact affirms the importance of history. God's guarantee of future permanent sanctions is supposed to change the way we believe *and live* on earth. We do not live apart from institutions. God in His grace grants increasing cultural authority to us as we progressively conform ourselves to His word (positive sanctions in history). As this extension of authority takes place, we must steadily reform our institutions. From those to whom much is given, much is required (Luke 12:47-48). This is the reason why pessimillennialists, especially fundamentalists, strongly resist the very suggestion of such an extension of authority in history. They do not want this added responsibility.

Biblical Rhetoric

Sometimes, in order to get an idea across (and to make it stick in people's minds), a writer has to make the same point by saying it several different ways. Sometimes he puts his statement in italics. He does whatever he can to make his point, because he knows that memories are weak and hostile prejudices are strong. This is the art of rhetoric.

Rhetoric is biblical. While he did not use italics, Paul adopted a similar technique. Then he even told his readers that he had adopted it! "See with what large letters I am writing to you with my own hand" (Gal. 6:11, NASB). Following Paul's lead, I will say it again, in a different way, and even tell you what I am doing: *the ethical continuities of history, both personal and cultural, are confirmed by the judicial and cosmic discontinuity that ends history.* God's judgments are coming, both temporal and final. This is not a denial of historical continuity; this is an *absolute affirmation* of historical continuity. God announced this affirmation in the second of His Ten Commandments.

> Thou shalt not bow down thyself to them, nor serve them: for I the LORD thy God am a jealous God, visiting the iniquity of the fathers upon the children unto the third and fourth generation of them that hate me; And shewing mercy unto thousands of them that love me, and keep my commandments (Ex. 20:5-6).

Mercy unto thousands: not thousands of people (there have been more of us than that), but *thousands of generations* (a symbolic reference, I presume, given a minimum figure of 2,000 generations – plural – times at least 30 years in a generation, which equals 60,000 years). Bible commentators, both Jewish and Christian, have interpreted this reference as thousands of generations, meaning *wholeness*, not literal generations. They cite Deuteronomy 7 as proof:

> The LORD did not set his love upon you, nor choose you, because ye were more in number than any people; for ye were the fewest of all people: But because the LORD loved you, and because he would keep the oath which he had sworn unto your fathers, hath the LORD brought you out with a mighty hand, and redeemed you out of the house of bondmen, from the hand of Pharaoh king of Egypt. Know therefore that the LORD thy God, he is God, the faithful God, which keepeth covenant and mercy with them that love him and keep his commandments *to a thousand generations*; And repayeth them that hate him to their face, to destroy them: he will not be slack to him that hateth him, he will repay him to his face. Thou shalt therefore keep

the commandments, and the statutes, and the judgments, which I command thee this day, to do them (Deut. 7:7-11). (emphasis added)

At this point, dispensational commentators will affirm their *occasional* commitment to symbolism in biblical interpretation: waiting another 56,600 years for the Rapture (60,000 minus 3,400 = 56,600) is a bit too much for them to handle.

What is my point? Simple: the Bible sometimes uses symbolic language as a rhetorical means of driving home an important theological point. So can we. But we must do this fairly and honestly. This ethical requirement is not always honored.

Reconstructionist Rhetoric

I come now to a consideration of a recent debate over biblical interpretation. That the Bible does use symbolic language in order to emphasize important truths was a point made by David Chilton – and made rhetorically – when he spoke of the supposed 36,600-year millennial era: not a literal 36,600 years but rather the Bible's use of symbolic language to describe God's long-suffering patience with rebellious mankind and His blessings to covenant-keepers. Chilton was quite clear: "Similarly, the **thousand** years of Revelation 20 represent a vast, undefined period of time. . . ." He cited Milton Terry, the respected commentator and master of biblical hermeneutics: "It may require a million years."[12] This means simply that the designation of one thousand years must not be taken exclusively in a literal sense. In *Paradise Restored*, citing Deuteronomy 7:9, Chilton writes of a long era of millennial blessings:

> The God of the Covenant told His people that he would bless them to the thousandth generation of their descendants. That promise was made (in round figures) about 3,400 years ago. If we figure the Biblical generation at about 40 years, a thousand generations is *forty thousand years*. We've got 36,600 years to go before this promise is fulfilled![13]

12. Chilton, *Days of Vengeance*, p. 507.

13. David Chilton, *Paradise Restored: A Biblical Theology of Dominion* (Ft. Worth, Texas: Dominion Press, 1985), p. 221.

Then, to make his point, Chilton's next paragraph spelled out his position on the use of the number one thousand:

> When God said that He owns the cattle on a thousand hills, He means a vast number of cattle on a vast number of hills – but there are *more* than 1,000 hills. The Bible promises that God's people will be kings and priests for a thousand years, meaning a vast number of years – but Christians have been kings and priests for *more* than 1,000 years (almost 2,000 years now). My point is this: the term *thousand* is often used symbolically in Scripture, to express vastness; but that vastness is, in reality, much *more* than the literal thousand.

Chilton's book is a model of rhetoric. He goes straight to the heart of his opponents' arguments in a few memorable words. You will not soon forget this highly rhetorical delivery. (The saying, "Never answer a question with a question!" is a favorite of those who lose all their arguments. Jesus answered a loaded question with an even more loaded question, and so devastated were his questioners that they never again asked Him another question: Matt. 22:41-46.) Chilton says that Psalm 50 speaks of God's ownership of the cattle on a thousand hills. Is this a literal number, limiting God? No. "God owns *all* the cattle on *all* the hills."[14] He asks a classic rhetorical question: "Does Hill No. 1,001 belong to someone else?" The self-professed hermeneutical literalist should now begin to feel the noose tightening around his neck. Then Chilton pulls the lever on the trap door:

> In the same way – particularly with regard to a highly symbolic book – we should see that the "1,000 years" of Revelation 20 represent a vast, undefined period of time. It has already lasted almost 2,000 years, and will probably go on for many more. "Exactly how many years?" someone asked me. "I'll be happy to tell you," I cheerfully replied, "as soon as you tell me exactly how many hills are in Psalm 50."[15]

Snap! There went dispensationalism's forced literalism of Revelation 20. The lifeless body is twisting slowly, slowly in the wind.

---

14. *Ibid.*, p. 199.
15. *Idem.*

He ended his discussion with this forthright statement: "I am not interested in setting dates. I am not going to try to figure out the date of the Second Coming. The Bible does not reveal it, and it is none of our business. What the Bible does reveal is our responsibility to work for God's Kingdom, our duty to bring ourselves, our families, and all our spheres of influence under the dominion of Jesus Christ."[16] *David Chilton is not a date-setter.* He made this inescapably clear – too clear for some.

Chilton's rhetoric is so clear that his dispensational critics have felt morally compelled to self-consciously distort his words and then attack their deliberate distortion. When doing Jesus' work, one apparently is under grace, not law, especially this law: "Thou shalt not bear false witness against thy neighbour" (Ex. 20:16).

Pop-Dispensationalist Rhetoric

Chilton's discussion has been deliberately misquoted and then ridiculed in print by such best-selling dispensational authors as Dave Hunt and Hal Lindsey. Dave Hunt sneers: "It seems the height of folly to be looking for Christ when we know, according to Reconstructionist writer David Chilton, for example, that He cannot come for at least 36,000 years. . . ."[17] *Cannot* come? Where did Chilton say this? He didn't, but for Hunt to admit this would reduce the impact of his rhetoric.

Hunt has a moral problem: Christians' rhetoric is supposed to emphasize the truth for the benefit of the listener or reader, *not to convey deliberate falsehoods*. Hunt did not honor this fundamental biblical principle of rhetoric in dealing with Chilton's careful, cogent, and fully explained interpretation of the duration of the millennial era. He prefers rhetoric to the truth. An appropriate biblical response to Mr. Hunt is Nehemiah's reply to Sanbalat: ". . . There are no such things done as thou sayest, but thou feignest them out of thine own heart" (Neh. 6:8b). It is also appropriate for Hal Lindsey's similar discussion.

16. *Ibid.*, p. 222.

17. Dave Hunt, *Whatever Happened to Heaven?* (Eugene, Oregon: Harvest House, 1988), p. 53.

Lindsey quotes Chilton's statement of 40,000 years and Terry's million years, but skips the explanation of the symbolic usage of "one thousand" in the Bible. He also fails to mention (or respond to) Chilton's devastating use of "the cattle on a thousand hills."[18] He then says that this kind of teaching makes the Reconstructionists "So earthly minded that they are no heavenly good." He insists that Reconstructionists "often seem to be more interested in political takeover than evangelizing and discipling people for a spiritual kingdom." This, despite Chilton's explicit statement in the chapter in *Days of Vengeance* that Lindsey relies on to attack him.[19] Chilton states as clearly and emphatically as possible that politics is not primary.

> It must be stressed, however, that the road to dominion does not lie primarily through political action. While the political sphere, like every other aspect of life, is a valid and necessary area of Christian activity and eventual dominance, we must shun the perennial temptation to grasp for political power. Dominion in civil government cannot be obtained before we have attained maturity and wisdom – the result of generations of Christian *self*-government.[20]

According to Chilton, how long will it take for Christians conceivably to be ready to exercise widespread political leadership as a self-conscious, organized group? *Generations*. Christian *self-government* first, he insists; then politics. He could not have made it any plainer. This has always been the view of the Christian Reconstructionists. But neither Hal Lindsey nor the myriads of other dispensational critics who attack Reconstructionism are willing to take our words seriously, no matter how many times we repeat ourselves. Our words simply do not register with them. (They are beyond the Bible; I suppose it should not surprise me that they are beyond our rhetoric.)

They see the word "dominion," and just like the political humanists, they automatically think "politics." Like the Jews of Jesus' day, these men are *judicially blinded*: ". . . seeing [they] see

---

18. Hal Lindsey, *The Road to Holocaust* (New York: Bantam, 1989), p. 232.
19. *Ibid.*, p. 292, footnote 15.
20. Chilton, *Days of Vengeance*, p. 511.

not; and hearing they hear not, neither do they understand" (Matt. 13:13b). They apparently incapable of comprehending what they read (I am here assuming they actually do read our books, which is probably naive), so they announce this grotesque misrepresentation to their followers: ". . . Dominionists believe that the Church must politically conquer the world. . . ."[21]

Do they have a moment's twinge of conscience? Not that I can detect. Lindsey allowed *The Road to Holocaust* to reprinted in paperback without bothering to correct even the incorrect names (e.g., his "John Rousas Rushdoony" instead of Rousas John Rushdoony) and other misstatements of fact. It was as if we had not published *The Legacy of Hatred Continues* just 30 days after *The Road to Holocaust* appeared. Anything for the cause (and their book royalties). Theirs is the "Sanballat Strategy."

And they wonder why they are losing the battle to half a dozen men with word processors!

Reconstructionists Deny Political Salvation

What do we teach? We teach that the gospel of Jesus Christ, *whenever empowered by the Holy Spirit*,[22] will progressively conquer the hearts *and minds* of men, and as a result, will conquer the cultural world, which includes politics. This is a very different perspective from the wholly perverse idea that the Church of Jesus Christ must use political power in order to conquer the world. But the critics, pessimillennialists and humanists alike, cannot imagine that the gospel possesses this degree of authority and power, even when the Holy Spirit imparts His irresistible saving grace to men.

The Calvinists tell us (implicitly) that God has foreordained the historic failure of His gospel. In contrast, the Arminians tell us (explicitly) that the mass of autonomous mankind will never convert to saving faith. (How they know this in a supposedly non-predestined world is a mystery.) The humanists tell us that

---

21. David Allen Lewis, *Prophecy 2000* (Green Forest, Arkansas: New Leaf Press, 1990), p. 282.

22. Greg L. Bahnsen, *By This Standard: The Authority of God's Law Today* (Tyler, Texas: Institute for Christian Economics, 1985), pp. 185-86.

Christianity is false, and therefore it should have no influence in politics or culture generally. But they are all agreed: *God will never bring the world to the foot of the cross on this side of the Second Coming of Christ.* Reconstructionists say that He will, that His kingdom's earthly triumph in history is foreordained. This is why Christian Reconstruction is a stumbling stone to everyone.

Here is what the debate is really all about: *the God-predestined victory of Christ in history*, as manifested by a wide acceptance of His covenant law, but not achieved through His bodily presence on a physical throne in Jerusalem. Reconstructionists argue that because God will accomplish this through His irresistible grace, politics is not very important. Our critics deny that God has foreordained His visible kingdom's victory in history, and so they imagine that *only* politics can serve as a tool sufficient to achieve a theonomic millennium. Denying the sovereignty of God in bringing His kingdom on earth to visible victory, they focus on politics, which they all agree is the ultimate power in history, given the assumption (which they all make) of the cultural impotence of the kingdom of God in history. It makes them ready to surrender to humanism in advance of defeat.

Pre-Emptive Surrender

What frightens some of the dispensational critics is their fear of persecution. David Allen Lewis warns in his book, *Prophecy 2000*, that "as the secular, humanistic, demonically-dominated world system becomes more and more aware that the Dominionists and Reconstructionists are a real political threat, they will sponsor more and more concerted efforts to destroy the Evangelical church. Unnecessary persecution could be stirred up."[23] In short, because politics is humanistic by nature, any attempt by Christians to speak to political issues as people – or worse, as *a* people – who possess an explicitly biblical agenda will invite "unnecessary persecution."

We see once again dispensational fundamentalism's concept of *evangelism as tract-passing*, a narrowly defined kingdom program

23. Lewis, *Prophecy 2000*, p. 277.

of exclusively personal evangelism that has one primary message to every generation, decade after decade: *flee the imminent wrath to come*, whether the Antichrist's (the Great Tribulation) or the State's ("unnecessary persecution"). This is a denial of the greatness of the Great Commission,[24] yet all in the name of the Great Commission: "Our vision is to obey and fulfill the command of the Great Commission."[25]

Mr. Lewis says that we can legitimately participate in politics *as individuals*, since our government is democratic: ". . . we encourage Christians to get involved on an individual basis, in all realms of society, including the political arena." Should our goal be to change society fundamentally? Hardly. This is an impossible goal. Our goal is to gain new contacts in order to share the gospel with them. "This is partly to insure that Christians are in place in every strata of society for the purpose of sharing the gospel message."[26] The purpose of political and social involvement is not to reform the world; it is to tell people about the imminent end of this pre-millennium world. We are apparently not supposed to say anything explicitly Christian or vote as an organized bloc (the way that all other special-interest groups expect to gain political influence).[27] "To be involved in our governmental process is desirable; however, it is quite another matter for the Church to strive to become Caesar."[28]

Mr. Lewis does not understand politics: one does not get involved in order to lose; one gets involved in order to win. He also does not understand society: one does not make the neces-

---

24. Kenneth L. Gentry, Jr., *The Greatness of the Great Commission: The Christian Enterprise in a Fallen World* (Tyler, Texas: Institute for Christian Economics, 1990).

25. Lewis, *Prophecy 2000*, p. 282.

26. *Idem.*

27. This is traditional democratic theory, but it has never really come to grips with the reality of political power. The Council on Foreign Relations and the Trilateral Commission do not organize voters into blocs. They simply make sure that they control who gets appointed to the highest seats of power and what policies are enacted. This raises other questions, which, being political, are not the focus of my concern here. See Gary North, *Conspiracy: A Biblical View* (Ft. Worth, Texas: Dominion Press, 1986; co-published by Crossway Books, Westchester, Illinois). See also Philip H. Burch, *Elites in American History*, 3 vols. (New York: Holmes & Meier, 1980-81); Carroll Quigley, *Tragedy and Hope: A History of the World in Our Time* (New York: Macmillan, 1966).

28. Lewis, *Prophecy 2000*, p. 277.

sary sacrifices in life that it takes to be successful if one is told that his efforts will not leave anything of significance to the next generation, if in fact there will be a next generation, which is said to be highly doubtful. Mr. Lewis and his pre-tribulational dispensational colleagues have paraphrased homosexual economist John Maynard Keynes' quip, "In the long run we are all dead." They say, "In the short run, we Christians will all be Raptured, and the Jews in Israel will soon wish they were dead, which two-thirds of them will be within seven years after we leave." (This view of the Jews is still taught by the retired, 30-year president of Dallas Theological Seminary.)[29]

Mr. Lewis' position on politics and social involvement is one more example of the long-term operational alliance between the escape religion and the power religion.[30] Both sides are agreed: Christians should not seek office as civil magistrates, except as *judicially neutral agents*. Yet at the same time, all but Liberty University's Norman Geisler (a former Dallas Theological Seminary professor) and the academic political pluralists (e.g., Richard John Neuhaus) admit there is no neutrality. This is schizophrenic.[31] This schizophrenia has left Christians intellectually helpless in the face of an officially neutral, officially pluralistic humanist juggernaut. This has been going on for over three centuries.[32] (An Islamic juggernaut might provide a cure.)

Continuity and Time

The two divisive millennial issues are *continuity* and *time*. The self-conscious premillennialist denies continuity and shortens time. He forthrightly declares, as Lewis has declared: "We are in the final era prior to the coming of Jesus and the establishing of the visible aspect of the Kingdom – the Millennium. We have no time to waste on wild experimentation with possible futures and

---

29. John F. Walvoord, *Israel in Prophecy* (Grand Rapids, Michigan: Zondervan Academie, [1962] 1988), p. 108.

30. North, *Moses and Pharaoh*, pp. 2-5.

31. Gary North, "The Intellectual Schizophrenia of the New Christian Right," *Christianity and Civilization*, I (1983).

32. Gary North, *Political Polytheism: The Myth of Pluralism* (Tyler, Texas: Institute for Christian Economics, 1989), Part 3.

postmillennial pipedreams."[33] In comprehensive contrast, the postmillennialist has a much longer time span in mind, and he also affirms covenantal continuity in history. He understands the power of *compound growth*. He believes that obedient Christians can accomplish great things in history, little by little, which is the strategy that the Bible requires.[34] Little by little, he is supposed to prepare himself and his fellow Christians to take advantage of the next major historical discontinuity, *when God's latest enemies will be thrown back, broken, snared, and taken*.

> Whom shall he teach knowledge? and whom shall he make to understand doctrine? them that are weaned from the milk, and drawn from the breasts. For precept must be upon precept, precept upon precept; line upon line, line upon line; here a little, and there a little: For with stammering lips and another tongue will he speak to this people. To whom he said, This is the rest wherewith ye may cause the weary to rest; and this is the refreshing: yet they would not hear. But the word of the LORD was unto them precept upon precept, precept upon precept; line upon line, line upon line; here a little, and there a little; that they might go, and fall backward, and be broken, and snared, and taken (Isa. 28:9-13)

Why Discontinuities?

The second commandment is clear: God grants four generations to workers of a particular culture's iniquity, and He grants thousands of generations for His covenant people:

> Thou shalt not bow down thyself to them, nor serve them: for I the LORD thy God am a jealous God, visiting the iniquity of the fathers upon the children unto the third and fourth generation of them that hate me; And shewing mercy unto thousands of them that love me, and keep my commandments (Ex. 20:5-6).

The covenant-keeper, legitimately thinking in terms of many generations, can operate in terms of the principle, "slow but sure." He thinks in terms of compound growth: the steady ex-

---

33. Lewis, *Prophecy 2000*, p. 279.

34. Ray R. Sutton, *That You May Prosper: Dominion By Covenant* (Tyler, Texas: Institute for Christian Economics, 1987), ch. 14.

pansion of God's kingdom, until it fills the earth. This was the meaning of the dream given to King Nebuchadnezzar by God.

> Thou sawest till that a stone was cut out without hands, which smote the image upon his feet that were of iron and clay, and brake them to pieces. Then was the iron, the clay, the brass, the silver, and the gold, broken to pieces together, and became like the chaff of the summer threshingfloors; and the wind carried them away, that no place was found for them: and the stone that smote the image became a great mountain, and filled the whole earth (Dan. 2:34-35).

God's kingdom will from time to time fall upon the imitation kingdoms of man, as Daniel explained to the king. It will fill the whole earth. The imagery of filling the earth is the imagery of continuity. The imagery of broken kingdoms and scattering is the imagery of discontinuity. So, *there will inevitably be discontinuities in history until all societies repent.* These discontinuities will break the kingdoms of self-proclaimed autonomous man. Persevering through these historical discontinuities is the growing kingdom of God. One by one, the broken kingdoms of man are replaced in history by God's universal kingdom-civilization.

The Hare's Strategy

To use Aesop's famous metaphor of the race between the tortoise and the hare, the humanist kingdoms must strive for rapid power. They will always be overtaken by the unstoppable tortoise, God's kingdom. Unlike the Christians, who have compound growth working for them, the humanists must bet everything, step by step, in their quest for short-term expansion. They must use borrowed money and borrowed vision in order to gain "leverage." It is all or nothing with them. It is "winner take all!" God says that none of them will ever take all. A tiny handful of them will gain something, medium-term. None of them will survive, long-term.

The humanist, like the pessimillennialist, is committed to the strategy of the hare. His believes that his time is short. "After me, the deluge!" Only those few covenant-breakers who have adopted the Bible's long-range view of kingdom-building – conspirators all – have even begun to imitate the success of

God's earthly kingdom.

Build the kingdom in history? Impossible, says the premillennialist. "We are here to win souls for the kingdom of God, which is eternal, invisible, within us now, but shortly to become visible when Jesus comes back. Time enough, then, under His command to witness His dominion over the nations."[35] When Jesus returns personally to set up His top-down, international, One World Order bureaucracy, which will be staffed exclusively by Christians, we can then profitably discuss Christian social theory. Not until then. Then we will have "time enough"; not today. And by "we" is meant *someone else*.

They resent being labeled defeatists in history. They speak of victory, but *they do not mean victory in history*. What they mean by victory is that God will deliver victory into "our" hands, but only representatively. He will deliver the world into the hands of those post-Rapture converts to Christianity who will reign with Jesus during the millennium. This means brand-new converts only; Raptured Christians will not return to earth until after the millennium.[36] Here is a message of *complete cultural discontinuity*: those pagans who have gone through the Great Tribulation, and who have only recently been converted to saving faith, will be given political power unprecedented in the entire history of mankind. The comparative failure of the gospel and God's Church in history will become obvious to everyone forever.

Faith in Bureaucratic Power

Here is the inescapable social message of all forms of premillennialism, dispensational and historic, but without the sugar-coating: *only **a pure power play** by God from heaven directly to earth is sufficient to create a Christian civilization*. In this sense, the premillennial escape religionists are at heart power religionists. They see the history of civilization only in terms of pure power: (1) escaping anti-Christian political power today, thereby aban-

35. Lewis, *Prophecy 2000*, p. 279.

36. John Walvoord, *The Rapture Question* (rev. ed.; Grand Rapids, Michigan: Zondervan, 1979), p. 86; J. Dwight Pentecost, "The Relation between Living and Resurrected Saints in The Millennium," *Bibliotheca Sacra*, vol. 117 (Oct. 1960), pp. 337, 341.

doning any attempt to build a Christian civilization; but then (2) exercising total, centralized political power during the millennium. As Dave Hunt says of the coming millennial political rule by the saints: "Justice will be meted out swiftly."[37] Power, not ethical continuity and the accumulated, Bible-informed wisdom of the ages (i.e., dispensationalism's designation of the "Church Age"), will alone make God's earthly kingdom a success.

In his book, *A Conflict of Visions*, Thomas Sowell makes this observation regarding fundamentalism, which he says is committed to an unconstrained (perfectionist, no trade-offs) view of society: "Fundamentalist religion is the most pervasive vision of central planning, though many fundamentalists may oppose human central planning as a usurpation or 'playing God.' This is consistent with the fundamentalist vision of an unconstrained God and a highly constrained man."[38] Sowell is correct on both counts. What he does not perceive is that the fundamentalist (i.e., premillennialist) defends a constrained vision of society and man today, on this side of the millennium, because Christ is in heaven and His enemies are on human thrones. On the other hand, during the millennium, Christ will sit on an earthly throne of total power. Then the fundamentalist vision switches to an unconstrained view: totalitarian power with a vengeance – God's vengeance. A Christian bureaucracy will rule the world. *But this will still be a world in which Christians do not exercise independent authority on their own responsible initiative in terms of God's law.* They will simply obey detailed orders handed down from a master bureaucrat, Jesus. This debate is not over bureaucracy; it is over how powerful it should be, who runs it, and when.

Today, both the humanists and the premillennialists agree: humanists should run it. But, the pessimillennial Christians say, this should be done fairly, honestly, and above all, *neutrally*. The humanists then cross their hearts (and fingers) and swear that they will be neutral. Then, when they start tyrannizing the

---

37. Dave Hunt, *Beyond Seduction: A Return to Biblical Christianity* (Eugene, Oregon: Harvest House, 1987), p. 250.

38. Thomas Sowell, *A Conflict of Visions: Ideological Origins of Political Struggles* (New York: William Morrow, 1987), p. 51.

Church and Christian schools, the premillennialists are simply amazed. "But you guys *promised*!" Yet they secretly rejoice. This is just additional proof that Jesus is coming soon. "*Then* Jesus gonna whip yo' ---!" *This* is premillennial social theory.

Dispensational social theory is even more explicit, at least in its non-academic form: "Then Jesus gonna let *me* whip yo' ---!" Comments Rev. Ice:

> My blessed hope, however, continues to be that Christ will soon rapture his Bride, the church, and that we will return with him in victory to rule and exercise dominion with him for a thousand years upon the earth. Even so, come Lord Jesus![39]

Notice that Rev. Ice has adopted the pop-dispensational view of the return to earth of Raptured saints. This means that they will be in their post-Rapture, perfect, sin-free, pain-free, death-free bodies, impervious to physical or other attacks by covenant-breakers or even demons. They will run the bureaucratic show then. This view has been rejected by the academic theologians of dispensationalism,[40] but it has been widely accepted by laymen and their pastors. This is a major appeal factor of the pop-dispensational movement, which is keeping the more academic version of dispensationalism afloat financially (which is why the seminary professors never publicly attack these paperback book theologians for having misled the public). This view of the millennium is the dispensationalist's equivalent of boys' comic book advertisements for Charles Atlas' *dynamic tension* (isometric) body-building techniques, but without any sweat or pain. The 98-pound fundamentalist weaklings will at last get even with the 250-pound humanist bullies who had kicked so much sand in their faces during the "Church Age." Once again, the issue is *sanctions*. Marx promised his readers that the currently expropriated will at last become the expropriators after the inevitable Revolution; the same psychology of revenge is present in pop-dispensationalism.

---

39. Thomas D. Ice, "Preface," H. Wayne House and Thomas D. Ice, *Dominion Theology: Blessing or Curse?* (Portland, Oregon: Multnomah Press, 1988), p. 10.

40. See footnote #36, above.

The humanists and the pessimillennialists agree on another point: God's kingdom is today *exclusively internal*, that is to say, *culturally irrelevant*. They all agree that time is not on the side of the Church, meaning there is not "time enough" for Christians to build a bottom-up, decentralized, biblical law-based, creedal, international, God-blessed social order.[41] This means that they agree on this fundamental point: *continuity within history favors covenant-breakers and the kingdom of autonomous man*.

Conclusion

Any millennial eschatology that proclaims the near-term return of Jesus Christ becomes a major ecclesiastical barrier to the development of Christian social theory. The supposed imminence of Jesus' physical return removes from God's people the crucial resource that they need to think about the future and plan for it: *time*. According to premillennial theologians, the looming eschatological discontinuity of Jesus' Second Coming works against the Church long-term and in favor of God's enemies, near-term. *Therefore, for the Church to accomplish anything of significance in history, it must drastically limit its vision of what it can accomplish*. It must plow shallow because there is not enough time to plow deep. Even so, they expect the Church to fail. Dispensationalists deeply (shallowly?) resent anyone who calls them to plow both deeper and longer. Common grace amillennialists do not resent being called to plow deeper, since they rejoice in deeply lost causes; they scoff, however, when they are told that Christians will finish plowing the field in history.

The biblical view of history is that God, who providentially controls all events in terms of His decree, brings discontinuous, negative, *historical* sanctions against covenant-breaking societies. These discontinuities are the social foundation of the long-term victory of His kingdom in history. While these discontinuities can and do bring great pain and consternation to covenant-keepers, they serve as the fire that burns off the dross of sin (Isa. 1:25-28). Jeremiah, Ezekiel, and Daniel all suffered during the

41. Gary North, *Healer of the Nations: Biblical Blueprints for International Relations* (Ft. Worth, Texas: Dominion Press, 1987).

period of the Babylonian captivity, but this discontinuity advanced the kingdom that was preached by all three of these prophets. Historical discontinuities are not threats against the long-term success of evangelism and social transformation. On the contrary, they are the basis of a positive, comprehensive, biblical, and *continuous* social transformation in history: Christian reconstruction.

The continuities of life favor covenant-keepers. So do the discontinuities. "And we know that all things work together for good to them that love God, to them who are the called according to his purpose" (Rom. 8:28). (This means, of course, that all things work together for bad to them who hate God, to them who are not called according to His purpose.) Historical discontinuities must be seen as God's negative sanctions against evil-doing societies in history. They are His means of *transferring the inheritance in history to His covenant people*.

The problem comes when Christians deny the existence of God's predictable, biblical law-governed, *covenantal*, corporate sanctions in history. Such a viewpoint explains God's historic corporate sanctions as random and inscrutable to man, even covenant-keeping man. The great historical discontinuities are not interpreted as advancing God's earthly kingdom. *Therefore, by default, God's negative sanctions in history must be seen as working to advance Satan's earthly kingdom*. There is no neutrality. Historic discontinuities are then viewed as mere reminders ("earnests") of the future *cosmic* discontinuity of Jesus' Second Coming. This future cosmic discontinuity is supposedly the only event that will enable God to bring His kingdom-civilization to earth, but only after history ends. In short, *God's civilization is defined a exclusively non-historical, while Satan's is exclusively historical*.

In conclusion, *whenever God's historical, covenantal sanctions are denied, history loses all meaning for covenant-keepers*. But there will always be discontinuities in history as God's kingdom advances. Thus, from a sanctions-denying perspective, history becomes a threat to Christians. This is exactly what has happened in our day. Here it is not primarily the apocalyptic premillennialists who are at fault; rather, it is the Calvinist amillennialists, as we shall see in the next chapter.

7

DENYING GOD'S PREDICTABLE SANCTIONS IN HISTORY

And meanwhile it [the common grace order] must run its course within the uncertainties of the mutually conditioning principles of common grace and common curse, prosperity and adversity being experienced in a manner largely unpredictable because of the inscrutable sovereignty of the divine will that dispenses them in mysterious ways.

Meredith G. Kline (1978)[1]

There is no better way for a Christian to proclaim his own personal and cultural irresponsibility in history than to proclaim the mystery of God's specific revelation. Mystery is defined as man's permanent ignorance. Mystery cannot be overcome. It does exist, of course: "The secret things belong unto the LORD our God: but those things which are revealed belong unto us and to our children for ever, that we may do all the words of this law" (Deut. 29:29). Notice that mystery and biblical law are contrasted. The impenetrable mysteries of God are not to discourage us, because we have His revealed law. But in denying the legitimacy of biblical law in New Testament times, modern antinomians are implicitly (and sometimes explicitly) substituting mystery in law's place. This can lead to mysticism: personal withdrawal into the interior recesses of one's incommunicable consciousness (escape religion). It can also lead to antinomian

1. Meredith G. Kline, "Comments on an Old-New Error," *Westminster Theological Journal*, XLI (Fall 1978), p. 184.

Pentecostalism: direct authoritative messages from God to a few uniquely gifted leaders (spokesmen in history: point two of the biblical covenant) – messages that replace God's law, since God's law is no longer binding. That this (power religion) leads again and again to ecclesiastical tyranny should surprise no one. In either case, there is an increase of personal irresponsibility.

To classify as one of "the secret things of God" the idea of God's predictable sanctions in history requires a leap of faith. The question is: Is such a leap of faith biblical? Or is the Old Testament's message of God's predictable sanctions in history itself part of our covenantal legacy from God, meaning "those things which are revealed belong unto us and to our children for ever, that we may do all the words of this law"?

In the Old Covenant, the sins of priests and kings could subject the society to God's negative sanctions (Lev. 4). Christian theologians believe that God no longer brings negative sanctions against society because of the unintentional sins of His priests, although He did do this under the Old Covenant (Lev. 4:1-3). (They might admit that certain kinds of sins by national political leaders could bring negative sanctions, but probably not God's.) But their rejection of God's historical, negative, corporate sanctions in history is more broadly conceived than this. The vast majority of Bible-affirming theologians today assume that there has been a radical New Covenant break from Old Covenant citizenship.[2] They assume (though seldom, if ever, attempt to prove exegetically) that the Old Covenant's close links between the social rewards of covenant-keeping and the social cursings of covenant-breaking are no longer operative in the New Covenant order. More than this: *there are supposedly no predictable covenantal sanctions in New Covenant history, meaning no sanctions applied in terms of biblical law*. Meredith G. Kline and his disciples argue that God does not bring predictable covenantal sanctions against a social order at all, i.e., that the historical sanctions in the New Covenant era are random from covenant-keeping man's point of view. "God's sanctions are mysterious."

---

2. On Old Covenant citizenship, see Gary North, *Political Polytheism: The Myth of Pluralism* (Tyler, Texas: Institute for Christian Economics, 1989), ch. 2.

What readers may not immediately recognize is that such an argument is a cover for a very different ethical conclusion, namely, that *historical sanctions should therefore be imposed in terms of some rival system of social theory*. There must always be sanctions in society, imposed by the State, the family, the market, and numerous other associations. The five covenantal questions are: (1) Who establishes these sanctions? (2) What agent or agency enforces them? (3) What is the moral foundation of these sanctions? (4) What sanctions apply to which acts? (5) Does the society prosper and expand its influence when these sanctions are enforced? To say that the Bible does not provide this covenant order in the New Testament era is to say that *some other covenant is legitimate for society*. But the opponents of biblical covenant social order never dare to admit this. They hide their implicit call for the establishment of *some other covenantal standard* in the language of ethical neutrality or judicial randomness. But there is no ethical neutrality. So, are God's sanctions in history really random, covenantally speaking?

In order to get a proper perspective on this question, let us consider the teachings of two of the most significant theologians (and culture-transformers) in history: Augustine and Calvin.

Augustine

Augustine's *City of God* discusses God's historical sanctions against *individuals* exactly where such a discussion should appear, in Chapter XX, on the last judgment. He therefore relates sanctions to *general eschatology*. He begins with a summary of the traditional creed, "that Christ shall come from heaven to judge quick and dead. . . ."[3] He asserts that men and devils are punished in this life and the next. He then limits himself to a discussion of the final judgment, "because in it there shall be no room for the ignorant questioning why this wicked person is happy and that righteous man unhappy."[4]

What ignorant questioning does he have in mind? He begins with a presupposition regarding individuals in history: "For we

3. Augustine, *The City of God*, XX:1 (Modern Library), p. 710.
4. *Ibid.*, XX;1, p. 711.

do not know by what judgment of God this good man is poor and that bad man is rich; . . ."[5] He lists a whole series of these apparent contradictions between righteous behavior and external adversity. "But who can collect or enumerate all the contrasts of this kind?"[6] What we must conclude, he insists, is that "rather on this account are God's judgments unsearchable, and His ways past finding out."[7] He cites Paul: "How unsearchable are his judgments, and his ways past finding out!" (Rom. 11:33b).[8] He cites Ecclesiastes on the vanity of life, concluding that the "calamities and delusions of this life, and the shifting nature of the present time, in which there is nothing substantial, nothing lasting. . . ."[9]

> But in these days of vanity it makes an important difference whether he resists or yields to the truth, and whether he is destitute of true piety or a partaker of it – important not so far as regards the acquirement of the blessings or the evasions of the calamities of this transitory and vain life, but in connection with the future judgment which shall make over to good men good things, and to bad men bad things, in permanent, inalienable possession.[10]

How Inscrutable Are God's Sanctions?

Augustine's view of God's *final* sanctions is individualistic rather than historical. He focuses on the coming judgment of individuals, which will be rigorously governed by ethical cause and effect, in contrast to the inscrutable outcome of personal ethics in history. Later in this chapter, he refers to the 73rd Psalm, Asaph's description of his former mental dilemma.[11] I cite this Psalm in its entirety, since it is a single unit expressing one message, namely, *the long-term predictability of God's sanctions in history*.

---

5. *Ibid.*, XX:2, p. 711.
6. *Ibid.*, XX:2, p. 712.
7. *Idem.*
8. *Ibid.*, XX:1, p. 711.
9. *Ibid.*, XX:3, p. 713.
10. *Idem.*
11. *Ibid.*, XX:28, p. 757.

> {A Psalm of Asaph.} Truly God is good to Israel, even to such as are of a clean heart. But as for me, my feet were almost gone; my steps had well nigh slipped. For I was envious at the foolish, when I saw the prosperity of the wicked. For there are no bands in their death: but their strength is firm. They are not in trouble as other men; neither are they plagued like other men. Therefore pride compasseth them about as a chain; violence covereth them as a garment. Their eyes stand out with fatness: they have more than heart could wish. They are corrupt, and speak wickedly concerning oppression: they speak loftily. They set their mouth against the heavens, and their tongue walketh through the earth. Therefore his people return hither: and waters of a full cup are wrung out to them. And they say, How doth God know? and is there knowledge in the most High? Behold, these are the ungodly, who prosper in the world; they increase in riches. Verily I have cleansed my heart in vain, and washed my hands in innocency. For all the day long have I been plagued, and chastened every morning. If I say, I will speak thus; behold, I should offend against the generation of thy children. When I thought to know this, it was too painful for me; Until I went into the sanctuary of God; *then understood I their end. Surely thou didst set them in slippery places: thou castedst them down into destruction*. How are they brought into desolation, as in a moment! they are utterly consumed with terrors. As a dream when one awaketh; so, O Lord, when thou awakest, thou shalt despise their image. Thus my heart was grieved, and I was pricked in my reins. *So foolish was I, and ignorant: I was as a beast before thee*. Nevertheless I am continually with thee: thou hast holden me by my right hand. Thou shalt guide me with thy counsel, and afterward receive me to glory. Whom have I in heaven but thee? and there is none upon earth that I desire beside thee. My flesh and my heart faileth: but God is the strength of my heart, and my portion for ever. *For, lo, they that are far from thee shall perish: thou hast destroyed all them that go a whoring from thee*. But it is good for me to draw near to God: I have put my trust in the Lord GOD, that I may declare all thy works. (emphasis added)

Having described the dilemma of the seeming prosperity of the wicked, Augustine then adds: "For in the last judgment it shall not be so; . . ."

The problem is, this Psalm makes it clear that there is no dilemma. God simply takes time to destroy the wicked. He gives them enough rope to hang themselves. He allows them to build up their evil, so that He can punish them even more. This procedure is true in both the Old Covenant and the New Covenant. Paul favorably cites Proverbs 25:22: "Therefore if thine enemy hunger, feed him; if he thirst, give him drink: for in so doing thou shalt heap coals of fire on his head" (Rom 12:20). God places covenant-breakers on slippery places. Their prosperity in history is temporary. He who fails to understand this, the Psalmist says, is foolish, ignorant, and like a beast. (Rhetoric!)

The emphasis of the Old Testament is the transition from wrath to grace in history. This is not to say that it completely ignores God's negative sanctions on the day of judgment, but surely this is not emphasized. Thus, to interpret Psalm 73 as if it were a psalm about the inscrutable prosperity of the wicked throughout history, with the emphasis on God's post-historical judgment, misses the point. The psalmist is describing history. *On average*, covenant-breakers are eventually brought under God's negative sanctions in history. But we must not expect to see instant sanctions. God is sometimes merciful to sinners, not giving them what they deserve. He sometimes also allows them extra time to fill their historical cup of wrath to the brim, just as He did with the Amorites (Gen. 15:16).

Is Augustine's view the biblical view of God's historical sanctions? What of the supposed inscrutability of God's historical sanctions? Doesn't the Bible affirm this inscrutability? With respect to any given individual, sometimes. With respect to covenanted corporate groups, no. What Augustine failed to consider in this section on God's final judgment is what his entire book is about: *God's negative historical sanctions against the city of Rome because of Rome's paganism and moral debauchery*. It should be clear why he focused on individuals in Chapter XX: he was explicitly dealing with God's final judgment against individuals, not God's historic judgments against corporate entities.

With respect to covenantal history, Augustine's *City of God* has served as the most important document in Church history. He makes it clear that God brings negative historical sanctions against all imitations of Christ's kingdom in history. They cannot survive in their rebellion against God. The city of God is not brought under comparable negative judgments in history.

It continues to the end of time, while God cuts down pagan kingdoms, one by one. This is why Augustine was at the very least implicitly postmillennial: God's kingdom in history wins by default. The rival cities of man collapse, one by one.

Calvin

Because Calvin wrote the single most effective theological summary in the history of the Church, *The Institutes of the Christian Religion*, its readers have tended to ignore the enormous compendium of writings that constitute his life's work. The 22 volumes of Bible commentaries published by Baker Book House only skim the surface of his total output. Much of his work has yet to be translated from the Latin. His 200+ sermons on Deuteronomy appeared in English in the late sixteenth century and were promptly forgotten.[12] Yet it is here, in his sermons on Deuteronomy, that we find the heart of Calvin's covenant theology. It is in Deuteronomy that God's covenant is presented most comprehensively.[13]

What is the nature of social change? This is *the* question of modern social theory.[14] Humanist scholars usually focus on the perceived dualism between mind and matter: ideas vs. the environment as the primary interaction leading to social development. The Bible, in contrast, focuses on the question of ethics: covenant-keeping vs. covenant-breaking. This raises the key issue in biblical social theory: God's sanctions in history.

Calvin's view of history was straightforward: God brings His sanctions – blessings and curses – in the midst of history in terms of each man's obedience to His law. *Each man reaps in history what he sows in history*. Calvin did not qualify this statement in any significant way, and he repeated the same sentiment over and over in his sermons on Deuteronomy:

---

12. These have been reprinted in the original small print by the Banner of Truth, London.

13. Ray R. Sutton, *That You May Prosper: Dominion By Covenant* (Tyler, Texas: Institute for Christian Economics, 1987), chapters 1-5.

14. Robert A. Nisbet, *Social Change and History: Aspects of the Western Theory of Development* (New York: Oxford University Press, 1969).

> For if any one of us should reckon up what he has suffered all the days of his life, and then examine the state of David or Abraham, doubtless he will find himself to be in a better state than were those holy fathers. For they, as the apostle says (Heb. 11:13), only saw things afar off, things that are right before our eyes. . . . We therefore have a much more excellent estate than they had who lived under the law. This is the difference of which I speak, which needed to be supplied by God because of the imperfection [lack of completion] that was in the doctrine concerning the revelation of the heavenly life, which the fathers only knew by outward tokens although they were dear to God. Now that Jesus Christ has come down to us, and has shown us how we ought to follow Him by suffering many afflictions, as it is told us (Matt. 16:24; Rom. 8:29), in bearing poverty and reproach and all such like things, and to be short, that our life must be as it were a kind of death; since we know all this, and the infinite power of God is uttered in His raising up Jesus Christ from death and in His exalting him to glory of heaven, should we not take from this a good courage? Should not this sweeten all the afflictions we can suffer? Do we not have cause to rejoice in the midst of our sorrows?

Calvin then called for Christians to obey God's law, just as the patriarchs were required to obey to secure their blessings.

> Let us note, then, that if the patriarchs were more blessed by God than we are, concerning this present life, we ought not to wonder at it at all. For the reason for it is apparent. But no matter how things go, yet is this saying of St. Paul always verified: that the fear of God holds promise not only for the life to come, but also for this present life (1 Tim. 4:8). Let us therefore walk in obedience to God, and then we can be assured that He will show Himself a Father to us, yea even in the maintenance of our bodies, at least as far as concerns keeping and preserving us in peace, delivering us from all evils, and providing for us our necessities. God, I say, will make us to feel His blessing in all these things, so that we walk in His fear.[15]

15. John Calvin, *The Covenant Enforced: Sermons on Deuteronomy 27 and 28*, edited by James B. Jordan (Tyler, Texas: Institute for Christian Economics, 1990), Sermon 154, pp. 100-1.

Historical Sanctions for Individuals

Calvin was not speaking merely of the great sweeping movements in mankind's history. He was speaking of the small things of each man's life. There is orderliness in a man's life because there is a coherent, predictable relationship between obedience and blessings. God does not limit His covenantal blessings to the afterlife:

> Let us therefore be persuaded that our lives will always be accursed unless we return to this point whereto Moses leads us, namely to hearken to the voice of our God, to be thereby moved and continually confirmed in the fact that He cares for our salvation, and not only for the eternal salvation of our persons, but also for the maintenance of our state in this earthly life, to make us taste at present of His love and goodness in such a way as may content and suffice us, waiting till we may have our fill thereof and behold face to face that which we are now constrained to look upon as it were through a glass and in the dark (1 Cor. 13:12). That is one more thing we ought to remember from this text, where it is said that we will be blessed if we hearken to the voice of the Lord our God.
>
> This is to be applied to all parts of our lives. For example, when a man wishes to prosper in his own person – that is, he desires to employ himself in the service of God and to obtain some grace so that he may not be unprofitable in this life but that God may be honored by him – let him think thus to himself: "Lord, I am Yours. Dispose of me as You will. Here I am, ready to obey You." This is the place at which we must begin if we desire God to guide us and create in us the disposition to serve Him, so that His blessings may appear and lighten upon us and upon our persons. So it is concerning every man's household.[16]
>
> The same thing is true concerning cattle, food, and all other things. For we see here [in this text] that nothing is forgotten. And God meant to make us to perceive His infinite goodness, in that He declares that He will deal with our smallest affairs, which one of our own equals would be loath to meddle with. If we have a friend, we should be very loath, indeed, and ashamed to use his help unless it were in a matter of great importance. But we see here that God

16. *Ibid*, p. 107.

> goes into our sheepfolds and into the stalls of our cattle and oxen, and He goes into our fields, and He cares for all other things as well. Since we see Him abase himself thus far, shouldn't we be ravished to honor Him and to magnify His bounty?[17]

Calvin was not only persuaded of the corporate cause-and-effect relationship between obedience to God's law and blessings in history; he was persuaded of the individual connection. In this sense, he went beyond Augustine. For Calvin, God's sanctions are not inscrutable; given enough time, they can be seen to conform to His covenantal promises in Deuteronomy 28.

Just two generations after Calvin died, the Puritans of New England began to apply Calvin's view of covenantal sanctions. They began their "errand into the wilderness" to build "a city on a hill."[18] They expected God visibly to bless their efforts, making them an example to the world, assuming that their heirs remained covenantally faithful. (They didn't, which had been the founders' greatest fear.) The founders hoped that New England would become the base of a worldwide covenantal revival. There were both theonomic and postmillennial.[19]

Have Calvin's modern disciples retained their commitment to Calvin's doctrine of God's individual sanctions in history? Have they even taken seriously Augustine's view on God's corporate sanctions in history? My conclusion: *no*. In abandoning both Augustine and Calvin, they have also abandoned faith in the possibility of devising a distinctly Christian social theory.

Muether's "Unleaven": Common Grace

Pay close attention to the explicit arguments of Reformed theologian John R. Muether. His essay appears in the quarterly magazine of Reformed Theological Seminary. Seminary magazines are aimed at donors and potential donors. If you are

---

17. *Ibid.*, p. 108.

18. Perry Miller, *Errand into the Wilderness* (Cambridge, Massachusetts: Belknap Press of Harvard University, 1956), chapters 1-3, 5.

19. Gary North (ed.), Symposium on Puritanism and Law, *Journal of Christian Reconstruction*, V (Winter 1978-79); Symposium on Puritanism and Progress, *ibid.*, VI (Summer 1979).

trying to raise funds from conventional Christian laymen, you do not publish radical articles. Muether's views are quite conventional in contemporary Reformed circles – indeed, in most Christian circles.

Muether's view of God's sanctions in history is representative of all pessimillennial theology, but especially common grace amillennialism. He has distinguished himself by spelling out in detail what the presuppositions and implications of pessimillennialism are in the field of Christian social ethics. His forthrightness is to be commended, even if his theology is not very commendable. His colleagues have been far more reticent to speak.

The Church's Exile, Yet God's Inscrutability

Muether speaks of the New Testament era as a period of exile for the Church. This is the language of pessimillennialism. Simultaneously, he speaks of God's random sanctions. "Our exile has no guarantees, few securities. It affords no occasion for triumphalism. We have no promise from God regarding our cultural achievements. Unlike the promises to the holy nation of Israel in the Old Testament, the common [grace] state possesses no special guarantees of a material blessing as a reward for its obedience to the law of God. Rather prosperity and adversity are experienced unpredictably through the inscrutable sovereignty of God's will."[20] Here is the familiar theme of Kline's common grace amillennialism: *the inscrutability of God in history*. Muether asserts the indeterminate nature of the New Covenant era's sanctions. "Things may improve, things may get worse. Common grace ebbs and flows throughout history."[21]

This in an important admission on the part of this disciple of Kline's. The *exile condition* of the Church in history is based on God's *random sanctions*. What I argue, here and in my book on common grace,[22] is that all amillennialists are in fact "exile"

20. John R. Muether, "The Era of Common Grace: Living Between the 'Already' and the 'Not Yet,' " *RTS Ministry*, IX (Summer 1990), p. 18.

21. *Idem.*

22. Gary North, *Dominion and Common Grace: The Biblical Basis of Progress* (Tyler, Texas: Institute for Christian Economics, 1987).

theologians. They believe that *God brings negative sanctions against His covenant people in history, no matter what they do*. Van Til said that these negative sanctions will grow progressively worse. Kline, the "optimist," insists only that there can be no victory of Christianity in history. Christians are in a cultural hole, and there is no reason to believe that God will ever pull us out of it in history. Van Til's version is Really Bad News Ahead, whereas Kline's is Bad News Ahead, With Occasional, Culturally Insignificant, Soon Overcome Victories.

Why say, then, that there are no guarantees in history? If you argue that history develops (or fails to develop) in a particular way, you are asserting a guaranteed scenario. If you are a Calvinist, and therefore believe in God's providential control of history, you *have* to believe in guarantees. Muether systematically misleads his readers when he says that there are no guarantees in history: "Our exile has no guarantees." Of course there are guarantees. If the Church is in a condition of permanent exile, we have a guarantee: no deliverance in history. The language of *no guarantees* is the language of *neutrality*. Neutrality is a myth, here as everywhere. There can be no neutrality in millennial speculation. Muether is a pessimillennialist, although he nowhere mentions this crucial fact in his essay. (Van Til also neglected to mention this same eschatological commitment in his "unleaven" essays.)[23] For all but the postmillennialists – that is, for all forms of pessimillennialism – there are indeed God-given guarantees: *guarantees of historical cultural failure for Christians in general and the Church specifically*. There is nothing random about exile.

Muether's theology of cultural defeat is self-conscious, for he thoroughly understands exactly what his pessimillennialism implies: "First, we cannot get caught up in the things of this world. This world is penultimate; it will pass away, and so we must eagerly await the new world to come."[24] He goes on: "The church in this world, in other words, is a people in exile. We are far short of the kingdom of God. . . . The church is

23. North, *Political Polytheism*, ch. 3.
24. Muether, p. 15.

called to suffer in this world."[25] From this we can legitimately infer what is never stated publicly by these defenders of Christianity's cultural impotence in history: *covenant-breakers are not in comparable exile and are not called to suffer nearly so much as the Church is.*

Muether's Total Discontinuity: Final Judgment

What is most significant about Muether's essay in terms of social theory is that he clearly asserts a radical discontinuity between what he calls the coming kingdom and this world of Church history. "The kingdom of God will come from above, not made with human hands, and no cultural activity, redeemed or unredeemed, will carry over into the new order."[26] This is a consistent and inescapable assertion of the common grace amillennialism's worldview: *the self-conscious denial of the eternal cultural relevance of anything men do in history.* All of mankind's cultural efforts are completely doomed, whether produced by covenant-keepers or covenant-breakers.

If this were the case, the works of covenant-keepers and the works of covenant-breakers would be *equal in historical impact.* There would be no cultural "earnest" – no cultural down payment by God – in history. God will pull victory out of the jaws of covenant-breakers at the last day. Christians could then learn nothing culturally from their experiences in history that will carry over into the final state, although Muether and his many common grace colleagues never put things so bluntly. Except for the personal salvation of individuals, history for them resembles what Macbeth said it is: a tale told by an idiot, full of sound and fury, signifying nothing.

This view of Church history is why modern Calvinism is not covenantal. It is individualistic. History for the amillennialist has meaning only as a means of distinguishing the saved from the lost in eternity. This is why amillennial Presbyterianism is basically an odd sect of Baptists that baptizes babies. It is Congregationalism with national committees.

---

25. *Idem.*
26. *Idem.*

The Non-Lessons of History

Let us think about Muether's assertions for a few moments. If we can learn nothing of eternal value culturally from history, since nothing of cultural value carries over into the resurrected state, then how can we have any confidence that we can learn anything useful regarding the success or failure of personal ethics in history? If Christians' social efforts in history are as devoid of eternal significance as those of non-Christians – a variant of the familiar neutrality hypothesis – then why not also Christians' personal ethical efforts? If there is no covenantal relationship between our *cultural* efforts in history and our rewards in history, then on what basis can we expect to discover a covenantal relationship between our *personal* ethical efforts and rewards in history?

Furthermore, what about our familistic and our ecclesiastical corporate efforts? Why single out politics as an area of Christianity's necessary historic irrelevance and impotence? Why not also include the Church and the family? Muether does not mention this obvious implication of his theology of God's random historical sanctions. Neither do his common grace amillennial peers. This would be too much for most Christians to swallow. "Pessimism, yes, but not *that* much pessimism!" To say that all our corporate (institutional) efforts are doomed would be to commit theological suicide in full public view, and no one wants to do this. So, they verbally concentrate on politics and culture, even though their pessimistic worldview cannot in principle be separated from all other covenantal and social institutions.

The critics of Christian Reconstruction imply (and sometimes explicitly state) that the primary concern of Christian Reconstructionists is political, even though we consistently deny this. (My slogan is "politics fourth.")[27] Muether, for example, calls his opponents "political utopians."[28] Why do these critics of

27. North, *Political Polytheism*, p. 559. It is my concern after individual salvation, church membership, and family membership.

28. Muether, p. 15. He does not identify exactly who he is talking about in this essay, perhaps because donors' money to Reformed Seminary is on the line. But he uses the phrase "political utopianism" to describe theonomists in his essay in the Westminster Seminary collection, published several months later: William S. Barker and W. Robert

theonomy persist in this misrepresentation? I contend that it is because their theological strategy is to call people's attention away from their comprehensive denial of Christianity's social relevance. They can readily sell their anti-theocratic views to people raised on the humanistic theology of pluralism, but they do not want to pursue the logic of their position to its inescapable conclusion: *the historical irrelevance of Christianity for both the Church and the family*. Thus, our affirmation of the relevance of the Bible for the civil covenant becomes the focus of their attempted refutations, ignoring the fact that this very affirmation is inextricably entwined with our affirmation of the relevance of the Bible for Church, family, and everything else. For rhetorical purposes (offensive), these anti-covenantal theologians and pastors attack our covenantal political stand. For equally rhetorical purposes (defensive), they remain prudently silent about the connection between our view of the covenant and all the other areas of society. They want to deny the covenantal relevance of Christianity for politics, while implicitly retaining faith in the covenantal relevance of Christianity for other institutions. They cannot do this logically or theologically, but they attempt it anyway. It makes for good editorial copy. It also makes for incoherent book-length studies. Hence, they refuse to write book-length studies. They refuse to say how their view of God's sanctions in history relates to social theory. This is why they offer no social theory.

Progressive Institutional Sanctification

The assumption of a radical historical discontinuity – this world vs. the next – is the theological foundation of the denial of progressive institutional sanctification in history. This view is promoted by amillennialists with respect to the entire post-resurrection era, and by premillennialists with respect to the era prior to Christ's physical return to earth in order to establish a

Godfrey (eds.), *Theonomy: A Reformed Critique* (Grand Rapids, Michigan: Zondervan Academie, 1990), p. 257. If there are repercussions from incensed donors, let Westminster bear the negative sanctions! The school no longer employs him. In this area, at least, Mr. Muether acted prudently. Westminster didn't.

millennial kingdom. We owe a debt of thanks to Muether for saying so clearly what his common grace peers have tended to muddle so systematically. He makes plain the theological and emotional foundations of the theology of cultural defeat.

An amillennialist who denied this discontinuity was Anthony Hoekema. He understood where such a view of history leads: *complete skepticism regarding the usefulness of any attempt to reform society*. Hoekema asked: "Is there, however, also some cultural continuity between this world and the next? Is there any sense in which we today can already be working for that better world? Can we say that some of the products of culture which we enjoy today will still be with us in God's bright tomorrow?" Here is his answer: "I believe we can. The new earth which is coming will not be an absolutely new creation, but a renewal of the present earth. That being the case, there will be continuity as well as discontinuity between our present culture and the culture, if so it will still be called, of the world to come."[29]

Hoekema understood the social implications of this position. "What all this means is that we must indeed be working for a better world now, that our efforts in this life toward bringing the kingdom of Christ to fuller manifestation are of eternal significance." Notice, however, that he did not say *historical* significance. As an amillennialist, he did not believe that these reform efforts will ever be successful. Nevertheless, in typical "Hold the fort, boys!" Progressively Bad News for Future Christian Man fashion, he optimistically proclaimed the usefulness of our mission: ". . . our mission work, our attempt to further a distinctively Christian culture, will have value not only for this world but even for the world to come." He should have written this: "Our mission work, our attempt to further a distinctively Christian culture, will have value not only for the world to come, but even for this world." But he would have sounded like a Christian Reconstructionist. Nobody at Calvin Seminary wants to sound like a Christian Reconstructionist.

Muether, as an advocate of Meredith G. Kline's "Random

29. Anthony Hoekema, *The Bible and the Future* (Grand Rapids, Michigan: Eerdmans, 1979), p. 39.

News for Future Christian Man" view of history, will have none of this. It is just too postmillennial for him to accept. Theologically, he is correct: Hoekema's language here is the language of postmillennial continuity, but it camouflages a Manichean view of history.[30] As I keep saying, chapter after chapter, this is schizophrenic. It is also intellectually dishonest.

Muether's Verbal Legerdemain

Muether's language of God's historical inscrutability, of *this world's historical open-endedness*, is a carefully contrived illusion, an example of verbal legerdemain. On the one hand, he says that the Church is in exile in history. This is a permanent condition. It is guaranteed by a Calvinistic, predestinating, totally sovereign God. On the other hand, he asserts that God's ethical randomness is manifested in history. "Things may improve, things may get worse. Common grace ebbs and flows throughout history."[31] He defines "exile" as an *indeterminate condition* in which things may get better or may get worse, yet on average stay pretty much the same throughout New Covenant history. (Would you like to construct an ethical system or social philosophy in terms of this view of history? How about a theory of business? Or technology? No? Neither would anyone else.)

This assertion of indeterminacy, as I have already argued, is a contrived illusion. If God applied His sanctions randomly, then the institutional, covenantal outcome would hardly be random; it would be perverse. Covenant-breakers would retain control over culture throughout Church history, despite the death, resurrection, and ascension of Christ to the right hand of God the Father. But this is precisely what Calvinist amillennialists say must happen. It is predestined by God this way.

Kline, Muether, and the Random Sanctions amillennialists are all bearers of Bad News. A *flatline eschatology* in a world presently dominated by covenant-breakers is bad news. It is also difficult to defend exegetically. No eschatological position that I am aware of has ever been defended exegetically which asserts

---

30. See Chapter 4, above, p. 91.
31. Muether, p. 18.

the existence of what is in effect a horizontal flat line for the social and cultural efforts of Christianity in history. Without exception, systematic theologians have argued that the Church's influence will either decline over time until Jesus comes again, or else increase. *There is no millennial neutrality*. Common grace does not "ebb and flow" apart from *history's directionality*: either inclining or declining. Like an electronic sine wave on a screen, common grace does indeed oscillate around a linear development, but this linear relationship is not flat; it is inclined over time, either up (postmillennialism) or down (traditional amillennialism and "Church Age" dispensational premillennialism). I assume that Muether, as a seminary professor, must know this, yet he refuses to mention it in his essay. In this sense, he follows the tradition of Meredith Kline, who has also steadfastly refused for well over a decade to pursue in print the implications of his theory of God's random sanctions in history.

A Progressing Church

At this point, I need to raise a fundamental issue: the question of the Church's advance in history. No orthodox theologian would ever argue that the Church did not advance culturally from, say, the year 100 to 325. Pietistic Protestants might argue that everything after Constantine went downhill until the Protestant Reformation, but not before then. (Question: Was the Protestant Reformation an advance in history? If so, how can an amillennialist account for this progress?) Culturally, I know of no scholar who would seriously argue that Christianity's influence on medieval culture was overwhelmingly negative compared with what preceded it, unless the historian, following Gibbon and rejecting Augustine, blames the supposed tragedy of the fall of Rome on the rise of Christianity. The prevailing view of modern historians, whether Christians or non-Christians, is that there was cultural and technological progress in the Middle Ages, and that much of this progress can be attributed to Christianity.[32] They all accept Augustine's defense of

32. Cf. Robert Latouche, *The Birth of the Western Economy: Economic Aspects of the Dark Ages* (New York: Harper Torchbooks, [1956] 1966), especially Pt. I, ch. iv; Pt. II, ch. ii.

linear history as a major legacy to Western civilization.

The problem for the amillennialist and the premillennialist is to identify when the decline from Christian social order began. There was cultural advance for centuries after A.D. 100, possibly for many centuries. Why and how must the prophesied decline be regarded as permanent prior to Jesus' Second Coming? Why can't there be a great reversal? What biblical passage implies that the decline we have seen cannot be turned around during the next thousand years? There has been Christian cultural advance in the past. Why not in the future?

There will be no cultural victory of the gospel in history, Mr. Muether insists. There will always be suffering in exile. "It is not always pleasant," he says, "to suffer in exile." (Not always pleasant? For psychologically normal people, it is *never* pleasant.) "It may seem much better to live with the confidence of the utopians. But that is a false and unbiblical confidence."[33] (Somehow, I suspect that when he says Christian "utopians," he means the Christian Reconstructionists, but as the seminary's librarian, he knows only too well what might happen were he to mention any of us by name, book, and page number. It might get a few of his brighter students to start reading the works of those whom he criticizes so confidently. So he refuses to say just exactly who he has in mind.[34] Extreme politeness is in this case *extreme prudence*. His prudence was quite obviously insufficiently extreme, as this chapter indicates. He will get caught anyway. Bright students always find out.)

A Rigged System of Justice

Here is what Kline and his disciples really believe. In order to keep the Church suppressed in history, God does not apply His sanctions according to the covenantal standards in Leviticus 26 and Deuteronomy 28. Why not? Because the randomness of

---

33. Muether, p. 18.

34. At least Charles Colson came close to forthrightness when he criticized the theonomists on page 117 of *Kingdoms in Conflict*, and then spoke of the need for "the church to avoid utopianism" on page 118. A few of his readers might conceivably put two and two together. Colson, *Kingdoms in Conflict* (New York: William Morrow; Grand Rapids, Michigan: Zondervan, 1987).

God's historical sanctions would guarantee the *non-neutrality of the outcome*, since God's non-neutrality (covenantal faithfulness) insures the victory of His covenant people in history.

But wait. Is it merely neutral or random for God to prevent the visible outcomes that He specified in Leviticus 26 and Deuteronomy 28? Can God go from *visible* covenantal faithfulness to *visible* randomness without becoming *visibly covenantally unfaithful* in history? Not if neutrality is a myth. But as Kline and his disciples know, Van Til proved biblically that neutrality is a myth. So, what they are really saying is that *God holds His finger on the scales of justice so that covenant-breakers can maintain both cultural and judicial control throughout history*. In short, according to the historical-judicial criteria of Leviticus 26 and Deuteronomy 28, God externally rewards covenant-breakers in history far more than they deserve, and He curses His covenant people far more than they deserve. Thus, Muether's language of God's judicial neutrality is a smoke-screen. *Random historical sanctions means a rigged system of justice*: rigged against covenant-keepers.

Hayek on Equality

F. A. Hayek has discussed the idea of equality before the law, as contrasted with equality of results. The defender of personal liberty insists on the need for equality before the law, in order to reduce the arbitrariness of the tyrant. The socialist insists on equality of outcomes. These two ideals of equality are in total opposition. His argument is extremely important for a discussion of biblical ethics, since the most fundamental principle governing biblical civil justice is that *God is not a respecter of persons*. This is repeated over and over in the Bible.

> Ye shall not respect persons in judgment; but ye shall hear the small as well as the great; ye shall not be afraid of the face of man; for the judgment is God's: and the cause that is too hard for you, bring it unto me, and I will hear it (Deut. 1:17).

> Thou shalt not wrest judgment; thou shalt not respect persons, neither take a gift: for a gift doth blind the eyes of the wise, and pervert the words of the righteous (Deut. 16:19).

> Wherefore now let the fear of the LORD be upon you; take heed and do it: for there is no iniquity with the LORD our God, nor respect of persons, nor taking of gifts (II Chron. 19:7).
>
> These things also belong to the wise. It is not good to have respect of persons in judgment (Prov. 24:23).
>
> To have respect of persons is not good: for a piece of bread that man will transgress (Prov. 28:21).
>
> For there is no respect of persons with God (Rom. 2:11).
>
> And, ye masters, do the same things unto them, forbearing threatening: knowing that your Master also is in heaven; neither is there respect of persons with him (Eph. 6:9).
>
> But he that doeth wrong shall receive for the wrong which he hath done: and there is no respect of persons (Col. 3:25).
>
> But if ye have respect to persons, ye commit sin, and are convinced of the law as transgressors (James 2:9).
>
> Then Peter opened his mouth, and said, Of a truth I perceive that God is no respecter of persons (Acts 10:34).

In short, *God applies His standards of justice impartially*, and so should the civil magistrate. Keeping this *permanent*, New Testament, judicial principle in mind, consider Hayek's warning:

> From the fact that people are very different it follows that, if we treat them equally, the result must be inequality in their actual position, and that the only way to place them on an equal position would be to treat them differently. Equality before the law and material equality are therefore not only different but are in conflict with each other; and we can achieve either the one or the other, but not both at the same time. The equality before the law which freedom requires leads to material inequality.[35]

Hayek is saying that if the legal basis of the inequality of economic results is formal judicial equality before the law, then

---

35. F. A. Hayek, *The Constitution of Liberty* (University of Chicago Press, 1960), p. 87.

the defense of inequality must be made in terms of both the legitimacy and necessity of *predictable judicial sanctions, equally applied*. I doubt that Professors Kline and Muether would disagree with this. I also presume that any Christian who opposes socialism would agree. Finally, I believe that most Christians oppose socialism. Why, then, have they adopted a view of God's sanctions in history that is the same as the socialists' view of civil justice: the denial of equality before the law? Answer: their pessimillennialism.

Is God a Respecter of Persons?

I come now to my most important conclusion in this book: by denying God's predictable sanctions in history, Christian theologians are attributing to God a blatant disregard of His own principle of civil justice, *equality before the law* (Ex. 12:49). They are saying that God's judgments in history produce the covenantal equivalent of socialism: *equality of results*. This is why I argue that amillennialism, even in its best interpretation, is Manichean. So is premillennialism. In such a view, civilization is *at best* morally indeterminate. This means that righteousness gets stalemated by the New Covenant, if in fact it does not lose.

The equality of results is precisely what Muether is arguing for. He argues, first, that Christianity does not triumph over its rivals in history. At best, Christianity gains a stalemate, but even this is illusory. Christianity does not have a stalemate today; it is under humanism's judicial and cultural authority. Pluralism guarantees this. Second, he insists that there is no difference in eternity between the cultural results of covenant-keeping in history and covenant-breaking. If he is correct in these two assertions, *then God Almighty is treating covenant-keepers differently from covenant-breakers*. He is rigging His sanctions in New Covenant history against them. In order for His sanctions to be unpredictable to mankind, they have to be unequally applied.

The *historical outcome* of God's system of rewards and punishments in history is not inscrutable for the pessimillennialist. The supposed inscrutability of God's historical sanctions guarantees a highly predictable – that is, *inevitable* – outcome: the defeat of Christianity in history. This is what pessimillennialism teaches.

This system of judicial sanctions is not merely random; it is *ethically perverse*. God is said to reward covenant-breakers with external success even if they break His covenant laws, and He drives covenant-keepers into "exile" even if they remain faithful to the terms of His covenant. It was not this way in the Old Testament, these theologians are forced to admit (Lev. 26; Deut. 28), but it is today. These are the inescapable ethical implications of common grace amillennialism, yet its defenders refuse to admit this.[36] Such a frank admission apparently hurts too much; also, it would make it difficult to gain new recruits, and they do not have many followers as it is. Calling Christians to a life of guaranteed cultural frustration is not a good way to gain disciples, especially activists.

Why would anyone believe in such a perverse system of justice? Because a person *must* believe this if he defends a pessimillennial eschatology: bad people win, despite the gospel and God's historical sanctions. The *ethical non-neutrality* of the outcome of the work of the gospel in history is the fundamental presupposition of all pessimillennialism. Bad fruit does not come from good trees. Similarly, bad results do not come from neutral sanctions. Conclusion: *these amillennial sanctions are neither neutral nor random*. God's historical sanctions must be rigged against Christianity in order for covenant-breakers to maintain cultural control. For evil to triumph in history, God must refuse to reward His covenant-keeping people and also refuse to retard the efforts of covenant-breakers. Pessimillennialists have therefore implicitly rewritten the Second Commandment:

> . . . *for the* Lord *thy God is* ***not*** *a jealous God, visiting the iniquity of the fathers upon the children unto thousands of generations of them that hate me; And* ***shewing mercy unto the third and fourth generation of them that love me, and keep my commandments.***

Muether is not alone in this view of the God's providence and the Church's future. This outlook – "God's inscrutability unto cultural irrelevance" – is in fact *an eschatology of inevitable*

36. This is my chief criticism of Cornelius Van Til's apologetic system: North, *Political Polytheism*, pp. 144-46.

historical defeat. Dispensational theology teaches the same thing about the cultural efforts of Christians during the so-called "Church Age."[37] (An exception: the premillennialist who has adopted Van Til's even more pessimistic vision.) But Muether's view is worse, for being both Calvinistic and amillennial, it offers no hope for Christians in history, not even the Rapture. Applying Rushdoony's dictum, John R. Muether is basically a premillennialist without earthly hope.

Where Is His Exegesis?

Two additional comments are in order regarding Muether's theological position. First, his view of God's inscrutable sanctions in history is precisely what needs to be demonstrated exegetically, not merely asserted authoritatively. Muether does not even attempt such a task, in this essay or in a book-length study.[38] Neither had his seminary colleagues at the time of publication of Muether's essay in the summer of 1990, seventeen years after the publication of Rushdoony's *Institutes of Biblical Law*, thirteen years after the publication of Bahnsen's *Theonomy in Christian Ethics*. Prudence can be abused.

Second, Muether does not cite a single book, author, or theological tradition in the essay. He cites only two Bible verses. One is Jeremiah 29:7, "And seek the peace of the city whither I have caused you to be carried away captives, and pray unto the LORD for it: for in the peace thereof shall ye have peace." This is precisely what the Christian Reconstructionist would advise to those in cultural captivity, but he would deny that this captivity period is permanent in history; surely it was temporary under the Old Covenant. Muether, in contrast, sees the cultural exile of Christians as a permanent historical condition. In short,

---

37. Douglas Oss has correctly noted the similarities between Kline's thesis of the common grace "intrusion" period of the New Covenant era and dispensationalism's "Church Age" or "great parenthesis." Oss, "The Influence of Hermeneutical Frameworks in the Theonomy Debate," *Westminster Theological Journal*, LI (Fall 1989), p. 240n.

38. Like all common grace amillennial theologians, he needs to respond in a detailed fashion to my book, *Dominion and Common Grace*. Like most of his common grace academic peers, he refuses to acknowledge its existence. This is the seminary professor's game of "let's pretend."

the resurrection of Jesus Christ has removed from covenantal history a glorious promise of God to His people under the Old Covenant: "And he shall judge among many people, and rebuke strong nations afar off; and they shall beat their swords into plowshares, and their spears into pruninghooks: nation shall not lift up a sword against nation, neither shall they learn war any more. But they shall sit every man under his vine and under his fig tree; and none shall make them afraid: for the mouth of the LORD of hosts hath spoken it" (Mic. 4:3-4). This was God's covenantal *guarantee*. Muether does not tell us why or how Christ's resurrection removed this guarantee; he simply assumes that this is what happened.

He expects the reader to accept his unsupported assumptions and assertions on their own merit. In short, he refuses to debate. He simply declares from on high (or at least from Orlando, Florida) what God does in history and what the Church can expect, irrespective of what God's word says that He has done in history and will do in history. This is not scholarship. This is not theological inquiry. *This is "hit and run" propaganda in the name of Jesus*. Yet this is what most Christian laymen have been subjected to for well over a century.

Academic Silence

That Professor Muether's essay should appear in a seminary's promotional magazine should surprise no one. The utter bankruptcy of Christian social theology today – for this is exactly what his essay is: *social theology* – has left Christians without any intellectual defenses against the comprehensive claims of the humanist world. Bible-affirming seminaries continue to encourage this situation. This has been going on for a long time. Theologically liberal seminaries promote liberal, activist, deeply political humanism in the name of Jesus, while conservative seminaries promote political passivity and covenantal silence – "Me, too" pluralist humanism – in the name of Jesus. The first side promotes the power religion, while the second side promotes the escape religion.[39]

---

39. Gary North, *Moses and Pharaoh: Dominion Religion vs. Power Religion* (Tyler, Texas:

Understandably, both sides are outraged by the idea of the reconstruction of society based on biblical law. These critics have intermittently attempted to dismiss the writings of the Christian Reconstructionists in a series unfootnoted three-page essays and brief book reviews.[40] They have steadfastly refused to challenge us line by line, doctrine by doctrine, *implication by implication*. Yet they propose no cultural alternatives to secular humanism. Problem: you can't beat something with nothing. They fully understand this principle, so they recommend our toleration of the general culture of secular humanism.

The Absence of Published Alternatives

Let me make what I believe is an important observation. Christian Reconstruction is at long last gaining a hearing because it presents a consistent position. It possesses a unified worldview. Its authors take this worldview and apply it to real-world issues. We are not afraid to follow the implications of our position, both logically and in terms of applied theology. We have published over a hundred volumes of books and scholarly journals stating our position. We will publish many more.

In contrast, our theological opponents, both Calvinists and Arminians, are unwilling to present their developed theological position before the general public. There has not been a systematic theology written by a major Calvinist scholar since Louis Berkhof's *Systematic Theology* (1941). It is generally regarded as quite conventional, having added no fresh insights to Dutch amillennial theology. Many seminarians are still being assigned Charles Hodge's three-volume systematics, published in 1873. Can you imagine any other academic discipline that still relies on a codifying text written well over a century earlier?

Meanwhile, in the dispensational camp, Lewis Sperry Chafer's *Systematic Theology* (1948) was taken out of print several

Institute for Christian Economics, 1985), pp. 2-5.

40. See, for example, John Walvoord's 2.5-page review of Bahnsen and Gentry's *House Divided: The Break-Up of Dispensational Theology* in *Bibliotheca Sacra* (July-Sept. 1990), in which he devotes two pages to a history of non-dispensational premillennialism. See my response in *Dispensationalism in Transition*, III (August 1990).

years ago; only an expurgated version remains. In any case, it is doubtful that many scholars ever relied heavily on the eight-volume original. We find very few references to it in the books written by other dispensational authors. Dispensationalism has relied on books written in the early 1950's to defend the position, such as Pentecost's *Things to Come*. This is indicative of a stagnant intellectual system. Dispensationalism is in transition. It is unlikely that whatever emerges will resemble Scofield's original system, with its sharp discontinuity between the Old and New Covenants and its total rejection of biblical law.

Furthermore, even these older works systematically refrained from applying any of their theological principles to real-world problems. This is a theological tradition stretching back to the end of the seventeenth century. Both Protestant and Roman Catholic casuistry died as a field of Christian ethics after 1700. Thus, those who oppose Christian Reconstruction do not possess a developed body of materials to offer as an alternative. They are in the position of fighting something with nothing. Yet they give the illusion of possessing a published heritage behind them that serves as the foundation of a comprehensive challenge to both theonomy and secular humanism. The leaders all know they are holding an empty book bag, but they never admit this to their followers. But word is getting out among those who read: *there is no published, Protestant alternative to the comprehensive worldview of Christian Reconstruction*. This is why our critics keep losing their brightest students to our camp. The pessimillennialists cannot beat something with nothing.

Conclusion

What prompted Muether's article? The theological errors of certain "utopians," he says – unidentified Christian "utopians" who promote "a reconstructed republic patterned after the civil law of Old Testament Israel. . . ."[41] (Can you guess who these authors might be?) These error-promoting people recommend that "Christians pick up the sword to achieve a political goal."

41. Muether, p. 14.

(Paul calls civil government "the sword" [Rom. 13:4], so there is no way to involve oneself with politics apart from trying to pick up "the sword." This does not seem to have occurred to Professor Muether.) He calls this error-laden impulse "political utopianism" and "theocratic utopianism."[42]

Was Old Covenant Israel also utopian? Did God impose utopian standards on Israel? If not, then why is it that a similar set of standards is illegitimate today? What it is that makes our task so utopian? Is the resurrection of Jesus Christ somehow irrelevant culturally? Is the presence of the Holy Spirit somehow irrelevant culturally? Are Christians less culturally empowered today than the Israelites were? When amillennialists at long last address these questions, we will have a much better understanding of the theological foundations of their eschatological system. We will know how seriously to take it. Until then, however, there is not much reason to take seriously Mr. Muether's accusation of Christian Reconstruction's utopianism.

Ever since the demise of New England Puritanism in the late seventeenth century, Protestant theology has ignored the fundamental covenantal issue of God's historical sanctions. The theologians of the twentieth century have been adamant: there are no predictable covenantal sanctions in history. This is an aspect of the myth of neutrality. But there is no neutrality. There are always covenant sanctions in history. Therefore, what the denial of God's predictable covenant sanctions in history really means is this: *an affirmation of Satan's exclusive, predictable covenantal sanctions in history*, meaning blessings for covenant-breakers and cursings for covenant-keepers.

A few common grace amillennial theologians have tried to hide the implications of their eschatology. They have said that the sanctions in New Testament history are random. But then they speak of the Church's "exile," which brings us back to the issue of negative sanctions in history. They do not want to be identified as men who have in fact adopted a perverse imitation of postmillennialism: *the progressive triumph in history of Satan's comprehensive kingdom-civilization*. This is not the way they want

42. *Idem.*

to put it, but it is exactly what their system implies. On the surface, however, this sounds bad. (Frankly, it *is* bad.) To cover themselves, they adopt the language of randomness and inscrutability in self-defense. This is the language of neutrality.

What these theologians need is biblical exegesis. They need to answer three sets of questions. *First*, how can common grace amillennialism be defended? If common grace is being withdrawn (Van Til's view), how can God's blessings to the lost increase? How do the lost gain and retain power in history, which they need in order to subdue Christian culture? If, on the other hand, common grace is not being withdrawn, then what connection does common grace have with biblical ethics? What connection does it have with special (soul-saving) grace? If common grace neither expands nor contracts in response to the Holy Spirit's gift of special grace in history, what does common grace have to do with history? It had a lot to do with history before the cross. What does it have to do with history today? Explain, please. Use the Bible to defend your answers, please. No more unsupported pronouncements from on high.

Second, how can amillennialism be anything but pessimistic with respect to the future of the Church? If God's sanctions are random, then history is *at best* a flat line. But covenant-breakers today control most of the world. An extension of present trends keeps the Church in a condition of permanent historical exile. In other words, how can there be such a thing as optimistic amillennialism? Isn't optimistic amillennialism a form of soft-core postmillennialism? Explain, please. Use the Bible to defend your answers, please.

Third, how can the amillennial version of common grace present God's historical sanctions as essentially random or at least inscrutable in a world in which the cultural leaven of covenant-keeping is supposedly being overcome progressively by the more powerful leaven of covenant-breaking? *Such a world is clearly not ethically random; it is merely ethically perverse.* History is either moving downward into the void or upward toward the heavenly Jerusalem. This is what millennialism teaches. So, how can God's covenant sanctions in this common grace world be random? Explain, please. Use the Bible to defend your answers.

These are fundamental questions that the common grace amillennialists have steadfastly ignored for over fifty years. It is time for them to produce some biblical theology. We have seen more than enough unsupported assertions. It is time for them to clarify their position. There is nothing clear about it yet.

8

HISTORICAL SANCTIONS: AN INESCAPABLE CONCEPT

Thus saith the LORD, *thy redeemer, and he that formed thee from the womb, I am the* LORD *that maketh all things; that stretcheth forth the heavens alone; that spreadeth abroad the earth by myself; That frustrateth the tokens of the liars, and maketh diviners mad; that turneth wise men backward, and maketh their knowledge foolish; That confirmeth the word of his servant, and performeth the counsel of his messengers; that saith to Jerusalem, Thou shalt be inhabited; and to the cities of Judah, Ye shall be built, and I will raise up the decayed places thereof: That saith to the deep, Be dry, and I will dry up thy rivers: That saith of Cyrus, He is my shepherd, and shall perform all my pleasure: even saying to Jerusalem, Thou shalt be built; and to the temple, Thy foundation shall be laid (Isa. 44:24-28).*

If Professor Muether's position on God's sanctions in history were true, then it would be impossible to construct an explicitly and uniquely biblical social theory, which is why, for over three centuries, those Christians who have espoused similar views of God's historical sanctions have failed to construct such a theory, and have rarely attempted to do so. This perspective on God's sanctions has been the dominant view within the modern Church. Theologians of all schools have been content to baptize this or that Enlightenment social theory, or else they have publicly abandoned the quest for social theory, only to import some Enlightenment variant in the name of common grace. There is no neutrality. There is, however, self-deception. I am suggesting here that Muether and all of his common grace amillennial colleagues are self-deceived.

Honesty as the Best Policy

Why do I argue that without the idea of predictable sanctions in history, there can be no social theory of any kind? Because, *first*, I am unaware of any social philosophy in history that has ever denied all forms of predictable sanctions.[1] Some system of predictable sanctions in history must exist if social theory is conceivable. The question is: Whose sanctions? *Second*, I cannot conceive of such a sanctions-less system. Neither can you. I think I can prove this. As a simple case study, consider the familiar aphorism Cervantes' *Don Quixote*, "Honesty is the best policy." (As in so many other instances, Ben Franklin is erroneously given credit for having said this first.) In what sense is this aphorism true? Personally? Culturally? Where is the proof? What are the legitimate criteria of proof?

What if God's corporate sanctions in history were perverse, which is what pessimillennialism teaches? What if honesty were to lead to economic poverty in most individual cases? Then it must also lead to poverty corporately. Would it still be the best policy? Only if we insist that only beyond the grave, though not in history, will honest individuals receive their appropriate rewards. (This is the pessimillennialist's assertion.) But then only those people who believe in God's sanctions in a world beyond the grave would take the aphorism seriously.[2] In the meantime – that is, *in time* – most people would pursue dishonesty. After all, dishonesty pays in history. Even if honesty and dishonesty were rewarded equally – i.e., Muether's inscrutability doctrine – this state of affairs would serve as *a subsidy to dishonesty* in a world in which original sin prevails. The dishonest person would not be any worse off in history than the honest person.

If we are to examine the truth of the aphorism that honesty is the best policy, we must ask, answer, and then apply to the aphorism the Bible's five covenantal[3] questions:

---

1. I have been working on a book, *Heaven or Hell on Earth: The Sociology of Final Judgment*. I have found that humanist societies immanentize the final judgment.

2. I regard it as ominous that in our day, ostensibly orthodox Christian theologians have begun to deny the doctrine of hell and the eternal lake of fire, into which hell's contents will be dumped on judgment day (Rev. 20:14-15).

3. On the five-point covenant model, see Ray R. Sutton, *That You May Prosper: Domin-*

1. Who defines "best" and "honesty"?
2. Who enforces honesty institutionally?
3. Which rules tell us what honesty is in any given case?
4. What visible evidence do we have that honesty really is the best policy?
5. What successful society can we find in history in which honesty has been rewarded? Did it survive?

Is there a God? If not, who assures us that honesty is the best policy? Who is impartial? The free market? The State? The forces of history? What? Any social philosophy that does not have a theory of sovereignty is not a serious social philosophy.

Who represents the sovereign in the social system? Who speaks in his (or its) name? Officials of the State? Businessmen? Church officers? Educators? How do we know what the true sovereign requires from us? How do we know where to find an accurate interpretation of his rules? Where do we appeal our case when we are in conflict with each other?

Then comes the question of historical sanctions. This is the central practical problem for social theory: *verification*.

Visible Sanctions and Truth

Without visible sanctions in history, there can be no public testimony to the truth or falsity of any assertion regarding the effectiveness of any proposed system of social organization. The theorist must be able to offer evidence from history that the application of his logic in history will have the positive results that he promises.[4] This is not philosophical pragmatism; this is *biblical covenantalism*: the nations can see the benefits that come from obeying God's law. They can also see the righteousness of this law-order (Deut. 4:4-8). The *work* of the law is written in their hearts (Rom. 2:14-15). Righteousness does not produce bad fruit: "For a good tree bringeth not forth corrupt fruit;

---

ion By Covenant (Tyler, Texas: Institute for Christian Economics, 1987).

4. At this point, I am rejecting the *a priorism* of Ludwig von Mises' economic epistemology. See Gary North, "Economics: From Reason to Intuition," in Gary North (ed.), *Foundations of Christian Scholarship: Essays in the Van Til Perspective* (Vallecito, California: Ross House Books, 1976), pp. 87-96.

neither doth a corrupt tree bring forth good fruit" (Luke 6:43).

In any free society, visible sanctions must be imposed in terms of a *publicly announced* system of law (Deut. 31:10-13). These public sanctions must be predictable. This is what law enforcement is all about: the imposition of negative sanctions against publicly proscribed behavior. Try to run a family or a business without law and sanctions. It cannot be done. But if you accept ("sanction") the idea that a legal order's sanctions can legitimately be *random in terms of fundamental law*, you have accepted the legitimacy of *tyranny and arbitrary rule*.[5]

Nevertheless, Christian theologians insist that there is neither a required system of biblical civil law nor corporate sanctions imposed by God in terms of this binding legal order.[6] The rejection of the idea of the reality of God's corporate covenantal sanctions in history parallels the rejection of the idea that biblical covenant law is supposed to govern society formally. Those who deny that biblical law is God's required corporate standard also hasten to assure us that God does not bring negative sanctions against societies that ignore this standard. (In order to avoid being labeled antinomians, they usually assure us that there *are* God-imposed sanctions against evil personal behavior, but then the same five covenantal questions still need to be answered. They never are.) If not God's sanctions, then whose?

The problem here is the problem of *formally specified judicial sanctions*. A person has the legal right to receive the specified sanctions, as Paul asserted in his trial (Acts 25:11). Punishment is a fundamental right. In a classic essay, C. S. Lewis warned against any concept of civil sanctions in which they are not spelled out in advance. The indeterminate prison sentence, he argued, is a license for State tyranny.

---

5. F. A. Hayek, *The Constitution of Liberty* (University of Chicago Press, 1960).

6. They may acknowledge the existence of corporate responsibility and God's negative sanctions against collectives. Berkhof writes: "We should always bear in mind that there is a collective responsibility, and that there are always sufficient reasons why God should visit cities, districts or nations with dire calamities." He cites Luke 13:2-5. But he does not mention biblical law. Louis Berkhof, *Systematic Theology* (London: Banner of Truth Trust, [1941] 1963), p. 260.

> To be taken without consent from my home and friends; to lose my liberty; to undergo all those assaults on my personality which modern psychoytherapy knows how to deliver; to be re-made after some pattern of "normality" hatched in a Viennese laboratory to which I never professed allegiance; to know that this process will never end until either my captors have succeeded or I grown wise enough to cheat them with apparent success – who cares whether this is called Punishment or not? That it includes most of the elements for which any punishment is feared – shame, exile, bondage, and years eaten by the locust – is obvious. Only enormous ill-desert could justify it; but ill-desert is the very conception which the Humanitarian theory has thrown overboard.[7]

In his novel, *That Hideous Strength,* Lewis has a weak-willed sociologist write a justification for the imposition of corrupt and total police rule in a local community. The ruling organization will come, wrote the young sociologist, "in the gracious role of a rescuer – a rescuer who can remove the criminal from the harsh sphere of punishment to that of remedial treatment."[8]

It is just such a concept of State tyranny that would result from the judicial prescriptions of Calvinist philosopher Robert Knudsen. He denies in the New Testament era any legitimacy of the formal requirements of the Old Covenant legal order. He insists: "In all their relationships New Testament believers do not have less responsibility than their Old Testament counterparts for obeying God's will as expressed in his law; in fact, they have greater responsibility, because it is not legally stipulated exactly what they should and should not do."[9] Our responsibilities to each other are open-ended. Yet in any covenant, there are legal aspects, as Knudson admits.[10] These laws restrain the legitimate demands made by one person on another. It is sig-

---

7. C. S. Lewis, "The Humanitarian Theory of Punishment," in Lewis, *God in the Dock: Essays on Theology and Ethics,* edited by Walter Hooper (Grand Rapids, Michigan: Eerdmans, 1972), pp. 290-91.

8. C. S. Lewis, *That Hideous Strength: A Modern Fairy-Tale for Grown-Ups* (New York: Macmillan, 1946), pp. 132-33.

9. Robert D. Knudsen, "May We Use the Term 'Theonomy' for Our Application of Biblical Law?" in William S. Barker and W. Robert Godfrey (eds.), *Theonomy: A Reformed Critique* (Grand Rapids, Michigan: Zondervan Academie, 1990), p. 34.

10. *Ibid.,* pp. 32-33.

nificant that he discusses the family, marriage, and the Church in this regard, but steadfastly ignores the State, as if it were not a covenant, as if Romans 13 did not describe the civil magistrate as a minister of God (Rom. 13:4, 6). Anyone who applies Knudsen's principle of open-ended personal responsibilities to civil law has created the foundation for arbitrary State power.[11]

The Rejection of Social Theory

Whenever any Christian social theorist – amateur or professional – asserts that the New Covenant has annulled the Old Covenant's clear-cut system of positive and negative corporate sanctions (Lev. 26; Deut. 28), he is thereby denying the very possibility of developing a uniquely Christian social philosophy. Since there are no cultural or judicial vacuums in history, he is opening the door for the acceptance by Christians of rival (anti-Christian) social theories.

Because the vast majority of Bible-believing Christian theologians have little awareness or interest in this process of social substitution – theological liberals *do* understand – they do not think carefully about the implications of their assertion regarding sanctions in history. They rarely adopt self-consciously the Hellenistic Greeks' natural law theory as a supplement to the Bible,[12] nor do they suggest some other hybrid system. They simply assert without evidence that the New Covenant era has no predictable sanctions by God. They tell us that Old Covenant civil law is today null and void, and that there has been no New Covenant resurrection of the Old Covenant's case laws. They strip the Church of any judicial authority in society at large, and then either call Christians to a life of sacrificial service (e.g.,

---

11. A quarter century ago, Knudsen taught a course, The Fate of Freedom in Western Philosophy. I have never forgotten the title of that course. By the end of the term, I was the only student still enrolled in the class. He would lecture at the podium, and I would take notes. I did not dare to cut *that* class! My absence would have been noticed. He was the one who first introduced me to Lewis' *That Hideous Strength*, for which I am grateful; it changed my life. What I did not fully comprehend then is that his commitment to Dooyeweerdianism meant that he, like his mentor, would not allow biblical law determine the content of his cultural worldview. But without God's law, there can be no permanent freedom in Western philosophy, or anywhere else.

12. Fundamentalist Norman Geisler is an exception.

common grace amillennialism) or else warn them that such sacrificial service outside the narrow confines of tract-passing is futile (e.g., pre-tribulational dispensationalism).[13]

What is astounding is that these same theologians, in order to avoid being labeled as socially irrelevant, then insist that they *do* have something relevant to say to society. Not biblical, of course, but relevant nonetheless. Muether insists that "We should address the social concerns of our day."[14] To which I ask: Precisely how, biblically speaking? By what standard? In what hope? At what price? With what results? Why bother?

Similarly, Hal Lindsey insists that he is deeply concerned about social issues, but in *The Late Great Planet Earth*, he contented himself with this one-paragraph reference to Christian involvement, on the very last page of his text: "Fifth, we should plan our lives as though Christ may come today. We shouldn't drop out of school or worthwhile community activities, or stop working, or rush marriage, or any such thing unless Christ leads us to do so. However, we should make the most of our time that is not taken up with the essentials."[15] Try building a comprehensive biblical social theory in terms of such a call to "Christian social involvement"! I ask: What exactly should we study in school, and why, biblically speaking? What are "worthwhile community activities," biblically speaking? Why should we bother if such activities are eschatologically doomed to failure? Lindsey and his pietistic colleagues – millions of them – do not say. (I include Muether and all the common grace amillennialists as colleagues of Lindsey, judicially speaking: they all deny God's predictable sanctions during the era of the Church.)

How could they say? They have created a theological system – on the question of the relevance of biblical social theory, it is a single system – that systematically and self-consciously denies both the possibility and the practicality of constructing a consis-

13. See especially Gary DeMar and Peter Leithart, *The Reduction of Christianity: A Biblical Response to Dave Hunt* (Ft. Worth, Texas: Dominion Press, 1988).

14. John R. Muether, "The Era of Common Grace: Living Between the 'Already' and the 'Not Yet,' " *RTS Ministry*, IX (Summer 1990), p. 18.

15. Hal Lindsey, *The Late Great Planet Earth* (Grand Rapids, Michigan: Zondervan, [1970] 1972), p. 188.

tent, comprehensive, Bible-based social theory. They insist that God will not bring unique negative sanctions against covenant-breakers this side of Christ's bodily return from heaven. He will also not bring unique positive sanctions to bless the cultural efforts of covenant-keepers prior to the Second Coming. I ask: Then who in his right mind would devote years of study and lots of personal capital to working out biblical principles of politics, education, economics, or anything else, given this kind of theology? We now have three centuries of accumulated evidence that provides the answer: *hardly anyone*.

This is the practical problem. It is a problem that pessimillennialists refuse to deal with. This is especially true of dispensational premillennialists, who have no tradition of academic excellence behind them, and who have not been pressured by their peers to deal with real-world social issues.

The Dispensational View of History

Alva J. McClain wrote a five-and-a-half-page essay on "A Premillennial Philosophy of History" for Dallas Seminary's *Bibliotheca Sacra* in 1956. McClain was the president of Grace Theological Seminary, a school which, along with Dallas, has dominated the training of dispensational pastors. His book on the dispensational kingdom would soon become a standard. He was a highly influential academic figure in these circles.

This essay should be read by every dispensationalist, not to learn what this view of history is, which the essay never says, but to learn that a major theologian of the movement did not bother to describe it. In this essay, McClain rejected postmillennialism, although he did admit that "Classical postmillennialism had plenty of defects, but it did make a serious attempt to deal with human history."[16] He then dismissed – in one paragraph per error – the following: modern liberalism, neo-orthodoxy,

16. Alva J. McClain, Th.M., D.D. [honorary], L.L.D. [honorary], "A Premillennial Philosophy of History," *Bibliotheca Sacra*, vol. 113 (April-June 1956), p. 112. A journal that has its authors list honorary degrees after their names is a journal aimed at readers with too much respect for academics and not enough knowledge about what the various academic degrees represent. It is aimed at a movement with an academic inferiority complex. *Bibliotheca Sacra* no longer does this, but it did in 1956.

amillennialism (Louis Berkhof), and all those who think "there will never be such a 'Golden Age' upon earth in history. . . ."[17] This left exactly half a page for a thorough discussion of the premillennial view of history. He never did say what this is. He simply concluded, "The premillennial philosophy of history makes sense. It lays a Biblical and rational basis for a truly optimistic view of human history."[18]

McClain refused even to mention the key historical issue for those living prior to the Rapture: *What is the premillennial basis for Christians' optimism regarding the long-term effects of their earthly efforts?* Clearly, there is none. The results of all of their efforts, pre-tribulational dispensational premillennialists would have to say if they had the courage to discuss such things in public, will all be swallowed up during the seven-year Great Tribulation after the Rapture. Even those people converted to Christ by today's evangelism will all be either dead or Raptured out of history. All that will be left behind is a temporary glut of used cars with "I brake for the Rapture" bumper stickers.

This is a self-consciously pessimistic view of the future of the Church, and it has resulted in the triumph of humanism whenever it has been widely believed by Christians; therefore, the intellectual leaders of dispensationalism refuse to discuss it forthrightly. It is just too embarrassing. They use the language of postmillennial optimism to disguise a thoroughgoing pessimism. They keep pointing to the glorious era of the millennium in order to defend their use of optimistic language, never bothering to admit out that *the seven years that precede the millennium will destroy the results of gospel preaching during the entire Church Age*. After all, every Christian will have been removed from the earth at the Rapture, whether it will be pre-trib, mid-trib, or post-trib. (This is an explicit denial of the historical continuity predicted in Christ's parable of the wheat and tares [Matt. 13:20, 38-43]). McClain's essay is representative of what has passed for world-and-life scholarship within dispensationalism since 1830. It avoided any discussion of the premillennial view

---

17. *Ibid.*, p. 115.
18. *Ibid.*, p. 116.

of history, which was its explicit topic.

The reader may be thinking to himself: "But how did Alva McClain get away with this? Why did the editor publish such a piece? How could anyone be fooled this badly?" The answer is simple: *because they wanted to be fooled*. They still do. They want to escape personal responsibility for the cultural success of the gospel of salvation in history. Anything that seems to further this end they are willing to accept uncritically. We are not witnessing an intellectual failure only; we are witnessing a moral failure. It has been going on for well over a century. McClain's essay was only one small example of a way of life and a way of thinking about the gospel in history. The good news of Jesus Christ for a comparative handful of individuals thus far in Church history is interpreted as bad news for the Church's efforts in the "Church Age" as a whole. There can be no fulfillment of the Great Commission in history. This is trend-tending with a vengeance, but not God's vengeance.

A Missed Opportunity

Consider when that article appeared. It was at the peak of the post-World War II period of American supremacy. Eisenhower was President. Khrushchev had only barely consolidated his power in the Soviet Union. His famous 1956 "secret speech" on Stalin's "cult of personality" had shaken the American Communist Party to the core, with many resignations as a result. In America, rock and roll was still in its Fats Domino-Bill Haley-Buddy Holly-early Elvis Presley phase. There was no conservative movement. William F. Buckley's *National Review* magazine was only a year old. No one outside of Arizona had heard of Barry Goldwater, whose run for the Presidency came in 1964.

Religiously, Dallas Seminary and Grace Seminary possessed something of a monopoly in fundamentalism. The neo-evangelical movement was less than a decade old. Billy Graham helped to start *Christianity Today* in 1956, but it had not yet begun its visible drift to its present middle-to-left position. Graham had not yet begun his cooperation at his crusades with local congregations that belong to the National Council of Churches. He was a strong anti-Communist in 1956, and the USSR had not yet started inviting him to give crusades that were followed by press conferences telling the world how there was no religious persecution in the Soviet Union. (Solzhenitsyn was politely scathing in 1983 in his denunciation of Rev. Graham's services to the Soviet Union's tyrants in this regard.)[19] There was no six-day creationist movement to speak of; Morris and Whitcomb's *Genesis Flood* was five years away. (Grace Seminary officially affirms the six-day creation; Dallas Seminary never has.) Fuller Seminary was a small, struggling school that had not yet begun its drift into liberalism, ecumenism, and influence.

Over the next fifteen years, Dallas Seminary, Grace Seminary, and the newly created Talbot Seminary in California sat immobile and culturally silent while the rest of the country went through enormous changes. The conservative political movement got rolling visibly in 1960. Liberalism consolidated itself in the Kennedy and early Johnson years, but it was blown apart ethically during the Vietnam War era. Kennedy was assassinated in November of 1963, and the myth of Camelot was retroactively created. The Beatles appeared on the Ed Sullivan Show the next February. Then all hell broke loose.

Black ghettos rioted, beginning in Harlem in the summer of 1964. Watts went up in flames in 1965. The Rolling Stones had their first big hit in 1966. The youth movement went crazy, 1965-70. It seemed that everyone under age 25 was asking the old social order to defend itself morally (it couldn't), and millions of people were asking many fundamental questions about life and society.[20] Throughout all of this, nothing was heard

---

19. In his 1983 speech to the Templeton Foundation, which had granted him its enormous award (close to $200,000) for a lifetime of religious service, Solzhenitsyn remarked toward the end of his presentation on the horrors of Communism: It is with profound regret that I must note here something which I cannot pass over in silence. My predecessor in receipt of this prize last year – in the very months that the award was made – lent public support to communist lies by his deplorable statement that he had not noticed the persecution of religion in the USSR. Before the multitude of those who have perished and who are oppressed today, may God be his judge." His predecessor was Billy Graham. Solzhenitsyn, *The Templeton Prize, 1983* (Grand Cayman Islands: Lismore Press, 1983), no page numbers.

20. Gary North, *Unholy Spirits: Occultism and New Age Humanism* (Ft. Worth, Texas: Dominion Press, 1986), pp. 4-11.

from dispensationalism. An opportunity, not of a lifetime but of a century, was missed. Dispensationalism lost its legitimacy, 1965-70. Its intellectual decline since then has been the result.

Cultural Irrelevance for Jesus' Sake

Then came what Tom Wolfe called the "me decade," and Hal Lindsey's *Late Great Planet Earth* (1970) sold tens of millions of copies. Having forfeited moral and intellectual leadership, 1965-70, the Dallas Seminary faculty saw one of its less gifted graduates become the voice of the movement.[21] Lindsey's career went into orbit, while two of his marriages failed. ("We're under grace, not law.") Its message: Jesus is coming back real soon.

Lindsey did not miss the social implications of dispensational theology. In his book, *The Liberation of Planet Earth* (1974), there is not one word on the liberation of planet earth. It is a 236-page book (no index, no Scripture index) dealing exclusively with the doctrine of individual regeneration. He did include a section on the crucifixion, "The Day the Planet Was Liberated," in his brief chapter on "Redemption," but then he limited his discussion to Christ's death for individuals. There is nothing on how Jesus' death, resurrection, and ascension to the right hand of God affects society. He did not even mention the family (understandable!) or the Church (also understandable). His book's title was as misleading as the title of McClain's essay. It did not deliver what was promised on the cover.

In 1973, the U. S. Supreme Court handed down its decision, *Roe v. Wade*. That decision legalized abortion on demand. The case had originated in Dallas. What was Dallas Seminary's response? Silence. No calls for picketing, no press releases, no books, nothing. This is still Dallas Seminary's official position on legalized abortion: silence. In 1973, Dallas Seminary publicly

---

21. There has a long-standing debate ever since: Did Lindsey borrow more heavily from Col. Bob Thieme's sermon notes or from J. Dwight Pentecost's lecture notes? Lindsey belatedly acknowledged Thieme's influence in the dedication of *The Road to Holocaust*. (Half the royalty money, plus interest, would also have been a decent gesture.) He has not, to my knowledge, acknowledged Dr. Pentecost's notes.

relegated itself to social irrelevance. It had been doing so in its journal and its classrooms for over forty years.

A Startling Contrast

In that same year, 1973, R. J. Rushdoony's *Institutes of Biblical Law* appeared. (So did my *Introduction to Christian Economics.*) To assess the magnitude of the opportunity that dispensationalism forfeited, consider what Rushdoony did with practically no money, no degree-granting institution, and no mailing list of graduates. He began his book ministry in 1959 with a book on Van Til's philosophy, *By What Standard?*, and followed this effort with these: *Intellectual Schizophrenia* (1961), *The Messianic Character of American Education* (1963), *This Independent Republic* (1964), *The Nature of the American System* (1965), *Freud* (1965), *The Mythology of Science* (1967), *Foundations of Social Order* (1968), *The Myth of Over-Population* (1969), *The Biblical Philosophy of History* (1969), *Politics of Guilt and Pity* (1970), *Law and Liberty* (1971), *The One and the Many* (1971), and *The Flight from Humanity* (1973). He wrote a column every other week for *The California Farmer*, from which a collection of essays was taken: *Bread Upon the Waters* (1969). He also intervened to get *The Genesis Flood* published by Presbyterian & Reformed after Moody Press turned it down.[22] He had begun his newsletter on a shoestring in 1965. Speaking hundreds of times each year, reading an average of a book a day, Rushdoony produced more books of lasting significance than the combined faculties of Dallas, Grace, and Talbot did in the same period, 1959-73 (and, I would also add, before or after).

How did he do it? It was not that Rushdoony was a genius or had a string of advanced academic degrees. (He had a B.A. in English and an M.A. in education from Berkeley, and a B.D. from the liberal Pacific School of Religion.) It was that he had a vision – a comprehensive, integrated worldview – and also the personal dedication to defend that worldview intellectually. His worldview was not one of corporate defeat and social irrele-

22. Henry M. Morris, *A History of Modern Creationism* (San Diego: Master Books, 1984), p. 154.

vance for Christianity, all in the name of Jesus. So, unlike Alva J. McClain and dispensationalism in general, Rushdoony really did have a philosophy of history. He still does.

Without the Sugar-Coating

While the title of McClain's essay may have given the impression that premillennialism has a philosophy of history, the troops in the pews have not been fooled. Dave Hunt is willing to say publicly what dispensationalism means, and without any apologies. Dispensational theology obviously teaches the defeat of all the Church's cultural efforts before the Rapture, since the millennium itself will be a cultural defeat for God, even with Jesus reigning here on earth in His perfect body.

> In fact, dominion – taking dominion and setting up the kingdom for Christ – is an impossibility, even for God. The millennial reign of Christ, far from being the kingdom, is actually the final proof of the incorrigible nature of the human heart, because Christ Himself can't do what these people say they are going to do. . . . [23]

Here we have it without any sugar-coating: there is no connection between God's exclusively spiritual kingdom and man's history, not even during the millennium. The world of fundamentalism is so radically divided between spirit and culture that even God Himself cannot bind the two together. Such a binding is an impossibility, says Hunt. In the best-selling writings of Dave Hunt, the legacy of C. I. Scofield has come to fruition: a cultural rose which is all thorns and no blooms. Of course, dispensational seminary professors can protest that this is not the "real" dispensationalism, but this complaint assumes that the movement's scholars have produced a coherent alternative to pop-dispensationalism. They haven't. They have forfeited

---

23. Dave Hunt, "Dominion and the Cross," Tape 2 of *Dominion: The Word and New World Order* (1987), published by Omega Letter, Ontario, Canada. See the similar statement in his book, *Beyond Seduction*: "The millennial reign of Christ upon earth, rather than being the kingdom of God, will in fact be the final proof of the incorrigible nature of the human heart." Dave Hunt, *Beyond Seduction: A Return to Biblical Christianity* (Eugene, Oregon: Harvest House, 1987), p. 250.

moral and intellectual leadership to paperback theologians. They are silent: neither critical of these amateurs nor positive about an alternative. They cling silently to their jobs and refuse to apply dispensational premises to their academic specialties. This keeps them out of trouble with the Board of Trustees. It also keeps them irrelevant. This, too, is consistent.

Dispensationalists say that Christians in principle are impotent to reverse the downward drift of history, and to attempt to do so would be a waste of our scarce capital, especially time. While the academic leaders of dispensationalism have been too embarrassed to admit what is obviously a consistent cultural conclusion of their view of history, the popularizers have not hesitated, especially in response to criticisms by the Reconstructionists. Here is what dispensationalist newsletter publisher Peter Lalonde says regarding a friend of his who wants Christians to begin to work to change the "secular world":

> It's a question, "Do you polish brass on a sinking ship?" And if they're working on setting up new institutions, instead of going out and winning the lost for Christ, then they're wasting the most valuable time on the planet earth right now, and that is the serious problem in his thinking.[24]

The Theology of the Rescue Mission

This is not the unique opinion of an obscure Canadian tabloid newspaper editor. Lalonde is simply voicing what the intellectual leaders of dispensationalism have always said. Consider the words of John Walvoord, former president of Dallas Theological Seminary. In the twilight of his career, he participated in a panel on the millennium, which was sponsored by *Christianity Today*. Kenneth Kantzer asked him a key question.

> Kantzer: For all of you who are not postmils, is it worth your efforts to improve the physical, social, political situation on earth?
>
> Walvoord: The answer is yes and no. We know that our efforts to

---

24. "Dominion: A Dangerous New Theology," Tape 1 of *Dominion: The Word and New World Order.*

> make society Christianized are futile because the Bible doesn't teach it. On the other hand, the Bible certainly doesn't teach that we should be indifferent to injustice and famine and to all sorts of things that are wrong in our current civilization. Even though we know our efforts aren't going to bring a utopia, we should do what we can to have honest government and moral laws. It's very difficult from Scripture to advocate massive social improvement efforts, because certainly Paul didn't start any, and neither did Peter. They assumed that civilization as a whole is hopeless and subject to God's judgment.[25]

He then went on to observe that premillennialists run most of the rescue missions. "Premillennialists have a pretty good record in meeting the physical needs of people." This is quite true, but there is no doubt from his words that he does not believe it is possible for Christians to influence the creation of a world in which there will be freedom, righteousness, and productivity – a world in which fewer rescue missions will be necessary. His vision of social action is to get people out of the gutter. This is because his view of the gospel is to take people out of this world – first mentally and then physically, at the Rapture. *For dispensationalism, this world is one gigantic gutter. It cannot be cleaned up during the "Church Age."* The best a Christian can hope for is to sit peacefully on a short, clean stretch of curbing on the sidelines of life.

In response, Professor John J. Davis of Gordon-Conwell Theological Seminary, a postmillennialist, replied: "But generally speaking, the premillennialist is more oriented toward helping those who have been hurt by the system than by addressing the systematic evil, while the postmillennialist believes the system can be sanctified. That's the basic difference with regard to our relationship to society."[26] This is exactly right.

Walvoord, a consistent representative of traditional dispensationalism, assures us: "We know that our efforts to make society Christianized are futile because the Bible doesn't teach it." He deliberately ignores the Old Testament prophets. He does not

---

25. *Christianity Today* (Feb. 6, 1987), pp. 5-I, 6-I.
26. *Ibid.*, pp. 6-I, 7-I

want Christians to preach prophetically, for the prophets called Israel back to obedience to biblical law, and dispensationalism rejects biblical law. Walvoord calls only for a vague, undefined "moral law" to promote an equally vague "honest government." Without specifics, this is meaningless rhetoric. This is *the theology of the rescue mission*: sober them up, give them a bath and a place to sleep, and then send them to church until they die or Jesus comes again. This is the "Christian as a nice neighbor" version of what should be "salt and light" theology: "Save individuals, but not societies."

> Kantzer: Are we saying here that the Christian community, whether premil, postmil, or amil, must work both with individuals as well as seek to improve the structures of society? In other words, is there nothing within any of the millennial views that would prevent a believer from trying to improve society?
>
> Walvoord: Well, the Bible says explicitly to do good to all men, especially those of faith. In other words, the Bible does give us broad commands to do good to the general public.[27]

Broad commands are worthless without specifics. A call to "do good" is meaningless without Bible-based standards of good. A Communist or a New Age evolutionist could readily agree with Walvoord's statement, since it contains no specifics.

The Truth Hurts

When dispensationalists are called pessimists by postmillennialists – as we postmillennialists unquestionably do call them – they react negatively. This is evidence of my contention that everyone recognizes the inhibiting effects of pessimism. People do not like being called pessimists. Walvoord is no exception. But his self-defense is most revealing: "Well, I personally object to the idea that premillennialism is pessimistic. We are simply realistic in believing that man cannot change the world. Only God can."[28] *Realism!* That sounds so much better. And what is

27. *Ibid.*, p. 6-I.
28. *Ibid.*, p. 11-I.

the message of this dispensational realism? Pessimism.

"Man cannot change the world." What in the world does this mean? That man is a robot? That God does everything all alone, for both good and evil? Walvoord obviously does not mean this. So, what does he mean? That men collectively can do evil but not good? Then what effect does the gospel have in history? If he does not want to make this preposterous conclusion, then he must mean that *men who act apart from God's will, God's law, and God's Holy Spirit* cannot improve the world, long-term. If God is willing to tolerate the victory of evil, there is nothing that Christians can do about it except try to get out of the way of the victorious sinners if we possibly can, while handing out gospel tracts on street corners and running local rescue missions. The question is: *Is* God willing tolerate the triumph of sinners over His Church in history? *Yes*, say premillennialists and amillennialists. *No*, say postmillennialists.

What Walvoord is implying but not saying is that the postmillennialists' doctrine of the historical power of regeneration, the historical power of the Holy Spirit, the historical power of biblical law, God's historical sanctions, and the continuing New Testament validity of God's dominion covenant with man (Gen. 1:26-28) is theologically erroneous, and perhaps even borderline heretical. But this, of course, is precisely the reason we postmillennialists refer to premillennialists as pessimistic. They implicitly hold the reverse doctrinal viewpoints: the historical lack of power of regeneration, the historical lack of power of the Holy Spirit, the historical lack of power of biblical law, and the present suspension of God's dominion covenant with man. (Carl McIntire's tiny, premillennial, Bible Presbyterian Church in 1970 went on record officially as condemning any New Testament application to society of God's cultural mandate of Genesis 1:28.)[29]

Walvoord says that only God can change the world. Quite true. But who does he think the postmillennialists believe will change the world for the better? Of course God must change

29. Resolution No. 13, reprinted in R. J. Rushdoony, *The Institutes of Biblical Law* (Nutley, New Jersey: Craig Press, 1973), pp. 723-24.

the world. Given the depravity of man, He is the only One who can. But how does He do this? Through demons? No. Through fallen men who are on the side of demons in their rebellion against God? No. So, what is God's historic means of making the world better? *The preaching of the gospel!*

This is what postmillennialists have always taught. And the comprehensive success of the gospel in history is what premillennialists have always denied. They categorically deny that the gospel of Christ will ever change most men's hearts at any future point in history. The gospel in this view is a primarily a means of condemning gospel-rejecting people to hell, not a program leading to the victory of Christ's people in history. The gospel cannot transform the world, they insist. Yet they resent being called pessimists. Such resentment is futile. They *are* pessimists, and no amount of complaining and waffling can conceal it.

A Perfect Pessimism

Pessimism regarding the transforming power of the gospel of Jesus Christ in history is what best *defines* pessimism. There is no pessimism in the history of man that is more pessimistic than this eschatological pessimism regarding the power of the gospel in history. The universal destruction of mankind by nuclear war – a myth, by the way[30] – is downright optimistic compared to pessimism with regard to the transforming power of the gospel in history. This pessimism testifies that the incorrigible human heart is more powerful than God in history, that Satan's defeat of Adam in the garden is more powerful in history than Christ's defeat of Satan at Calvary. It denies Paul's doctrine of triumphant grace in history: "Moreover the law entered, that the offence might abound. But where sin abounded, grace did more abound" (Rom. 5:20). In pesssimillennial theologies, grace struggles so that sin might more abound in history. Few have said it more fearlessly than Lehman Strauss in *Bibliotheca Sacra*, Dallas Seminary's scholarly journal:

---

30. Arthur Robinson and Gary North, *Fighting Chance: Ten Feet to Survival* (Ft. Worth, Texas: American Bureau of Economic Research, 1986).

> We are witnessing in this twentieth century the collapse of civilization. It is obvious that we are advancing toward the end of the age. Science can offer no hope for the future blessing and security of humanity, but instead it has produced devastating and deadly results which threaten to lead us toward a new dark age. The frightful uprisings among races, the almost unbelievable conquests of Communism, and the growing antireligious philosophy throughout the world, all spell out the fact that doom is certain. I can see no bright prospects, through the efforts of man, for the earth and its inhabitants.[31]

What is Christian man's hope? The Rapture. And what of the vast majority of non-Christian men who will not participate in the Rapture? No dispensationalist likes to discuss this publicly. The question answers itself. Armageddon. The Great Tribulation. And if they survive this, a thousand years under Jesus' One World bureaucratic State. Will they be saved then? Probably not. The social answer is a future millennial bureaucracy, for which there are no operational blueprints this side of the Second Coming of Christ.

Because this attitude toward social change steadily became ascendant after 1870,[32] those who dominate modern society – non-Christians – have had few reasons to take Christians very seriously. American Christians have been in self-conscious cultural retreat from historic reality and cultural responsibility for most of this century.[33] Meanwhile, as non-Christians have become steadily more consistent with their own worldview, they have begun to recognize more clearly who their enemies really are: Christians who proclaim the God of the Bible, i.e., the God of final judgment. Thus, we are now seeing in the United States an escalation of the inherent, inevitable conflict between covenant-keepers and covenant-breakers. (This conflict can be cut

---

31. Lehman Strauss, "Our Only Hope," *Bibliotheca Sacra*, vol. 120 (April/June 1963), p. 154.

32. George Marsden, *Fundamentalism and American Culture: The Shaping of Twentieth-Century Evangelicalism, 1870-1925* (New York: Oxford University Press, 1980), chapters 20-23.

33. See, for example, Douglas W. Frank, *Less Than Conquerors: How Evangelicals Entered the Twentieth Century* (Grand Rapids, Michigan: Eerdmans, 1986).

short, of course: by God's negative sanctions against the society and/or by the conversion of large numbers of present covenant-breakers. There is always an "if" element in every supposedly inevitable trend.)

The Quest for Relevance

Nevertheless, pessimillennial pietists publicly profess concern regarding the irrelevance of Christianity today. They know that Christians should have answers to the dilemmas of the day, even if pagans refuse to accept our answers. This may be why Hal Lindsey's publisher insisted on a relevant-sounding title, *The Liberation of Planet Earth*, even though the book said nothing about it. The problem facing those who would mobilize the evangelical Christian community is that this community has taken its pietism very seriously. The people in the pews have assimilated the teaching of a century of pietism. Its leaders therefore have devoted little effort and less money to developing specific answers to obvious social problems.

Example: Where are the uniquely Christian medical schools and hospitals when sick people seek healing? Oral Roberts built a hospital and medical school, but he lost tens of millions of dollars (maybe much more). He wound up with an unfinished hospital with a statue of praying hands in front of it. What uniquely Christian approaches to healing and health maintenance should Christian medical treatment provide? No answers. No one in the evangelical world even tries to discover such answers.[34] This is consistent.

Another example: Where are the Christian lawyers? Today churches and Christian day schools are visibly under attack by humanist politicians and bureaucrats. Where are the certified defenders? Oral Roberts started a law school, lost a fortune, and shut it down. Furthermore, what uniquely Christian legal principles – as distinguished from medieval Roman Catholic scholastic natural law theory or eighteenth-century Jeffersonian and Madisonian political theory[35] – should a Christian law school

---

34. Perhaps the Seventh Day Adventists do a better job at Loma Linda University Medical School. I hope so.

35. I refer here to the present curriculum of the Regent University Law School

teach? No one says. No one holding a pietistic theology can say. Pietism denies that anything so worldly can or should be said.

This is why every attempt on the part of theological pietists to create interest in Christian social involvement leads their brighter recruits directly into the camp of either the Christian Reconstructionists or the liberation theologians. These newly motivated recruits do understand that you can't beat something with nothing. But the pietists offer Christians nothing specific, nothing concrete, nothing uniquely biblical on which to build alternatives to a collapsing social order. The theonomists do.[36]

The Shaking of the Foundations

A recent book from the dispensational camp illustrates the growing problem faced by the movement. Kerby Anderson, a dispensationalist, is also a strong defender of Christian social involvement. He has edited a book titled *Living Ethically in the '90s*.[37] Surely this is a worthy goal. But the book's title presents a monumental problem for dispensationalists. How does one live ethically? This was Schaeffer's unanswered question: How should we then live? If biblical law is not morally binding in the New Covenant era, then how do Christians know what righteous living is? The book raises the question of ethical standards, meaning permanent ethical principles. This is the question of *law*. For a Christian, it is this issue: *biblical law vs. non-biblical law*. It is a question that dispensationalists have done their best to avoid asking, let alone answer, since 1830.

(formerly the CBN University Law School). See Gary Amos' book, *Defending the Declaration: How the Bible and Christianity Influenced the Writing of the Declaration of Independence* (Brentwood, Tennessee: Wolgemuth & Hyatt, 1989). Amos teaches in the Regent University School of Law and Government, though not in the law school itself.

36. The liberation theologians appear to, but when pressed, they have no biblical answers. See David Chilton, *Productive Christians in an Age of Guilt-Manipulators: A Biblical Response to Ronald J. Sider* (4th ed.; Tyler, Texas: Institute for Christian Economics, 1986). Worse; they even deny that there is any need or warrant to search the Old Testament for relevant case laws. See the three critical responses to my essay in Robert Clouse (ed.), *Wealth and Poverty: Four Christian Views of Economics* (Downers Grove, Illinois: InterVarsity Press, 1984).

37. J. Kerby Anderson (ed.), *Living Ethically in the '90s* (Wheaton, Illinois: Victor Books, 1990).

The book reveals the escalating theological schizophrenia within the dispensationalist camp. Gary R. Williams writes an essay defending the efficacy of the Old Testament's penal sanctions. They are better than the modern humanist civil sanctions of prison, he insists (correctly). This, of course, has been the Christian Reconstructionist view since the beginning of the movement. "The prison system," writes Rushdoony in *The Institutes of Biblical Law*, is "a humanistic device. . . ."[38]

Norman Geisler, seeing exactly where such an argument leads – to Bahnsen's theonomy and possibly even to Tyler's covenant theology – defends Thomistic natural law theory. Geisler recognizes that if you begin to defend Old Testament civil sanctions for any reason, you have taken a major step in the direction of affirming the New Testament authority of Old Testament law in general. He sees that *the covenant is a package deal*. You cannot accept Old Testament law pragmatically and then expect people to believe that Old Testament laws are not also morally and judicially binding. You cannot tell people that Old Testament civil law works better than all the non-biblical alternatives, and then repeat the heart of dispensational ethical theory, namely, "we're under grace, not law." (Of course we are under grace. The question that non-theonomists do not wish to face is this: Whose *civil law* should Christians be under? God's or man's? They prefer the myth of neutrality and pluralism.)

Dr. Geisler instinctively sees that you cannot pragmatically defend the legitimacy of Old Testament laws on the basis of *sanctions* (point four of the biblical covenant model), and then expect to deny successfully biblical law's moral legitimacy based on its *authority* (point two). But Geisler is fast becoming a voice crying in the antinomian wilderness of the traditional dispensational camp. His colleagues, tired of wandering in the ethical wilderness, want to stop at a judicial oasis and get a drink. But Geisler sees the risk involved: the theonomists bought up all the judicial oases back in the 1970's, when they were cheap, and will now extract monopoly rents. The theonomists will demand

---

38. Rushdoony, *Institutes of Biblical Law*, p. 228. See also Gary North, *Victim's Rights: The Biblical View of Civil Justice* (Tyler, Texas: Institute for Christian Economics, 1990).

a high price: the *operational abandonment* of the dispensational system. This will eventually lead to a quiet, unnanounced, but nonetheless effective *theological abandonment* of the system.

The Impossible Dream

The pessimillennialists want Christianity to be relevant in history, yet they have publicly denied the theological foundations of historical relevance: (1) the continuing New Covenant relevance of God's Old Covenant social and civil laws; (2) God's historical sanctions applied in terms of these laws; and (3) historical continuity between the present and the prophesied era of millennial blessings that will take place *on earth and in history*. How can they sensibly expect their followers to take seriously their assertion of Christianity's historical relevance, let alone the historical relevance of their own efforts? C. S. Lewis described about a similar problem in his 1947 essay, "Men Without Chests":

> In a sort of ghastly simplicity we remove the organ and demand the function. We make men without chests and expect of them virtue and enterprise. We laugh at honour and are shocked to find traitors in our midst. We castrate and bid the geldings be fruitful.[39]

Conclusion

Social theory requires a unified, authoritative concept of good and bad, right and wrong, efficient and inefficient. To be consistent, it must affirm the existence of known or at least knowable standards, and it must also affirm that there is a sanctioning process that rewards the good (or the efficient) and penalizes the bad (or the inefficient). If the standards are affirmed without also affirming appropriate sanctions, then there is no way for society to insure justice. There is also no way for it to insure progress.

Modern Christian theology has denied both biblical law (the standards) and God's historical sanctions. It has therefore sought the standards of society elsewhere. Occasionally, Chris-

39. C. S. Lewis, *The Abolition of Man* (New York: Macmillan, 1947), p. 35.

tian social commentators appeal openly to Stoic-medieval natural law theory to provide the standards. Mostly, they do not identify the source of their standards. If they seek standards elsewhere than in the Bible, they are forced to import modern, post-Newtonian standards into their social theories. But this leaves them vulnerable to post-Darwinian standards, which is to say, vulnerable to the "tender mercies" of either free market social Darwinism, with its doctrine of the "survival of the fitest" (Herbert Spencer, William Graham Sumner), or elitist, scientifically planned, State-directed, tax-financed social Darwinism (Lester Frank Ward).[40]

Dispensationalists have generally avoided even discussing social theory. They recognize their theological dilemma and have prudently remained silent. Neo-evangelical social scientists have spoken out in the name of Jesus, and have sounded very much like a cassette tape of some abandoned political program of a decade earlier. Amillennialists have generally done what the neo-evangelical premillennialists have: baptized secular humanism, meaning politically liberal humanism. They have generally adopted the worldview of the professors who certified them at humanist universities. There has to be a better way. Christians will never beat something with nothing.

40. Gary North, *The Dominion Covenant: Genesis* (2nd ed; Tyler, Texas: Institute for Christian Economics, 1987), pp. 289-318.

9

THE SOCIOLOGY OF SUFFERING

And there was also a strife among them, which of them should be accounted the greatest. And he said unto them, The kings of the Gentiles exercise lordship over them; and they that exercise authority upon them are called benefactors. But ye shall not be so: but he that is greatest among you, let him be as the younger; and he that is chief, as he that doth serve. For whether is greater, he that sitteth at meat, or he that serveth? is not he that sitteth at meat? but I am among you as he that serveth. Ye are they which have continued with me in my temptations. And I appoint unto you a kingdom, as my Father hath appointed unto me; That ye may eat and drink at my table in my kingdom, and sit on thrones judging the twelve tribes of Israel (Luke 22:24-30).

Before we get to a more detailed consideration of this passage, let me note briefly that the Lord's Supper is a sacrament, meaning it is a God-authorized means of God's imposing His negative sanctions in history: "For he that eateth and drinketh unworthily, eateth and drinketh damnation to himself, not discerning the Lord's body. For this cause many are weak and sickly among you, and many sleep" (I Cor. 11:29-30). The Protestant Church does not really believe this – a testimony to its commitment to philosophical nominalism: the sacrament as a memorial and nothing more, surely not a judicially significant ritual. This sacrament is not taken very seriously as a means of bringing God's judicial sanctions in history. Neither, for that matter, are the imprecatory psalms taken seriously as the Church's means of bringing God's negative sanctions in society. So thoroughly has nominalism corrupted the Church that its spokesmen no longer recognize the Church as an agent lawfully authorized to invoke God's direct negative sanctions. This means that the Church in the New Covenant era is no longer seen as the agent authorized by God to bring His covenant lawsuit against covenant-breakers in history, unless the lawsuit is redefined: stripped of all suggestion of God's historical sanctions. This is exactly what amillennial theology does.

In the previous chapter, I argued that God's predictable negative sanctions in history are an inescapable concept. It is never a question of God's predictable historical sanctions vs. no sanctions. The question rather is this: *Against whom* will God's negative sanctions be predictably imposed, covenant-keepers or covenant-breakers? There can be no neutrality. The amillennialist and the premillennialist both insist that prior to the next prophesied eschatological discontinuity, which they insist is Christ's Second Coming or the Rapture, God's negative sanctions will be imposed either *equally* against covenant-keepers and covenant-breakers (Kline's Random News) or *progressively* against covenant-keepers, with covenant-breakers acting as God's appointed agents (Van Til's Bad News). The familiar denial of God's predictable negative sanctions in history is in fact an affirmation of the inevitability of His negative sanctions against the Church, from Pentecost to the bodily return of Christ in power and glory.

The postmillennialist, in sharp contrast, denies that covenant-keepers will be the primary targets of God's negative sanctions throughout history. He argues that the message of the Bible is covenantal: faithfulness brings God's blessings, while rebellion brings God's curses (Deut. 28). This is the message of the Old Testament prophets. They brought covenant lawsuits against Israel and Judah, judicially calling all covenant-breakers back to covenantal faithfulness, and threatening them with direct, culture-wide, negative sanctions if they refused. Furthermore, in a shocking disregard of the non-theonomists' principle that only ancient Israel was under the judicial requirements of God's covenant, Jonah was sent to Nineveh to announced the same message: in 40 days, God would bring His sanctions against them. Jonah, initially acting in a non-theonomic fashion, remained faithful to his principle that God was not really interested in bringing Nineveh under the terms of His covenant. He steadfastly refused to bring this covenant lawsuit against Nineveh, and he suffered an unpleasant three-day experience as a result of this refusal. He was given time to rethink his position, which he did, becoming theonomic. He then was given another opportunity to prosecute God's lawsuit, which turned out to be successful – unique in the Old Covenant era.

What if I were to come to you and try to recruit you to a difficult missionary field, namely, the city of Sodom. No, I don't mean San Francisco; I mean the original city. I would then tell you that in fact the whole world is Sodom, or will progressively become so in the future. You are being be asked to spend your life there, just as Lot spent his days there: *vexed*. I assure you that no angels will come to lead you out. There will be no widespread conversion of the city, either – not in your lifetime or in anyone else's lifetime. There will be no fiery judgment until the last day, and I refuse to tell you when that will be. The best news I can tell you about your assignment – indeed, the only good news – is that your wife will not be under any risk whatsoever of being turned to salt. I then assure you that this program is called a *victory assignment*, part of a missionary program known as *realized eschatology*. What would you think of my recruiting strategy? You would probably regard me as either a madman or a Calvinistic seminary professor.

A Covenant Lawsuit Without God's Historic Sanctions

The amillennialist ("realized millennialist") insists that it is illegitimate to appeal to the Old Testament in search of a message of visible, historical, covenantal faithfulness on God's part. Amillennialists understand what the Old Testament says, but they are compelled by their eschatology to deny that we should accept the Old Testament's covenantal message at face value. They contrast the New Testament's supposed message of humiliation and exile for the Church with the Old Testament's far more straightforward message of covenantal predictability. Writes Richard Gaffin, Professor of Systematic Theology at Westminster Seminary:

> Briefly, the basic issue is this: Is the New Testament to be allowed to interpret the Old – as the best, most reliable interpretive tradition in the history of the church (and certainly the Reformed tradition) has always insisted. . . . Or, alternatively, will the Old Testament, particularly prophecies like Isaiah 32:1-8 and 65:17-25, become the hermeneutical fulcrum?[1]

Gaffin knows where the soft underbelly of amillennialism is. He never attempts to explain this pair of problem passages; he just presumes them away. We need to review them, although I have already commented on them in Chapter 5.

> Behold, a king shall reign in righteousness, and princes shall rule in judgment. And a man shall be as an hiding place from the wind, and a covert from the tempest; as rivers of water in a dry place, as the shadow of a great rock in a weary land. And the eyes of them that see shall not be dim, and the ears of them that hear shall hearken. The heart also of the rash shall understand knowledge, and the tongue of the stammerers shall be ready to speak plainly. The vile person shall be no more called liberal, nor the churl said to be bountiful. For the vile person will speak villany, and his heart will work iniquity, to practise hypocrisy, and to utter error against the LORD, to make empty the soul of the hungry, and he will cause the drink of the thirsty to fail. The instruments also of the churl are evil: he deviseth wicked devices to destroy the poor with lying words, even when the needy speaketh right. But the liberal deviseth liberal things; and by liberal things shall he stand (Isa. 32:1-8).

> For, behold, I create new heavens and a new earth: and the former shall not be remembered, nor come into mind. But be ye glad and rejoice for ever in that which I create: for, behold, I create Jerusalem a rejoicing, and her people a joy. And I will rejoice in Jerusalem, and joy in my people: and the voice of weeping shall be no more heard in her, nor the voice of crying. There shall be no more thence an infant of days, nor an old man that hath not filled his days: for the child shall die an hundred years old; but the sinner being an hundred years old shall be accursed. And they shall build

---

1. Richard B. Gaffin, Jr., "Theonomy and Eschatology: Reflections on Postmillennialism," in William S. Barker and W. Robert Godfrey (eds.), *Theonomy: A Reformed Critique* (Grand Rapids, Michigan: Zondervan Academie, 1990), pp. 216-17.

> houses, and inhabit them; and they shall plant vineyards, and eat the fruit of them. They shall not build, and another inhabit; they shall not plant, and another eat: for as the days of a tree are the days of my people, and mine elect shall long enjoy the work of their hands. They shall not labour in vain, nor bring forth for trouble; for they are the seed of the blessed of the LORD, and their offspring with them. And it shall come to pass, that before they call, I will answer; and while they are yet speaking, I will hear. The wolf and the lamb shall feed together, and the lion shall eat straw like the bullock: and dust shall be the serpent's meat. They shall not hurt nor destroy in all my holy mountain, saith the LORD (Isa. 65:17-25).

The latter is the passage that so confounded Professor Hoekema. It is *the* unanswerable passage in the Bible for the amillennialist, so Professor Gaffin, like the vast majority of his eschatological colleagues, refuses to comment on it. They know how bad his attempted exposition made Professor Hoekema look, and they do not wish to experience similar public humiliation. (Perhaps some energetic, tuition-paying student will ask Dr. Gaffin to explain either or both of these passages in class sometime. I hope so. I hope he sends me a copy of the answer.)

But what of his initial presupposition, that the New Testament teaches suffering and cultural defeat for the prosecutors of God's covenant lawsuit (the gospel of Jesus Christ) throughout history? Can this claim be substantiated exegetically? No. But it has been repeated so often in the twentieth century that most Christians probably think that it can be or has been substantiated exegetically.

Exercising Judgment

Let us return to Christ's words regarding the Lord's Supper. The covenantal postmillennialist looks in confidence to the primary manifestation of God's blessings in history, the sacrament of the Lord's Supper. He makes his case for God's sanctions in the New Covenant era in terms of this extraordinary blessing and this extraordinary power. More than a mere memorial (nominalist-Anabaptist), but judicial rather than metaphysical (realist-Roman Catholic), the Lord's Supper is proof that God brings His sanctions in history. The postmillennialist then appeals to Christ's the words in Luke 22 that link the Lord's Supper to judicial rule in history.

Christ's words in Luke regarding the Lord's Supper appear in no Church liturgy, as far as I know. I have never heard any reference to this passage prior to taking communion. We are usually told to do this in rembrance of Him, but not in expectation of exercising judgment against His enemies as agents of His kingdom. Yet the message that Christ gave to His disciples in Luke 22 was certainly consistent with His entire ministry. *First*, it presents the contrast between the basis of authority wielded by covenant-breakers and covenant keepers: power vs. service. We are not to rule as the gentiles do. Jesus' ministry was grounded in the ultimate service: His death for His friends. "Greater love hath no man than this, that a man lay down his life for his friends" (John 15:13). "For scarcely for a righteous man will one die: yet peradventure for a good man some would even dare to die. But God commendeth his love toward us, in that, while we were yet sinners, Christ died for us" (Rom. 5:7-8). *Second*, His appointment of them as rulers of His kingdom, even as He received such an appointment from His Father. *Third*, the connecting of Holy Communion with Jesus' rulership in history: "That ye may eat and drink at my table in my kingdom, and sit on thrones judging the twelve tribes of Israel."

This reference to rulership has to be historical. The twelve tribes of Israel were still a political unit. The Church would soon be persecuted by Israel, Jesus had warned them. "But take heed to yourselves: for they shall deliver you up to councils; and in the synagogues ye shall be beaten: and ye shall be brought before rulers and kings for my sake, for a testimony against them. And the gospel must first be published among all nations. But when they shall lead you, and deliver you up, take no thought beforehand what ye shall speak, neither do ye premeditate: but whatsoever shall be given you in that hour, that speak ye: for it is not ye that speak, but the Holy Ghost" (Mark 13:9-11). There would come a time of suffering under the synagogue of Satan.

A generation later, John was instructed by God to write this to the Church of Smyrna: "I know thy works, and tribulation, and poverty, (but thou art rich) and I know the blasphemy of them which say they are Jews, and are not, but are the synagogue of Satan. Fear none of those things which thou shalt suffer: behold, the devil shall cast some of you into prison, that ye may be tried; and ye shall have tribulation ten days: be thou faithful unto death, and I will give thee a crown of life" (Rev. 2:9-10). Ten days of tribulation, and even the possibility of death, but they had God's assurance of victory. But would this mean *victory in history* for those who would survive the persecution, as well as victory in heaven for those who would die? Yes. The book of Revelation presented the Church with a promise from God: the persecution of the Church under Israel would soon end, when Israel would be brought under final judgment nationally.[2] That event took place within a matter of months.[3] Thus, the period of prophesied persecution in John's day was short. Then came God's predicted, negative, culture-wide sanctions against Old Covenant Israel: the Great Tribulation.[4]

There will be persecution of Christians, but the end result is the destruction of evil-doers. They persecute us, but in doing so, they grow *progressively deceived* and *progressively impotent*:

> Now as Jannes and Jambres withstood Moses, so do these also resist the truth: men of corrupt minds, reprobate concerning the faith. But they shall proceed no further: for their folly shall be manifest unto all men, as theirs also was. But thou hast fully known my doctrine, manner of life, purpose, faith, longsuffering, charity, patience, persecutions, afflictions, which came unto me at Antioch, at Iconium, at Lystra; what persecutions I endured: but out of them all the Lord delivered me. Yea, and all that will live godly in Christ Jesus shall suffer persecution. But evil men and seducers shall wax worse and worse, deceiving, and being deceived (II Tim. 3:8-13).

Representation

In what way did the disciples judge Israel in history? By

---

2. David Chilton, *The Days of Vengeance: An Exposition of the Book of Revelation* (Ft. Worth, Texas: Dominion Press, 1987).

3. Kenneth L. Gentry, Jr., *Before Jerusalem Fell: Dating the Book of Revelation* (Tyler, Texas: Institute for Christian Economics, 1989).

4. David Chilton, *The Great Tribulation* (Ft. Worth, Texas: Dominion Press, 1987).

representing God and Christ in history. Persecution first, Jesus and John warned; then the godly exercise of righteous judgment. In this case, the Church was spared God's negative sanctions. The Church survived, and by surviving, exercised judgment against Old Covenant Israel. Just as Lot brought judgment against Sodom by surviving, just as Moses brought judgment against Egypt in the Red Sea by surviving, just as Daniel brought judgment against Babylon on that final night by surviving, so does the Church of Jesus Christ bring judgment against the false kingdoms of this world by surviving. The Church announces God's covenant lawsuit, and then it awaits God's negative sanctions against that society which refuses to repent.

But what about Mark 13:10? "And the gospel must first be published among all nations." This has to happen in the days of the looming persecution. Until this kingdom program is fulfilled, we are still in the era of persecution, eschatologically speaking. Isn't this fulfillment still in the future? Not according to Paul's interpretation the Church of his day. "If ye continue in the faith grounded and settled, and be not moved away from the hope of the gospel, which ye have heard, and which was preached to every creature which is under heaven; whereof I Paul am made a minister" (Col. 1:23). *Which was preached*: his words could not be any plainer. Paul's words are no doubt figurative; they refer to a *representative* hearing: ". . . the hope of the gospel, which ye have heard, and which was preached to every creature which is under heaven." No one takes all of his words literally, i.e., every creature under heaven: bugs, mice, etc. Most theologians choose the safer path: to ignore the verse. But however interpreted, Paul made it clear that these words of Christ had already been fulfilled in Paul's day: "And the gospel must first be published among all nations." All of these prophesies were fulfilled by A.D. 71: the looming persecution, the preaching of the gospel to the whole world, the delivery of the disciples before judges, and their sitting in final judgment over Old Covenant Israel. Their sitting in judgment over Israel was fulfilled representatively, yet no less definitively, for Old Covenant Israel is no more.

My conclusion is this: while there can be and is persecution in this life, it is no more of an eschatological certitude that we shall be persecuted in the future than that God will put His words in our mouths when we are delivered up before judges. Persecution of the Church by covenant-breakers is no more assured eschatologically in the future than the Great Tribulation is – and the Great Tribulation is behind us. I doubt that Gaffin believes that we can wait on God to put words in our mouths rather than hire defense attorneys. I presume that he would admit that this prophecy applied only to the transition era between Pentecost and the fall of Jerusalem. But persecution of Christians? This is supposedly a category of Christian existence, an eschatological imperative. And if he follows Van Til, progressive persecution is eschatologically inevitable.

I prefer progressive sanctification to progressive persecution.

Progressive Sanctification

Because this doctrine is so often ignored by Christians, especially those few who bother to comment on the covenantal meaning of New Covenant history, I need to remind the reader one more time of the biblical doctrine of sanctification. God grants the *perfect humanity* of Christ to each individual convert to saving faith in Christ. This takes place at the point of his or her conversion. Subsequently, this implicit, *definitive* moral perfection is to be worked out in history. We are to strive for the mark. We are to run the good race (strive to win it, by the way, not in hope of a covenantal tie, i.e., pluralism).[5] We are to imitate Christ's perfect humanity, though of course not His divinity, which is an incommunicable attribute.

The doctrine of definitive sanctification taken by itself would mean that an individual is perfect. Certain perfectionist sects and cults have taught this, but this is clearly not Christian orthodoxy. "If we say that we have no sin, we deceive ourselves, and the truth is not in us" (John 1:8). On the other hand, if progressive sanctification is not balanced by the doctrine of definitive sanctification as a pure gift of God, then it would

5. Gary North, *Political Polytheism: The Myth of Pluralism* (Tyler, Texas: Institute for Christian Economics, 1989).

appear as though man can save himself by his own efforts, i.e., that he is not the recipient of God's grace. It would also leave him without permanent standards. We need both doctrines.

It is my argument in this study and in my book, *Dominion and Common Grace*, that these same dual concepts of definitive and progressive sanctification apply to corporate groups, especially covenantal associations, and above all, the Church. Thus, the fact that the Church has been definitively granted Christ's moral perfection does not deny the possibility and moral necessity of its progressive sanctification in history. Similarly, the fact that there is progressive sanctification in history does not in any way deny the fact of Christ's perfection, which was definitively granted to the Church at the point of its covenant-based creation. This applies also to the family and the State.

This simple concept completely baffles Professor Gaffin. He has read *Dominion and Common Grace*, for he offers a brief, exegetically unsupported sentence criticizing its cover, but, predictably, refuses to refer to its thesis or its documentation, and even this he confines to a footnote.[6] He ignores the book's documentation. (It should be noted that in his essay against Christian Reconstruction, Gaffin does not once cite any Reconstructionist author in the body of the text, and includes only three brief footnote references, one to the book cover and two to David Chilton's *Paradise Restored*. In fact, most of the essays in this compilation are remarkably devoid of actual citations of our writings, except Bahnsen's *Theonomy*. To say that this is a peculiar way to respond to a movement that has published well over one hundred volumes of books and scholarly journals, plus 25 years of newsletters is, to say the least, revealing. But, as I always say, you can't beat something with nothing. I think the faculty at Westminster Seminary understands this, so they have avoided direct confrontations with the primary sources of Christian Reconstructionism.)[7] Here is Dr. Gaffin's position:

---

6. Gaffin, p. 216n.

7. This has been going on for well over two decades. For my comments on the practice, see my Publisher's Foreword to Greg L. Bahnsen and Kenneth L. Gentry, Jr., *House Divided: The Break-Up of Dispensational Theology* (Tyler, Texas: Institute for Christian Economics, 1989), pp. xxxvii-xli, "Dealing With the Academic Black-Out."

> Nothing has been more characteristic of current postmillennialism than its emphasis on the kingship of the ascended Christ; nothing fires the postmil vision more than that reality. Yet it is just this reality that postmillennialism effectively compromises and, in part, even denies. . . . Emphasis on the golden era as being entirely future leaves the unmistakable impression that the church's present (and past) is something other than golden and that so far in its history the church is less than victorious.[8]

Less than victorious? If what the Church has experienced over the past 1,900 years is a victory equal to what the Bible promises for covenantal faithfulness, then I would surely hate to see a defeat! He then insists that "The New Testament, however, will not tolerate such a construction." What he means is that *he* will not tolerate such a construction. The New Testament is quite in conformity with such a construction:

> For he must reign, till he hath put all enemies under his feet. The last enemy that shall be destroyed is death. For he hath put all things under his feet. But when he saith all things are put under him, it is manifest that he is excepted, which did put all things under him. And when all things shall be subdued unto him, then shall the Son also himself be subject unto him that put all things under him, that God may be all in all (I Cor. 15:25-28).

This footstool condition of God's enemies is definitive, as Gaffin knows, for he correctly cites Ephesians 1:22: "And hath put all things under his feet, and gave him to be the head over all things to the church."[9] But why does he deny the progressive aspect of this definitive victory? Because he rejects the idea of the kingdom's victory in history. He is an amillennialist.

Progress in the Creeds?

If I were to ask Professor Gaffin if he has a great appreciation for the Westminster Confession of Faith, he would tell me that he does. I would then ask him: "Do you appreciate it more than the Athanasian Creed or the Nicene Creed?" If he says yes,

---

8. Gaffin, p. 202.
9. *Ibid.*, p. 203.

he has just accepted the concept of creedal progress in history. If he says no, he has just submitted his resignation from Westminster Seminary. So, I suppose he would answer that "each has its proper place in the Church," as indeed each does. (I would hate to have to sing the Westminster Confession of Faith each Sunday morning, the way I sing the Nicene Creed!) But if I were to ask him if the Westminster Confession is more theologically rigorous than earlier creeds, he would tell me it is. It was the product of centuries of creedal advance.

So, Professor Gaffin, I now ask you this: Can you imagine the possibility that the Westminster Confession will be improved upon as time goes on? Yes? Then are you now ready to begin working on such an improvement? I know I am. But more to the point, do you think such improvements in creedal formulations will parallel and reinforce the maturation of the Church? Finally, will such maturation have positive effects in society? If not, then are you saying that the progress of the Church and the creeds is socially irrelevant? Please be specific. And when you have got your answers ready, don't forget to discuss them with your students. Perhaps some of them may remind you of this assignment periodically. They do pay your salary.

Let us continue, this time with the family. The marital vows are definitive. The working out of these vows in the lives of a married couple is progressive: love, honor, obey, cherish, etc. Are we to say that an older couple has in no way matured covenantally since their wedding day? No. But does this in any way denigrate the integrity of those vows? No. This is so clear that even seminary professors ought to be able to understand it. They won't, of course. They acknowledge dual sanctification with respect to the individual Christian, but as soon as you raise the possibility that sanctification in both aspects also applies to institutions, you get a blank stare – what we might call *blank stare apologetics*. (If pressed hard, the professor might respond, "I see." He really doesn't, however.)

Outside the Cloister and the Family

Now, let us get to the heart of the matter: the world outside the Church and the family. Here is where the pietist gags. The pessimillennialist cannot tolerate the suggestion that the same principle of definitive and progressive sanctification applies to Christian societies, despite the fact that it applies to the Church and to the Christian family. What biblical principle do they invoke to prove the existence of such an interpretive discontinuity between the world outside Church and family and inside the Church and family? None. There is none. They simply refuse to discuss what they have done. They assert, as Gaffin asserts, that any concept of covenantal progress in history outside the Church and family is biblically illegitimate. His language is so strong in this regard that he could become as confrontationally rhetorical as I am, if he would just work at it. He has clearly displayed the basic talent; now he just needs to develop it.

Gaffin's problem is that he holds to the theology of Eastern Orthodoxy with respect to history: *moral progress only through suffering*. No Calvinist amillennial theologian has articulated this position any more clearly. He has developed an entire worldview based on this presupposition. He calls this his most substantial reservation against postmillennialism.[10] It has taken seventeen years of theological pressuring since Rushdoony's *Institutes of Biblical Law* was published to get so forthright a statement out of a Calvinist amillennialist. No one has demonstrated more visibly the accuracy of Rushdoony's judgment: amillennialists are premillennialists without earthly hope.

Personal Moral Progress Only Through Suffering

Gaffin calls amillennialism *inaugurated eschatology*, a variant of realized eschatology. Understand, this is the equivalent of *definitive eschatology*. There would be nothing wrong with it if it had the necessary complement, *progressive eschatology*. But he is appalled by the very thought of progressive eschatology, for it would necessarily deny the heart of his ethical system: personal maturation through suffering. We *need* persecution in history.

> The inaugurated eschatology of the New Testament is least of all the basis for triumphalism in the church, at whatever point prior to

10. *Ibid.*, p. 210.

> Christ's return. Over the interadvental period in its entirety, from beginning to end, a fundamental aspect of the church's existence is (to be) "suffering with Christ"; nothing, the New Testament teaches, is more basic to its identity than that.[11]

He cites II Corinthians 4:7: "But we have this treasure in earthen vessels, that the excellency of the power may be of God, and not of us." This imagery of man as a vessel is familiar in Scripture. Paul uses it in Romans 9:

> Nay but, O man, who art thou that repliest against God? Shall the thing formed say to him that formed it, Why hast thou made me thus? Hath not the potter power over the clay, of the same lump to make one vessel unto honour, and another unto dishonour? What if God, willing to shew his wrath, and to make his power known, endured with much longsuffering the vessels of wrath fitted to destruction: And that he might make known the riches of his glory on the vessels of mercy, which he had afore prepared unto glory, Even us, whom he hath called, not of the Jews only, but also of the Gentiles? (Rom. 9:20-24).

The question is not whether we are vessels. The question is: *Which vessels get progressively smashed by God in history, the vessels of wrath or the vessels of glory?* The answer to this question is biblically clear, and nowhere is it clearer than in Psalm 2, one of the most disconcerting Bible passages for the amillennialist:

> Why do the heathen rage, and the people imagine a vain thing? The kings of the earth set themselves, and the rulers take counsel together, against the LORD, and against his anointed, saying, Let us break their bands asunder, and cast away their cords from us. He that sitteth in the heavens shall laugh: the Lord shall have them in derision. Then shall he speak unto them in his wrath, and vex them in his sore displeasure. Yet have I set my king upon my holy hill of Zion. I will declare the decree: the LORD hath said unto me, Thou art my Son; this day have I begotten thee. Ask of me, and I shall give thee the heathen for thine inheritance, and the uttermost parts of the earth for thy possession. *Thou shalt break them with a rod of*

11. *Ibid.*, pp. 210-11. He cites his essay, "The Usefulness of the Cross," *Westminster Theological Journal*, vol. 41 (1978-79), pp. 228-46.

> *iron; thou shalt dash them in pieces like a potter's vessel.* Be wise now therefore, O ye kings: be instructed, ye judges of the earth. Serve the LORD with fear, and rejoice with trembling. Kiss the Son, lest he be angry, and ye perish from the way, when his wrath is kindled but a little. Blessed are all they that put their trust in him (Psa. 2). (emphasis added)

Lest we imagine that this is merely another Old Testament proof text,[12] consider Revelation 2:26-29: "And he that overcometh, and keepeth my works unto the end, to him will I give power over the nations: And he shall rule them with a rod of iron; as the vessels of a potter shall they be broken to shivers: even as I received of my Father. And I will give him the morning star. He that hath an ear, let him hear what the Spirit saith unto the churches." Let him hear, indeed.

Clay jars, Gaffin writes, are believers "in all their mortality and fragility."[13] Well, so what? What does this professor of systematic theology think covenant-breakers are made of, stainless steel? But, as with every amillennialist, *he gets his biblical imagery backwards*. He sees the Christians as clay pots and the covenant-breakers as rods of iron, *from now until doomsday*. It is true that the covenant-breaker is sometimes employed by God as a rod against us (negative sanctions in history), but never apart from the promise of a future reversal of the sanctioning relationship:

> And it shall come to pass in that day, that the remnant of Israel, and such as are escaped of the house of Jacob, shall no more again stay upon him that smote them; but shall stay upon the LORD, the Holy One of Israel, in truth. The remnant shall return, even the remnant of Jacob, unto the mighty God. For though thy people Israel be as the sand of the sea, yet a remnant of them shall return: the consumption decreed shall overflow with righteousness. For the Lord GOD of hosts shall make a consumption, even determined, in the midst of all the land. Therefore thus saith the Lord GOD of hosts, O my people that dwellest in Zion, *be not afraid of the Assyrian: he shall smite thee with a rod, and shall lift up his staff against thee, after the manner of Egypt*. For yet a very little while, and the indignation

---

12. A *proof text* is a biblical text proving something that you don't like one little bit.
13. *Ibid.*, p. 211.

> shall cease, and mine anger in their destruction. And the LORD of hosts shall stir up a scourge for him according to the slaughter of Midian at the rock of Oreb: and as his rod was upon the sea, so shall he lift it up after the manner of Egypt. And it shall come to pass in that day, that his burden shall be taken away from off thy shoulder, and his yoke from off thy neck, and the yoke shall be destroyed because of the anointing (Isa. 10:20-27). (emphasis added)

After the manner of Egypt. Every covenant-keeper is supposed to remember what happened to Egypt after that nation broke the Israelite vessels: destruction in history. But such a message of reversed roles, of victory, Gaffin says is strictly limited to Old Testament history; it has nothing to do with the history of the Church of the resurrected Christ. How do we know this? Because of Philippians 3:10: "That I may know him, and the power of his resurrection, and the fellowship of his sufferings, being made conformable unto his death."[14] He then spends several pages explaining Christ's sufferings and His death. *He defines Christ's resurrection in terms of His suffering.* Here is without a doubt the heart of the amillennial message, a message of incomparable pessimism: "By virtue of union with Christ, Paul is saying, the power of Christ's resurrection is realized in the sufferings of the believer; sharing in Christ's sufferings is the way the church manifests his resurrection-power."[15]

Prior to World War II, the great amillennial Dutch theologian Klaas Schilder wrote a trilogy: *Christ in His Suffering, Christ on Trial*, and *Christ Crucified*. He needed three more volumes: *Christ in the Grave, Christ Resurrected*, and *Christ Ascended*. But there is not much to say about Christ in the grave, and amillennialists get very nervous discussing Christ resurrected, let alone Christ ascended. They interpret the history of the Church in terms of Schilder's three volumes. They do not think culturally and socially except in these terms. The Dutch in Kuyper's day and Schilder's day tried to design a Christian culture, but without Old Testament law. World War II and its aftermath ended all such attempts. Schilder's trilogy was resurrected in Van

14. *Ibid.*, p. 212.
15. *Ibid.*, p. 213.

Riessen's sociology of suffering.[16]

The Meek Shall Inherit the Earth, Not the Wimps

Gaffin rejects triumphalism, as do all amillennialists. It has been absent for generations, but now Christian Reconstructionism has revived it. Reconstructionists expect God's highly divisive historical sanctions. They expect New Covenant history to realize *visibly* the promise of Old Covenant cultural restoration.

> Behold, I will gather them out of all countries, whither I have driven them in mine anger, and in my fury, and in great wrath; and I will bring them again unto this place, and I will cause them to dwell safely: And they shall be my people, and I will be their God: And I will give them one heart, and one way, that they may fear me for ever, for the good of them, and of their children after them: And I will make an everlasting covenant with them, that I will not turn away from them, to do them good; but I will put my fear in their hearts, that they shall not depart from me. Yea, I will rejoice over them to do them good, and I will plant them in this land assuredly with my whole heart and with my whole soul. For thus saith the LORD; Like as I have brought all this great evil upon this people, so will I bring upon them all the good that I have promised them (Jer. 32:37-42).

This is what David taught:

> Fret not thyself because of evildoers, neither be thou envious against the workers of iniquity. For they shall soon be cut down like the grass, and wither as the green herb. Trust in the LORD, and do good; so shalt thou dwell in the land, and verily thou shalt be fed. Delight thyself also in the LORD; and he shall give thee the desires of thine heart. Commit thy way unto the LORD; trust also in him; and he shall bring it to pass. And he shall bring forth thy righteousness as the light, and thy judgment as the noonday. Rest in the LORD, and wait patiently for him: fret not thyself because of him who prospereth in his way, because of the man who bringeth wicked devices to pass. Cease from anger, and forsake wrath: fret not thyself in any wise to do evil. For evildoers shall be cut off: but those that wait upon the LORD, they shall inherit the earth. For yet a little

16. See Chapter 5, above.

> while, and the wicked shall not be: yea, thou shalt diligently consider his place, and it shall not be. *But the meek shall inherit the earth; and shall delight themselves in the abundance of peace.* The wicked plotteth against the just, and gnasheth upon him with his teeth. The Lord shall laugh at him: for he seeth that his day is coming. The wicked have drawn out the sword, and have bent their bow, to cast down the poor and needy, and to slay such as be of upright conversation. Their sword shall enter into their own heart, and their bows shall be broken. A little that a righteous man hath is better than the riches of many wicked. For the arms of the wicked shall be broken: but the LORD upholdeth the righteous. The LORD knoweth the days of the upright: and their inheritance shall be for ever. They shall not be ashamed in the evil time: and in the days of famine they shall be satisfied. But the wicked shall perish, and the enemies of the LORD shall be as the fat of lambs: they shall consume; into smoke shall they consume away. The wicked borroweth, and payeth not again: but the righteous sheweth mercy, and giveth. For such as be blessed of him shall inherit the earth; and they that be cursed of him shall be cut off (Psa. 37:1-22). (emphasis added)

This is why the amillennialist has his heart turned against the Old Testament. It allows us to understand the covenantal foundation of Christ's teachings, such as this one: "Blessed are the meek: for they shall inherit the earth" (Matt. 5:5). Those who are *meek before God* and therefore *active toward His creation* shall exercise dominion in history, if they obey His laws. God's promise of victory to His Church is tied to His covenant. This cannot be understood apart from His covenantal sanctions in history, both positive and negative.

Resurrection, Then Crucifixion

Gaffin insists that the Bible's "eschatology of victory is an eschatology of suffering. . . ." Then he adds what he regards as his *coup d'grace*: "Until Jesus comes again, the church 'wins' by 'losing.' " He then asks a rhetorical question: "What has happened to this theology of the cross in much of contemporary postmillennialism?"[17] I shall provide him with the answer: *it has been modified by the theology of resurrection and ascension.*

---

17. *Ibid.*, p. 216.

Professor Gaffin has managed to reverse the sociological order of events at Calvary. In his sociology of suffering, the crucifixion follows Christ's death and resurrection. He argues as clearly as anyone ever has that our historical condition is to be crucified with Christ; resurrection is strictly a post-historical experience. But Gaffin has a problem: *Jesus Christ announced the Great Commission only **after** His resurrection*. Gaffin's sociology of suffering would reverse Matthew 27 and 28. For Gaffin, the Great Commission is a message of cultural crucifixion. In all honesty, the Roman Catholic crucifix should be Gaffin's symbol of the Great Commission, not the empty cross of Protestantism. The crucifix is appropriate for the Roman Church, which is also amillennial. Those of us who are postmillennial much prefer the symbol of the empty cross. It conforms to our eschatology. So does the empty tomb.

Yes, we take up our cross to follow Him. But that burden is easy (Matt. 11:30). It is not a burden so crushing that Christians are beaten down historically. Carrying the cross of Christ means extending His kingdom in history, *not* being pushed out by Satan's leaven. It is Satan's doom in history to suffer progressive frustration, not the Church's. It is his representatives who are called upon to suffer as God's kingdom unfolds in history. *Christ was nailed to the cross so that Satan could be nailed to the wall.*

I began this chapter with Luke 22, on the Lord's Supper and our lawful exercise of authority in history. Gaffin also places the Lord's Supper at the heart of his eschatology. "According to Jesus, the church will not have drained the shared cup of his suffering until he returns."[18] Gaffin's theological problem is not with postmillennialism as such; it is with what Jesus taught about the judicial implications of His Supper.

He adds this rhetorical question: "Is it really overreacting to say that such triumphalism is repugnant to biblical sensibilities?"[19] Now, there are perfectly good uses for rhetorical questions, even aggressive questions. But there are risks, too. Your target may have an opportunity to respond. He may re-work

18. *Ibid.*, p. 218.
19. *Ibid.*, p. 216.

your rhetorical question, changing only one word, making you the target. He may ask: "Is it really overreacting to say that such *masochism* is repugnant to biblical sensibilities?" Some readers may prefer triumphalism to masochism. Not Gaffiin:

> Suffering is a function of the futility/decay principle pervasively at work in the creation since the fall; suffering is everything that pertains to creaturely experience of this death-principle. . . . Until then, at Christ's return, the suffering/futility/decay principle in creation remains in force, undiminished (but sure to be overcome); it is an enervating factor that cuts across the church's existence, including its mission, in its entirety. The notion that this frustration factor will be demonstrably reduced, and the church's suffering service noticeably alleviated and even compensated, in a future era before Christ's return is not merely foreign to this passage; it trivializes as well as blurs both the present suffering and the future hope/glory. Until his return, the church remains one step behind its exalted Lord; his exaltation means its (privileged) humiliation, his return (and not before), its exaltation.[20]

Christ is now resurrected; the Church will continue to be humiliated. Christ has ascended; the Church will continue to be crucified. Was Christ's resurrection and ascension historical? Yes, says orthodox Christianity. Will the Church experience a progressive taste of either resurrection or ascension in its effect on culture in history? No, says the amillennialist. The Great Commission is a commission to a millennium of defeat.

Understand what this means. Gaffin says it well: the Church of Jesus Christ in history remains *one step behind* the Lord. But the Church's experience is humiliation throughout history. So, what does this tell us of Jesus Christ's influence in history, just one step ahead of the Church? Except for saving individual souls, this influence is nil. Zip. Nada. "Satan 1,000, Christ 0." This is the essence of the amillennial view of history. It reduces covenant theology to pietistic Anabaptism: *save souls, not culture.* It is premillennialism without earthly hope.

20. *Ibid.*, pp. 214-15.

Incurable Schizophrenia; or, St. Verbiage's Dance

Sadly, Gaffin simply could not leave it at this. It was not in him. Having produced a masterpiece of amillennial masochism, he could not resist the lure of the standard Dutch doubletalk. He shifts to the familiar language of optimism. In the appropriately titled subsection, "The Church in the Wilderness," he denies that he has proclaimed "an anemic, escapist Christianity of cultural surrender. Without question, the Great Commission continues fully in force, with its full cultural breadth, until Jesus returns; . . . That mandate, then, is bound to have a robust, leavening impact – one that will redirect every area of life and transform not only individuals but, through them corporately (as the church), their cultures; it already has done so and will continue to do so, until Jesus comes."[21]

Leaven, again. The leaven of victory. The leaven of victory in history. The leaven of victory in culture. But he has already denied this possibility with respect to the general culture. So, what does he mean here by "culture"? He means the institutional Church. What this means is this: *the only culture that the Great Commission of Christ's gospel actually leavens in history is the institutional Church*. "It's ghetto time!"

What, then, is the true meaning of history? We never get a straight answer from the amillennialist. What we get, first, is *doubletalk*. Gaffin denies that his view of Christ's kingdom is static. "If, as some charge, this position is 'staticism,' involving a 'static' view of history, so be it. But it is not a staticism that eliminates real, meaningful progress in history." Second, we get *verbiage*: "It is, we may say, the 'staticism of eschatological dynamism,' staticism in the sense of the kingly permanence of the exalted Christ being effectively manifested – in its full, diverse (and ultimately incalculable, unpredictable) grandeur – over the entire interadvental period, from beginning to end."[22]

"What does this mean?" you ask. It means that Calvinistic amillennialism has no doctrine of historical progress and no doctrine of covenantal cause and effect in history. It means that

21. *Ibid.*, p. 230.
22. *Ibid.*, p. 205.

the *covenantal promise* of God to enforce His law by means of direct sanctions (Deut. 28) was *chronologically limited* to the Old Covenant era, and even then, only inside national Israel (except for that one confounding case of Nineveh). It means that Dr. Gaffin is as embarrassed as all the other pessimillennialists are by the obvious implications of their eschatologies. They do not want to be called cultural defeatists just because they happen to be cultural defeatists. They want to clothe themselves in the optimistic language of postmillennialism. So, the amillennialist's strategy is to spray verbiage all over the page. (The premillennialist keeps talking about how great it is going to be on the far side of Armageddon.)

There is another academic strategy, however: to offer no cultural alternative, but criticize the present humanist world order relentlessly. This does not change anything, but at least it allows Christians, in Gaffin's words, to get in a few licks.[23]

The Consequences of Christ's Resurrection and Ascension

For many years, I have taunted non-theonomists with this slogan: "You can't beat something with nothing." They have said nothing public in response, but they have not needed to. Their implicit answer is clear; it is based self-consciously on their two (or three) pessimillennial eschatologies: "With respect to social theory, we know we have nothing culturally to offer, but since God does not really expect the Church to defeat anything cultural in history anyway, nothing is all we need."

The more intellectually sophisticated among them have contented themselves with writing critical analyses of modern humanist culture. By implication, they are calling Christians to avoid the pits of Babylon. But calling Christians to "Come out from among them!" without also providing at least an outline of a cultural alternative to come *in to* (i.e., to construct) is simply to mimic the fundamentalism of an earlier era: no liquor, no cigarettes, no social dancing, and no movies. It is a scholarly version of fundamentalism's old refrain: "We don't smoke; we don't

---

23. *Ibid.*, p. 222n.

chew; and we don't go with the boys who do!" We cannot seriously expect to recruit dedicated, intellectually serious people into "full-time Christian service" with a worldview that says little more than "we don't go to R-rated movies."[24] So, what good are these negative intellectual critiques? They serve as outlets for highly frustrated Christian intellectuals to produce other highly frustrated Christian intellectuals.

We can see this dilemma in the publishing career of Herbert Schlossberg. His *Idols for Destruction* (1983) is by far the most eloquent criticism of modern humanist thought that anyone has written. Nothing matches it for the number of insights per page. It is like a horde of gems sown in a magnificent tapestry. It even has footnotes ("bottom of the page" notes). Its only defect is that some of its crucial footnotes are missing. But after five years, its publisher, Thomas Nelson, decided not to reprint it. So, a conservative but non-Christian publisher picked it up, a firm with a vision broader than mere financial profit.

The Hermeneutic of Persecution

The problem is not with the book. The problem is with its sequel, *Altars for Construction*. It never got written. I suggested the title to Schlossberg, but he decided instead to begin a long-term research project on the history of the persecution of the Church. This would be a worthy project for a Greek Orthodox scholar. Greek Orthodoxy teaches that maturity comes only through suffering. God gave them into the hands of the Turks to let them test their theology, just as He gave the Russian Orthodox Church into the hands of the Communists. Nevertheless, Schlossberg's new task is consistent with his amillennialism. What is seldom admitted by amillennialism's adherents is this: amillennialism is a theology that proclaims *personal maturation*

24. I am not exaggerating about the continuing prevalence of such views. Writes one critic of Christian Reconstruction, one of the leading pastors in England, who holds the pulpit in Spurgeon's Metropolitan Tabernacle: "In many cases it [Christian Reconstruction] leads in a subtle way to worldliness. (After all, if Christians are commissioned to take dominion over the arts, and so on, they had better start by participating in them and enjoying them.)" Peter Masters, "World Dominion: The High Ambition of Reconstructionism," *Sword & Trowel* (May 24, 1990), p. 19.

through suffering rather than through exercising dominion. It does not have a concept of institutional development.

Schlossberg, as an amillennialist, has made a crucially important presupposition, one that governs all amillennial views of Church history: "The Bible can be interpreted as a string of God's triumphs disguised as disasters."[25] We see this principle of the disguised victory illustrated most graphically at the cross: what appeared to be Satan's greatest victory was in fact his judicial seal of doom. But this was true only because of what followed: Christ's bodily resurrection and ascension to the right hand of God in heaven. If these historical events had not followed, then the amillennial hermeneutic of persecution would be valid. Had Jesus not risen from the dead in history, Christianity would be a vain faith, as Paul said: ". . . we have testified of God that he raised up Christ: whom he raised not up, if so be that the dead rise not. For if the dead rise not, then is not Christ raised: And if Christ be not raised, your faith is vain; ye are yet in your sins" (I Cor. 15:15b-17). The reason why the hermeneutic of persecution is a legitimate tool of biblical interpretation for events that took place before the death and bodily resurrection of Jesus Christ is that it is not an equally valid tool of historical interpretation for events that have taken place after the bodily resurrection and ascension of Jesus Christ.

I shall put it as bluntly as I can: *Amillennialism is an eschatology that ignores the theological, intellectual, and social consequences of the fact that both Christ's resurrection and His ascension were events in history*. These were trans-historical events, too, but they were events in history. Deny this, and you remove the very heart of Christianity. If Christ did not rise in history, then our faith is vain. Theological liberals, like the Pharisees before them, fully understand this. They deny the historicity of Christ's resurrection in their attempt to destroy the Church. They are following the rival "Great Commission" of the enemies of Christ, which is recorded in the text of Matthew's gospel immediately prior to

25. Herbert Schlossberg, *Idols for Destruction: Christian Faith and Its Confrontation with American Society* (Nashville, Tennessee: Nelson, 1983), p. 304. Reprinted by Regnery Gateway, 1990.

Jesus' issuing of His Great Commission to the Church:

> Now when they were going, behold, some of the watch came into the city, and shewed unto the chief priests all the things that were done. And when they were assembled with the elders, and had taken counsel, they gave large money unto the soldiers, Saying, Say ye, His disciples came by night, and stole him away while we slept. And if this come to the governor's ears, we will persuade him, and secure you. So they took the money, and did as they were taught: and this saying is commonly reported among the Jews to this day (Matt. 28:11-15).

Bible-believing Christians must publicly affirm the reality of the bodily resurrection and ascension of Jesus Christ in history. This means that *Christians must also affirm the* ***consequences*** *of both the resurrection and the ascension, including their social and cultural consequences*. Amillennialism's hermeneutic of persecution is therefore not valid as a primary classification device to evaluate the entire work of the Church in history. There is more to the progress of the Church in history than its persecution. In short, *there is more to Christianity's victory in history than its hypothetical cultural defeat in history*. But this is what amillennialism explicitly and self-consciously denies. It proclaims cultural defeat.

Schlossberg understands that there has to be more to the interpretation of history. But as an amillennialist and a non-theonomist, he does not speculate in public about what this might be. He writes: "We need a theological interpretation of disaster."[26] The Church has needed this for many centuries. So have the humanists. The devastating Lisbon earthquake of 1755 shook not just the foundations of Lisbon; it shook the foundations of Enlightenment optimism. So have major catastrophes ever since. If man is essentially good, then why do such terrible things happen to large numbers of us?

What the Bible has given us is a *covenantal* theory of disaster: men will be called to account in history by God whenever they systematically refuse to obey His Bible-revealed laws. But this is too much to swallow for millions of Christians and billions of

26. *Idem.*

non-Christians, who agree on one thing: God's Bible-revealed laws for society are null and void today. So are His sanctions.

Conclusion

Gaffin ends his essay with a footnote, one which makes a very important point, though astoundingly misleading. He argues that the final judgment is part of history. Now, nothing could be farther from the accepted use of language. The final judgment is the consummation of history, a radical, discontinuous event that cannot be accelerated or retarded by any normal, continuous actions by men in history. It is exclusively God's intervention into the historical process that will abolish the historical process. "The enemy that sowed them is the devil; the harvest is the end of the world; and the reapers are the angels. As therefore the tares are gathered and burned in the fire; so shall it be in the end of this world" (Matt. 13:39-40). This is *the end of*, not *an aspect of*, the historical process.

He offers his theory of why people become premillennialists and postmillennialists: they seek evidence of God's sanctions in history. I believe he is correct. This is surely what this book is all about. But this search, in Gaffin's eyes, is a major misunderstanding of the Bible. He pulls no punches. (I really do appreciate his vitriolic confrontational style, so unlike the normal academic discourse of theologians; it helps to keep the readers awake. My only regret is that he put this gem in a footnote; vitriol ought to be right up there in the middle of the text, where it belongs. As I said before, Gaffin has the polemical gift. My only disappointment is his use of a wishy-washy, academic phrase, "it seems.")

> My surmise is that, for many, a significant factor disposing them toward either a premil or a postmil position stems from etherialized, even insipid, less-than-biblical understandings of the eternal state. Such rarified, colorless conceptions give rise to the conviction – compounded by a missing or inadequate awareness of the realized eschatology taught in Scripture – that eventually God must somehow "get in his licks" and "settle things" in history, as distinct from eternity. But what is the eternal order other than the consummation of *history*, the historical process come to *its* final fruition? The

> new heavens and earth, inaugurated at Christ's return, will be the climactic vindication of God's covenant and, so, his final historical triumph, the ultimate realization of his purposes for the original creation, forfeited by the first Adam and secured by the last. Inherent in both a postmil and a premil outlook, it seems, is the tendency, at least, toward an unbiblical, certainly un-Reformed separation or even polarizartion of creation and redemption/eschatology.[27]

The New Heavens and New Earth are exclusively future, he insists, contrary to Isaiah 65:17-23. Professor Gaffin preaches a "realized eschatology," except when it actually comes to *real* realized eschatology. Then he preaches *deferred eschatology*: victory beyond history.

He tells us that Jesus secured what Adam forfeited. Indeed, Christ regained title to the whole world.[28] Adam had the legal authorization from God to leave an inheritance to his heirs. So does Jesus. But amillennialists insist that Jesus merely secured title; *title will not be transferred to His people progressively in history*. Again, this is "definitivism" apart from progressivism; it is the fundamental theological error of all amillennialism. It has no vision of the progressive realization of Christ's definitive conquest in history. Christ's conquest in history is assumed to be based exclusively on power, not on covenantal faithfulness, and it will be achieved only *ultimately*, i.e., outside of history: in heaven (Church Triumphant) and at the end of history (Church Resurrected). It supposedly has nothing to do with the Church Militant (history). In amillennialism, there is no progressive *kingdom* development in history toward the present triumphant condition of the Church in heaven. While our citizenship is in heaven, this heavenly "passport" progressively entitles us only to the kinds of rights and benefits given to someone in Iraq who holds an Israeli passport. (This defeatist outlook on Church history is equally true of premillennialism.) The result is predictable: the Church Militant has become in our day the Church Wimpetant.

---

27. Gaffin, p. 222n.

28. Gary North, *Inherit the Earth: Biblical Blueprints for Economics* (Ft. Worth, Texas: Dominion Press, 1987), pp. 61-62.

If this is "realized" eschatology, I'd prefer another option. So would a lot of other Christians, which is why Calvinistic amillennialism cannot recruit and keep the brighter, more activist students. Gaffin tells his disciples that they, like the Church, have a lifetime of frustration ahead of them. This comforts the pietists among them, but it drives the activists in the direction of covenantal postmillennialism, which offers a consistent and Bible-based alternative. Gaffin's amillennialism of pre-1940 Holland cannot compete effectively against it.

Westminster Seminary and Reformed Presbyterian in general need to return to the optimistic vision presented by J. Gresham Machen in 1932, in the midst of his courageous battle against theological liberalism in the Northern Presbyterian Church. As a postmillennialist of the Princeton Seminary variety, he believed in a coming discontinuity, a burst of new power:

> We who are reckoned as "conservatives" in theology are seriously misrepresented if we are regarded as men who are holding desperately to something that is old merely because it is old and are inhospitable to new truths. On the contrary, we welcome new discoveries with all our heart; and we are looking, in the Church, not merely for a continuation of conditions that now exist but for a burst of new power. My hope of that new power is greatly quickened by contact with the students of Westminster Seminary. There, it seems to me, we have an atmosphere that is truly electric. It would not be surprising if some of these men might become the instruments, by God's grace, of lifting preaching out of the sad rut into which it has fallen, and of making it powerful again for the salvation of men.[29]

Sadly, he failed to articulate his eschatology, and his successors at Westminster abandoned it. The amillennialism of Dutch Calvinism soon triumphed at Westminster. His academic and ecclesiastical successors have had no faith in the burst of new power that he dreamed of. In this sense, it is the Christian Reconstruction movement that is the spiritual heir of Machen.

---

29. J. Gresham Machen, "Christianity in Conflict," in Vergilius Ferm (ed.), *Contemporary American Theology* (New York: Round Table Press, 1932), I, pp. 269-70.

10

PIETISTIC POSTMILLENNIALISM

A holy disposition and spiritual taste, where grace is strong and lively, will enable the soul to determine what actions are right and becoming Christians, not only more speedily but far more exactly than the greatest abilities without it. . . . He has, as it were, almost a spirit within him that guides him. The habit of his mind is attended with a taste by which he immediately relishes that air and mien which is benevolent, and disrelishes the contrary. . . . Thus it is that a spiritual disposition and taste teaches and guides a man in his behaviour in the world.

Jonathan Edwards (1747)[1]

By what standard?

R. J. Rushdoony (1959)[2]

The postmillennial viewpoint is committed to optimism regarding the outcome of the Church's efforts in history. As is the case in so many movements, there is a division within the camp. There is a biblical law-oriented, social reform-oriented wing and a more antinomian, socially non-committal, personal transformation-oriented wing. Both believe in the power of the Holy Spirit to transform men and societies, but there is a great division over the nature of the link between personal transformation and social transformation. We can call one wing the *judicialists* and the other wing the *pietists*.

---

1. Jonathan Edwards, *A Treatise Concerning the Religious Affections*, vol. III of *Select Works of Jonathan Edwards* (London: Banner of Truth Trust, [1746] 1961), p. 209.

2. R. J. Rushdoony, *By What Standard?: An Analysus of the Philosophy of Cornelius Van Til* (Tyler, Texas: Thoburn Press, [1959] 1983).

Postmillennialism is an ancient view of eschatology, going back at least to Eusebius (early 4th century). It was not, as is charged by dispensational theologians (though never by dispensational Church historians holding the Ph.D.), invented in the early eighteenth century by the Unitarian, Daniel Whitby. I mention this because it has been part of the dispensational apologetic to lie, decade after decade, about Whitby's supposed inventing of postmillennialism. Because the dispensationalists' rhetoric equates postmillennialism with theological liberalism (e.g., the late nineteenth-century social gospel movement),[3] it has been embarrassing for them to admit to their students that postmillennialism was pioneered in part by Augustine and John Calvin, and developed more fully by the Puritans of the seventeenth century. The Puritans were the most orthodox Protestants in history, so this creates a major problem for the dispensationalists when they try to equate liberalism and postmillennialism. Any time you see some author write that Whitby invented postmillennialism, you can be absolutely sure that this person has never studied Church history or the history of doctrine from a specialist in either field, unless he is a self-conscious, deliberate liar and dispensational propagandist who has decided to mislead his readers for the sake of "the cause."[4]

---

3. They seldom explain that the social gospel movement was a self-consciously secularization of postmillennialism, just as the Enlightenment's optimism was. Liberalism has been successful because it borrowed from postmillennialism, not pessimillennialism. The liberals have understood that a vision of assured defeat is antithetical to the idea of cultural conquest. So have the pietists, who hate the very idea of cultural conquest, as we see in the writings of the English Baptist, Peter Masters: "May the Lord keep us all dedicated wholly to the work of the Gospel, and deliver us from taking an unbiblical interest in social affairs (especially out of frustration at the poor progress of our evangelistic labours!)." Masters, "World Dominion: The High Ambition of Reconstructionism," *Sword & Trowel* (May 24, 1990), p. 21. The humanist-pietist alliance continues.

4. This myth of Whitby as the founder of postmillennialism, while known to be false by the better-informed adherents of dispensationalism, is simply too tempting for some of them to resist, since it was what they were taught at Dallas Seminary way back when. House and Ice repeat it in their book, *Dominion Theology: Blessing or Curse?* (Portland, Oregon: Multnomah Press, 1988), p. 209. Kenneth Gentry, a former dispensationalist, shows in detail why this traditional myth of dispensational apologetics is historically false, and why anyone with the barest understanding of Church history would know it to be false: Greg L. Bahnsen and Kenneth L. Gentry, Jr., *House Divided: The Break-Up of Dispensational Theology* (Tyler, Texas: Institute for Christian Economics, 1989), pp. 245-50,

The great promoters of early modern postmillennialism were the Scottish Calvinists and English Puritans of the seventeenth century. It was they who wrote the Westminster Confession of Faith and the Larger Catechism, Answer 191 of which is postmillennial. It was dispensationalism that appeared late – about 1830 – rather than postmillennialism.[5] Postmillennialism has been linked to a defense of biblical law only in the case of the Puritans, especially the New England Puritans,[6] and the Christian Reconstruction movement. In this sense, Christian Reconstruction is socially (judicially) neo-Puritan.[7] It is not an heir of the other Puritan tradition, best represented by the mid-seventeenth-century pietist expositor, William Gurnall.[8] The pietist wing of Puritanism emphasized the discipline of personal introspection, extended prayer, and personal, individualistic ethics to the exclusion of programs for social transformation. It was more Baptist-individualist in outlook than Presbyterian-covenantal. It is with us still.[9]

253-54, 306-7. I had challenged Ice on this point several months before *Dominion Theology* appeared, in our debate in Dallas. Ice said absolutely nothing in response, yet he dishonestly repeated the myth in his book later in the year. (Audiotapes of this nationally broadcast radio debate are available from the Institute for Christian Economics.) The myth is repeated by Marvin Rosenthal, *The Pre-Wrath Rapture of the Church* (Nashville, Tennessee: Nelson, 1990), p. 50, and by David Allen Lewis in his book, *Prophecy 2000* (Green Forest, Arkansas: New Leaf Press, 1990), p. 275. Mr. Lewis cites as proof *Dominion Theology*. The myth is also promoted by Robert P. Lightner, Th.D., a professor at Dallas Seminary: *The Last Days Handbook* (Nashville, Tennessee: Nelson, 1990), p. 80. These authors are not well read in Church history. Professors House and Lightner have no excuse.

5. In response, the standard dispensational apologetic is to point to the ancient origins of premillennialism, thereby deflecting attention from the main historical question: the date of the origin of dispensationalism. This deflection technique has worked quite well in dispensational seminary classrooms, at least with C-average students, so the defenders of dispensationalism continue to repeat the refrain outside the classroom. Then they wonder why other theologians and serious Bible students do not take them or their theology seriously. See, for example, John Walvoord's review of *House Divided* in *Bibliotheca Sacra* (July-Sept. 1990), almost all of which is devoted to a recapitulation of the history of non-dispensational premillennialism.

6. Gary North (ed.), Symposium on Puritanism and Law, *Journal of Christian Reconstruction*, V (Winter 1978-79).

7. Christian Reconstruction's adoption of the presuppositional apologetics of Cornelius Van Til distinguishes it from the older Puritanism, which was still infused with secular rationalism.

8. William Gurnall, *A Christian in Complete Armour*, 2 vols. (London: Banner of Truth Trust, [1655-62] 1964).

9. The Banner of Truth Trust in Scotland and England defends this older, pietistic

The indivisible covenantal link between biblical law and postmillennialism, as I have argued, is the presence of God's sanctions in history. If there were no guaranteed historic sanctions, then the two positions could be held independently, but covenant theology does not allow this. Logically, the two may somehow be separated; theologically, they cannot be. There is positive corporate feedback in history for covenant-keepers and negative corporate feedback for covenant-breakers.[10]

Revivalism

The kind of Calvinistic postmillennialism preached by Jonathan Edwards was non-theonomic. It relied entirely on the movement of the Holy Spirit in men's hearts. The revivalist preachers of the Great Awakening did not discuss the possibility of progressive cultural transformation in response to widespread communal covenantal faithfulness to the stipulations of biblical law. This was the great defect with the postmillennial revival inaugurated by Edwards and his followers. They fully expected to see the blessings of God come as a result of strictly individualistic conversions. They had no social theory relating personal salvation and social transformation. In this sense, Jonathan Edwards was not the last New England Puritan; he was a pietist to the core. He and his followers destroyed the cultural remnants of Puritanism in New England.[11]

Consider Edwards' *Treatise on the Religious Affections*. There is nothing on the specifics of the law of God for culture. Page after page is filled with the words "sweet" and "sweetness." A diabetic reader is almost risking a relapse by reading this book in one sitting. The words sometimes appear three or four times on a page. Consider these phrases: "sweet entertainment," "sweet ideas," "sweet and ravishing entertainment," "sweet and admirable manifestations," "glorious doctrines in his eyes, sweet

---

Puritanism. It is revivalist in orientation. For a recent example, see Errol Hulse, "Reconstruction, Restprationism or Puritanism," *Reformation Today*, No. 116 (July-Aug. 1990).

10. Ray R. Sutton, *That You May Prosper: Dominion By Covenant* (Tyler, Texas: Institute for Christian Economics, 1987), ch. 4.

11. Richard L. Bushman, *From Puritan to Yankee: Character and the Social Order in Connecticut, 1690-1765* (Cambridge, Massachusetts: Harvard University Press, 1967).

to the taste," "hearts filled with sweetness." All these appear in just two paragraphs.[12] And while Edwards was preaching the sweetness of God, Arminians were "hot-gospeling" the Holy Commonwealth of Connecticut into political antinomianism.[13] Where sweetness and emotional hot flashes are concerned, we learn that Calvinistic antinomian preaching is no match for Arminian antinomian preaching.

The Great Awakening of the mid-1700's faded, and it was followed by the Arminian revival of the early 1800's – the Second Great Awakening – leaving emotionally burned-over districts and cults as its devastating legacy to America.[14] Because the postmillennial preaching of the Edwardsians was culturally antinomian and pietistic, it crippled the remnants of Calvinistic political order in the New England colonies, helping to produce a vacuum that Arminianism and then Unitarianism filled.[15]

This is not to argue that these revivals were uniformly negative in their effects. People did get saved. The Holy Spirit was at work. But so was Satan. In the end, culturally speaking, the negative forces won out. The antinomianism of the two Great Awakenings triumphed institutionally. Peter Leithart is correct: "Antinomian revivalism shifted the basis for social theory from the theocratic and authoritarian Puritan emphasis to a democratic one."[16] A common-ground, religiously neutral political order became the new ideal. Thus was born the American civil religion. The pietist-humanist alliance became law.

The Calvinistic postmillennialism of the nineteenth century was only marginally superior to Edwards' version. It rejected

12. Edwards, *Religious Affections*, pp. 175-76.

13. On the opposition to Edwards' toleration of revivalism, not from theological liberals but from orthodox Calvinistic pastors, see Bushman, *From Puritan to Yankee*, Parts 4 and 5. Bushman also explains how the Great Awakening was a disaster for the legal remnants of biblical law in the colony of Connecticut. The political order was forced into theological neutralism, which in turn aided the rise of Deism and liberalism.

14. Whitney R. Cross, *The Burned-Over District: The Social and Intellectual History of Enthusiastic Religion in Western New York, 1800-1850* (Ithaca, New York: Cornell University Press, [1950] 1982).

15. Gary North, *Political Polytheism: The Myth of Pluralism* (Tyler, Texas: Institute for Christian Economics, 1989), pp. 355-62.

16. Peter J. Leithart, "Revivalism and American Protestantism," *Christianity and Civilization*, No. 4 (1985), p. 58.

(i.e., rarely discussed) the Old Testament case laws. It was not tied explicitly to biblical creationism, so Warfield's acceptance of Scottish common sense rationalism and his acceptance of long ages of geological and biological history undercut the Princeton Seminary apologetic.[17]

Without explicitly biblical standards of righteousness – point three of the biblical covenant model[18] – meaning standards for *corporate* righteousness, there has to be an appeal to some sort of common sense, natural law-based ethical system. This idea undermines the idea of a uniquely biblical social ethics. It is Trojan horse ethics, or borrowing from Van Til, the nose of the covenant-breaking camel inside the covenant-keeper's tent. The Bible-believing postmillennialist who rejects the legally binding character of the case laws of the Old Testament finds himself epistemologically helpless in the face of the proposed reform program of the social gospel postmillennialist or the liberation theology postmillennialist. All he can do is propose some version of the right-wing Enlightenment (free market economics) or medieval guild socialism as an alternative. The debate becomes a shouting match of "I like this program best!"

Boettner's Postmillennialism

No better example of the ideological helplessness of the non-theonomic postmillennialist can be found in recent history than Loraine Boettner. His chapter, "The World Is Growing Better," gives away the store to the humanists, and all in the name of Jesus. Ignoring the case laws of the Old Testament, on what compelling basis could Boettner have opposed the looming rise of the humanists' New World Order? He cites the following as evidence of Christian social progress: "A spirit of cooperation is much more manifest among the nations than it has ever been before."[19]

17. Gary North, *Dominion and Common Grace: The Biblical Basis of Progress* (Tyler, Texas: Institute for Christian Economics, 1987), Appendix: "Warfield's Vision of Victory: Lost and Found."

18. Sutton, *That You May Prosper*, ch. 3.

19. Loraine Boettner, *The Millennium* (Philadelphia: Presbyterian & Reformed, 1958), p. 39.

He offers as proof of this argument the post-World War II growth of compulsory, tax-financed, government-to-government foreign aid programs. "As evidence of international good will witness the fact that the United States this fiscal year (July, 1957 to July, 1958) appropriated more than three billion dollars for the foreign aid and national security program, and since the end of World War II has given other nations more than sixty billion dollars for those purposes." (This surely sounds like a defense of political liberalism.) Added to this, he says, was lots of voluntary international giving. "This huge amount of goods and services has been given freely by this enlightened and predominantly Protestant nation to nations of other races and religions, with no expectation that it will ever be paid back, an effective expression of unselfishness and international good will."[20] Boettner was not a political liberal; he was merely a traditional pietistic postmillennialist.[21]

Twenty years later or thereabouts, a friend of Ray Sutton's phoned Boettner and asked him some questions. "How do you believe the millennium will come?", he asked. Boettner replied (in good Edwardsian fashion): "I believe that a great revival will sweep the earth." The friend then asked: "Yes, but how will you know when that great revival has come?" Boettner replied: "I don't know. I never thought about that question before." This is the problem. Without biblical law, we have no biblical standards of corporate transformation.

When Sutton related his account of this discussion, he was unaware that Boettner was still alive.[22] A few weeks later, he received a letter from Boettner, one of the last that he ever wrote. He denied having said such a thing. His explanation of how he knew he could not have said it is worth reprinting, and Sutton reprinted it:

---

20. *Idem.*

21. Murray N. Rothbard has made a cogent case for a link between early twenteith-century Progressivism-statism and a szecularized version of pietistic postmillennialism. Rothbard, "World War I as Fulfillment: Power and the Intellectuals," *Journal of Libertarian Stidies*, IX (Winter 1989), pp. 83-87, 95, 102-3.

22. Ray R. Sutton, "Covenantal Postmillennialism," *Covenant Renewal*, III (Feb. 1989), p. 3.

> In this book, *The Millennium*, page 58, I state that the millennium comes by imperceptible degrees, and I liken it to the coming of spring and summer, that there are many advances and many apparent setbacks as the winter winds give way to the gentler spring breezes "and after a time we find ourselves in the glorious summer season." And we certainly do know that we have passed from winter to summer. I add that we cannot pinpoint the arrival of the millennium any more than we can pinpoint certain great events in history, and that over the long term the millennium comes as the Gospel is preached over the world and the Holy Spirit brings more and more people into the kingdom. So it is incorrect to quote me as having said that I had never thought about that question before.[23]

Sutton points out that Boettner's response indicates that Sutton's account of the phone conversation had been on target. Boettner reverts to a metaphor of seasonal change instead of offering explicitly biblical standards of covenantal justice and prosperity. Sutton comments: "Saying you perceive the kingdom just as you would realize that it is Summer is not exactly telling *how* a person knows. Nor is it telling you how to know it is Summer. In the February issue of *Covenant Renewal*, this was my initial point: What are the concrete indicators that the millennium has arrived? . . . He argues like the romantic who simply says, 'I know I'm in love because I know. Love is like the Summer that follows the cold wintry winds of infatuation. You know when it has arrived, and I'm telling you that I know I'm in love.' "

Sutton has identified Boettner's theological problem: his unwillingness to use the biblical covenant in his analysis of history. "The real problem, however, is that Dr. Boettner has an individualistic view of the millennium, which is opposed to a covenantal perspective." So did virtually all the postmillennialists in modern history, except for the Puritans activists. To demonstrate the advent of the millennial era of blessings, traditional postmillennialists would apparently add up the number of professing Christians, and then compare this figure with the

---

23. Sutton, "A Letter from Loraine or a Covenantal View of the Millennium," *ibid.*, III (May 1989), p. 1.

number of professing non-Christians. In response to such thinking, Sutton cites Isaiah 2:2-4:

> And it shall come to pass in the last days, that the mountain of the LORD'S house shall be established in the top of the mountains, and shall be exalted above the hills; and all nations shall flow unto it. And many people shall go and say, Come ye, and let us go up to the mountain of the LORD, to the house of the God of Jacob; and he will teach us of his ways, and we will walk in his paths: for out of Zion shall go forth the law, and the word of the LORD from Jerusalem. And he shall judge among the nations, and shall rebuke many people: and they shall beat their swords into plowshares, and their spears into pruninghooks: nation shall not lift up sword against nation, neither shall they learn war any more.

The issue is not merely personal conversion; the issue is the law of God. *There must be institutional conversion to God, not simply personal conversion*. "Isaiah says that it is when the nations of the world come to Christ and to the *Law of God* that we not only know they have truly come to Christ, but we know that the millennium has arrived. I don't agree that we will not definitively be able to mark the beginning of the millennium. It is when the nations of the world give up natural law. . . . It is when the nations of the world turn to the Law of God for their politics, their economics, their science, their everything."[24] In short, "Isaiah not only describes conversions, he speaks about *Law-abiding conversions*. He not only discusses converted people, he describes converted nations with *converted laws*, converted politics, converted economics, converted education and so forth. And, each converted sphere is known to be converted by its compliance to the *Law of God*. As Scripture says, 'By this we know that we know Him, if we keep His commandments' (I John 2:3). Converted Christians are not enough! Converted Christians involved in politics or any number of activities is not enough! Converted Christians who keep God's commandments, however, is more than enough! For too long, Christians have naively thought that all they need is a moral majority. Yes, we

24. *Ibid.*, p. 2.

need a majority of Christians, but we need Christians committed to the Biblical *covenant* and who have the opportunity, authority and grace to apply God's *Law* in the societies of the world. Until they do, the millennium has not begun."[25]

It is worth noting that Rev. Jerry Falwell's Moral Majority organization was officially shut down by its board of trustees three months after Sutton's newsletter appeared. America's majority is not moral, biblically speaking, and common-ground morality is in any case insufficient to redeem a civilization that remains under a centuries-old, self-malectory oath to God.[26]

Conclusion

Ever since the demise of the original Puritan theological and cultural vision, based on an affirmation of Old Covenant law, postmillennialism in Anglo-American history has been deeply antinomian. It has not affirmed the continuing validity of the Old Covenant case laws. It has therefore had nothing except the Spirit-led feelings of the individual human heart to test both behavior and institutional operations. It has had no concept of institutional justice. It has affirmed progress, but it has not affirmed specific standards of progress. It predicts that things will eventually get better, yet it has no formal, judicial standards of "better."

This implicit individualism has been out of conformity with biblical covenantalism. Nineteenth-century Presbyterian postmillennialism rested on the presupposition of the validity of Scottish common sense rationalism. This philosophical system, like all the other philosophical products of Newtonianism, did not survive the effects of Kantianism, Darwinism, and modern quantum physics. Thus, postmillennialism faded rapidly after the death of B. B. Warfield until Christian Reconstruction's revival of a neo-Puritan postmillennialism in the 1970's.

It is not enough to predict the coming of a wave of mass conversions. It is not enough to pray and work for them. It is mandatory that specifically biblical categories be used to distin-

25. *Idem.*
26. North, *Political Polytheism*, ch. 11.

guish a work of God from a spiritual counterfeit. Professed conversions apart from the ethical and judicial requirements of the biblical covenant are counterfeits. We have seen antinomian revivals before, and they do not last. They leave in their wake spiritually burned-over districts, emotional exhaustion, and humanism. What we need are mass conversions to Christ which lead men to ask the two crucial questions: "How should we then live?" and "What is to be done?" Then the new converts must be directed to the Bible – all of it, not just the New Testament – for their answers.

11

WILL GOD DISINHERIT CHRIST'S CHURCH?

Beware of false prophets, which come to you in sheep's clothing, but inwardly they are ravening wolves. Ye shall know them by their fruits. Do men gather grapes of thorns, or figs of thistles? Even so every good tree bringeth forth good fruit; but a corrupt tree bringeth forth evil fruit. A good tree cannot bring forth evil fruit, neither can a corrupt tree bring forth good fruit. Every tree that bringeth not forth good fruit is hewn down, and cast into the fire. Wherefore by their fruits ye shall know them (Matt. 7:15-20).

For many decades, a series of sensational prophecies have been made in the name of biblical revelation. Few of these events have come true. The predictors have identified antichrist after antichrist, and each one has died. For over 70 years, they have identified the Soviet Union as the prophesied aggressor from the north,[1] yet overnight, in July of 1990, they switched to Saddam Hussein's Iraq. Hal Lindsey told a reporter that Hussein is rebuilding Babylon, which Zechariah prophesied.[2] And so it goes, and has gone, throughout the twentieth century.

These prophecies-predictions are not harmless. They embarrass the Church. But my objection to them is not my concern over public relations with the secular world. My concern is ethical. I argue that the motivation of these false teachers is not merely their desire to sell books and become famous men after

---

1. Dwight Wilson, *Armageddon Now!: The Premillenarian Response to Russia and the Soviet Union and Israel Since 1917* (Grand Rapids, Michigan: Baker, 1977).

2. Scott Baradell, "Prophets of doom: We're a leg up on Armageddon," *Dallas Times Herald* (Sept. 8, 1990), p. A-14.

the prophesied events take place. Their goal is ethical. Their goal is to deflect Christians from the Great Commission, as defined by the Bible rather than by the gospel tract association. They wish to substitute a very narrow plan of salvation for the Bible's comprehensive plan. Pessimillennialism is basic to this strategy of deflection.

Narrowing One's Ethical Vision

Marvin Rosenthal has written a book that defends what seems to be a mid-tribulational view of the Rapture, although he wants to avoid the term "tribulation." In the Introduction to his book, he makes this statement: "The importance of understanding still unfulfilled prophecy for contemporary Christian living cannot be overstated."[3] He then spends three hundred pages (no subject index) describing his new interpretation of the seventieth week of Daniel, etc. But there is nothing in the book that tells us what difference, specifically, any of this makes for contemporary Christian living. He never bothers to discuss contemporary Christian living. (Prophecy books never do.) Chapter 20 is titled, "The Prewrath Rapture: Catalyst for Holy Living." Yet there is not one word on any specifically ethical application of his thesis. He tells us only to be godly, for Jesus is coming soon. The chapter is basically a plea to the reader to accept the author's thesis. He offers us his thesis of the seven churches of the Book of Revelation: more discussion of the timing the Rapture. That is all. End of chapter. End of book.

He tells us – as four or more generations of dispensational preachers have assured us – that "At the present moment of history, the planet Earth is in grave crises. This celestial ball is on a collision course with its Creator. Man has pushed the self-destruct button."[4] What is the Church to do? He does not say. But he assures us, once again, that "Jesus is coming again. That is the blessed (living) hope. At his coming (*parousia*), He will raise the dead and rapture the righteous. Then He will pour

---

3. Marvin Rosenthal, *The Pre-Wrath Rapture of the Church* (Nashville, Tennessee: Nelson, 1990), p. xi.

4. *Ibid.*, p. 295.

out His wrath on the wicked before physically returning to the earth. *Even so, come, Lord Jesus* (Rev. 22:20)."[5] End of book.

So, he says confidently, "The importance of understanding still unfulfilled prophecy for contemporary Christian living cannot be overstated." Then what, exactly, is its importance? *How should we then live?* The answer from the world of dispensationalism has been the same from the beginning: "This world is doomed, we are running out of time, there is no earthly hope, so attend a prophecy conference soon." *Ethically, dispensationalism is self-consciously an empty box.* Yet it has been the dominant millennial position in modern fundamentalism, which in turn has been the dominant force in American (and Western) Protestant evangelicalism. It is these churches that will probably be the pioneers of any imminent revival. (This thought is almost sufficient to make an amillennialist out of me.)

One major consolation is this: when the great revival comes, and these premillennial churches start growing, they will shift their eschatology. They have been premillennial in order to explain the Church's obvious failure to evangelize the world. Pessimillennialism's two main functions are these: (1) to justify failure in the past and (2) to minimize responsibility in the present. Success will transform the churches' millennial views. When they no longer see themselves as losers in history, Christians will discard their eschatologies of guaranteed defeat.

But is dispensationalism really a theology of defeat? Dave Hunt has answered this better than anyone else: *yes.*

God's Supposed Disinheritance of His Church

I have said earlier that a major incentive for believing the doctrine of the Rapture is that people want to get out of life alive. There is another factor: *the desire to leave nothing valuable behind.* This is not a normal motivation in life. It is not a biblical motivation for a good man. "A good man leaveth an inheritance to his children's children" (Prov. 13:22a). But this is not an acceptable goal if you reject the truth of the second half of the

5. *Ibid.*, p. 297.

proverb, "the wealth of the sinner is laid up for the just." If you think God's plan for history is the opposite, that *the wealth of the just is laid up for the sinner* (pessimillennialism's thesis), then logically you would prefer to cut off the legacy of Christians to their heirs. You would much prefer to see God disinherit His Church in history. An insane view? Not at all, *given the initial covenant-denying assumption*. This is *consistent* pessimillennialism.

Am I exaggerating? Not if Dave Hunt isn't. He writes of the psychological importance of the doctrine of the pre-tribulation Rapture. The Rapture's total cultural discontinuity is far better than death's personal discontinuity, he insists. "The expectancy of being caught up at any moment into the presence of our Lord in the Rapture does have some advantages over a similar expectancy through the possibility of sudden death."

> (1) If we are in a right relationship with Christ, we can genuinely look forward to the Rapture. Yet no one (not even Christ in the Garden) looks forward to death. The joyful prospect of the Rapture will attract our thoughts while the distasteful prospect of death is something we may try to forget about, thus making it less effective in our daily lives.
>
> (2) While the Rapture is similar to death in that both serve to end one's earthly life, the Rapture does something else as well: it signals the climax of history and opens the curtain upon its final drama. It thus ends, in a way that death does not, all human stake in continuing earthly developments, such as the lives of the children left behind, the growth of or the dispersion of the fortune accumulated, the protection of one's reputation, the success of whatever earthly causes one has espoused, and so forth.[6]

It could not be any clearer. When believed, the idea of the pre-tribulation Rapture destroys *all* hope in Christian progress in history. It is the climax of history, Hunt insists. In fact, its more forthright defenders actually say that this is one of its great *advantages* for Christian living. Belief in the pre-tribulation Rapture ends "all human stake in continuing earthly developments." Hunt has not hesitated to tell us the psychological

6. Dave Hunt, "Looking for that Blessed Hope," *Omega Letter* (Feb. 1989), p. 14.

appeal of the Rapture for the average dispensationalist.

Hunt forgets that personal death ends our worrying about earthly things. There are no more tears in heaven. But this future freedom from pain and concern is not good enough to satisfy him. No, he wants more: the utter destruction of every trace of the work of Christians and God's Church in history. He wants *total historical discontinuity* as a result of the coming cosmic discontinuity of the Rapture and the subsequent earthly horrors of the Great Tribulation.[7] He says plainly that the Rapture "signals the climax of history." The dispensationalist equates the so-called "Church Age" with history. We Reconstructionists take Hunt at his word. This is how we have always understood the dispensational view of the Church. This is why we call dispensationalism historically pessimistic: it is pessimistic about God's Church in history. There can be no greater pessimism than this.

Over and over, we Reconstructionists have said that this is what faith in the Rapture produces in *consistent* dispensational theology. Dispensationalists have replied (when they have even bothered to reply) that we are exaggerating, that the dispensational system teaches nothing of the kind. Dave Hunt has spelled it out in no uncertain terms. We were correct. This is exactly the worldview that the dispensational system produces. It took Dave Hunt, the most widely read spokesman for the position in the 1980's, to follow the logic of dispensational theology to its inescapable conclusion. While he is not a theologian, as he freely admits when debating complex topics, his exposition of "plain vanilla" dispensational theology is the view that the average fundamentalist in the pew holds dear. Hunt knows what sells. He sells it. Seminary theologians can protest from now until premillennial kingdom come that Hunt is not a representative thinker. On the contrary, the publicly silent seminary theologians are the ones who are not representative. No one has ever heard of them. The man the dispensational movement's troops read and believe is Dave Hunt.

---

7. This is equally true of John R. Meuther's amillennialism, with its Rapture-like radical discontinuity culturally between history and the post-resurrection world. See above, Chapter 7, pp. 165-67.

The Theological Threat of Activism

Why is Hunt so concerned about people's continuing faith in the Rapture? Because, he says, they are rapidly abandoning it. He goes so far as to call it "One of the most unpopular doctrines today, in stark contrast to its prominence only a few years ago. . . ."[8] Hunt feels the theological ground shaking beneath him. He is in close contact with the fundamentalist world. While he is exaggerating the degree of abandonment, there is little doubt that dispensationalism has lost its appeal in the lives of many of its former adherents. The paperback book writers cried "Antichrist!" too often, and this endless sensationalism produced a de-sensitizing effect in the victims. They are burned out.

What has caused this shift in opinion? From what Hunt indicates in his essay, Christian Reconstructionism. (Would that it were so!) Hunt knows that Jerry Falwell is whistling past the graveyard by telling his followers that it is harder to find a postmillennialist now than a Wendell Willkie button.[9] In two instances, volumes in the Biblical Blueprint Series have been assigned as textbooks to students at Falwell's university. It is dispensationalism, not postmillennialism, that is on the wane.

What would be more accurate for Hunt to say is that the 1980's produced a more activist-minded American fundamentalism. The world around the Church is clearly disintegrating, and a growing minority of Christians sense that they do have some degree of responsibility to reverse this drift. This is a major break from pre-1980 American fundamentalism, and it appalls Hunt. He blames it on the one Christian group that has systematically articulated the *only* theologically consistent justfication for Christian social involvement. He recognizes that theology counts, even when its defenders are presently few in number.

Hunt is extremely upset by Christian Reconstruction's view of historical progress, which he correctly perceives as a direct assault on traditional dispensationalism's view of history:

---

8. Hunt, p. 14.

9. Quoted by Ed Dobson and Ed Hindson, "Apocalypse Now?" *Policy Review* (Fall 1986), p. 20. Both men were employed at the time by Falwell's Liberty University.

> The whole dominion/reconstruction movement is too wedded to an ongoing earthly process stretching into the indeterminate future to be truly faithful to the totality of what Scripture says about being sufficiently disengaged from this world to leave it at a moment's notice.[10]

As is true of premillennialists generally, Hunt does understand the significance of a Christian's personal unwillingness to disengage from this world *before the time that God calls his soul home to heaven because his work is completed* (Phil. 1:20-24). Hunt understands that we are supposed to want to finish our tasks. So, in order to make it easy for us to end all such concerns, he proclaims the doctrine of the Rapture and the subsequent Great Tribulation: events that will bury all of the Church's work in history. He calls this an end to history. But, unlike the amillennial view of Christ's Second Coming, the premillennialist says that Christ has at least a thousand years of work ahead of Him. But this work will be utterly discontinuous from anything the Church achieves in history. This view is wrong.

Our work does have great significance in history. We are building up God's kingdom in history, an idea that Hunt denies in his recent books. He recognizes that we Reconstructionists have a world-transforming vision. He wants to cut that vision short. "Look up!" he shouts. This means, "Stop looking forward to society here on earth through future generations."

Comic Book Theology

Like those plantation slaves in the American South back in 1850, we Christians are told to look up for our deliverance. This means that in the meantime, we should say to the humanists who dominate society, "Yes, massa. We be good, massa. We jus' keep lookin' up, massa. We don' cause you no problems, massa. Jus' don' use that whip, massa!"

And deep down inside, we may think, "Someday, Jesus gonna whip yo' ---! And maybe I will, too." Hunt does:

---

10. Hunt, p. 15.

> Our hope is not in taking over this world, but in being taken to heaven by our Lord, to be married to Him in glory and then to return with Him as part of the armies of heaven to rescue Israel, destroy His enemies and participate in the Millennial reign.[11]

Yes, it is that old Charles Atlas *dynamic tension* syndrome, this time for grown-ups, and without any sweat: new, superhuman bodies for all the saints! "Our hearts should be in perpetual wonder and joy at the prospect of being suddenly caught up to be with Christ, our bodies transformed to be like His body of glory. . . ." And more: "And in our transformed bodies, made like His body of glory, in which we will share His resurrection life, we will reign with Him over this earth for 1,000 years."[12] The trouble is, this is a child's dream. It is the *Shazam* syndrome of the old Captain Marvel comic books. After saying "Shazam," wimpy Billy Batson instantly becomes the invulnerable Captain Marvel. The bad guys tremble. Justice is meted out swiftly. Today's Christians become part of the *Millennial Justice League*. Someday soon, someday soon. . . . Meanwhile, Christians are stuck in the culturally irrelevant bog of history. History is the era of the Church, of Billy Batson, but not of Captain Marvel.

A comic book view of the future has been the dominant outlook of twentieth-century evangelicalism. It has not produced Christian social theory. Today, as Hunt recognizes, some of the troops in the pews have decided that they are too old to be reading comic books. Even some of the seminary professors who teach the future shepherds are having doubts. Time is running out for dispensationalism, one way or another. Either the Rapture confirms it very soon, or else the troops will refuse to renew their subscriptions. Their leaders have cried "Wolf!" too often, just as boys back in 1947 shouted "Shazam!" too often. Nothing happened. Rapture fever eventually cools.

The Premillennialists' Response

Premillennialism does have some understanding of the resur-

---

11. *Idem.*
12. *Idem.*

rection and ascension. The premillennialist expects the good times to come to earth when Christ returns bodily to overcome the weakness of the Church in history. What premillennialism ignores is the doctrine of the Holy Spirit. It also denies the doctrine of God's irresistible grace. What the premillennialist ignores is the question of the two angels to the witnesses of Christ's ascension: "Ye men of Galilee, why stand ye gazing up into heaven. . . ?" (Acts 1:11a). Then the witnesses returned to Jerusalem to await the coming of the Holy Spirit. But premillennialists are still standing around culturally, gazing in hope at heaven.[13] In the meantime, their pockets are being picked by the humanists. "Just keep on looking up," the humanists tell them. "Let us know if you see something."

Dispensationalists do not see persecution as a means of advancing the Church. They see it as one of Satan's means of thwarting the Church. The Church does not advance, in their view. The Church, they insist, will fail in carrying out the Great Commission, even the narrowly defined Great Commission of modern pietism. What they pray for is the Great Escape from persecution during the supposedly imminent Great Tribulation. They want to stop hearing about the need for mass evangelism today. They want to stop having to answer social questions. The way that they are able to do this in good conscience is to deny that there is sufficient time remaining for implementing any fundamental changes in either Church or society.

No Theoretical or Practical Answers

In response to the challenge from Christian Reconstruction, the less well-informed critics have said: "These people have substituted politics for evangelism." This is a lie that cannot be supported from our writings, which is why you never see a single direct quotation from a Reconstructionist source to support this accusation. But this criticism does raise a legitimate question: Do Christian Reconstructionists believe that the "positive feedback" process within a culturally Christian social order

---

13. Dave Hunt, *Whatever Happened to Heaven?* (Eugene, Oregon: Harvest House, 1988).

can be sustained apart from continuing widespread conversions to saving faith? The answer is *no.*[14] Without continuing evangelism and a manifestation of the irresistible grace of God in history, we can expect nothing better than what New England experienced: a slow erosion from Calvinism to the rule of lawyers and merchants, to Arminianism, to Unitarianism, and finally to Teddy Kennedy. There must be divine intervention from outside of history (discontinuity) in order to sustain the blessings of God in history (continuity). Meanwhile, we must obey God. Continuously. Our job is continuity. God's job is discontinuity.

The Christian Church today faces a horrendous problem: it has no answers to the question, "What is to be done?" It has not even thought about an appropriate answer. It has denied the only foundation for constructing a working alternative to humanism: the biblical covenant model. Its theologians and leaders have consistently and publicly denied: (1) the continuing validity of Old Testament law in New Covenant society, (2) God's predictable historical sanctions, and (3) the coming of a millennial era of blessings inaugurated by the Holy Spirit through the preaching of the gospel and the application of God's law to human problems.

Because Christian scholars have denied these fundamental biblical doctrines, they have been unable to formulate a specifically biblical social theory. They have generally denied that such a formulation is even possible. They have repeated the liberals' refrain, "The Bible gives us no blueprints for society." This of necessity has led to a fruitless quest to discover *non-biblical humanist blueprints* that can somehow be made to fit "biblical principles," carefully undefined. This is baptized humanism, and it has been a way of life for the Church for almost two millennia.

No Time for Silence

With the escalating epistemological, moral, and institutional collapse of Western humanism, and the growing skepticism that

---

14. Gary North, *Dominion and Common Grace: The Biblical Basis of Progress* (Tyler, Texas: Institute for Christian Economics, 1987), ch. 6.

threatens to engulf the West, the Church must not remain silent. It must no longer tie its future to a sinking ship: the reigning humanist social order. But to escape the fate of modern humanism – and by "fate," I mean God's historic sanctions – Christians must categorically reject every form of humanism. They must reject the present social order.

This leaves them with the familiar dilemma of all social reformers: *You can't beat something with nothing*. Yet Bible-believing Christians have self-consciously proclaimed the empty condition of their social bag for well over a century. Worse: they have proudly proclaimed its emptiness. They have insisted that all social theories must be constructed apart from the Bible. There are no knowable biblical models, we are assured, even by those who call themselves Calvinists. As Errol Hulse has asked rhetorically: "Who among us is adequately equipped to know which political philosophy most accords with biblical principles?"[15] This professed agnosticism has left the Church with nothing except mumbled platitudes to offer a civilization in crisis. *Evangelism by platitude* is their chosen strategy.

The Great Commission is comprehensive – as comprehensive as all the sins that engulf the world.[16] Redemption is comprehensive – also as comprehensive as all the sins that engulf the world.[17] Therefore, biblical theology is equally comprehensive. It must include the principles – *laws* – by which society can and must be reconstructed. Any theological system that abandons the very idea of such principles of social restoration has understood neither the comprehensive rebellion of modern autonomous man nor the comprehensive redemption offered to him.

Where are Christians supposed to search for these permanent, authoritative social laws? In Aristotle's *Politics*? In Thomas Aquinas' *Summa Theologica*? In Thomas Hobbes' *Leviathan?* In

---

15. Errol Hulse, "Reconstructionism, Restorationism or Puritanism," *Reformation Today*, No. 116 (July-Aug. 1990), p. 25.

16. Kenneth L. Gentry, Jr., *The Greatness of the Great Commission: The Christian Enterprise in a Fallen World* (Tyler, Texas: Institute for Christian Economics, 1990).

17. Gary North, *Is the World Running Down? Crisis in the Christian Worldview* (Tyler, Texas: Institute for Christian Economics, 1988), Appendix C: "Comprehensive Redemption: A Theology for Social Action."

Sir Isaac Newton's *Principia*? In John Locke's *Second Treatise on Government*? In Jean Jacques Rousseau's *Social Contract*? In Thomas Jefferson's *Notes on Virginia*? In Karl Marx's *Capital*? In John Rawls' *A Theory of Justice*?[18] Or in the Bible? When we get direct answers to this question from today's Christian intellectual leaders, depending on the content of their answers, we may begin to move away from the dominant political humanism of our day. Not until then, however.

Without considerable pressure, they will not provide these answers. They haven't in the last two centuries, except when identifying Aquinas or Locke as the proper source. There is no independent biblical social theory. Pessimillennialism and the myth of neutrality have done their work very well. A series of major catastrophes perhaps will undo it.

Biblical Blueprints

What is the alternative? Biblical blueprints.[19] We must proclaim the fact that the Bible does provide biblical blueprints for the reconstruction of society. If this were not true, then there could not be an explicitly biblical social theory. There could not be explicitly biblical social action. This is why the concept of biblical blueprints is anathema to all sides: fundamentalists, neo-evangelicals, Lutherans, traditional Calvinists, and of course secular humanists. The idea of biblical blueprints, when coupled with the idea of God's historical sanctions and postmillennialism, threatens the existing alliance between the humanist power religion and the pietist escape religion. This is why the idea is opposed so consistently in recent Christian social commentary.

Those Christians who maintain that there are no biblical blueprints have a major problem. They live in a society that is operated in terms of non-biblical blueprints. There is no neutrality. There will always be blueprints. Blueprints are an ines-

---

18. It is easy today to dismiss Hitler's *Mein Kampf*. It was not so easy in Germany in 1942. The problem was, not enough Christian leaders said so, authoritatively, from 1924 to 1933. After 1933, it was too late.

19. Gary North, (ed.): *Biblical Blueprint Series*, 10 vols. (Ft. Worth, Texas: Dominion Press, 1986-87).

capable concept. Therefore, Christians must either remain in "exile," or else they must seek deliverance. To seek *deliverance* is necessarily to seek *dominion*. There is no neutrality. *To seek dominion is to seek a biblical social alternative*. Today, most Christians, like their spiritual forebears in Egypt, Assyria, and Babylonia, much prefer exile. They prefer the leaks and onions of Egypt to the responsibility of comprehensive reconstruction.

God requires much more from His people. He required more from them in the wilderness of Sinai, and He requires more today. But like the Israelites in the wilderness, modern Christians, especially the leaders, do not want to hear a message of comprehensive responsibility, let alone preach one. Such a message of responsibility means confronting the Canaanites who control the Promised Land (the whole earth: Matt. 28:18-20). Fed up with today's manna, they are nevertheless unwilling to risk conquering Canaan. After all, as Mr. Lewis so aptly put it: "Unnecessary persecution could be stirred up."[20]

Until the amillennialists and premillennialists offer Bible-based suggestions for Christians to pursue God's comprehensive redemption in New Testament times, their millennial systems will remain fringe theologies for cultural ghettos. There is a lesson in Western history that is dangerous to ignore: where there are ghettos, there will eventually be pogroms of one kind or another. Far better to win the whole society to Christ.

What about God's sanctions in history? What about the future? With the history of God's redemptive acts in history as our background, one thing seems certain: we can expect a major discontinuity. Soon. And I don't mean the Rapture. This discontinuity probably will not be exclusively positive.

Comprehensive Salvation

Salvation is more than just personal. It is institutional. It is even national. We know this has to be the case because of the nature of God's final judgment.

---

20. David Allen Lewis, *Prophecy 2000* (Forest Green, Arkansas: Green Leaf Press, 1990), p. 277.

> When the Son of Man comes in His glory, and all the holy angels with Him, then He will sit on the throne of His glory. All the nations will be gathered before Him, and He will separate them one from another, as a shepherd divides his sheep from the goats. And He will set the sheep on His right hand, but the goats on the left. Then the King will say to those on His right hand, "Come, you blessed of My Father, inherit the kingdom prepared for you before the foundation of the world" (Matt. 25:31-35; New King James Version).

Many people have interpreted such verses as Matthew 25:31-35 as referring exclusively to individual salvation, but the language of the text indicates God's judgment of collectives, not just individual souls. *The text indicates institutional salvation, meaning national restoration*. To restrict the meaning of salvation to the human soul is to misread Scripture.

The passage is clear: the sheep and the goats are symbolic terms for saved and lost *nations*. "All the nations will be gathered before Him, and He will separate them one from another, as a shepherd divides his sheep from the goats. And He will set the sheep on His right hand, but the goats on the left." He will separate nations, one from another. People will enter the resurrected kingdom of Christ as members of nations, just as they enter it as members of racial and cultural groups. History does have meaning in eternity.

> And I saw no temple therein: for the Lord God Almighty and the Lamb are the temple of it. And the city had no need of the sun, neither of the moon, to shine in it: for the glory of God did lighten it, and the Lamb is the light thereof. And the nations of them which are saved shall walk in the light of it: and the kings of the earth do bring their glory and honour into it. And the gates of it shall not be shut at all by day: for there shall be no night there. And they shall bring the glory and honour of the nations into it. And there shall in no wise enter into it any thing that defileth, neither whatsoever worketh abomination, or maketh a lie: but they which are written in the Lamb's book of life (Rev. 21:22-27).

This has to refer to the post-resurrection kingdom, though it may refer also to the present preliminary manifestation of the

New Heaven and New Earth.[21] There are only saints in the city. But these saints are referred to as members of nations: "And the nations of those who are saved shall walk in its light."

Those who confess Christ at judgment day make up one group of nations. Those who refuse to confess Him as Savior make up the other group. Note that there are only two possible confessions ("lip" = confession of faith: Gen. 11:1) – Christ or Satan – but there are numerous nations. There is one kingdom of God, but numerous national representatives of His kingdom.

This points to God's covenantal dealing with mankind as *members of nations*. The division of tongues (languages) at the Tower of Babel is a permanent phenomenon in history. Mankind remains divided into recognizable cultural groups even after the resurrection. Most of us accept this implicitly. We expect to meet relatives beyond the grave. We expect them to resemble whoever they had been on earth. When families are reunited, the children of white caucasians will not be orientals, and the children of blacks will not be eskimos.

This means that some elements of our historical experience are permanent, in the same way that God's eternal rewards to us for our earthly performance are permanent (I Cor. 3:11-14). It also means that *some aspects of nationhood persist beyond the grave* – not the geographical boundaries, but people's shared cultural experiences and presumably also shared memories.

Nations slowly change in history, and borders also change, but nations will always be part of history. While some humanists emphasize the need for internationalism – the ideology of the Tower of Babel – while other humanists emphasize nationalism – a development of the last two centuries – we need to recognize that both internationalism and nationalism are biblically legitimate.[22]

What we have lost in the modern world is the commitment to *localism* – psychologically, judicially, and economically. In the

---

21. David Chilton, *The Days of Vengeance: An Exposition of the Book of Revelation* (Ft. Worth, Texas: Dominion Press, 1987), ch. 21.

22. Gary North, *Healer of the Nations: Biblical Blueprints for International Relations* (Ft. Worth, Texas: Dominion Press, 1987)

medieval period, few people ever journeyed as far as 25 miles from their village. As history has advanced, this restricted mobility has steadily disappeared. So has people's psychological commitment to a home town. The growing mobility of capital and people within nations has overcome geographical localism. Localism will presumably not be a major factor at the resurrection. In a future millennial era characterized by high per capita income, freedom of movement, freedom of trade, and international peace based on one public "lip" – a public confession of Trinitarian faith – we can expect to see nationalism go the way of clannism (tribalism) and localism. Localism will not disappear, but its hold on people's minds will decrease. A vision of God's international kingdom in history will replace the competing regional commitments. It will also replace the humanists' vision of a one-world kingdom.

In the kingdom-expansion phase, however, this may not be true. If men become committed to the four-corners strategy of urban conquest, quadrant by quadrant,[23] they may develop local sympathies and commitments that are stronger than those that exist today, in the Church's passive, pessimillennial phase. A three-way commitment may replace today's unitary nationalism: local (the church's parish), national (the mother tongue), and international (the civilization of God).

If all men have one public "lip," how will there be any anti-Christian nations to divide on Judgment Day? Why will there be goats? First, because there have been evil nations in the past. Their members will be judged. Second, because some members of the future covenanted communities of Christian nations will lie about their faith and commitment. There will be a final falling away at the last day.[24] The public confessions of some groups will change. But this does not mean that a long period in between cannot be confessionally and culturally Christian.

He Shall Overcome

We know there is only one kingdom of God, and it has many

23. See Chapter 12.
24. North, *Dominion and Common Grace*, Preface, pp. 189-90, 248-50.

enemies in history:

> Then cometh the end, when he shall have delivered up the kingdom to God, even the Father; when he shall have put down all rule and all authority and power. For he must reign, till he hath put all enemies under his feet. The last enemy that shall be destroyed is death (I Cor. 15:24-26).

The final overcoming of all rival authorities by Jesus Christ comes at the last judgment, when He triumphs over His enemies, and He delivers His kingdom to God the Father. *Christ's kingdom at last absorbs all other kingdoms.* But the word "absorbs" is metaphorical, related to some organic process. The expansion process of Christ's triumphant kingdom in history is neither mechanical nor organic. It is covenantal. God's kingdom triumphs *judicially*.

The kingdom of God is real. It is a factor in human history. It is something that Christ literally delivers to God. Such a transfer of authority is covenantal. Christ subdues the earth; then He transfers this subdued earth to God the Father. This transfer is a kind of dowry which Christ pays to the "Father of the Bride," His Church. His inheritance from God becomes the "bride price" for His Church, *a visible payment at the end of history* that in principle was paid for covenantally at Calvary.[25] This payment on the Church's behalf is *definitive*, *progressive*, and *final*: at Calvary, in history, and at the final judgment.

There is of necessity a disinheritance at that time. Like the inheritance concept, *covenantal disinheritance* is also definitive (Calvary), progressive (historical), and final. "Let both [wheat and tares] grow together until the harvest: and in the time of harvest I will say to the reapers, Gather ye together first the tares, and bind them in bundles to burn them: but gather the wheat into my barn" (Matt. 13:30). The tares are finally and eternally disinherited at the final judgment. The nations will be divided at that time (Matt. 25:31-35).

25. On the economics of the bride price system, see Gary North, *Tools of Dominion: The Case Laws of Exodus* (Tyler, Texas: Institute for Christian Economics, 1990), pp. 225-28, 250-59, 266-76, 647-57.

The Process of Overcoming

This overcoming of His enemies is progressive over time. The last enemy to be subdued will be death. So, Christ's enemies are not subdued all at once. This process of overcoming takes place in history.

With respect to the nations, there can be little doubt of how the kingdom of God will be manifested: through men's public confession and their covenanting together. Confessing Christ ecclesiastically means confirming the Church covenant through baptism and renewing it periodically (preferably weekly) through the Lord's Supper. Confirming Christ in the realm of civil government means a periodic public affirmation of God's covenant law (Ex. 31:10-13). There is no legitimate escape from the covenant and its ethical requirements.[26]

As men strive together in their various national covenants to work out their salvation in fear and trembling (Phil. 2:12), they extend Christ's kingdom on earth. As they become covenantally faithful by honoring God's law in word and deed (James 1:19-27), God's visible, external blessings cover each formally covenanted society. Deuteronomy 28 teaches that these blessings are clearly national and external: military (v. 7), weather (v. 12), and financial (v. 12). The rain will not fall only on the converted, after all. The locus of covenant blessings is the *nation*.

This means that nations as covenantal institutions will eventually overcome the enemies of Christ. The *positive feedback* of covenantal blessings produce wealth, authority, and influence for covenantally faithful institutions: churches, civil governments, and families. These external, visible blessings are designed by God to reinforce men's faith in the reliability of God's covenant promises in history: "But thou shalt remember the Lord thy God: for it is he that giveth thee power to get wealth, that he may establish his covenant which he sware unto thy fathers, as it is this day" (Deut. 8:18).

26. Gary North, *Political Polytheism: The Myth of Pluralism* (Tyler, Texas: Institute for Christian Economics, 1989), ch. 11.

Who Gets Rich?

The socialists adopted a highly successful slogan, "The rich get richer, and the poor get poorer." It is a big lie. The Bible teaches that in the long run, the *covenantally faithful* get richer, and the *covenantally rebellious* get poorer. This is denied by the humanists, who deny any visible manifestations of God's covenant in history, and it is also denied by Christian pietists and retreatists, who also want no public, national manifestations of God's covenant in history. God's covenantal system of blessings and cursings is designed to produce long-term victory for Christ's people in history. This *long-term increase in Christians' personal responsibility to extend God's dominion on earth* is opposed by both humanists and Christian pietists. The humanists do not want Christians to inherit authority in history, for they want to retain monopoly power over history. Christian pietists also do not want Christians to inherit authority in history, for with authority necessarily comes responsibility.

Men are responsible before God, and this means that we are responsible *in terms of permanent standards*. This means God's law. The more cultural authority that Christians inherit from God, the harder they must strive politically to enact God's revealed laws in the legal codes of each nation. A Christian society's legal order should reflect the requirements of revealed biblical law. So should the international legal order that is established progressively by Christian nations. The implicit covenantal division between sheep and goats – national entities – must be made increasingly visible as time goes by, "in earth as it is in heaven" (Matt. 5:10b). This process of *kingdom conquest through covenantal separation in history* must include the realm of politics, although politics is not to be regarded as primary.

Apocalypticism and Social Change

When people believe that whatever they are capable of accomplishing in history is minimal, they will tend not to strive to achieve very much: high expected costs coupled with very low expected returns. This outlook is hostile to the idea of historical progress. *Societies that have no concept of historical prog-*

ress tend not to be progressive. But what if men believe that great things are attainable in history? What if they believe that God has made available to them the tools of dominion? Then a minority of them will try to improve their world, and this vision can become the standard for the majority. This is exactly what happened in the West.

The question is one of *history*. If the coming great day is seen as the co-product of continuous work and investment by the faithful and the Spirit's sovereign, discontinuous grace into history, then apocalypticism is not basic to their thinking. The process of Spirit-reinforced compound growth is their hope of the future. But when men believe that they can speed up the historical process by violent action, the revolutionary impulse is furthered. Faith in a discontinuous event imposed by man replaces faith in the eventual outcome of compound growth: the exponential curve.

If people believe that a great day is coming, but they also believe that the tools of dominion are not available to them in history, then their great temptation is the adoption of apocalypticism. Apocalypticism, like revolution, rests on *a lack of faith in the possibility of a systematic, progressive dominion of the earth*. It comes in two forms: *passive* and *active*. The passive apocalyptics peacefully wait on God, Amish-like. They do not attempt to change the society around them. They adopt a ghetto mentality. In contrast, the revolutionary apocalyptics perform acts that they believe will hasten God's revolutionary transformation of the social cosmos. They adopt a Communist cell-like mentality. They view themselves as God's "vanguard of the future." Both attitudes show a loss of faith in the masses of men; both show a loss of faith in the familiar social processes of history. God is seen as accomplishing His goals outside of history, apart from the continuities of His Bible-mandated covenantal civil order.

The best examples we have in Western history of both of these apocalyptic approaches are found in one movement: sixteenth-century Anabaptism. In 1525, the revolt of the German peasants began, led by John of Leyden. This apocalyptic and activist wing of the Spiritualist movement[27] soon became communist, revolutionary, and finally polygamous. It was openly opposed by Luther and Calvin.[28] Similar movements had sprung up in Europe ever since the thirteenth century. It took a decade for the combined military forces of Europe to crush them. The revolt ended in the city of Münster (1534-35). From that time on, the bulk of the spiritualist Anabaptists have been passivists and even pacifists; they have also tended to hold property in common.[29] The Amish, Hutterites, and Mennonites are products of this passivist Anabaptist tradition.

Who, then, are the apocalyptic millennialists today?

Pessimillennialism

The pessimillennialist denies that there is a co-partnership between God and the Church in bringing discontinuous social change. Personal transformation, yes: faith cometh by hearing, and hearing by the word of God (Rom. 10:17). The Church preaches the gospel, and the Holy Spirit then moves men to respond. But this is supposedly not God's means of social transformation. To achieve God-honoring social transformation, the pessimillennialist believes, God must unilaterally impose a *cosmic* discontinuity. "The work of Christians in history has very little directly to do with this cosmic discontinuity. It is solely the work of God. The continuity of the Church's work in history has little or nothing to do with the positive transformation of society."

Amillennialism. The amillennialist is an apocalyptic, but a passivist. He believes in the legitimacy traditional order, but he expects little from it. The best he can hope for is social peace. He sees himself as a member of a spiritual ghetto. He adopts the mentality of the Amish. He may drive a car and have electricity in his home, but he sees no hope in the future. His only

27. On the Spiritualists, see Henning Graf Reventlow, *The Authority of the Bible and the Rise of the Modern World* (London: SCM Press, [1980] 1984), ch. 1.

28. Martin Luther, "Against the Robbing and Murderous Hordes of Peasants" (1525), *Luther's Works* (Philadelphia: Fortress Press, 1967); Willem Balke, *Calvin and the Anabaptist Radicals* (Grand Rapids, Michigan: Eerdmans, 1981).

29. Leonard Verduin, *The Reformers and Their Stepchildren* (Grand Rapids, Michigan: Baker, [1964] 1980), ch. 7.

relief from history is found in his hope in God's calling history to an end. He may send his children to Christian schools, but not because he regards these schools as boot camps for cultural conquest. These schools are instead regarded as ports in history's endless storms, and also as marriage centers. In the case of denominational colleges, they are useful for keeping local, rural, "called out" communities from genetic inbreeding. The local gene pool is broadened when sons return from college with wives from different communities. This goal is especially true of immigrant churches that want to keep their accents alive in their children: continuity, which is point five of the immigrant Church's covenant. The accent is on accents, not theology.

Premillennialism. The premillennialist is also an apocalyptic. He sees no hope in the processes of history. The Church is a refuge, not a boot camp. He may sing "Onward, Christian Soldiers," but he believes "I'm just a poor wayfaring stranger, just travelling through this world of woe." He may send his children to public schools because of his faith in the American civil religion and its faith in zero-tuition education, but he has no real hope in such schools, except perhaps as "free" sports centers. His hope is in the imminent return of Jesus. Generally, the premillennial mentality is passive. There is nothing we can do to hasten Christ's return, they believe, except possibly missions work and public support for the state of Israel.

According to premillennialism, raw political power, not the transforming work of the Holy Spirit, is God's chosen method of social transformation. This power will be exercised by Jesus personally during the millennium. A political bureaucracy, not the Church, will become the means of peace. God refuses to coerce men's saving faith in His Son; His saving grace is not irresistible. His political power will be irresistible, however. As Dave Hunt promises, "Justice will be meted out swiftly."[30] But until the millennium, there is no way to transform culture, for only Jesus in person is allowed by God to compel men to obey. "All power corrupts, and absolute power corrupts absolutely,

30. Dave Hunt, *Beyond Seduction: A Return to Biblical Christianity* (Eugene, Oregon: Harvest House, 1987), p. 250.

but not if you are Jesus." The Christian's goal, then, is to shun political power during Church history; it is far too corrupting. Until the millennium, Christians must be content with political rule by covenant-breakers. Jesus is the solution; until then, we must make many political trade-offs. God's theocracy then, but humanism's theocracy today (political pluralism).[31]

Dispensationalism. The preservation of the state of Israel is basic to the eschatology of the pre-tribulational dispensationalist. Why? So that the Antichrist will be able to wipe out two-thirds of Israel's population after the Rapture of the Church and during the Great Tribulation.[32] *The Jews of the state of Israel are to serve as God's cannon fodder in the inevitable war of Armageddon.* Without the Jews' service as future sitting ducks, pre-tribulational dispensationalists would lose all faith in the imminent Rapture. The Antichrist would have no ducks in a barrel if there were no barrel. *The state of Israel is the Antichrist's barrel.* The leaders of dispensationalism do not say in public that this is what their support for Israel is all about, but it is.[33] Based on Zechariah 13:8-9, among other passages, dispensationalists conclude that the two-thirds of the Jews are doomed. This is standard teaching from the pulpits.[34]

Dispensational fundamentalism's support for the state of

---

31. North, *Political Polytheism, op. cit.*

32. This scenario of slaughter is found in former Dallas Seminary president John Walvoord's book, *Israel in Prophecy* (Grand Rapids, Michigan: Zondervan Academie, [1962] 1988), p. 108.

33. In their essay for a conservative secular magazine, dispensationalists Ed Dobson and Ed Hindson try to sugar-coat this concern for national Israel. They admit that "The Tribulation will largely consist of the Antichrist persecuting the Jews and the nation of Israel." They quote Dallas Seminary's J. Dwight Pentecost: "God's purpose for Israel in this Tribulation is to bring about the conversion of a multitude of Jews, who will enter into the blessings of the kingdom and experience the fulfillment of Israel's covenants." What they do not discuss is that according to pre-tribulational dispensationalism, this conversion of the Jews only takes place in the midst of the slaughter of two-thirds of the entire population of the state of Israel. Dobson and Hindson, "Apocalypse Now?" *Policy Review* (Fall 1986), pp. 20-21.

34. Grace Halsell, a non-Christian who went on two of Jerry Falwell's tours to the state of Israel, got into a discussion with one young man on the tour who assured her that two-thirds of all Jews would be killed during the battle of Armageddon: Grace Halsell, *Prophecy and Politics: Militant Evangelists on the Road to Nuclear War* (Westport, Connecticut: Lawrence Hill & Co., 1986), p. 26.

Israel is governed by this unique presupposition: "No national Israel, no Armageddon; no Armageddon, no imminent Rapture." This is *three-stage apocalypticism*: the Rapture of the Church (cosmic discontinuity), the slaughter of the Jews (historical discontinuity), and the return of Christ to set up His millennial kingdom seven years after the Rapture (cosmic discontinuity). But the Church's work in history has nothing to do with any of this.

One piece of evidence for my contention is the almost total absence of evangelism by dispensational groups in or to the state of Israel. They do not beam Christian broadcasts in from Cyprus or other areas, the way they beam programs to the Islamic world. They do not advertise any such campaigns, the way that the "Jews for Jesus" and similar "Messianic Jews" organizations do. They are happy to evangelize Jews outside of the state of Israel, but not inside. Why not? One reason is that if the Jews of the state of Israel were converted before the Rapture, there could be no Armageddon.[35] The Antichrist could invade Palestine, but there would be no national Jewish state of Israel there. If the bulk of the Jews of the state of Israel were converted to saving faith before the Rapture, it would destroy dispensationalism, both pre-tribulational and post-tribulational.

Dispensational theology creates a major incentive to write off the state of Israel as a target of mass evangelism. This is a direct consequence of a particular millennial viewpoint. Here is my contention: *any millennial viewpoint that in any way writes off any group or nation at any point in time is a defective eschatology*. Today is the day of salvation (II Cor. 6:2), not at the beginning of the millennium after Armageddon.

When the postmillennialist cites Romans 11 and argues that the Jews will be converted in history, leading to unprecedented

35. Another is that the Israeli government frowns on such evangelism. It would not cooperate with dispensational tour programs if this kind of evangelism were conducted by the leaders. This systematic ignoring of Christians in the state of Israel by the Falwell tours was noted by Halsell, *ibid.*, pp. 55-58. The local Baptist minister in Bethlehem was introduced by Falwell to his tour. He is an evangelist only to Arabs, according to Halsell's report of her interview with the man. The Israelis, he said, do not permit him to share the gospel with Jews (p. 64).

blessings for the Church,[36] the dispensationalist dismisses this view of the future as utopian. Why is it utopian? Is it because in our millennial system, not enough Jews get slaughtered before a handful of survivors gets converted? Is it because we refuse to single out the Jews as the targets of persecution in a coming era of tribulation? Is it because we deny that the Great Tribulation is in the future? I think so. Yet Lindsey calls us anti-Semitic![37]

Postmillennialism: Is It Utopian?

The postmillennialist is anti-apocalyptic. He knows that God breaks into history, but God does this by using the familiar processes of Church history: evangelism, the sacraments, Church discipline, civil justice, and family order. He will send the Holy Spirit to transform billions of individual hearts, and the regenerate then use the familiar tools of dominion to extend God's kingdom in history. This is *conquest by conversion*. It is utopian only in the sense that if God refuses to send the Holy Spirit in history to achieve this transformation, the God-authorized techniques of evangelism will fail to bring in the era of kingdom blessings, which requires the Holy Spirit's miraculous intervention: *covenantal revival*. But the postmillennialist always has hope that God will eventually send the Holy Spirit. He does not adopt either a utopian or an apocalyptic mentality. He places his faith in God's gift of the tools of dominion (continuity) and the Holy Spirit's means of transforming rebellious hearts in history (discontinuity).

Postmillennialists are labeled as utopians. But who does the labeling? The apocalyptics. They come in two theological forms, Calvinist amillennialists[38] and Arminian premillennialists (and

---

36. Charles Hodge, *Commentary on the Epistle to the Romans* (Grand Rapids, Michigan: Eerdmans, [1864] 1950), p. 365; Robert Haldane, *An Exposition of the Epistle to the Romans* (Mad Dill Air Force Base, Florida: MacDonald Pub. Co., [1839] 1958), pp. 632-33; John Murray, *The Epistle to the Romans*, 2 vols. (Grand Rapids, Michigan: Eerdmans, 1965), II, pp. 65-103.

37. Hal Lindsey, *The Road to Holocaust* (New York: Bantam, 1989).

38. Writes "realized millennialist" (amillennialist) Jay E. Adams: "If the millennium is a present reality, it is most certainly of the non-utopian type." Adams, *The Time Is at Hand* (Nutley, New Jersey: Presbyterian & Reformed, 1966), p. 9.

a scattering of amillennialists). The Calvinist apocalyptic denies that God will ever send His Holy Spirit to transform men and society. The failure of the gospel in history is predestined by God, he insists (privately). The Arminian apocalyptic argues that even if God planned to transform men and society in this way (doubtful), the Holy Spirit's efforts would inevitably be thwarted by the free wills of the vast majority of covenant-breakers. This is the Arminian's doctrine of *predestination by Satan* (inevitability = predestination). Satan has predestined the failure of God's Church in the "Church Age"; God, however, cannot predestine the success of His Church. This is why He has to intervene by pulling the Church to heaven and starting over. The Church is rotten wood. It has to be removed from history before anything culturally positive can be accomplished.

Kingdom and Church

Here is the basis of Christ's progressive overcoming of His enemies in history: the steady expansion of the authority of His covenant people on earth and in history. This is the principle of *leaven*. God's holy leaven steadily replaces Satan's unholy leaven in history. "Another parable spake he unto them; The kingdom of heaven is like unto leaven, which a woman took, and hid in three measures of meal, till the whole was leavened" (Matt. 13:33). The imagery of leaven is the imagery of continuity. It is a denial of dispensationalism's future cosmic discontinuity of the Rapture.[39]

We now come to Paul's re-statement of God's "footstool theology." *God triumphs in history through the expansion of Christ's international kingdom*. "Now when all things are made subject to Him, then the Son Himself will also be subject to Him who put all things under Him, that God may be all in all" (I Cor. 15:28). This is not pantheism; it is covenant dominion. God is not infused into His creation; His kingdom in heaven progressively becomes covenantally identified with Christ's kingdom on earth. Our prayer is finally answered at the end of history: "Thy king-

39. O. T. Allis, "The Parable of the Leaven," *Evangelical Quarterly*, XIX (Oct. 1947).

dom come. Thy will be done in earth, as it is in heaven" (Matt. 6:10). But it is also answered progressively in history.

This is the society of man's long-term earthly future, no matter what difficulties Christians may experience between now and then. God's kingdom comes; His will is done.

For proclaiming such a view of history, the Reconstructionists have come under heavy fire from pietists. An English pastor announced to his magazine's readers: "Reconstructionist writers all scorn the attitude of traditional evangelicals who see the church as something so completely distinct and separate from the world that they seek no 'authority' over the affairs of the world."[40] He is correct on this point, though on few others in his essay. This is *exactly* what we scorn, and for explicitly theological reasons.

That the Church is distinct from the world institutionally is not a major insight. It alone lawfully administers the holy sacraments. But what has this got to do with the other half of his assertion, namely, that they (Christians) therefore need seek no authority over the affairs of this world? It is *because* the Church is distinct from this world that God has called Christians, as His disciples, to baptize *nations*, bringing whole societies under God's authority: the Great Commission (Matt. 28:18-20). If the Church had its origins in this world, we could not lawfully claim to represent God legally in history. We would be *of* this world, and therefore incapable of bringing a heaven-originated process of healing and restoration to this world. It is the *very distinctness of the Church* and its God-assigned task of discipling the nations that authorizes Christians progressively to seek authority over the affairs of this world.

A False Definition of God's Kingdom

We do not argue, as this critic argues to defend his own position of cultural isolation, that "The kingdom of God is the church, small as it may sometime appear, not the world. . . ." This definition of the kingdom of God is the Roman Catholic

40. Peter Masters, "World Dominion," *Sword & Trowel* (May 24, 1990), p. 18.

definition of the kingdom, and it has led in the past to ecclesiocracy. It places everything under the institutional Church. The Church in principle absorbs everything. This same definition can also lead to the ghetto mentality and cultural isolation: it places nothing under Christianity, because the kingdom is narrowly defined as merely the institutional Church. Because the institutional Church is not authorized to control the State (correct), and because the kingdom is said to be identical to the Church (incorrect), the kingdom of God is then redefined as having nothing to do with anything that is not strictly ecclesiastical. This is our critic's view of the kingdom.

Let me ask three rhetorical questions. Is the family under God's lawful authority? Is the family part of the kingdom of God? Is the family to be governed by biblical law? The family is not the institutional Church. It is a separate institution. Would our critic like to go before his readers and announce that the Christian family has nothing to do with the kingdom of God? I do not think this is what he is ready to do. I would not expect any pastor to do this. But if he hesitates to remove the Christian family from kingdom status because it is not identical to the Church, then he is a theological dead duck if he is a pietist. He now has moved boundaries of the kingdom of God beyond the confines of the institutional Church, and so his argument dies.

What the Bible teaches is the *civilization of God*, which is in historical warfare with the *civilization of Satan*. It is broader than the institutional Church, as surely as Satan's kingdom is broader than this or that cult or temple. God calls every Christian into service. Each person has some talent that can be used to build the kingdom. Each person must build one kingdom or the other. *There is no neutrality*. Christians are called to build God's institutional Church. But we are also called to build His families. What enrages our critics, pietists and Christians alike, is that Christian Reconstructionists say that Christians are also called to build His civil government. For them, this is the ultimate heresy. Why? Because it involves more responsibility than they choose to bear. The pietist's goal in life is to reduce the claims of Christ on him, his vision, and his pocketbook.

Yet there is no escape in the mythical realm of neutrality. As

C. S. Lewis has one of his most self-conscious anti-heroes say in his 1946 novel about the war between the New Age, New World Order and Christianity, "If you try to be neutral you become simply a pawn."[41] *It is not our task as Christians to serve as pawns in this "game."* Yet this is what modern pietism insists that we must be, on principle; anything else is the heresy of power. Pietists would rather see us all sacrificed – the strategic purpose of pawns. So would the humanists. The alliance continues.

If pietists regarded their family responsibilities with the same attitude of contempt that they regard their civic responsibilities – to exercise dominion under God's sovereign authority in terms of God's law – why, we would see divorce and adultery go unpunished in God's Church! Pastors caught in adultery would then be regarded as no more culpable than someone caught embezzling church funds. Maybe even less culpable!

Oops. Sorry. Scratch that. This is *exactly* what we see today, and have seen for a century. The adulterers in the pulpit have an implicit alliance of silence with the adulterers in political office, and Reconstructionists threaten this alliance. That Jimmy Swaggart was exposing the "evils" of dominion theology every weekend on national television at the same time that he was visiting a prostitute was at least theologically consistent. "We're under grace, not law!" By God's grace (and also by means of a private investigator who had been hired by another formerly adulterous pastor, whose escapades Rev. Swaggart had exposed publicly), the now-expelled Mr. Swaggart can no longer attack dominion theology, or anything else, on national television. God stopped using Swaggart as a middleman to subsidize sin.

Conclusion

It is always hard to sell personal responsibility. This has been a continuing problem facing the Christian Reconstructionists. Christians will do almost anything to escape added responsibilities, even if this means: (1) abandoning hope in a worldwide revival, (2) adopting the myth of neutrality, (3) abandoning the

---

41. C. S. Lewis, *That Hideous Strength: A Modern Fairy-Tale for Grown-Ups* (New York: Macmillan, 1946), p. 41. The character is Lord Feverstone.

world in history to the devil, but all in the name of biblical prophecy and narrowly defined evangelism. They have rejected the nation-discipling aspect of the Great Commission, but in the name of the Great Commission.[42]

Society can never be Christian, we are told, because it never has been. (Forget about the medieval world; forget about the Holland in the sixteenth century; we are apparently not talking about Western Civilization here.) "Where Christians have previously attempted to construct even a very limited Christian society their efforts have been sadly frustrated."[43] It is the same old humanist-pietist story: the progress of the West is seen as having nothing to do with the spread of the gospel and men's post-conversion construction of Christian social institutions.

This is the textbook history of the West as written by Voltaire and Diderot. It is the modern textbook version of the past – a past devoid of Christianity and God's covenantal sanctions (*especially* His sanctions). And it is presented to Christian laymen by pastors with doctorates (earned and honorary) in theology. This is another example of the continuing alliance between the power religion and the escape religion. The power religion always establishes the standards in this alliance. There is no neutrality. The power religionists understand this; the escape religionists never do. They become outraged when another Christian points out their non-neutrality to them.

It is the great offense of the Christian Reconstructionists to remind Christians of just how unneutral humanism is, how comprehensive Christ's salvation is, and how much God expects from us. When it comes to the task of discipling the nations, the pietist responds: **"Not on our Agenda."**[44] In the name of God, sir, if you are a Christian, it sure as heaven is.

---

42. Kenneth L. Gentry, Jr., *The Greatness of the Great Commission: The Christian Enterprise in a Fallen World* (Tyler, Texas: Institute for Christian Economics, 1990).

43. Masters, "World Dominion," p. 19.

44. *Idem.*

12

OUR BLESSED EARTHLY HOPE IN HISTORY

For every high priest is ordained to offer gifts and sacrifices: wherefore it is of necessity that this man have somewhat also to offer. For if he were on earth, he should not be a priest, seeing that there are priests that offer gifts according to the law: Who serve unto the example and shadow of heavenly things, as Moses was admonished of God when he was about to make the tabernacle: for, See, saith he, that thou make all things according to the pattern shewed to thee in the mount. But now hath he obtained a more excellent ministry, by how much also he is the mediator of ***a better covenant****, which was established upon* ***better promises****. For if that first covenant had been faultless, then should no place have been sought for the second. For finding fault with them, he saith, Behold, the days come, saith the Lord, when I will make a new covenant with the house of Israel and with the house of Judah: Not according to the covenant that I made with their fathers in the day when I took them by the hand to lead them out of the land of Egypt; because they continued not in my covenant, and I regarded them not, saith the Lord. For this is the covenant that I will make with the house of Israel after those days, saith the Lord; I will put my laws into their mind, and write them in their hearts: and I will be to them a God, and they shall be to me a people: And they shall not teach every man his neighbour, and every man his brother, saying, Know the Lord:* ***for all shall know me, from the least to the greatest*** *(Heb. 8:3-11).* (emphasis added)

In principle, this prophecy of Jeremiah the prophet (Jer. 31:31-34) has been fulfilled in Jesus Christ. It has been fulfilled *definitively*. It has not yet been fulfilled *progressively*. This is analogous to Christ's perfection, which is imputed judicially to each new convert as the legal basis of his regeneration. This definitive fulfillment must become progressive in his life. He must run the race, fight the good fight, and persevere to the end. This is also true of the prophecy of the transformation of human hearts. "I will put my laws into their mind, and write them in their hearts: and I will be to them a God, and they shall be to me a people: And they shall not teach every man his neighbour, and every man his brother, saying, Know the Lord: for all shall know me, from the least to the greatest." Similarly, the Church must persevere to the end, preaching the gospel in the expectation that God will eventually bring this prophecy to pass in history across the face of the earth. This is the Christian's blessed earthly hope.

The Continuity of Jesus' Heavenly Enthronement

Jesus the High Priest is in heaven. Jesus the King of kings is in heaven. He must stay at God's right hand until the end of history. *His presence at God's right hand in heaven is the sign of His sovereignty over history.* He will not return physically to earth until His kingdom is fully developed in history, thereby ending history. His timing can be derived from the word *until.*

> Then cometh the end, when he shall have delivered up the kingdom to God, even the Father; when he shall have put down all rule and all authority and power. For he must reign, *till* he hath put all enemies under his feet. The last enemy that shall be destroyed is death. For he hath put all things under his feet. But when he saith all things are put under him, it is manifest that he is excepted, which did put all things under him. And when all things shall be subdued unto him, then shall the Son also himself be subject unto him that put all things under him, that God may be all in all (I Cor. 15:24-28). (emphasis added)

This is Paul's amplification of Psalm 110:

> {A Psalm of David.} The LORD said unto my Lord, Sit thou at my right hand, *until* I make thine enemies thy footstool. The LORD shall send the rod of thy strength out of Zion: rule thou in the midst of thine enemies (Ps. 110:1-2). (emphasis added)

How long must Jesus remain at God the Father's right hand? Until God the Father makes His enemies Jesus' footstool (Psa.

110:1). How long will Jesus reign? Until God the Father has put all enemies under His feet (I Cor. 15:25). Jesus therefore must remain at God's right hand until history ends: so a *literal* reading of the two texts demands. (Are dispensationalists really committed to a literal hermeneutic? Hardly. Their principle of interpretation is this: "Literal, except whenever inconvenient.") This passage, along with Matthew 13 on the continuity of God's kingdom,[1] is the key passage for postmillennialism's rejection of premillennialism, just as Isaiah 65:20 is the key passage in postmillennialism's rejection of amillennialism: "There shall be no more thence an infant of days, nor an old man that hath not filled his days: for the child shall die an hundred years old; but the sinner being an hundred years old shall be accursed."[2]

Because postmillennialism is true, Christians have two blessed earthly hopes: one historical, the other post-historical. The blessed post-historical yet earthly hope is the end of history, the last judgment, and the transition to the post-resurrection consummation of the *already existing* New Heaven and New Earth (II Pet. 3:10-13). But first, we should pray for and work toward the *historical* fulfillment of the already existing New Heaven and New Earth (Isa. 65). This is the blessed historical earthly hope. (There is a heavenly hope: heaven after death. This is not what is commonly called the *blessed* hope.)

The Work of the Holy Spirit

What do we have at our disposal that can be used in the historical fulfillment of the blessed earthly hope? What we have, above all (literally), is Jesus Christ, sitting enthroned at the right hand of His Father.[3] He has sent the Holy Spirit to empower us.[4] This was crucial and remains crucial to the empowering of Christians in history:

---

1. See below, pp. 296-98.
2. See above, pp. 98-106.
3. Francis Nigel Lee, *The Central Significance of Culture* (Nutley, New Jersey: Presbyterian & Reformed, 1976), pp. 49-53.
4. *Ibid.*, pp. 53-54.

> Nevertheless I tell you the truth; It is expedient for you that I go away: for if I go not away, the Comforter will not come unto you; but if I depart, I will send him unto you. And when he is come, he will reprove the world of sin, and of righteousness, and of judgment: Of sin, because they believe not on me; Of righteousness, because I go to my Father, and ye see me no more; Of judgment, because the prince of this world is judged (John 16:7-11).

The Comforter is of course the Holy Spirit. *The Holy Spirit maintains ecclesiastical and therefore also historical continuity.* He was not sent until the three judicial discontinuities between Christ and His Father were completed. These judicial discontinuities are now behind us. *These three discontinuities are more important than anything else in history or eternity.* Everything that has taken place since then, or will take place in the future, has been or will be an extension of these discontinuous judicial events.

What were these cosmically crucial judicial discontinuities? First, the completed transaction of Christ's death on the cross: sin's full payment to His Father. Second, His bodily resurrection: His visible testimony of redeemed mankind's victory over the second death (Rev. 20:14-15). Third, His ascension to the right hand of His Father: His enthronement as both High Priest and King of kings.

The completion of these three judicial discontinuities led to the next major historical discontinuity, Pentecost, when the Holy Spirit was sent in power to inaugurate the Church. This was point five of the biblical covenant model: *succession*. Then, a generation later, came the institutional completion of the Old Covenant at the destruction of the temple in Jerusalem in A.D. 70.[5] Covenantally, this was also point five: *disinheritance*. This event completed the Old Heavens and Old Earth. No discontinuous event of comparable covenantal magnitude will take place in history until the Second Coming of Christ at the last judgment. Jesus will remain at God's right hand until then: the guarantee of covenantal continuity in history. This guarantees the Holy Spirit's presence with His Church in history.

---

5. David Chilton, *The Great Tribulation* (Ft. Worth, Texas: Dominion Press, 1987).

A Question of Continuity

Institutionally, what do we possess to aid us in our work of evangelism and cultural conquest? *First*, we have the Holy Spirit, who is God. This means we are in God's presence at all times. This is point one of the covenant: transcendence, yet presence. *Second*, we have the three covenantal, hierarchical institutions established by God: Church, State, and family. *Third*, we have God's law and His revelation of Himself in the Bible. *Fourth*, we have earthly access to the implements of God's heavenly sanctions: the sacraments of baptism (covenantal discontinuity and a new inheritance) and the Lord's Supper (special covenantal presence and renewal). *Fifth*, we have God's promise of both historical continuity and cultural victory in history.

The premillennialist affirms victory but not historical continuity. The amillennialist affirms historical continuity but not victory. *Only the postmillennialist affirms both historical continuity and victory*. This three-way division within the Church has led to the abandonment of biblical covenantalism. The churches have therefore adopted one of the two rival views of society: organicism or contractualism.[6] Organicism favors *ecclesiocracy* (unity of Church and State), while contractualism favors *religious pluralism* (the legal separation of Christianity and State). Covenantalism separates Church from State and fuses Christianity and State. There can never be separation of religion and State in any system. The question is: *Which religion?*

The goal of the biblical covenantalist is to bring all the institutions of life under the rule of God's covenant law. The State imposes negative sanctions against specified *public* acts of evil. The churches preach the gospel and proclaim God's law. The family acts as the primary agent of dominion. Voluntary corporations of all kinds are established to achieve both profitable and charitable goals. Working together under the overall jurisdiction of God's revealed law, these institutions can flourish. Biblical covenantalism produces an open society. It did in Old Covenant times; it does today. To deny this is to argue that God

6. See Chapter 2, pp. 34-37, 38-39.

required a closed, unfree society in ancient Israel. The following unstated assumption is made all too often by anti-theonomic commentators, and it is probably presumed by the vast majority of contemporary Christians: "Israel was a tyrannical nation." But it was the other pagan city-states of ancient history that were closed, not Israel. In a biblically covenantal society, there will be one law for all residents with respect to the imposition of negative civil negative sanctions (Ex. 12:49). I have called this system *Athanasian pluralism*.[7]

When this kind of *corporate, judicial subordination to God* takes place, society can expect God's corporate blessings. This is the only foundation of long-term positive feedback in history: from victory unto victory. This is the vision of *compound ethical growth in history*. It is basic to covenantal postmillennialism.

How to Overcome the Continuity of Evil

God's kingdom and Satan's are locked in mortal combat. Both kingdoms seek continuity. Both seek victory. Neither is ready to surrender to the other. But the terms of battle, like the terms of surrender, are covenantal. This is not a battle that will be decided in terms of political power or any other kind of power. It is not a power play. *It is an ethical battle in history based on rival covenantal commitments*. If it were a power play, the conflict would have ended in Eden. There are, however, negative corporate sanctions that are applied by God in history to His covenantal enemies. These sanctions are applied because of corporate covenant-breaking by people in history. He breaks the continuity of corporate evil. He may replace one society's corporate evil with another society's corporate evil, but He does not allow the compound growth of the same social evil.

Meanwhile, He shows kindness unto thousands of generations of those who love Him and keep His commandments. This is God's compound growth process for covenant-keeping in history. Little by little (with occasional discontinuities), God's kingdom expands over time.

---

7. Gary North, *Political Polytheism: The Myth of Pluralism* (Tyler, Texas: Institute for Christian Economics, 1989), pp. 594-97.

Negative Corporate Sanctions

Because we have no biblical examples of the imposition of God's positive, historical, corporate sanctions apart from the imposition of negative, historical, corporate sanctions, it is difficult (foolish) to predict with confidence that the millennial reversal away from humanism and toward Christianity will take place during an era of unprecedented peace and prosperity. The more common condition of man is to forget God in times of external success. Success creates pride; pride leads to forgetfulness and the claim of autonomy:

> And thou say in thine heart, My power and the might of mine hand hath gotten me this wealth. But thou shalt remember the LORD thy God: for it is he that giveth thee power to get wealth, that he may establish his covenant which he sware unto thy fathers, as it is this day. And it shall be, if thou do at all forget the LORD thy God, and walk after other gods, and serve them, and worship them, I testify against you this day that ye shall surely perish. As the nations which the LORD destroyeth before your face, so shall ye perish; because ye would not be obedient unto the voice of the LORD your God (Deut. 8:17-20).

We live in an era of unprecedented prosperity. The average resident of an industrial nation lives longer and more comfortably than kings did a century ago. The air conditioner alone has made a major difference in productivity. At some price, residents of every climate can experience the 80-degree temperature that is most conducive to high economic output.

Can we legitimately expect a discontinuous movement of the Holy Spirit in the middle of economic and political continuity? Will large numbers of covenant-breakers be persuaded by the message of the gospel apart from some social disruption that calls into question the sovereignty of whatever god they worship? We have no example of this in Church history, and none in the Bible, with the exception of Nineveh, which feared imminent judgment.

If the churches continue their present evangelism programs, should we expect a major cultural transformation? Only if God intervenes into history in a discontinuous way. But if He does this, the churches will have to learn to do things differently. They will be inundated with too many new converts who need too much attention.

What is needed today is a preliminary transformation of the Church, worldwide. But this is also unlikely. What would prompt such a change, apart from either the pressures of a worldwide revival or the coming of calamity? Churches are like other institutions; successful programs – by conventional standards – are hard to change, while unsuccessful programs, even if successfully altered before a worldwide crisis, are too small and isolated to serve as immediate models. The time of model-testing will probably be lengthy.

The Threat of Being Swamped

Only specialists in the early history of Darwinism know who Fleeming Jenkin was, but Charles Darwin knew. Jenkin, an engineer, asked a devastating question of Darwin, one which neither Darwin nor his followers could begin to answer before Mendel's work on genetics was rediscovered around 1900. Jenkin asked: How can the single member of a species who alone possesses the unique biological trait that will better enable it and its progeny to survive ever be able to overcome the huge numbers of the existing species? Unless almost the entire species dies off immediately, leaving the one uniquely endowed member as the dominant survivor, its offspring will be forced to mate with the conventional members of the species. So will their offspring. The unique attribute will then be swamped by the conventional attributes of the species. Loren Eiseley summarizes Jenkin's position:

> Jenkin set forth the fact that a newly emergent character possessed by one or a few rare mutants would be rapidly swamped out of existence by backcrossing with the mass of individuals that did not possess the trait in question. Only if the same trait emerged *simultaneously* throughout the majority of the species could it be expected to survive.[8]

8. Loren Eiseley, *Darwin's Century: Evolution and the Men Who Discovered It* (Garden

The answer that Mendel's laws of genetic variation provides is that genes can be recessive, but they do not get swamped out of existence. This raises another question: the statistical likelihood of a positive genetic mutation. But Jenkin's point was on target in 1867, as Darwin knew all too well, without Mendel to bail out Darwin's theory of natural selection.

A similar problem faces the Church today. The churches of the world present so many different models that not one of them has attained anything like universal acceptance. No one evangelism plan seems to work everywhere. There is no agreed-upon vision of the future, let alone a common program to deal with it. The Church international is rather like that species that Darwin said was no longer most fit for its changing environment. How can one lonely "member" change the "species," even if it does possess the unique characteristic that would give its heirs a competitive advantage in the new environment?

Here are two solutions. First, the Holy Spirit may change large sections of the Church in a brief period of time (institutional discontinuity). Second, it may be that certain churches will be ideally suited to certain cultural environments, so that when the Spirit at long last moves, He can move into many cultures simultaneously without changing all the churches to resemble a single model. (This is my presumption.)

The third possibility is Darwin's original view: all the other competitors will die off, leaving in command of the environment the heirs of the original mutant. This, however, takes many generations, both biologically and institutionally. Men's institutions do not change rapidly except in cultural cataclysms.

The Three Questions

When anyone wants to make a major change in his goals, he needs to ask himself three questions:

> What do I want to achieve?
> How soon do I want to achieve it?
> How much am I willing to pay?

City, New York: Anchor, [1958] 1961), p. 210.

The faster you want to achieve it, the more you will have to pay. It is like building a retirement portfolio: the longer you have until retirement, the less capital you need (given a fixed rate of compound growth) to begin with. Alternatively, the higher the rate of compound growth, the later you can wait before beginning. But there are always trade-offs among *time remaining*, the size of the *capital base*, and the *rate of growth*.

The modern Church believes that it has very little time remaining. It also knows that it is being swamped by its rivals: secular humanism, occultism, Islam, cults, and all the rest. It has a small visible capital base, in every sense: buildings, influence, money, dedicated personnel, training materials, etc. What does the modern Church conclude? "Not very much can be accomplished!" It has no vision of either compound growth or a long period of growth. Its leaders say to the members, "What we see today is all the Church will ever get in history."

In contrast, the postmillennialist sets his sights very high: the conquest (transformation) of the world, spiritually *and therefore institutionally*. He can take two approaches: (1) continuity with lots of time; (2) discontinuity soon, followed by lots of time.

Continuity. He can think, "slow growth, but very long term": little by little. If so, he must hypothesize that at some point in the future, all covenantal rivals stop growing or shrink. They die off. Christianity then wins by slow attrition. But what about the six billion people already alive today?

All the other millennial viewpoints dismiss them. It's "Sorry, Charlie," to about 5.5 billion of them (more, if the Second Coming is delayed). This is at the very least cold-blooded, if not actually callous. But the pure little-by-little postmillennialist has the same problem. He thinks that there is a lot of time before Jesus Christ comes again. What will happen in the centuries ahead to all of these people and tens of billions more of their biological heirs? Is the compounding process working today to fill up hell? If things do not change, and change soon, *yes*: for a long, long time. He, too, must write off today's billions.

Discontinuity. The postmillennialist therefore prefers a massive historical discontinuity, but not one outside of the familiar historical processes of evangelism and church-planting. He wants God's positive historical sanction of personal regeneration on a scale not seen before in human history. Yet he knows that in all previous cases, such positive, discontinuous, historical sanctions have come only *during or shortly after extensive corporate negative sanctions*. Wycliffe began the Lollard movement only one generation after the bubonic plague had disrupted the West as nothing ever had before (1348-50), and two generations after Europe's three years of famine (1315-17). Luther was successful because of the culture-disrupting syphilis that had been brought back by Columbus' crew and the other world sailors (a negative sanction),[9] the invention of the printing press (a positive sanction), and the threat of the Turks (a negative sanction). Also, the Reformation was cut short by wars, the Counter-Reformation, and the rise of Renaissance rationalism and magic (both at the same time, and sometimes in the same men).[10]

Each of the great wars has secularized society, from the crusades to the present. Wars are bad times for morality in general. There may be no atheists in foxholes, but there are few Christians on shore leave.

So, what should we consciously expect? Pessimillennialism says "the same as ever": muddling through, with billions lost eternally. But what should we work toward? *A massive covenantal revival*. How can we do this? By prayer, fasting, hard work, tithes and offerings, charitable works, Christian education, and pulling the TV plug to give ourselves back 20-40 hours a week for more productive uses. Yes, a few tracts would be useful. Maybe some pamphlets, too. But be sure they have tear-out mail-in sheets and order blanks, please. Never violate North's Prime Directive: "Every piece of paper should sell another piece of paper."

There is continuity in history. There is also discontinuity. The Holy Spirit provides both.

---

9. Within five years, it had spread across Europe. By 1506, it had struck China. Fernand Braudel, *Civilization and Capitalism: 15th-18th Century*, 3 vols. (New York: Harper & Row, [1979] 1981), vol. I, *The Structures of Everyday Life*, pp. 81-82.

10. Stephen A. McKnight, *Sacralizing the Secular: The Renaissance Origins of Modernity* (Baton Rouge: University of Louisiana Press, 1989).

Strategies: "Russian" vs. "Guerilla"

Russia has fought its wars the hard way in the twentieth century: by massing huge armies of underequipped men, and then throwing these men against the enemy's front lines. Wave upon wave of them die. Eventually, the enemy army suffers a break in the lines, and the Russian general is supposed to order his troops into the breach, to cut the enemy's army in half. In contrast, the guerilla has limited resources. He has to wage a war of attrition against invaders. His tools are the tools of low-intensity warfare: sniper rifles, land mines, spies, propaganda materials, confidence in his cause, and an extremely long-range time perspective. He needs to proclaim the moral high ground.

The problem for the Church today is that it needs a full-scale frontal assault against all its enemies, but it does not have the troops or the equipment. Their millennial views long ago shortened the time-perspective of fundamentalists, who were already anti-intellectual, and also the Calvinists, who were not very successful in evangelism, and who had been compromised by rationalism to some extent.[11] The various immigrant, amillennial ghetto churches were culturally defensive operations from the beginning, and have not changed significantly. This is especially true of Dutch-North American Calvinism. After all, if you have been told that time is short, that the world will not be brought to saving faith, that preaching the gospel to the lost will lead to persecution, and that all of this is predestinated by God, you have only minimal incentives to evangelize the world outside your cozy ghetto. Besides, all those outsiders speak with peculiar accents!

The fundamentalists never did consider a frontal assault against humanism as possible or even desirable. They did not think they would be around even this long. But they are still here. So are their enemies, but many times more numerous, and now financed by tax money. The public schools have done their secularizing work exactly as designed in the 1830's.[12]

---

11. Gary North, *Dominion and Common Grace: The Biblical Basis of Progress* (Tyler, Texas: Institute for Christian Economics, 1987), pp. 261-68.

12. R. J. Rushdoony, *The Messianic Character of American Education* (Phillipsburg, New

(The on-campus crime and drugs are extra added features, the better to keep Christians appropriately humble before their masters: "It isn't as bad in our local high school as it is across town,[13] so we're generally satisfied.")

We are forced to adopt guerilla strategies in most areas, especially anything to do with thought and culture. We publish books (small runs), newsletters, pamphlets, and inexpensive cassette tapes. We conduct home Bible studies. We imitate the early Church, not David's Jerusalem. We conserve our financial resources, since we do not have many. A Russian strategy is appropriate only for those with lots of resources, either numerically or through the media.

Consider the electronic media. The electronic media have important uses, but for the most part, they are overrated by Christians. The average viewer of the typical TV evangelist is female, over 65 years old, on a pension, and supports several programs. Radio has been used successfully only by a handful of specialists, notably James Dobson, who is not a pastor, but who meets the daily family needs of mothers. This kind of ministry is crucial in building a "home base" for long-term dominion, but it is not sufficient to launch a frontal assault against sophisticated, well-entrenched, tax-financed enemies. Yet Christians seem to think there is something nearly magical about the electronic media. "If I could only get a Christian talk show," the more naive Christian leaders say to themselves. Well, what if they could? Would their ratings be higher than the prime-time schlock that now dominates? Not very likely.

Negative Sanctions and the Samaritan Strategy

This leaves cultural crises. What this world needs today is a really big plague, *if* such a plague would bring men face to face with mankind's impotence in the face of God's judgments in history. An economic collapse would not be a bad thing, either, *if* men learned to rely on the providence of God to sustain them. A little covenantal terror and consternation in history

Jersey: Presbyterian & Reformed, [1963]).

13. Where *those* children live!

never does any lasting harm to people who are headed for eternal terror and consternation. But terror is not enough. India has had its fair share of famines and floods over the centuries, but there has been no Christian revival and no change of heart. Terror is not enough; *there must also be a major positive move by the Holy Spirit.* Even those who knew exactly who God is did not repent in the face of God's unprecedented negative sanctions against them in A.D. 70:

> And I beheld when he had opened the sixth seal, and, lo, there was a great earthquake; and the sun became black as sackcloth of hair, and the moon became as blood; And the stars of heaven fell unto the earth,[14] even as a fig tree casteth her untimely figs, when she is shaken of a mighty wind. And the heaven departed as a scroll when it is rolled together; and every mountain and island were moved out of their places. And the kings of the earth, and the great men, and the rich men, and the chief captains, and the mighty men, and every bondman, and every free man, hid themselves in the dens and in the rocks of the mountains; And said to the mountains and rocks, Fall on us, and hide us from the face of him that sitteth on the throne, and from the wrath of the Lamb: For the great day of his wrath is come; and who shall be able to stand? (Rev. 6:12-17).

They preferred burial by rocks to repentance. Men did not covenant with the Lamb except when moved to do so by the Holy Spirit's irresistible grace. It is no different today. Such events, though never again on the same order of *covenantal* magnitude, can happen to any nation, just as they happened to Old Covenant national Israel: "The whole land has rejected Christ, and the whole land is being excommunicated."[15] This was the final fulfillment of Hosea's prophecy against Israel the harlot. "The high places also of Aven, the sin of Israel, shall be destroyed: the thorn and the thistle shall come upon their altars; and they shall say to the mountains, Cover us; and to the hills, Fall on us" (Hos. 10:8).

So, the Church must prepare for both: unprecedented nega-

---

14. No one takes this literally, for obvious reasons.

15. David Chilton, *The Days of Vengeance: An Exposition of the Book of Revelation* (Ft. Worth, Texas: Dominion Press, 1987), p. 198.

tive sanctions, worldwide, and an unprecedented positive move of the Holy Spirit. The Church must pray imprecatory psalms against the wicked, even if their fall means national or international collapse. We must be biblically reasonable in our expectations: there are no known cases of God's widespread positive discontinuities in man's history apart from His widespread negative sanctions. There have only been emotional revivals that accelerated the society's drift into greater cultural and judicial rebellion. On this point, we must display the banner of historical truth.

If such crises hit, this means that Christians must be ready to take enormous economic and maybe personal risks (e.g., nurses during a plague), giving of their time and money way out of proportion to what is considered normal. They must be ready to serve. They must be dedicated in order to exercise local or regional leadership.

The Churches must get "Help" ministries operating now.[16] They must learn the procedures of successful giving. They must learn to recognize the difference between a hustler and a person in need. They must be ready to impart the vision and skills that are basic to personal restoration. They must be ready to make a difference in the local community. They must adopt the Samaritan Strategy.[17] There is no other way. If the Church is not significantly better than any other institution, why should it expect God's blessings in history?

The problem is, Christians for over a century have been convinced by the Church's pessimillennial theologians and popular writers that the Church should not expect God's blessings in history; consequently, its members see it as not significantly better than any other institution. Christians now believe what they have been told: the Church of Jesus Christ has been,

---

16. George Grant, *In The Shadow of Plenty: The Biblical Blueprint for Welfare* (Ft. Worth, Texas: Dominion Press, 1986; co-published by Thomas Nelson Sons); Grant, *The Dispossessed: Homelessness in America* (Dominion Press, 1986; co-published by Crossway Books); Grant, *Bringing in the Sheaves: Transforming Poverty into Productivity* (Brentwood, Tennessee: Wolgemuth & Hyatt, [1985] 1988).

17. Colonel V. Doner, *The Samaritan Strategy: A New Agenda for Christian Activism* (Brentwood, Tennessee: Wolgemuth & Hyatt, 1988).

and will continue to be, *disinherited by God in history*. This is a denial of the plain teaching of Scripture. It is also a denial of extensive responsibility for Christians in in history.

The Promise of Inheritance

Isaiah brought bad news to ancient Judah. God's negative sanctions were coming in history. But after her chastisement, he said, there will come blessings, not just for Israel but for the whole world. These blessings will be based on the world's recognition of the reliability of God's law. When the world at long last obeys God's law, it will escape the ruin of war.

> The word that Isaiah the son of Amoz saw concerning Judah and Jerusalem. And it shall come to pass in the last days, that the mountain of the LORD'S house shall be established in the top of the mountains, and shall be exalted above the hills; and all nations shall flow unto it. And many people shall go and say, Come ye, and let us go up to the mountain of the LORD, to the house of the God of Jacob; and he will teach us of his ways, and we will walk in his paths: for out of Zion shall go forth the law, and the word of the LORD from Jerusalem. And he shall judge among the nations, and shall rebuke many people: and they shall beat their swords into plowshares, and their spears into pruninghooks: nation shall not lift up sword against nation, neither shall they learn war any more. O house of Jacob, come ye, and let us walk in the light of the LORD (Isa. 2:1-5).

This promise was one tied directly to *God's law-based sanctions in history*: ". . . for out of Zion shall go forth the law, and the word of the LORD from Jerusalem. And he shall judge among the nations, and shall rebuke many people." This coming of God's judgment in history will bring unprecedented blessings. These blessings are listed in the section immediately following Isaiah's description of the sufferings of the Messiah (Isa. 53). The message could not be plainer. The Messiah's covenant people will inherit the wealth of the covenant-breakers, not just in eternity but in history.

> Sing, O barren, thou that didst not bear; break forth into singing, and cry aloud, thou that didst not travail with child: for more

are the children of the desolate than the children of the married wife, saith the LORD. Enlarge the place of thy tent, and let them stretch forth the curtains of thine habitations: spare not, lengthen thy cords, and strengthen thy stakes; For thou shalt break forth on the right hand and on the left; and thy seed shall inherit the Gentiles, and make the desolate cities to be inhabited (Isa. 54:1-3).

O thou afflicted, tossed with tempest, and not comforted, behold, I will lay thy stones with fair colours, and lay thy foundations with sapphires. And I will make thy windows of agates, and thy gates of carbuncles [crystal], and all thy borders of pleasant stones. And all thy children shall be taught of the LORD; and great shall be the peace of thy children. In righteousness shalt thou be established: thou shalt be far from oppression; for thou shalt not fear: and from terror; for it shall not come near thee. Behold, they shall surely gather together, but not by me: whosoever shall gather together against thee shall fall for thy sake. Behold, I have created the smith that bloweth the coals in the fire, and that bringeth forth an instrument for his work; and I have created the waster to destroy. No weapon that is formed against thee shall prosper; and every tongue that shall rise against thee in judgment thou shalt condemn. This is the heritage of the servants of the LORD, and their righteousness is of me, saith the LORD (Isa. 54:11-17).

Continuity and Discontinuity

If the amillennialist is correct, these passages refer to the world beyond the final judgment. This inheritance would surely be a peculiar form of continuity: the post-resurrection wealth left behind by the "gentiles" will be insignificant compared to the deliverance from sin and sin's cosmic curse. But if these passages refer to the realm of history, as the context indicates, then there is no escape from either premillennialism or postmillennialism. *Covenant-keepers will inherit the wealth and authority of covenant-breakers in history*. The law of the Proverbs will be fulfilled corporately and individually in history: "A good man leaveth an inheritance to his children's children: and the wealth of the sinner is laid up for the just" (Prov. 13:22). The debate now shifts to the question of the continuity between today's Church and the coming millennial era of blessings: premillennialism (discontinuity) vs. postmillennialism (continuity).

I have already discussed the reasons why we must insist on such a continuity. Here is my final argument: there will be no negative cosmic discontinuity between now and the final judgment, meaning no removal of the Church from history (the Rapture). The wheat and tares will grow together in the same field until the final judgment.

> Another parable put he forth unto them, saying, The kingdom of heaven is likened unto a man which sowed good seed in his field: But while men slept, his enemy came and sowed tares among the wheat, and went his way. But when the blade was sprung up, and brought forth fruit, then appeared the tares also. So the servants of the householder came and said unto him, Sir, didst not thou sow good seed in thy field? from whence then hath it tares? He said unto them, An enemy hath done this. The servants said unto him, Wilt thou then that we go and gather them up? But he said, Nay; lest while ye gather up the tares, ye root up also the wheat with them. *Let both grow together until the harvest*: and in the time of harvest I will say to the reapers, Gather ye together first the tares, and bind them in bundles to burn them: but gather the wheat into my barn (Matt. 13:24-30). (emphasis added)

The disciples were not sure what this parable meant (neither are today's premillennialists), so Jesus explained it to them:

> Then Jesus sent the multitude away, and went into the house: and his disciples came unto him, saying, Declare unto us the parable of the tares of the field. He answered and said unto them, He that soweth the good seed is the Son of man; The field is the world; the good seed are the children of the kingdom; but the tares are the children of the wicked one; The enemy that sowed them is the devil; *the harvest is the end of the world*; and the reapers are the angels. As therefore the tares are gathered and burned in the fire; so shall it be in the end of this world. The Son of man shall send forth his angels, and they shall gather out of his kingdom all things that offend, and them which do iniquity; And shall cast them into a furnace of fire: there shall be wailing and gnashing of teeth. Then shall the righteous shine forth as the sun in the kingdom of their Father. Who hath ears to hear, let him hear (Matt. 13:36-43). (emphasis added).

Notice the placement of the harvest. Covenant-breakers and covenant-keepers will work in society together until the final harvest. When will this be? At the end of the world. There is no possibility that there can ever be a Rapture that is separate from the final judgment.

The prophesied disinheritance of covenant-breakers therefore must take place in history. Why? Because covenant-keepers must inherit the earth from those who possess it today. "What man is he that feareth the LORD? him shall he teach in the way that he shall choose. His soul shall dwell at ease; and his seed shall inherit the earth" (Psa. 25:12-13). But this inheritance cannot be relegated exclusively to the post-judgment world, as amillennialists would insist that it must be. What value would such an cursed inheritance be in that perfect world? Some value (there is continuity between this world and the next), but not very much. The main continuity is ethical – lessons learned in history – not economic. So, title must transfer before the eternal disinheritance of the lost.

The problem today is that the Church is totally unprepared to inherit, let alone administer this inheritance. Christians have been taught that covenant-breakers lawfully disinherited covenant-keepers from the day of Adam's fall, and Jesus' death, resurrection, and ascension of have not altered this covenantal disinheritance. Neither has the arrival of the Holy Spirit at Pentecost. The covenantal message of Noah's Flood – a vast disinheritance of covenant-breakers and an opportunity for comprehensive reconstruction by covenant-keepers – does not register in their thinking. Neither do Christ's words: "All power is given unto me in heaven and in earth" (Matt. 28:18).

We should pray for the conversion of covenant-breakers. This is the most glorious means of their disinheritance. The old man in Adam will die. This will enable God's earthly kingdom to inherit the whole of their wealth when they repent, including their personal skills, which are far more valuable than their material possessions. But this will not happen in history, the pessimillennialists assure us.

Here is the cultural message of pessimillennialism: *the New Covenant is actually worse than the Old Covenant was with respect to covenant-keepers' inheriting in history*. In the Old Covenant, at least the theoretical possibility of inheritance was set before God's people, as we can see in the above passages in Isaiah. However, because of the New Covenant (we are never told exactly why), God has removed even this theoretical prospect. All of this we have been assured, in no uncertain terms, by the pessimillennialists. Calvinist pessimillennialists toss in the doctrine of God's predestination, just to wrap up the case. Arminians, in this unique instance, assume that the Calvinists are correct.

Conclusion

A meaningful, culture-transforming spread of the gospel is unlikely to happen without the crises. The churches are not ready for either a crisis or the harvest. They have little incentive to change. They do not even think change is necessary. Most of them believe in the pre-tribulation Rapture. The others hold to one or another pessimillennial view. They have no developed body of materials on social theory. They will therefore have to learn what to do when (1) they have no moral alternative before God, (2) they recognize that they have no moral alternative, (3), God removes the false alternatives anyway; (4) they switch their millennial viewpoints; and (5) they actually obey God's law. They will resort to on-the-job training; they will have no choice unless they begin to change now.

We will then see the sudden appearance inside the churches of men and women who can be productive in the midst of crises. It is not possible to know in advance who they will be. But to enable them to rise to the top, churches will have to learn to decentralize. They will have to allow the creation of new areas of service within the organization, probably self-financed from the offerings above the tithes of the members.

We can imagine such responses in a flood or short-term emergency. I am not talking about a short-term emergency. I am talking about a new way of life for at least a generation. The bubonic plague forced this in 1347-48, and it returned, generation after generation, for over three centuries, until the last major outbreak in London in 1665. The next year, London burned to the ground.

It will be a time of despair for billions of people. This is the softening-up process that has always been necessary in advance for widespread repentance.

Will the crises come? Let me ask another question. If crises do not come, and women continue to execute 50 to 60 million unborn infants a year, worldwide,[18] what does this say about the God of the Bible? If this level of transgression does not bring massive negative sanctions in history, then the Random News common grace amillennialists are correct: the sanctions of God are ethically inscrutable in history. And if this is true, there cannot be any explicitly biblical social theory that would differentiate a covenant-keeping society from a covenant-breaking society. God's kingdom would be aborted by Satan in history.

An economic crisis would be ideal. Few people would die, but millions of people in the West would be filled with fear. They might then turn to God for deliverance. The false god of this age, material prosperity, would be publicly dethroned. Its prophets, the economists and politicians, would be scattered. The reigning paradigms of this era would be broken. In such a crisis, a new worldview could become dominant. But it would have to present a comprehensive, consistent social theory to deal with the nature of the crisis. Neither amillennialism nor premillennialism can offer such a theory.

Must the crises come? No. It is conceivable that God will launch His era of millennial blessings by adopting a unique, historically unprecedented technique: covenantal revival apart from widespread negative sanctions. We should not assume that He will do this, but He might. This would produce an unprecedented disinheritance/inheritance: the transfer of the assets of today's worldwide satanic kingdom directly to God's kingdom by means of billions of individual conversions to saving faith. "Save souls *and* assets!" I personally pray that He will do this, but He does not answer all of my prayers favorably.

We need a great revival. What kind of revival must it be? A controversial one. The theologically conservative Presbyterian

---

18. *World Population and Fertility Planning Technologies: The Next 20 Years* (Washington, D.C.: Office of Technology and Assessment, 1982), p. 63.

leader of the 1920's and 1930's, J. Gresham Machen,[19] said it well in 1932, four years before he and his associates were expelled from the Presbyterian Church, U.S.A. for their non-compliance with that denomination's growing theological liberalism:

> The presentation of that body of truth necessarily involves controversy with opposing views. People sometimes tell us that they are tired of controversy in the Church. "Let us cease this tiresome controversy," they say, "and ask God, instead, for a great revival." Well, one thing is clear about revivals – a revival that does not stir up controversy is sure to be a sham revival, not a real one. This has been clear ever since our Lord said that He had come not to bring peace upon earth but a sword.[20]

The curse of God in history against His Church would be this: He will bring neither the crises nor a covenantal revival. This would maintain the original satanic disinheritance: from Adam's fall to the present. It would mean that the Incarnation, death, resurrection, and ascension of Jesus Christ *in history* were culturally irrelevant divine discontinuities. It would mean that the Church of Jesus Christ is merely a rescue mission. Yet it is this historic outcome of gospel preaching that the pessimillennialists defend. They preach Satan's defeat of the Great Commission.

If you choose to believe the pessimillennial version of the Church's history, that is your self-imposed burden in life. As for me, I choose optimism. I preach Christ's resurrection in history.

---

19. J. GRESSum MAYchen.

20. J. Gresham Machen, "Christianity in Conflict," in Vergilius Ferm (ed.), *Contemporary American Theology* (New York: Round Table Press, 1932), I, p. 271.

13

WHAT IS TO BE DONE?

Look down from heaven, and behold from the habitation of thy holiness and of thy glory: where is thy zeal and thy strength, the sounding of thy bowels and of thy mercies toward me? are they restrained? Doubtless thou art our father, though Abraham be ignorant of us, and Israel acknowledge us not: thou, O LORD, *art our father, our redeemer; thy name is from everlasting. O* LORD, *why hast thou made us to err from thy ways, and hardened our heart from thy fear? Return for thy servants' sake, the tribes of thine inheritance. The people of thy holiness have possessed it but a little while: our adversaries have trodden down thy sanctuary (Isa. 63:15-18).*

For three centuries, the enemies of God have steadily gained control over the sanctuaries: in Church, State, and culture. They have been invited inside the gates, not as conquerors, but as colleagues and fellow-heirs of the kingdom's promises. But now they have begun visibly trampling on the sanctuaries. Slowly, very slowly, a small contingent of the true heirs of God's kingdom have begun to perceive the nature of the problem, but they have no idea what the solutions may be.

The solutions begin with straight thinking. The solutions are more than intellectual; they are moral and institutional. But we must begin with straight thinking. It does no good to begin to make needed repairs if we have no repair manual. But we have this manual. Unfortunately, today's Church rejects five-sixths of it (or more) as no longer operational.

Here are three conclusions that I hope this book has proven. First, theology is not a rarified intellectual exercise that can be safely contained inside the four walls of a church building.

Second, biblical theology is *applied* theology. Third, by their fruits are we to distinguish competing theologies.

One of the most neglected fruits of theology in the history of the Church has been social theory. There are many reasons for this. First, as I have attempted to show in this book, there has been a commitment to millennial views that deny the very possibility of the expansion of God's *institutional* kingdom in history. Christians have denied that *kingdom* means *civilization*, at least with respect to God's kingdom. God's kingdom is not acknowledged as a civilization, even though Satan's kingdom is freely acknowledged as a civilization. Second, there has been a denial of God's predictable sanctions in history, either applied directly by God or representatively by His covenant people. Third, there has been a denial of covenant law in the New Testament era.

To remove biblical law from eschatology is to castrate the kingdom of God. Without biblical law, the idea of God's predictable sanctions in history inevitably disappears. The rule is this: *no law, no sanctions*. More to the point: no *written* law, no *predictable* sanctions. Each millennial view requires a particular concept of God's sanctions in history. Deny that God brings predictable positive and negative sanctions in history – sanctions that are governed by the terms of His Bible-revealed law – and you deliver Christians into the hands of covenant-breakers. Either you argue, as premillennialists and amillennialists do, that the effects of the gospel will not be culture-transforming, or else you wind up as non-theonomic postmillennialists have: incapable of specifying the judicial conditions by which we can correctly evaluate the coming of God's millennial blessings. Without a biblical, judicial theology, the New Age millennium[1] and/or the New World Order could not be distinguished from God's age of millennial blessings. Neither pessimillennialism nor pietistic postmillennialism can provide the theological foundation for the establishment of God's kingdom in history.

Then what is the alternative?

---

1. Alberto Villoldo and Ken Dychtwald (eds.), *Millennium: Glimpses into the 21st Century* (Los Angeles: J. P. Tarcher, 1981).

Two Practical Questions

In 1902, Lenin wrote a book with a question for its title: *What Is to Be Done?* Forty years earlier, that same title had been chosen by the radical Cherneshevsky for a novel that he began writing upon his imprisonment in the Peter and Paul Fortress. His book had become a favorite of Lenin's revolutionary older brother, who attempted to assassinate the Czar, and was lawfully executed.[2] It then became a favorite of Lenin's. But Lenin did not write a novel; he wrote a revolutionary manifesto.[3] This was to become the most important of his works. It was subtitled, *Burning Questions of Our Movement*. Things burned for Lenin. His newspaper was called *The Spark* (*Iskra*). As James Billington says, there was fire in the minds of men.[4]

In 1976, Francis Schaeffer also wrote a book with a question for a title: *How Should We Then Live?* This is the burning question of our movement: Christianity. This burning is different from the radical's burning: ours is fire initiated by the Spirit of God, man's only alternative to the consuming fire of final judgment (Rev. 20:14-15).

Schaeffer did not answer his own question. His book does not even attempt to do so; it is merely a brief popular history of Western culture. It surveys the rise of authoritarianism, tells us that we must speak out against it, warns us that we may well be executed for doing so, and offers no alternative political program. He suggested no specific, concrete, Bible-based, comprehensive ethical system. Lenin, in contrast, did answer his question, but his answers are now exposed to all mankind as productive of political tyranny and economic poverty. Leninism is just one more version of the power religion, one more attempt to build Babylon's empire: the god that fails.

So, what is to be done by all those who call themselves Christians? What do they do as individuals, as I hope to show, mat-

---

2. Robert Payne, *The Life and Death of Lenin* (New York: Simon & Schuster, 1964), pp. 65-72.

3. It was not noticeably Marxist; it was elitist-terrorist: *ibid.*, pp. 148-54.

4. James Billington, *Fire in the Minds of Men: Origins of the Revolutionary Faith* (New York: Basic Books, 1980).

ters far less than what they do as members of the Church. I begin with a presupposition: *the Church is primary*. Anyone who does not accept this premise will not appreciate this chapter. The family is important; the State is important; neither one is even remotely as important as the Church.[5]

A Loss of Authority

In the *Washington Times* (July 25, 1990), columnist Georgie Anne Geyer warns of a new threat to America, a national criminal gang structure that will soon rival the Mafia. Some 100,000 youths in Los Angeles County have already joined 900 of these violent criminal gangs. They are now spreading out across the nation. Highly disciplined, it is almost impossible for the police to penetrate them. These gangs command unqualified loyalty from their members. They have become substitute families. Captain Raymond Gott of the L. A. Sheriff's Department says, "One of my concerns, particularly in high-gang areas, is that parents totally abdicate parental responsibility, and they've given it to anyone who will pick it up." The problem, Geyer speculates, is a breakdown of authority.

> But the core of this problem seems to me to be simple in analysis and difficult in execution: We have become a society that refuses to socialize or acculturate its young because we have degraded all authority, and these far-out gangs symbolize the failure in stark terms that should warn us of larger reverberations.

How can Christians successfully bring the gospel to gang members and thereby undermine the gangs? In part, this is an organizational and tactical question, but more fundamentally, it is theoretical and strategic. It must be answered, and answered correctly, very soon. The price of our failure will be high.

---

5. It is disagreement over this issue that divides Rushdoony's version of Christian Christian Reconstruction from *all* the other major writers in the movement. They all belong to a local church. He refuses. They all take the Lord's Supper regularly in a local church. He refuses. None of them attends a Sunday morning home Bible study as a substitute for attending a morning or evening church worship service. He does. This is why none of them places the family, Christian education, or politics above the Church as the primary agency of Christian Reconstruction.

First and foremost, what message should we bring? It must include an appeal to the misdirected sense of loyalty that these gangs are able to call forth from their members. The Church of Jesus Christ must be presented as a valid institutional option, one with a better authority structure than the gangs can offer. *We can't beat something with nothing*. Yet the institutional Church today neither calls for such loyalty nor expects it. Churches do not honor each other's excommunications, nor do they expect their own excommunications to carry weight, either on earth or in eternity. Their impotent sanctions and lack of respect for other churches' sanctions reflects this lack of any real authority today. Churches have little sense of authority, so they cannot compete effectively with organizations that do possess this sense, whether gangs, cults, or secret societies.

There is a scene in the movie "Becket" where Thomas Becket, the late twelfth-century Archbishop of Canterbury, is confronted by some of the king's officers, who have been sent by the king to arrest him. Becket draws a circle around himself and announces, "The man who crosses this line will have his soul condemned to hell." Not one of them dares to cross. Today's Archbishop of Canterbury may not even believe in hell. Surely, some of his recent predecessors haven't, and most of those prelates under his authority do not. The Church no longer commands the respect due to an agency that represents God in history. God's sanctions are not taken seriously, so why should the Church's authority be taken seriously?[6]

The Church, by not taking itself very seriously, is not taken seriously by anyone else. The West's churches suffer from a distinct disadvantage. Behind the Iron Curtain, churches are beginning to recognize the power they possess to affect history. This realization has not yet penetrated the Western churches. Evangelism therefore suffers. If this self-imposed cultural and judicial impotence of the churches continues, their members are going to suffer persecution. The "equal time for Satan" rhetoric

---

6. Meredith G. Kline's theory of God's inscrutable historical sanctions has played its small role in undermining the authority of the Church today. While few people have ever heard of him, they share his view of God's historical sanctions.

of the political pluralists is rapidly becoming "no time for Jesus" in every public institution. Meanwhile, every institution is steadily being redefined by the messianic State either as inherently public or else under no other jurisdiction than the State.

The Prophesied Revival

For well over a decade, I have heard major Church and parachurch leaders predicting that there will soon be a great worldwide revival. So, where are their recommended plans to accommodate this revival? Nobody has one. Leaders make these glowing prophecies with all the confidence that they predict the imminent Rapture. Yet they do not restructure their lives, debts, and retirement investment portfolios in terms of an imminent Rapture. Why not? *Because they do not really believe in an imminent Rapture.*

If you believe that something is going to take place, you plan for it. You take steps to finance your plan. If you do not plan for it and begin to execute the plan, you simply do not believe it. It is just one option among many, and not one very high on your list of probabilities.[7]

Here is my premise: if God-honoring social change comes to this nation and then to the world (or vice versa), it must come through the institutional Church, with its sacraments and discipline. What is this discipline? The threat of excommunication: keeping people away from the communion table. To enforce its discipline, it must close communion to all non-Christians and Christians under Church sanctions.

The Church is primary. The Church, alone among human institutions, survives the final judgment intact. God-honoring social change will not come primarily through Christian education, Christian publishing, or Christian television networks. The Church will use all of these tools; they will not be allowed by

---

7. The reason why I devote as much time and money as I do to writing and publishing Christian Reconstruction books instead of spending time managing my investment portfolio is that I am persuaded that the need for such materials will take an historically discontinuous leap before I die. If I am wrong, the books will still produce some fruits, but it is my belief in, and hope for, a discontinuous move by the Holy Spirit that keeps me at my word processor eight hours a day, six days a week (then I go home and read).

God to use the Church, unless He is bringing it under judgment. Whatever happens, *it is the Church that will bear the brunt of the responsibility*. So, we do not need to be geniuses to conclude that one of four things must take place:

1. The revival will reshape the Church unexpectedly and totally when it hits.
2. The Church will prepare for it well in advance.
3. The Church will prepare, but the revival will not come.
4. The Church will not prepare; therefore, the revival will not come.

The fourth possibility is the chilling one. For that failure, we will be held accountable.

I think it is time to begin thinking about the kinds of institutional changes that a worldwide revival would probably force upon the Church. We should now begin to make plans for these preliminary changes, so that when it comes, we will not be caught flat-footed.

My bet: the Church will be caught flat-footed.

Satan Wins By God's Default

Maybe God does not intend to send a revival. Maybe we are dealing with a God who calls men to be fruitful and multiply (Gen. 1:28), and then gives them Western technology that enables them to meet this requirement. This brings over five billion people into the world (still growing), nine-tenths of whom (minimum) will spend eternity in hell and the lake of fire if no revival comes. The longer this rate of population increase continues, the smaller the percentage of Christians, at present growth rates. This is "the population bomb": not physical starvation but spiritual starvation. High temperature physical starvation will follow, however: God's negative sanctions beyond history. Covenant-breakers will move into eternity just as they lived: *covenantally dead*. There is only escape: saving faith.

To win this cosmic war, Satan merely has to see to it that no revival comes. What specifically does he have to do? Nothing. He can retain the covenantal allegiance of the vast majority of men merely by standing pat. People are automatically born into his covenantal kingdom. They are lost by default because of Adam's rebellion. *God therefore has to act positively in order to win the souls of men*. Satan doesn't. He can win by remaining passive, just so long as God refuses to send the Holy Spirit to bring His irresistible grace in history. Satan wins by God's default.

So, here is the choice of agendas: a God who wins in history by sending grace by His Spirit, or a God who loses in history by standing pat. If nothing changes, the mere birth rate differentials between the saved and the lost will guarantee the triumph of Satan's kingdom in history. Add up the populations of China, India, and the Islamic world. Toss in most of Latin America. Toss in Europe. Don't forget New York City, Los Angeles County, and San Francisco. What do the numbers tell us? Christianity is losing. *Continuity means historical defeat for God's kingdom in history*.

Amillennialism teaches that this is all we can legitimately expect. Premillennialism teaches that Christ's coming earthly kingdom will be marked only by the outward obedience of men. Premillennialism does not teach that most people will be converted to saving faith in Christ. In fact, given the Arminian views of most premillennialists, they cannot possibly assert that the coming of the earthly kingdom will automatically lead to mass revival. Some, like Dave Hunt, say specifically that the hearts of most men will not be changed, and that in this sense, the millennial earthly reign of Christ should not be equated with the kingdom of God.[8]

Then where are we? More to the point, where are they? Five billion souls are here. We cannot send them back. The question is: Are they going to perish eternally by the billions? Are we living in the most horrible period in man's history, when hell starts filling up in earnest? World population keeps growing. Will we live to see 10 billion people ready for eternal fire? Will we not see a great harvest?

What is to be done?

---

8. Dave Hunt and T. A. McMahon, *The Seduction of Christianity: Spiritual Discernment in the Last Days* (Eugene, Oregon: Harvest House, 1985), p. 250.

The Postmillennial Hope

I prefer to believe that in the coming millennium, the seventh since creation, God is going to send His Spirit. I cannot be sure, but it seems to me that this is the way God works.

I think this will happen fairly soon. If it doesn't, then Satan will be able to boast: "They obeyed your rule (Gen. 1:28), and therefore I will spend eternity with vastly more souls." The multiplication of mankind, minus the saving work of the Holy Spirit, means the overwhelming defeat of God's gospel and His Church in history. This is not prophecy; this is simply applied covenant theology. You do not need a degree in theology to figure this out; a hand-held calculator is sufficient.

I do not tell God what to do. I do make strong suggestions to Him from time to time. My number-one suggestion today is: "Don't sit on Your hands too much longer. Otherwise, people's faithfulness to the external terms of the dominion covenant – their multiplication – will become Satan's most successful jiu-jitsu operation against You in history."

I think the long-predicted but institutionally unexpected revival is imminent. Psychologically, I have to think this way; it is the only way I can see for God not to be defeated in history by the very success of the world's population in meeting the requirements of God's biological command to be fruitful and multiply. I do not choose to believe in the historic victory of Satan as a direct result of people's obedience to the external demographic requirement of God's law. I choose instead to believe in a coming historical discontinuity: mass revival.

The Mindset of the Critics

Non-Christians may be surprised to learn how hostile most Christians are to such a view of God's work in history. In his scathing attack on Christian Reconstruction, Dr. Masters, the heir of Calvinist Charles Spurgeon, who now occupies the pulpit of London's Metropolitan Tabernacle, has this to say about people who believe that God will save the souls of large numbers of people in our day. He is visibly contemptuous of those who foresee a future outpouring of God's salvation:

> Even now this restoration is underway, or so they believe. After nineteen hundred years of marking time or edging forward at a snail's pace, the kingdom of God is now back on the march, heading toward a season of spectacular evangelism and social dominion.[9]

Notice the tone of this remark. Anyone who believes in a discontinuous breakthrough of the Holy Spirit in history is supposedly naive in the ways of God. Masters points to the slow movement of the gospel in history, but he also assumes that this is normative throughout history. There is no question that for the billions of people now alive ever to be saved, it will take a monumental, *historically unprecedented* move of the Holy Spirit. But so adamant are the critics of postmillennialism that nothing like this can ever take place that they heap ridicule on those who sincerely believe that God may not necessarily have as His eternal decree the destruction of today's billions of lost souls. The more Calvinistic these critics, the more contemptuous their dismissal of these billions. If these lost souls were converted, this would verify postmillennialism. The critics would rather see them perish. There is no eschatological neutrality.

Let us recognize the unstated mental assumption that must be in the mind of anyone who calls himself a Calvinist, yet who ridicules the idea of a discontinuous break into history by the Holy Spirit: "These five billion people are lost, they're going to stay lost, they therefore *deserve* to stay lost, and anyone who says anything different is a postmillennial utopian." I am, indeed.

My concern is with evangelism. I am not willing to write off automatically (prophetically) the souls of five-plus billion people. God has this prerogative; I do not. Again, let me say it as plainly as I can: my hostility to amillennialism and premillennialism is not based on my disagreements with their interpretations of this or that verse in Scripture. Good men have disagreed for a long time over the proper interpretation of Bible verses. My hostility is to the mindset that has to underlie any Calvinist who says that God will not move large numbers of souls into His kingdom at

---

9. Peter Masters, "World Dominion: The High Ambition of Reconstructionism," *Sword & Trowel* (May 24, 1990), p. 13.

some point in history. He is saying, in no uncertain terms: "To hell with the whole world. I'm in the Book of Life, and that's what counts for me." It is a bad attitude, but it underlies all pessimillennial Calvinism. The Arminian pessimillennialists have an excuse: they do not believe in God's irresistible grace. But the Calvinist who thinks in pessimillennial terms has necessarily adopted an elitist attitude: a world in which he assumes, and sometimes even says publicly, that "God will not fill up heaven with the people of my generation. But I've got mine!"

My attitude is different. I think: "Oh, God, if you were willing to let me in, why don't you let billions in? It's no more difficult for you to let five billion more in than to let me in." I can pray in confidence that God might do this in my day because I know he will do it someday. Pessimillenialists do not pray for the conversion of the world with my degree of confidence, even those Presbyterian elders who take a public oath that they do believe in the Westminster Larger Catechism (Answer 191).

Deflecting Evangelism

The Rapture could solve one aspect of the evangelism problem, of course. The post-Rapture millennium would get the message of personal salvation to the lost, though it would not necessarily get them saved. (A top-down political bureaucracy run by Christians is hardly the equivalent of widespread, personal regeneration.) Most dispensationalists say that they believe the Rapture is imminent. Fair enough, but then they should not keep predicting the imminent revival. The imminent Rapture is the *alternative* to the imminent revival, not its means. If Jesus is coming to set up an earthly kingdom, then the revival, if it actually occurs, will be a post-"Church Age" phenomenon. The Christians who are on earth today will not be here to see it, promote it, or respond to it. We will be in heaven, or wherever it is the raptured Church will be sent for cosmic rest and recreation.

Institutionally, theologically, and emotionally, an appeal to the imminence of the Rapture is the removal from the Church of any responsibility for preparing for a great revival. Such a revival cannot be prepared for today; it is a post-Rapture event. If you wonder what I have most against premillennialism, this is it. By its very nature, it keeps Christians from praying about, planning for, and then financing the worldwide event that could overturn Satan's kingdom in the very period in which he expects to capture 6-10 billion souls. A vision of a post-Rapture revival motivates Christians to do little more than the equivalent of passing out gospel tracts. It does not prepare them for serious results from their evangelism. It is *evangelism for an elite*: those few who will be Raptured out of history. It is *lifeboat evangelism*, not "save the whole passenger list (let alone the crew and the ship)" evangelism. It is evangelism that explicitly assumes "to hell with the world on this side of the Rapture."

The premillennialist can always say that he is praying for the only discontinuous event (cosmic) that can conceivably allow the gospel to spread across the world in time. Even though Christ's millennial rule will not guarantee the widespread conversion of men, we are told (correctly) that it can at least guarantee that everyone on earth will hear the gospel. But the problem of the need for a discontinuous move by the Holy Spirit in history is not evaded by an appeal to the premillennial version of the millennium. Why does the Holy Spirit need a cosmic discontinuity in order to achieve His work? He still must impose His historic discontinuity. This is the great discontinuity, not the cosmic transformation. But modern Christians are hypnotized by the thought of a cosmic discontinuity. They forget that their own conversion to saving faith was a far greater discontinuity that the Second Coming of Christ. They do not recognize how great a salvation they possess. It is too common for them. They do not psychologically recognize the magnitude of man's sin and the magnitude of God's grace in history. They may say they do, but they have not integrated this into their thinking.

If this eschatology is wrong, then it necessarily deflects our concern for evangelism from the "Church Age," where we are responsible, to a non-existent, post-Rapture, bureaucratic, millennial age, for which we are not in any way responsible and to which we can contribute very little except writing handbooks for millennial civil government, which premillennialists do not choose to write. Here is the problem: the Great Commission was given to the *Church*, not to an international army of Christian civil bureaucrats with headquarters in Jerusalem.

The Turning Point?

I think history is coming to a head. I believe in the 6,000-year-old earth. I believe in a millennium of visible, worldwide covenantal blessings. I believe in the sabbath. I believe in the *sabbath millennium.*[10] But these chronological and symbolic biblical references do not weigh heavily upon me. If I turn out to be wrong, my embarrassment will be posthumous. I can live with that. What weighs upon me is not prophecy; rather, it is the inescapable reality of today's worldwide population. *God will lose 6 to 10 billion souls over the next 75 years if the revival does not come.* Apart from revival, the only thing that could change these numbers is some sort of demographic catastrophe. This does nothing eternally positive for the billions who are already here.

What is to be done?

The Traditional Consequences of Revivals

North America has had two great revivals, the First Great Awakening (1735-55?) and the Second Great Awakening (1800-50?). There have been similar revivals elsewhere, notably the Welsh revival at the turn of this century. They had common features. The main feature they all have shared is that they did not produce Christian societies.

Consider the two Great Awakenings in North America. They shared the following common features. First, a downgrading of theology. The "new light" preachers were rarely theologians; more often than not, they were untrained itinerant preachers who had no biblical doctrine of the institutional Church. If they had possessed a biblical doctrine of the institutional Church, they would not have been itinerant preachers.

Second, a downgrading of Church discipline. The "new light" preachers emphasized the experiential moment, not the hard work of a lifetime of service. The churches to a great extent

10. Gary North, *The Sinai Strategy: Economics and the Ten Commandments* (Tyler, Texas: Institute for Christian Economics, 1986), pp. 86-92.

were uncooperative with these wandering outsiders, and they suffered the consequences: church splits, attacks from "revived" saints, and the creation of lowest-common-denominator rival congregations.[11]

Third, a wave a sexual debauchery. The rise of illegitimate births nine months after a local revival was noted by observers during both Great Awakenings, and modern historians have confirmed this statistical relationship.

Fourth, the subsequent falling away of many. The heat of the moment cooled. The converts left the churches. These people could not be called to repentance. This phenomenon led to what were called "the burned-over districts" by Charles Finney, who had personally burned over many of them.

Fifth, the rise of political liberalism and non-Christian social transformation. The First Great Awakening led to the American Revolution and then to the Unitarian-Masonic Federal Constitution, with its abolition of Christian oaths of office (Article VI, Section 3).[12] The Second Great Awakening led to abolitionism as the primary focus of Christian political action, and then to the Unitarian-led Civil War (1861-65). American Christianity split in the decades after the War: a worldly social gospel paralleled by an escalating pietist-fundamentalist retreat from all social and political concerns. Common-ground (anti-creedal) religious experientialism leads to common-ground (neutral) ethics and common-ground (humanistic) politics.

A lot of people got saved. American society didn't. The unique period of widespread conversions did not last. Not many people got saved after 1860. God expects more than this from revivals.

The Transfer of Cultural Authority

The two great revivals of the American past led to a transfer of cultural authority from orthodox Christians to Unitarians and

11. By far, the most theologically perceptive history of these events is Charles Hodge, *The Constitutional History of the Presbyterian Church in the United States of America*, 2 vols. (Philadelphia: Presbyterian Board of Publication, 1851), II, chapters 4-6.

12. Gary North, *Political Polytheism: The Myth of Pluralism* (Tyler, Texas: Institute for Christian Economics, 1989), Part 3.

then to humanists. The First Great Awakening broke the civil authority of the older Calvinistic holy commonwealths of New England. Then the Civil War broke the cultural authority of Arminian Christianity. The parallel rise of the social gospel movement and dispensational pietism delivered the nation into the hands of the humanists.[13]

Why did this occur? Because the revivals promoted the *lowest common denominators*: theologically, ecclesiastically, judicially, and emotionally. There was no vision of a holy commonwealth in the preaching of the revivalists. Everything was focused on gaining from individuals a one-time profession of faith by whatever means. The revival meetings were like medieval fairs: everyone came. The unconverted masses came mostly for excitement, secondarily for entertainment, and only belatedly for a religious conversion. The revivalists gave them what they wanted. The pastors surely couldn't and still remain faithful to God.

There was an ecclesiastical transfer of authority after 1800. The waves of revival spread westward, just as the population had. The mainline denominations did not move fast enough, except for the Cumberland Presbyterians, who were not very Calvinistic and did not require advanced academic degrees for their pastors. The old saw goes like this: "The Baptist evangelists walked into the West, the Methodists rode on horseback, the Presbyterians went by covered wagon, and the Episcopalians waited for regularly scheduled train service. The Congregationalists stayed home." The more rigorous the academic requirements to serve as a pastor, the slower the comparative growth of the denomination during the revival. Presbyterians, New England Congregationalists, and Episcopalians, who had been the dominant influences as late as 1790, were dwarfed by the Baptists and Methodists during the next half century.

The pietism of these new churches was uniquely suited to the humanists' demand that Christians, *as Christians*, withdraw from public life over the next century and a half. Except for one doomed crusade – Prohibition – nothing of a social or political

---

13. C. Gregg Singer, *A Theological Interpretation of American History* (Nutley, New Jersey: Craig Press, 1964), ch. 5.

nature motivated these groups after World War I. Only with the Supreme Court's legalization of abortion has a small minority of these groups, usually laymen and especially laywomen, begun to re-enter American political life. Only with the accelerating reduction of the lowest common denominator of American public morality have a few Christians begun to challenge the establishment's humanist elite, which now has a huge majority of public school graduates, meaning a growing army of functional illiterates, solidly behind it.

What we have seen in past revivals does not inspire optimism about future revivals. The revivalism of the past has been *antinomian* to the core. Without exception, the great revivals have accelerated the drift into secularism, by separating personal conversion from biblical law. This antinomianism has undermined Church, family, and State. In short, *revivalism has never been covenantal.* It has always been individualistic. It has undermined the primary covenantal institution, the Church, and from there it has undermined everything else. *Revivalism has invariably transferred authority away from the existing Church order, yet always in the name of Christianity.*

So, what is to be done?

From Apprenticeship to Seminary

We have adopted a bureaucratic standard for pastoral training, one modeled by the university system: the theological seminary. The university is a failed Christian experiment. It is an institution which was invented by Christians, but which has without exception in over eight centuries led to institutional surrender to the humanists. Not one major university has retained its Christian roots. Without exception, colleges and universities have fallen to the humanists within a few generations. The history of the university has been a history of unrelieved theological failure. Yet churches have almost universally adopted the certification system designed for the university as our model for screening candidates for the ministry. Also, to get into most seminaries, you first need a college degree: a double witness to the evil of the day.

The seminary is bureaucratic. It follows the model of all the other modern certification institutions. In law, medicine, and theology, the older training system of apprenticeship has been replaced by the classroom lecture and the formal, written examination. This move *from personalism to impersonalism* has been a universal phenomenon, one that reflects the impersonalism of Newtonian thought. The cosmic personalism of creationism has been replaced by the cosmic impersonalism of mechanism. To gain autonomy for scientific man the modern world has paid a dear price.

But God is still on His throne. Today, the decentralization of technology is making possible the overcoming of the existing bureaucratic educational system. When we can put 1,000 volumes of books on a plastic disk (CD-ROM) that costs about $2 to reproduce, and then use a 4-pound portable computer to search any word or combination of words on those 1,000 volumes within a few seconds, the end of the old education is in sight. It is simply too expensive.

Today, the entire verbal and visual content of seminary education can be put on videotape. Eventually, it will be on CD-ROM disks. A few courses, such as biblical languages, need classroom instruction, but since the teaching of these languages is basically a charade, little is lost by relying on electronic teaching. A year after graduation, few pastors retain more than a crib-note (Bagster's helps) knowledge of Greek and Hebrew. How many pastors still use Greek and Hebrew Bibles to do their sermon preparation? About as high a percentage as American Ph.D.'s who keep up with their German and French.

At least in this case, we know what is to be done.

Covenantal Evangelism

The continuing disintegration of the churches in our day points to a failure of evangelism and church-planting in this century. Why has everything we seem to have tried failed to make a dent in today's humanist civilization? Why has revivalism failed, time after time? Why has Church discipline almost ceased to exist? Why have the churches not dominated evangelism, leaving it instead to the parachurch ministries? Where have the churches gone wrong?

I contend that we have failed to understand the five-point biblical covenant model: (1) transcendence/presence, (2) hierarchy/representation, (3) law/ethics, (4) oath/judgment, and (5) inheritance/continuity. How should this model be applied to the Church? More to the point, how should the modern Church be reconstructed in order that it might conform better to this five-point model?

We have had many competing models of Church government: independency, Presbyterian committees, Episcopalian and Methodist personalism, Pentecostal personalism. All of them have failed to produce what the Bible says is mandatory: *dominion by covenant*. We need to solve the problems of the one and the many: coherent Church order with individual initiative, international strategy with local tactics. How can we do it?

I believe that a fundamental flaw exists in contemporary Church order, one which would lead to a military defeat if the same flaw existed in an army, or to bankruptcy in a business. There is no agreed-upon strategy of conquest, no integration of dispersed efforts, no Bible-based performance standards, and above all, no system of pinpointing personal responsibility for actual performance in the field.

The Principle of the Four Corners

I believe that the principle of the four corners is perhaps the most neglected strategic principle in the Bible. We are told that a river went out of Eden (downhill, obviously, indicating that Eden was a mountain) to water the garden, where it became four rivers (Gen. 2:10). We are also told that there are four corners of the earth, a phrase which I freely confess I do not believe is to be taken literally: "And he shall set up an ensign [banner] for the nations, and shall assemble the outcasts of Israel, and gather together the dispersed of Judah from the four corners of the earth" (Isa. 11:12). In Numbers 15:38, there is a requirement that all Hebrews wear robes. The New King James Version translates this verse more clearly than the King James: "Speak to the children of Israel: Tell them to make tassels on the corners of their garments throughout their generations, and to put a blue thread in the tassels of the corners." Corners? On robes? Surely this is symbolic. There is only one sensible way to interpret this: they wore four *tassels* on their robes. These garments were to hang so as to make the garments symbolically like the four corners of a house. In principle, these garments were like the four corners of the world.

Why four corners? To indicate the task of God-given *worldwide conquest*. Maps are structured in terms of four corners and four primary directions. The four corners reflect the symbolic structure of the rivers of Eden, which pointed to worldwide dominion. Those four rivers flowed out to the four corners of the earth. Adam and his family were to go our from the garden in all four directions, progressively subduing the earth to the glory of God.[14]

Targeting the Cities

Evangelism is the historical and institutional basis of continuity across time and geography. It is man's part of the two-part contribution to the continuity of Church and culture. (The other part is the Holy Spirit's program of coercive discontinuities.) Without the proclamation of the gospel, this world would be lost to Satan. A positive program of evangelism is necessary to defeat Satan. Because of original sin, Satan wins by default. Where the gospel is not proclaimed, men automatically perish. Faith comes by hearing, and hearing by the word of God.

The missionary is the Church's "point man" in a long-term strategy of spiritual and cultural conquest. Where does the original missionary come from? Who sends him? Under whose authority does he operate? These are difficult organizational questions. Most important, *who finances him?* A "mother" congregation? The national missions organization? A combination of financial support and judicial authority over him? Financing will heavily inflence the structure of authority. It always does.

If he wants relative independence to build locally, he had better begin with financial independence. This is what Paul taught. This is why he was a tentmaker (Acts 18:3). Probably the

14. James B. Jordan, *The Sociology of the Church: Essays in Reconstruction* (Tyler, Texas: Geneva Ministries, 1986), p. 86.

best way to achieve this is for the pastor and his wife to set up a local day care center. This will finance them, and it will create initial contacts in the community. Then, as the local church grows, the pastor spends more time pastorally. The wife carries on with the day care center, making a decent income. (I help people to do this as a missionary venture.)

The missionary needs a long-range strategy. This is the four-corners strategy. The churches have long ignored this four-corners principle of outreach. I need to outline it.

Quadrants

Let us begin with the case of a single missionary to a particular city or town. The missionary takes the map of the city and divides it into four section by drawing the familiar cross hairs of telescopic sights on rifles. He "scopes out" the city. *His long-range goal is nothing less than the systematic conquest of that city*. He begins by setting up quadrants. Everything on that map is under God judicially; everything is to be brought under God historically. This is *comprehensive geographical evangelism*.

He then begins to set up Bible studies, one in each section of the city, if he can possibly do it. He doesn't ignore any area. Most cities have certain races or income groups in particular quadrants. No group, no race, no class is outside of Christ's jurisdiction. This is why the city must be self-consciously divided into quadrants by the missionary. There must be a plan.

The missionary's next major goal is to establish a church in each of the four sections of city. He uses local Bible studies to recruit people. He may also bring in other missionaries to set up day care centers in the other quadrants.

He acknowledges that he is a limited creature. He needs to make use of the division of labor in order to conquer the city for Christ. One local church per quadrant is hardly sufficient. Therefore, he needs to reproduce himself covenantally. How does he do this? By recruiting and discipling men to become pastors in each of the four quadrants. In each quadrant, he hopes to establish at least one church.

But this is only the beginning. Each of the churches in the four quadrants must plan a similar program of conquest inside its quadrant. From the day any church is begun, its goal must be to launch a minimum of three other churches in its quadrant. Then each of these churches targets its newly designated quadrant. There has to be a plan.

Once the first church becomes legally independent of the mother church's umbrella (if any), the missionary has become a pastor. He sits down with the heads of households in his congregation and tells them that it is his goal to equip at least three other men to become pastors of their own local congregations. They must meet the criteria of I Timothy 3: be married men (or widowers), be hospitable, etc. As he recruits and trains elders, he identifies those who might be capable of becoming pastors. He selects them and trains these few for the pastorate, but with this proviso: each of them must begin his own Bible study, either in the local quadrant or across the city in a yet-unevangelized quadrant.

This is why pastoral training must be decentralized, computerized, and personalized. We must return to the original ideal of apprenticeship. A pastor is best trained by a person in his own city who has a vision for that city. The training must be geared to the specific needs of that city. We need specialization.

A quadrant is a local church's parish. Each new pastor's goal is to repeat this process internally in his quadrant. This must be agreed to well in advance. The long-term goal is to have every person in the city worshipping weekly in a local congregation of some Trinitarian denomination. Nothing less than this meets the minimum requirements of the Great Commission. Any program of church-planting that settles for less than this is a victim of pessimillennialism. Today, they all are.

No More Megachurches

This means that no local congregation should be larger than about 400 members. A local church that is larger than this is not dividing in order to evangelize its quadrant. As soon as a church hits 200 members, it should begin planning a congregational division. Members must be approached and asked to move to the new congregation when it is launched. Each member must regard himself from the beginning as part of God's spiritual army of conquest. He is not to see his membership as passive. He is not there to be entertained.

The Church of Jesus Christ is not a biblical substitute for the theater, no matter how successful modern ecclesiastical entertainment centers appear to be today, when there is no crisis. Entertainment churches will not survive a major crisis unless they become serious. Such churches would not have made it during the bubonic plague in 1348-50, and they will not survive God's coming negative sanctions to serve as base camps for subsequent Christian reconstruction.

The ecclesiastical goal is clear: we must abandon the modern bureaucratic ideal of the megachurch-entertainment center, which has too many problems in continuity when the church's ringmaster-pastor leaves, retires, dies, or runs off with the choir director's teenage daughter. The modern megachurch concentrates Christian resources too much, especially human resources. While a large, well-equipped building is legitimate for the occasional multi-congregation services in the region, it should not be a permanent local church. In between common services, it should function as a regional Christian high school, into which "feeder schools" can send their graduates.

In 1986, a study of membership growth in Brazilian churches revealed this fact: the smaller the member-to-leader ratio, the faster the growth. The Assemblies of God had a 50-to-one ratio, while Lutherans were at 1,000-to-one. The Roman Catholics were 9,000-to-one.[15]

Organic analogies are dangerous unless they are governed by the principles of biblical covenantalism. This analogy is. The Church's goal is to imitate the amoeba. An amoeba does not die; it just divides. These new units then divide. Then they also divide. The species multiplies within its host. The churches need to do something very similar. Eventually, modern humanist culture will develop a terminal case of Trinitarian intestinal flu ("Augustine's Revenge").

15. "Protestants Create an Altered State," *Insight* (July 16, 1990), p. 14.

Bishops

The process of church-planting is repeated until each of the city's quadrants is saturated. The initial goal is to create clusters of four local congregations per city, each with its own pastor. Above each cluster of four is a senior pastor, or bishop (presbyter), but always under the authority of the whole denomination. Bishops must not be legally independent of the denomination's general assembly, which must include laymen.

I know, the word "bishop" terrifies independents and Presbyterians. They equate the office with sacerdotalism. The fact is, the office of bishop is inescapable – as inescapable as a single captain of a ship. In the independent churches, the local pastor is first among equals. Any Baptist pastor who is not strong enough to give primary direction to his deacons is a soon-to-be-dismissed pastor. A new man will be brought in, and this man becomes first among equals. (For want of a better name, let us call this the Spurgeon Effect.)

The office of bishop is inevitable in Presbyterian churches, too; it is just not called by that loathed name. Three-office Presbyterianism – teaching elder, ruling elder, and deacon – makes this office inescapable: ruling elders are not allowed to offer the sacraments apart from the teaching elders. A Presbyterian pastor answers to the presbytery, not to the local congregation. He has a seminary degree; his elders do not. The disciplinary system is more academic and bureaucratic than pastoral, but it is surely hierarchical. The Presbyterian pastor becomes a bishop operationally. But instead of answering to another bishop, he answers to a series of committees. *He is a pastor without a pastor*. Above the local congregation, Presbyterian rule becomes impersonal, and speedy justice is institutionally unobtainable. If Presbyterian committees would each appoint a representative foreman who could make decisions in the name of the committee, yet remain subject to oversight by the committee, this complaint would not be valid. But these foremen would then be bishops.

The goal is to create a judicial system in which quick decisions by pastors is encouraged – the goal of speedy justice (Ex. 18) – but always with the denomination's general assembly, which includes laymen, in the wings to hear appeals. No individual gets a final word. Thus, the organizational goal is to escape all three of the traditional ecclesiastical evils: local one-man rule, sacerdotal episcopacy, and bureaucracy.

The Principle of Decentralization

Christ is the head of the Church. There is no institution that can function without a personal, living head. The Church is described as a body with many members, but with a sovereign Head. Each member has specialized skills (Rom. 12; I Cor. 12). All are to be put to use to serve God. The integration of these skills is achieved through a covenant with a sovereign God through His ordained representatives. God authorizes three institutions with three covenants: Church, family, and State. God decentralizes through multiple covenants. God, being omnipotent, omniscient, and omnipresent, can afford to allow self-government to men and angels. God is not dependent on His subordinates, so He has the ability to delegate responsibility. Because He is absolutely sovereign, He can safely delegate partial sovereignty to His representatives. This is the great mystery of God's sovereignty: God is totally sovereign, yet He delegates authority. Those under His authority are responsible to Him.

Satan, in contrast, imposes only one covenant. He imitates God's sovereignty, but he cannot imitate it to the extent that he can afford to decentralize. He imitates it as a creature must, centralizing power rather than delegating it. Satan's system of control is a top-down bureaucracy. It has to be. He is not omnipotent, omniscient, or omnipresent. He has to rely on his subordinates to provide him with information and to execute his commands. Yet they are all liars and rebels, just as he himself is a liar and a rebel. He has to manage incompetents.[16] So he must use terror and coercion to achieve his goals. This is why Satan's model is always the State, which has the power of the sword, of life and death.

Satan's attempt at God's cosmic personalism results in the personalism of the tyrant who seeks to substitute his will for the will

16. As Peter Cook, playing the devil, told Dudley Moore in "Bedazzled": "I just can't hire decent help. This may have something to do with the wages they receive."

of his subordinates. Satan is a rebel against lawful authority. So are his followers. He therefore dares not allow his subordinates freedom. He must control them from the top down, which means that *Satan's system of rule is power-oriented, not ethics-oriented.* He exercises power in history through terror; God exercises power through service. Jesus Christ is the archetype servant in history; Satan is the archetype tyrant and terrorist. Thus, Satan has to centralize power. He could govern his hierarchy in no other way. Initiative remains at the distant top.

How can Christians conduct an organized campaign of cultural conquest without becoming either a scattered occupation force or a top-down bureaucracy? Only by honoring the principle of decentralization, meaning *local initiative* with a bottom-up appeals court for settling disputes. This means that Christians must also honor the principle of *lawful jurisdiction.* Each institution, as well as each individual, has an exclusive God-given area of lawful authority. To violate these boundaries is to invite tyranny.

If government begins with self-government under God, then Christian churches must start honoring each other's discipline. Pagan civil governments have mutual extradition treaties to deal with criminals who escape across borders. There is a great need for such arrangements. Churches, unfortunately, have yet to think through the implications of Church discipline in a world of competing denominations. Churches must recognize each other's excommunications. If the excommunicated member can walk across the street and join another God-ordained church, then God's judgments against individuals in history is thwarted. He therefore goes to stage two: collective (corporate) judgment in history. We read of this in Deuteronomy 28:15-68. It is not pleasant reading. Churches that refuse to honor each other's excommunications are like people who would try to stop a series of little earthquakes when the only alternative is a truly massive earthquake later on.

Oath and Government

We must begin with this premise: *the institutional Church is a lawful government.* It possesses lawful authority to administer an oath, which only the institutions of the family and civil government lawfully share. The covenant oath is always *self-maledictory*: the individual promises to uphold the terms of the covenant, and if he fails to do so, he calls down upon himself the negative sanctions of God, including those lawfully administered through lawful human government. God grants this authority to invoke and demand an oath only to families, churches, and civil governments. The sanctions of each institution are different: families apply the rod (corporal punishment short of execution), civil governments apply the sword (corporal punishment, including execution), and churches restrict access to the communion table (excommunication).

This Church oath involves the visible sign of baptism. Because it possesses the lawful authority to cut people off from the Lord's Supper, it is a government. Because it is a government, it possesses an institutional system for adjudicating disputes among local members and between members and members in other congregations and denominations. Here is where the breakdown in Church order has become obvious, and has been obvious for centuries. But churches pay no attention.

The gangs of Los Angeles do much better.

Conclusion

We have a tremendous opportunity today. We are seeing the death of a major faith, salvation through politics.[17] While the rhetoric of the imminent, transnational New World Order is escalating, the economic vulnerability of all government welfare programs becomes more and more visible. The reality of modern political life does not match the reality, any more than the reality of Roman political life in the third century A.D. matched the messianic announcements on the coinage.[18] Reality will soon triumph. Humanism as a rival religion is breaking down even as it asserts the apotheosis of the New Humanity.

Something must be put in its place. There is no neutrality. There can be no covenantal vacuums. The gangs of Los Angeles

17. Peter F. Drucker, *The New Realities* (New York: Harper & Row, 1989), ch. 2.
18. Ethelbert Stauffer, *Christ and the Caesars* (Philadelphia: Westminster Press, 1955).

testify loudly to this. The Church, however, is not equally confident about this. Christians look at the religion of humanism as if it were unbeatable. They have forgotten what God does each time in history when covenant-breaking men begin building the latest Tower of Babel.[19] They no longer believe in God's negative corporate sanctions in history.

Churches today are not prepared for the coming of mass revival: theologically, institutionally, financially, educationally, or morally. If we get a mass revival, new converts will inevitably ask: "How Should We Then Live?" If this new life in Christ is defined as "meet, eat, retreat, and hand out a gospel tract," the revival will leave one more egg on the face of God's Church.

None of this is perceived by the churches, which are not ready for revival. Yet revival may come nonetheless. If it does, we will see the most remarkable example of on-the-job-training since the early Church gathered in Jerusalem to meet, eat, and wait for the Holy Spirit to put them to work. They were waiting to receive power (Acts 1:8); today's Church is waiting for late-night reruns of "Ozzie and Harriet."

If revival comes, millions of new converts will ask: "Now what should we do?" What will pastors tell them? "Pray while you're plowing the fields"? Hardly. Ours is not a frontier wilderness. The division of international labor is the most developed in mankind's history. Platitudes will not suffice. Yet platitudes are all that Bible-believing Christians have offered mankind for a century. Christians have rejected biblical law, so all they can do is baptize the prevailing humanism. But baptized humanism will not suffice next time; humanism is too clearly bankrupt.

What is to be done? Solomon told us three millennia ago: "Let us hear the conclusion of the whole matter: Fear God, and keep his commandments: for this is the whole duty of man" (Eccl. 12:13-14). Jesus told us two millennia ago: "If ye keep my commandments, ye shall abide in my love; even as I have kept my Father's commandments, and abide in his love" (John 15:10). The churches have not listened. They need to, soon.

---

19. C. S. Lewis, *That Hideous Strength: A Modern Fairy-Tale for Grown-Ups* (New York: Macmillan, 1946), ch. 16.

CONCLUSION

Thou sawest till that a stone was cut out without hands, which smote the image on his feet that were of iron and clay, and brake them to pieces. Then was the iron, the clay, the brass [bronze], the silver, and the gold, broken to pieces together, and became like the chaff of the summer threshing floors; and the wind carried them away, that no place was found for them. And the stone that smote the image became a great mountain, and filled the whole earth (Dan. 2:34-35).

We conclude where we began, with the fundamental theme of the Bible: the transition from wrath to grace. This takes place in history: definitively and progressively. It is not limited to personal transformation. It involves every area of life in which sin presently reigns.

The definitive transition took place at the death, resurrection and ascension of Jesus Christ. The sending of the Holy Spirit and the destruction of the Old Covenant's World Order at the fall of Jerusalem in A.D. 70 completed the definitive foundation of Jesus Christ's New Covenant World Order.[1] This New World Order is still dominant in history. It will remain dominant. It will smash every earthly imitation New World Order, just as it smashed the Roman Empire.

> Ask of me, and I shall give thee the heathen for thine inheritance, and the uttermost parts of the earth for thy possession. Thou shalt break them with a rod of iron; thou shalt dash them in pieces like a potter's vessel (Psa. 2:8-9).

---

1. David Chilton, *The Days of Vengeance: An Exposition of the Book of Revelation* (Ft. Worth, Texas: Dominion Press, 1987).

The fifth kingdom belongs to Jesus Christ, not to autonomous man. God warns the rulers of the earth: "Be wise now therefore, O ye kings: be instructed, ye judges of the earth. Serve the LORD with fear, and rejoice with trembling. Kiss the Son, lest he be angry, and ye perish from the way, when his wrath is kindled but a little. Blessed are they that put their trust in him" (Psa. 2:10-12). But covenant-breaking man refuses to learn this lesson from either history or the Bible. The messianic rhetoric of political salvation is ingrained in modern man, despite men's loss of faith in the theology of political salvation. As Drucker says, "Political slogans outlive reality. They are the smile on the face of politics' Cheshire Cat."[2] More to the point: "The slogans can still serve as brakes on action. They are unlikely any longer to provide guides to action or motive power."[3] We must be ready for a masssive paradigm shift culturally.

We now see the ultimate unreality: a return to the rhetoric of the Tower of Babel, just before its builders were scattered. In the midst of an unprecedented budget crisis and political deadlock, and in the midst of a military confrontation between the U.S. and Iraq, President Bush announced to Congress:

> A new partnership of nations has begun. We stand today at a unique and extraordinary moment. The crisis in the Persian Gulf, as grave as it is, also offers a rare opportunity to move toward an historic period of cooperation. Out of these troubled times, our fifth objective – a new world order – can emerge: a new era, freer from the threat of terror, stronger in the pursuit of justice, and more secure in the quest for peace. An era in which the nations of the world, east and west, north and south, can prosper and live in harmony.
>
> A hundred generations have searched for this elusive path to peace, while a thousand wars raged across the span of human endeavor. Today that new world is struggling to be born. A world quite different from the one we've known. A world in which the rule of law supplants the rule of the jungle. A world in which nations recognize the shared responsibility for freedom and justice. A world where the strong respect the rights of the weak.

---

2. Peter F. Drucker, *The New Realities* (New York: Harper & Row, 1989), p. 8.
3. *Ibid.*, p. 9.

> This is the vision I shared with President Gorbachev in Helsinki. He, and other leaders from Europe, the gulf and around the world, understand how we manage this crisis today could shape the future for generations to come.[4]

He speaks of a hundred generations. This takes us back to the era of Abraham or thereabouts, in the days when Egypt rocked the cradle of civilization. From Egypt to 1990: a lengthy gestation period. I think Mr. Bush was not deliberayely exaggerating, as messianic as his extended timetable may initially appear. The model of Egypt is always the covenant-breaker's preferred alternative to decentralized biblical civilization. It is time to recall the words of the great German sociologist Max Weber, in a speech he delivered in 1909:

> To this day there has never existed a bureaucracy which could compare with that of Egypt. This is known to everyone who knows the social history of ancient times; and it is equally apparent that to-day we are proceeding towards an evolution which resembles that system in every detail, except that it is built on other foundations, on technically more perfect, more rationalized, and therefore more mechanical foundations. The problem which besets us now is not: how can this evolution be changed? – for that is impossible, but: what is to come of it?[5]

Our generation is about to get the answer to Weber's question. We now face the looming threat of Egypt revisited. This is far more of a threat to the enemies of Christ than to the Church. "Thus saith the LORD; They also that uphold Egypt shall fall; and the pride of her power shall come down: from the tower of Syene shall they fall in it by the sword, saith the Lord GOD" (Ezek. 30:6). The towers of this world shall crumble, and those who trust in them shall fall.

---

4. "Text of President Bush's Address to Joint Session of Congress," *New York Times* (Sept. 12, 1990).

5. Max Weber, "Speech to the *Verein für Sozialpolitik*" (1909); reprinted in J. P. Meyer, *Max Weber and German Politics* (London: Faber & Faber, 1956), p. 127. Cf. Gary North, "Max Weber: Rationalism, Irrationalism, and the Bureaucratic Cage," in North (ed.), *Foundations of Christian Scholarship: Essays in the Van Til Perspective* (Vallecito, California: Ross House Books, 1976), ch. 8.

Kingdom vs. Empire

History manifests a war between two organizational principles of international civil government, kingdom and empire. Christ's international kingdom is decentralized. Satan's international kingdom is centralized, characterized by a top-down bureaucratic system: issuing commands. Satan does not possess God's omniscience, omnipotence, and omnipresence, so he must rely heavily on his own hierarchy (or as C. S. Lewis calls it in *The Screwtape Letters*, "the lowerarchy"). The larger that Satan's empire becomes, the more overextended he becomes. Like a man who attempts to juggle an increasing number of oranges, Satan cannot say no to his assistants, who keep tossing him more decisions. Eventually, every empire collapses. The principle of empire cannot long sustain human government: Church, State, or family.

In the colloquial phrase, empires always bite off more than they can chew. The Bible teaches that human empires were always replaced by other empires, until the advent of Christ's kingdom. From that time forward, it is the kingdom principle that is dominant in history.

The "thousand-year reich" of Nazi Germany lasted twelve years (1933-45). The Communist empire of the Soviet Union is a creaking economic hulk, one which relies on the threat of nuclear war and a strategy of criminal subversion in order to extend its power, and which has steadily bankrupted itself by supporting its bankrupt client states. Empires are parasitic, relying on their conquest of productive nations in order to keep its bureaucracies well fed. But as their political power grows larger with the growth of empire, these bureaucracies steadily strangle the productivity of those who have already fallen to the empire. The empire cannot sustain its expansionist impulse. Meanwhile, its enemies multiply and strengthen their will to resist, unless they have already begun to worship the gods (world-and-life view) of the conquerors.

A Loss of Faith

Christianity, in its orthodox form, challenges all forms of the power religion. Christianity is the religion of Christ's kingdom (civilization). It offers a better way of life and temporal death, for it offers the only path to eternal life. It offers comprehensive redemption – the healing of international civilization.[6] It is the dominion religion.[7]

When Christianity departs from its heritage of preaching the progressive sanctification of men and institutions, it abandon's the idea of Christ's progressively revealed kingdom (civilization) on earth in history. It then departs into another religion, the escape religion. This leaves the battle for civilization in the hands of the various power religionists. Russia saw the defeat of the visible national Church when the theology of mysticism and suffering (kenotic theology) at last brought paralysis to the Russian Orthodox Church. It had been infiltrated by people holding pagan and humanistic views of many varieties.[8] The Church was incapable of dealing with the power religion of Lenin, and especially Lenin's successor, the former seminary student, Joseph Stalin.

We are seeing today a replay of those years written large. The war for the hearts and minds of men continues to escalate internationally. The technology of nuclear destruction competes with the technology of economic healing and the mass communication of the gospel. But, contrary to Marx, it is not the substructure of the mode of production that determines the superstructure of religious faith; the contrary is the case. The battle

6. Gary North, *Is the World Running Down? Crisis in the Christian Worldview* (Tyler, Texas: Institute for Christian Economics, 1988), Appendix C: "Comprehensive Redemption: A Theology for Social Action."

7. On escape religion, power religion, and dominion religion, see my analysis in *Moses and Pharaoh: Dominion Religion vs. Power Religion* (Tyler, Texas: Institute for Christian Economics, 1985), pp. 2-5.

8. Ellen Myers, "Uncertain Trumpet: The Russian Orthodox Church and Russian Religious Thought, 1900-1917," *Journal of Christian Reconstruction*, XI (1985), pp. 77-110. She writes: "Russian pre-revolutionary religious thought was thus generally suspended between the poles of materialist-Marxist and mystic-idealist monism. It partook of fundamentally anarchist Marxist and also Buddhist-style withdrawal from reality; an infatuation with hedonistic classical paganism over against Christian supposedly joyless morality; a 'promethean' desire to raise mankind to godlike superman status; and, concomitant to all three, an 'apocalyptic,' nihilist rejection of the entire existing order in Russia in anticipation of an imminent new, other, and better utopian state of affairs." *Ibid.*, p. 93.

is over covenants and ethics, not economics.

Conquest Through Service

An empire is necessarily threatened by the gospel. The gospel challenges the theology of man as divine, a theology that always undergirds every empire. But to stamp out their Christian enemies, the bureaucrats must take great risks. The bureaucrats who run the economy always want to meet their production quotas and earn their bonuses. If they persecute Christians, they threaten their organizations' output. Time and again, the most productive citizens of any empire are the hated Christians. They are the ones who are not addicted to alcohol, or absenteeism, or other forms of passive resistance. The biblical idea of service serves Christianity well. The failing productivity of the empire makes the bureaucratic functionaries increasingly dependent on Christians in order to meet the assigned production quotas. Like Jacob in Laban's household, like Joseph in Potiphar's household and in the Egyptian prison, competent service to others creates dependency on the servant. Dominion is by service. "But he that is greatest among you shall be your servant" (Matt. 23:11).

Satan believes that dominion is by power. He seeks to control others. Their resistance slows his ability to bring others under his power. There is built-in resistance to expansion in every empire. Territory and people once captured cannot be held captive indefinitely. They find ways of thwarting the bureaucratic system.

Empires do not survive for long. Their masters must work very fast and take high risks in order to extend the power of their empires. In contrast, Christians have plenty of time. Slow growth multiplies over many generations. This is God's promise: "For I the LORD thy God am a jealous God, visiting the iniquity of the fathers upon the children unto the third and fourth generation of those who hate me, and showing mercy unto thousands [of generations],[9] of them that love me, and

9. This is the standard interpretation. See the Jewish commentator U. Cassuto, *A Commentary on the Book of Exodus* (Jerusalem: The Magnes Press, The Hebrew University,

keep my commandments" (Ex. 20:5-6). "Know therefore that the LORD thy God, he is God, the faithful God, which keepeth covenant and mercy with them that love him and keep his commandments to a thousand generations; and repayeth them that hate him to their face, to destroy them. He will not be slack to him that hateth Him, he will repay him to his face" (Deut. 7:9-10).

Pagan empires are invariably cut off in the midst of history. They try to achieve world dominion, but there are always new empires rising up to challenge them (Dan. 8). God will not permit any nation to achieve total world dominion in history. The one-State world is a denial of God's universal sovereignty over man, and also a denial of Christ's progressive kingdom in history. The pagan empire cannot tolerate rivals. It cannot be content with a federation. It cannot share the glory of power. It therefore cannot succeed in history.

The kingdom of Christ imposes the requirement of modesty on the nations that compose it. No Christian nation can hope to impose its will by force on the whole world. Such pride is recognized as being evil, as well as self-destructive. Dominion is by service. Thus, the decentralized earthly kingdom of Christ can grow over time to fill the earth, but without becoming an empire. No one nation can hope to achieve dominance, though one or two may achieve primary influence temporarily, through adherence to the principle of service. Long-term cooperation among nations is possible only if all of them realize the inherent, God-imposed limitations on the power wielded by any one nation. The Christian nation faces the same warning that Christian individuals face: "Pride goeth before destruction, and an haughty spirit before a fall" (Prov. 16:18).

The residents of each nation must regard their own nation as mortal, just as men regard themselves. The more closely a nation conforms to biblical ethical standards, the longer it will survive as a separate entity. This is the biblical principle of inheritance. The heirs of any national group will retain their separate character only so long as God continues to grant the

---

[1951] 1974), p. 243.

nation His grace. Rebellion against Him brings destruction and national obliteration. As always, dominion is by covenant.[10]

> LORD, You will establish peace for us, for You have also done all our works in us. O LORD God, other masters besides You have had dominion over us; but by You only we make mention of Your name. They are dead, they will not live; they are deceased, they will not rise. Therefore, You have punished and destroyed them, and made their memory to perish. You have increased the nation, O LORD, you have increased the nation; You are glorified; You have expanded all the borders of the land (Isa. 26:12-15; New King James Version).

Christians have good reasons to be confident about the earthly future of Christ's kingdom. Pagans do not have much of anything to be confident about. Time is against them. So is God.

Time and Self-Confidence

If people believe that they are doomed as individuals, they find it difficult to survive in a life-threatening crisis. This is also true about civilizations. Self-confidence rests heavily on an optimistic view of the future. The vision of time that a society shares is very important for understanding how it operates. If you think you are running out of time, you will do certain things; if you think you have all the time in the world, you will do different things. Your vision of the future influences your activities in the present.

The Bible teaches that time is linear.[11] It also teaches that everything that takes place in history is governed by the absolute sovereignty of a personal God. Thus, Christians rest their earthly hope in the providence of God. History is neither random nor determined by impersonal forces. It is governed by the God who created the universe.[12]

---

10. Ray R. Sutton, *That You May Prosper: Dominion By Covenant* (Tyler, Texas: Institute for Christian Economics, 1987).

11. Gary North, *Unconditional Surrender: God's Program for Victory* (3rd ed.; Tyler, Texas: Institute for Christian Economics, 1988), ch. 4.

12. Gary North, *The Dominion Covenant: Genesis* (2nd ed.; Tyler, Texas: Institute for

The Bible teaches the doctrine of creation, meaning creation out of nothing. It teaches that man rebelled against God, and both nature and man now labor under God's historical curse. It tells of Jesus Christ, the Son of God: His birth, ministry, death, resurrection, and ascension to heaven to sit at the right hand of God. It tells of Pentecost, when He sent His Holy Spirit. It tells us of Christ's Church in history, and of final judgment. There is direction in history and meaning in life.

Christians are told to believe in "thousands of generations" as their operating time perspective. This is probably a metaphorical expression for history as a whole. Few if any Christians have taught about a literal 60,000-year period of history (2,000 times 30 years). The point is, the Bible teaches that the kingdom of God can expand for the whole of history, while Satan's empires rise and fall. There is no long-term continuity for Satan's institutional efforts. He has nothing comparable to the Church, God's monopolistic, perpetual institution that offers each generation God's covenantal sacraments.

If growth can be compounded over time, a very small capital base and a very small rate of growth leads to the conquest of the world. Growth becomes exponential if it is maintained long enough.[13] This is the assured basis of the Christianity's long-term triumph in history. God is faithful. The temporary breaks in the growth process due to the rebellion of certain generations of covenanted nations do not call a halt to the expansion of the kingdom.

The errors, omissions, and narrow focus of any particular Christian society need not inhibit the progress of Christ's earthly kingdom. These limitations can be dealt with covenantally. The international Church can combine its members' particular skills and perspectives into a world-transforming world and life view (Rom. 12; I Cor. 12). Modern telecommunications and modern airborne transport are now making this possible.

Christianity has in principle a far more potent view of time

Christian Economics, 1987), ch. 1: "Cosmic Personalism."

13. Gary North, *The Sinai Strategy: Economics and the Ten Commandments* (Tyler, Texas: Institute for Christian Economics, 1986), pp. 101-3.

than any other religion. If Christians fully understood the implications of the Bible's view of time, and if they also possessed the covenantal faithfulness to translate this vision into institutional action, then the world would soon fall to the gospel. It is only because of corruption by anti-Christian outlooks that the universal Church and Western civilization are visibly in retreat today.

A Vision of Victory

Because the West has lost its faith in God, it has lost its faith in the future. Only with a revival of covenantal Christianity is the West likely to reverse the drift into despair. Such a revival is possible, and there are signs that it is coming.

The Communists are suffering from their own waning of faith in Marxism, as Solzhenitsyn has said repeatedly. The problem is, when there is a contest between two empires, or two non-Christian systems, the one that has greater self-confidence, and overwhelming military superiority to back up this confidence, is likely to be the winner. The escape religion (Western humanism) until late 1989 was no match for the power religion (Communist humanism). It took the economic collapse of Communism, despite hundreds of billions of dollars in loans from Western governments and banks, to bring down *visible* Communist rule in Eastern Europe and to restructure it in the Soviet Union, at least for a time.

The West is losing faith in five major premises concerning history, Robert Nisbet writes: "There are at least five major premises to be found in the idea's [of progress] history from the Greeks to our day: belief in the value of the past; conviction of the nobility, even superiority, of Western civilization; acceptance of the worth of economic and technological growth; faith in reason and in the kind of scientific and scholarly knowledge that can come from reason alone; and, finally, belief in the intrinsic importance, the ineffaceable *worth* of life on this earth."[14]

14. Robert Nisbet, *History of the Idea of Progress* (New York: Basic Books, 1980), p. 317.

How will the West defend itself against the effects of skepticism, boredom, immorality, and economic crises? The West has lost faith in the future, so it finds it difficult to defend itself morally in the present. Western intellectuals perceive the West as morally bankrupt. Guilt is eroding the moral foundations of a successful defense of Western civilization, Nisbet says: "What is in all ways most devastating, however, is the signal decline *in America and Europe themselves* of faith in the value and promise of Western civilization. What has succeeded faith is, on the vivid and continually enlarging record, guilt, alienation, and indifference. An attitude – that we as a nation and as a Western civilization can in retrospect see ourselves as having contaminated, corrupted, and despoiled other peoples in the world, and that for having done this we should feel guilty, ashamed, and remorseful – grows and widens among Americans especially, and even more especially among young Americans of the middle class. For good reasons or bad, the lay clerisy of the West – the intelligentsia that began in the eighteenth century to succeed the clergy as the dominant class so far as citizen's beliefs are concerned – devotes a great deal of its time to lament, self-flagellation, and harsh judgment upon an entire history: Western history."[15]

Because Western men have lost their faith in God, biblical law, and God's sanctions of cursing and blessing in history, they have also lost their faith in the future. The West has begun to lose confidence in its past, its present, and its future. This has paralyzed Western foreign policy for over a generation. The West has lost its faith in progress.

The question today is this: Has the process of moral and ideological disintegration behind the Iron Curtain accelerated to the point that Communist rule really has collapsed of its own weight, despite its overwhelming superiority in the technology of destruction? Have we seen the turning point? Has the planned deception of the West that was described by the KGB defector Golitsyn in 1984 now backfired on the Communists?[16]

---

15. *Ibid.*, p. 331.
16. Anatoliy Golitsyn, *New Lies for Old: The Communist Strategy of Deception and Disin-*

If so, who will inherit the rotting hulk: Christianity, humanist democracy, international bureaucracy, or Islam?

Conclusion

The Bible teaches that God deals covenantally with nations, even at the final judgment and beyond. Thus, nations are under the terms of the covenant, either explicitly (ancient Israel) or implicitly (all nations under God as Judge). The covenant process of blessings and cursings is therefore called into operation in the history of nations. National continuity and discontinuity must be viewed as an outworking of this fourth point of the biblical covenant.

History has seen the rise of empires. They have all failed. They are satanic imitations of the definitively (though not historically) unified kingdom of Christ on earth. The tendency of Christ's kingdom is toward expansion. This leavening process is also a feature of Satan's imitation kingdom. But his kingdom has been on the defensive since Calvary. Whenever Christian nations remain faithful to the terms of God's covenant, they experience blessings leading to victory over time. Whenever they have apostatized, they have faced judgment and have had their inheritance transferred to other nations, either through military defeat or economic defeat.

The West now faces its greatest challenge since the fall of the Roman Empire. The formerly Christian West has abandoned the concept of the covenant, and with it, Christianity's vision of victory in history. The humanists cling to a waning worldview, announcing their New World Order even as the moral and intellectual foundations of such confidence are lost. Like the coins issued by Roman emperors, one after another, that kept announcing the dawn of a new age, a new political salvation, the dross is replacing the silver.[17] This is a religious crisis, and it has become visible in every area of life.

Peter Drucker has identified both the nature of this crisis and the opportunity: "The death of the belief in salvation by society,

---

formation (New York: Dodd, Mead, 1984).

17. Ethelbert Stauffer, *Christ and the Caesars* (Philadelphia: Westminster Press, 1955).

which for two hundred years had been the most dynamic force in the politics of the West and increasingly in politics worldwide, creates a void."[18] He insists that "we are not going to return to a belief in salvation by faith as a major political factor," but he is wrong. Salvation by faith is going to become the major factor in every area of life, including politics. The present historical trends, which Drucker probably understands better than any other contemporary social commentator, do not tell him what he needs to know. These trends are going to be disrupted by a divinely imposed discontinuity. The question is *when*, not *if*.

There is only one long-term solution to modern man's crisis: a comprehensive revival leading to the transformation of all things and the healing of all the nations.[19] This means that Christianity needs to offer the people of this world a better promise than "pie in the sky by and by," yet this is all that premillennialism and amillennialism can honestly offer to those who join the Church. While premillennialists and amillennialists may resent this statement, they need to show why I am wrong, not merely by writing a defense of the theoretical possibility of pessimillennial social theory (though I doubt that this can be done), but by actually writing biblical social theory. They have neglected to do so for over three centuries. Our enemies have noticed this silence. They correctly conclude that the modern Church is suffering from both a defective epistemology and a defective ethical system, and they have dismissed the gospel as a message fit only for children and old women of both sexes.

Christianity needs to offer a detailed, comprehensive cultural alternative to the existing humanist social order. We cannot beat something with nothing. The Church needs to offer covenant theology and social theory based forthrightly and consistently on the biblical covenant model. Until it does, the Church will continue to suffer from pie in the face in history.

18. Drucker, *The New Realities*, p. 16.

19. Gary North, *Healer of the Nations: Biblical Blueprints for International Relations* (Ft. Worth, Texas: Dominion Press, 1987).

Appendix

THE LAWYER AND THE TRUST

You may still be confused regarding the implications of the various millennial views. Why does each of them lead to a particular view of social theory?

I have decided to follow Van Til's lead. While his books are slow going, and his classroom lectures were fast sinking, his analogies are masterful. He has packed more meaning into an analogy than the reader initially recognizes, yet the analogy is what sticks in the memory, not his supporting arguments.

Back in the 1950's, there was a popular American television show, "The Millionaire." It centered around a billionaire who would give a million dollars away, tax free, each week to some unsuspecting subject. He would then send Michael Anthony to deliver the check. Then he waited to see how this money would affect the person. (A million dollars then would have had the purchasing power of about five million today.) Each week, there was a new story. The public liked the show because viewers recognized that a million dollars would radically change their lives. They knew that it would change the average person's environment completely, including his personal relationships.

I will use a similar analogy. Let us assume that you receive a letter from a lawyer. He informs you that he has some good very news for you. A distant trillionaire has set up a trust, and you have been named as one of the beneficiaries. You go to his office to get the details. The details of the trust will vary in terms of the millennial system under discussion. The lawyer's name is Fred Smurd.

Common Grace Amillennialism: Kline's Version

Smurd: Well, sir, I have good news for you. You have named as a beneficiary of my client's worldwide trust. All taxes have been paid. This is a pure windfall to you.

You: This is tremendous news. I've been having a terrible time making ends meet. I'm behind on some of my payments. This money is just what I need.

Smurd: Ah, yes. The money. Well, there is a lot of it, I can assure you. But there are certain conditions of this trust.

You: Conditions? What kind of conditions?

Smurd: Well, you must obey the stipulations of the trust. These are found in this book I am handing you.

You: It's a Bible.

Smurd: Yes, it's a Bible. You must obey it.

You: You mean all of it?

Smurd: In principle, all of it.

You: Specifically, what parts?

Smurd: Specifically, I am not allowed to disclose such information to you at this time.

You: When, then?

Smurd: Only at the time when the full capital value of the trust is transferred to the beneficiaries.

You: When will that be?

Smurd: After you are all dead.

You: This must be a joke.

Smurd: It's no joke. It is what the trust document requires.

You: You're telling me that I don't get any money until we're all dead?

Smurd: Why, not at all! You have misunderstood me. I was speaking only of the trust's full capital value. You will be given periodic distributions from the trust's income.

You: When?

Smurd: Periodically.

You: How large will these distributions be?

Smurd: Well, that depends on the profitability of the trust.

You: What has it been in the past.

Smurd: Up and down.

You: I just have to wait until I get paid.

Smurd: That's correct. But there's another aspect of the trust that you need to know about.

You: What now?

Smurd: The payments are profit-sharing grants. Sometimes there are losses.

You: Losses?

Smurd: Yes, and you will have to pay into the trust your proportional share in order to make up any of these losses.

You: You mean sometimes I can be assessed money to remain in the trust as a beneficiary.

Smurd: That is correct.

You: Well, what has the trust required in the past? How much comes out as distributions, and how much is assessed from the beneficiaries.

Smurd: On average, it's about even.

You: Do you mean it is statistically random?

Smurd: That is correct.

You: How many people are in this trust?

Smurd: Only Christians are named as final beneficiaries.

You: What about intermediate beneficiaries?

Smurd: Everyone on earth is named.

You: So, the trust pays out randomly and assesses randomly until final distribution?

Smurd: That is correct.

You: What about the Bible? If I obey the Bible, do I get special consideration?

Smurd: Only at the final distribution.

You: But what about those who actively disobey it? What happens to them?

Smurd: They do not participate in the final distribution of the trust.

You: But what about the intermediate distributions?

Smurd: Payments are randomly distributed.

You: As I understand this, I get no predictable benefits from this trust until I die.

Smurd: That is correct.

You: But when I die, I collect my share.

Smurd: You will indeed. And there is one benefit that I've neglected to mention.

You: What's that?

Smurd: No death duties!

Common Grace Amillennialism: Van Til's Version

Smurd: Well, sir, I have good news for you. You have named as a beneficiary of my client's worldwide trust. All taxes have been paid. This is a pure windfall to you.

You: This is tremendous news. I've been having a terrible time making ends meet. I'm behind on some of my payments. This money is just what I need.

Smurd: Ah, yes. The money. Well, there is a lot of it, I can assure you. But there are certain conditions of this trust.

You: Conditions? What kind of conditions?

Smurd: Well, you must obey the stipulations of the trust. These are found in this book I am handing you.

You: It's a Bible.

Smurd: Yes, it's a Bible. You must obey it.

You: You mean all of it?

Smurd: In principle, all of it.

You: Specifically, what parts?

Smurd: Specifically, I am not allowed to disclose such information to you at this time.

You: When, then?

Smurd: Only at the time when the full capital value of the trust is transferred to the beneficiaries.

You: When will that be?

Smurd: After you are all dead.

You: This must be a joke.

Smurd: It's no joke. It is what the trust document requires.

You: You're telling me that I don't get any money until we're all dead?

Smurd: Why, not at all! You have misunderstood me. I was speaking only of the trust's full capital value. You will be given periodic distributions from the trust's income.

You: When?

Smurd: Periodically.

You: How large will these distributions be?

Smurd: Well, that depends on the profitability of the trust.

You: What has it been in the past.

Smurd: Up and down.

You: I just have to wait until I get paid.

Smurd: That's correct. But there's another aspect of the trust that you need to know about.

You: What now?

Smurd: There are other named beneficiaries of the intermediate payments.

You: Who are they?

Smurd: Everyone on earth.

You: You mean, my share is diluted by everyone?

Smurd: Not exactly.

You: Why, "Not exactly"?

Smurd: Because the periodic distributions are not made randomly.

You: How are they distributed?

Smurd: The people who obey the terms of the trust instrument are paid less than those who do not obey it.

You: That means that the person who does what the Trustor wants him to do will lose.

Smurd: Only with respect to the periodic distributions.

You: This seems unfair.

Smurd: You must not call the Trustor unfair.

You: But what good does it do to obey the trust's stipulations?

Smurd: Those of you who obey will be the only ones to participate in the final distribution of the trust's assets.

You: Then what about the periodic assessments? Are they distributed randomly.

Smurd: I'm afraid not.

You: The people who break the terms of the trust pay more?

Smurd: I'm afraid not.

You: Are you telling me that the Trustor has set up this trust so that those of us who do what He says pay more to cover any losses than the people who disobey Him?

Smurd: That is correct.

You: But what if I do not want to participate?

Smurd: It's too late. You have already signed the trust agreement.

You: When?

Smurd: When you became a Christian.

You: What about my children? They are Christians.

Smurd: Then they will participate.

You: Do you expect their preliminary distributions will be larger.

Smurd: Certainly not larger.

You: Smaller?

Smurd: That is my expectation.

You: What about their payments into the trust? I suppose they will be larger than mine.

Smurd: I see that you're getting the picture.

You: I have never heard of anything like this arrangement in my life. What is the principle underlying it?

Smurd: Dutch treat.

Premillennialism: Dispensational

Smurd: Well, sir, I have good news for you. You have named as a beneficiary of my client's worldwide trust. All taxes have been paid. This is a pure windfall to you.

You: This is tremendous news. I've been having a terrible time making ends meet. I'm behind on some of my payments. This money is just what I need.

Smurd: Ah, yes. The money. Well, there is a lot of it, I can assure you. But there are certain conditions of this trust.

You: Conditions? What kind of conditions?

Smurd: Well, you must obey the stipulations of the trust. These are found in this book I am handing you.

You: It's a Bible.

Smurd: Yes, it's a Bible. You must obey it.

You: You mean all of it?

Smurd: Hardly! Most of it has been annulled.

You: Then what part?

Smurd: Just the New Testament.

You: All of it?

Smurd: Why no, just the parts that apply to the Church.

You: Which parts are those?

Smurd: Well, there's considerable debate over that.

You: Who is winning the debate?

Smurd: Theologically or institutionally?

You: Both.

Smurd: Institutionally, those who write off only the gospels.

You: And theologically?

Smurd: Those who write off everything except Paul's prison epistles.

You: What do I get if I obey only the prison epistles?

Smurd: The same that you get if you obey all the epistles.

You: Which is what?

Smurd: Assessments.

You: What assessments?

Smurd: The assessments to cover the operational costs of the trust fund.

You: You mean the trust fund makes no profits?

Smurd: Not in the last three hundred and seventy years.

You: When did it make any profits?

Smurd: From the year 100 A.D. until about 325. Then again, very briefly, from 1517 to 1618.

You: After that?

Smurd: After that it has been all downhill.

You: You mean that all the beneficiaries have lost money?

Smurd: No. Only those who obey the New Testament epistles.

You: You mean the Christians.

Smurd: Precisely.

You: And what about the non-Christians?

Smurd: They have done quite well.

You: So, why not get them to pay operational costs?

Smurd: This is not what the Trustor wants.

You: Then it pays to be part of the non-Christian beneficiaries.

Smurd: Not forever.

You: What changes things?

Smurd: The Trustor's Son will return and collect all the due assessments from those who haven't previously paid.

You: But what about those who have been paying?

Smurd: They are taken to heaven.

You: And then what happens to us?

Smurd: The trust document does not say exactly. But you will be taken care of, I assure you.

You: And what about those left on earth?

Smurd: They get hammered.

You: Well, I certainly don't want to get hammered.

Smurd: Of course not. Of course, they don't get hammered forever.

You: What do you mean?

Smurd: They get hammered for seven years. Or possibly three and a half years. There's some debate over this.

You: And then what?

Smurd: They inherit the earth.

You: You mean they get all of the trust's intermediate distributions?

Smurd: That is correct.

You: What about assessments?

Smurd: Only the evil-doers pay.

You: But that's the way it ought to be now!

Smurd: You aren't the first person to say that.

You: You mean others have objected?

Smurd: They used to.

You: Why not any longer?

Smurd: They all died off during World War I.

You: Who were these people?

Smurd: Postmillennialists.

You: And they left no heirs?

Smurd: Only a handful.

You: Who are these people?

Smurd: Christian Reconstructionists.

You: Aren't they legalists?

Smurd: Horrible: lawyers who believe in permanent law.

You: We're under grace, not law!

Smurd: Not exactly. You're under lawyers.

Premillennialism: Historic

Smurd: Well, sir, I have good news for you. You have named as a beneficiary of my client's worldwide trust. All taxes have been paid. This is a pure windfall to you.

You: This is tremendous news. I've been having a terrible time making ends meet. I'm behind on some of my payments. This money is just what I need.

Smurd, Ah, yes. The money. Well, there is a lot of it, I can assure you. But there are certain conditions of this trust.

You: Conditions? What kind of conditions?

Smurd: Well, you must obey the stipulations of the trust. These are found in this book I am handing you.

You: It's a Bible.

Smurd: Yes, it's a Bible. You must obey it.

You: You mean all of it?

Smurd: Hardly! Most of it has been annulled.

You: Then what part?

Smurd: Just the New Testament.

You: All of it?

Smurd: In principle, yes.

You: And specifically?

Smurd: Specifically, nobody says exactly.

You: Why not?

Smurd: Because they all subscribe to *Christianity Today*, and *Christianity Today* is careful never to say.

You: Are you telling me that *Christianity Today* is the only arbiter of what the Bible says?

Smurd: I wouldn't put it that way.

You: How would you put it?

Smurd: I'm not at liberty to say.

You: Why not?

Smurd: Lawyer-client secrecy.

You: Who is your client?

Smurd: I'm not at liberty to say.

You: Well, then, if I do what *Christianity Today* recommends, what do I get?

Smurd: Assessments.

You: What assessments?

Smurd: The assessments to cover the operational costs of the trust fund.

You: You mean the trust fund makes no profits?

Smurd: Not in the last three hundred and seventy years.

You: When did it make any profits?

Smurd: From the year 100 A.D. until about 325. Then again, very briefly, from 1517 to 1618.

You: After that?

Smurd: After that it has been all downhill.

You: You mean that all the beneficiaries have lost money?

Smurd: No. Only those who obey.

You: You mean the Christians.

Smurd: Precisely.

You: And what about the non-Christians?

Smurd: They have done quite well.

You: So, why not get them to pay operational costs?

Smurd: This is not what the Trustor wants.

You: Then it pays to be part of the non-Christian beneficiaries.

Smurd: Not forever.

You: What changes things?

Smurd: The final distribution.

You: But what about on earth?

Smurd: There are complications.

You: What kind of complications?

Smurd, Well, for one thing, Armageddon.

You: Armageddon?

Smurd: Yes, Armageddon.

You: What is Armageddon?

Smurd: That's when the people who haven't paid any assessments come and rob everyone who has.

You: We all get robbed?

Smurd: The fortunate ones, yes.

You: What about the unfortunate ones?

Smurd: You don't want to know.

You: Yes, I do.

Smurd: No, you don't.

You: Why not?

Smurd: It tends to lead to reduced productivity.

You: Is this bad?

Smurd: Oh, yes. It reduces the amount of wealth remaining for the non-assessed to extract from the victims.

You: At Armageddon?

Smurd: And before.

You: You mean now. Today. Tomorrow.

Smurd: Correct.

You: Then what's the advantage of being named a beneficiary?

Smurd: You get to participate in the final distribution of the trust's assets.

You: Yes, I know that. I mean before then.

Smurd: You get to go to heaven.

You: All Christians go to heaven.

Smurd: Yes, but I mean you get to go to heaven right after Armageddon. And you don't have to die first, either! I mean, assuming that you don't get killed during Armageddon.

You: How will that work?

Smurd: The Trustor's Son will return to take you there.

You: And then what happens to us?

Smurd: The trust document does not say exactly. But you will be taken care of, I assure you.

You: And what about those left on earth?

Smurd: They inherit the earth.

You: You mean they get all of the trust's preliminary distributions?

Smurd: That is correct.

You: What about assessments?

Smurd: Only the evil-doers pay.

You: But that's the way it ought to be now!

Smurd: You aren't the first person to say that.

You: You mean others have objected?

Smurd: They used to.

You: Why not any longer?

Smurd: They all died off during World War I.

You: Who were they?

Smurd: Postmillennialists.
You: And they left no heirs?
Smurd: Only a handful.
You: Who are these people?
Smurd: Christian Reconstructionists.
You: But they complain about everything.
Smurd: So I'm told.

Postmillennialism: Pietistic

Smurd: Well, sir, I have good news for you. You have named as a beneficiary of my client's worldwide trust. All taxes have been paid. This is a pure windfall to you.

You: This is tremendous news. I've been having a terrible time making ends meet. I'm behind on some of my payments. This money is just what I need.

Smurd: Ah, yes. The money. Well, there is a lot of it, I can assure you. But there are certain conditions of this trust.

You: Conditions? What kind of conditions?

Smurd: Well, you must obey the stipulations of the trust. These are found in this book I am handing you.

You: It's a Bible.

Smurd: Yes, it's a Bible. You must obey it.

You: You mean all of it?

Smurd: In principle, all of it.

You: Specifically, what parts?

Smurd: Specifically, I am not allowed to disclose such information to you at this time.

You: When, then?

Smurd: Only at the time when the full capital value of the trust is transferred to the beneficiaries.

You: When will that be?

Smurd: After you are all dead.

You: This must be a joke.

Smurd: It's no joke. It is what the trust document requires.

You: You're telling me that I don't get any money until we're all dead?

Smurd: Why, not at all! You have misunderstood me. I was speaking only of the trust's full capital value. You will be given periodic distributions from the trust's income.

You: When?

Smurd: When society improves.

You: When will that be?

Smurd: That's difficult to say.

You: Well, how will I know when it happens?

Smurd: That's also difficult to say.

You: But I *will* get the money.

Smurd: You or your heirs.

You: So the fund is transferrable property?

Smurd: If your heirs continue to have faith in it.

You: What exactly are they to have faith in?

Smurd: That when things improve in society, they will get their money.

You: What will make things get better?

Smurd: Having lots of people believe in the trust and the Trustor.

You: What are they supposed to believe about Him?

Smurd: Why, that things will get better when people believe in Him.

You: I am having trouble following this. We have to believe that things will get better in order to make things get better.

Smurd: That is correct.

You: And why should we believe that things will get better?

Smurd: Because lots of people will be getting payments from the trust.

You: I see. Then the trust makes things get better.

Smurd. You don't seem to understand. People's faith in the trust is what makes things better.

You: But when things get better, won't people be, well, you know, better? I mean, will they be better people?

Smurd: Of course!

You: How will they be better?

Smurd: They will be sweet.

You: Believing in the trust makes them sweet?

Smurd: No, *being* sweet makes them sweet. But believing in the Trust and the Trustor shows to everyone that they think the whole thing is one sweet deal.

You: That's nice.

Smurd: So, are you in or out?

You: I'm not sure.

Smurd: You need to be sure.

You: Sure, sure.

Smurd: No, I really mean it. You need to be sure.

You: About what?

Smurd: That things will get better.

You: All right, I believe that things will get better. They will begin to get better just as soon as I get my money. When do I get my money?

Smurd: Just as soon as things get better.

You: I'm wondering: Do a lot of people believe in this? I mean, have a lot of people signed up for this deal?

Smurd: Not since World War I.

You: Look, give me an advance on my share of the funds, and it will help society to improve. I promise.

Smurd: I'm authorized to write you a check for five dollars.

You: But it cost me ten dollars to get down here and park.

Smurd: Well, that's the best we can do. Things haven't been too good lately.

Postmillennialism: Christian Reconstruction

Smurd: Well, sir, I have good news for you. You have named as a beneficiary of my client's worldwide trust. All taxes have been paid. This is a pure windfall to you.

You: This is tremendous news. I've been having a terrible time making ends meet. I'm behind on some of my payments. This money is just what I need.

Smurd, Ah, yes. The money. Well, there is a lot of it, I can assure you. But there are certain conditions of this trust.

You: Conditions? What kind of conditions?

Smurd: Well, you must obey the stipulations of the trust. These are found in this book I am handing you.

You: It's a Bible.

Smurd: Yes, it's a Bible. You must obey it.

You: You mean all of it?

Smurd: Yes, unless something is said in the New Testament that would exclude some law in the Old Testament.

You: What do I get if I obey?

Smurd: You get your share of the preliminary trust distributions.

You: Immediately?

Smurd: Not necessarily.

You: What's the catch?

Smurd: The catch is, the Trustor wants to make sure you are serious about obeying Him, long-term.

You: So He doesn't pay off, cash on demand?

Smurd: Not your demand, no.

You: But I do get paid off eventually?

Smurd: That is the normal procedure.

You: What is abnormal?

Smurd: Occasionally, some Bible-obeying beneficiaries do not get paid off until the final distribution.

You: Why not?

Smurd: The Trustor does not say exactly. I suppose it is designed to test people's obedience even if there is a possibility that they will not receive preliminary distributions.

You: What is the purpose of that?

Smurd: So that they won't get greedy, I suppose.

You: That's an odd thing for a lawyer to say.

Smurd: I'll ignore that remark.

You: But you say that most people who obey do get paid their preliminary distributions.

Smurd: Yes.

You: What about people who do not obey?

Smurd: Christians or non-Christians?

You: Both.

Smurd: Disobedient Christians sometimes get paid enough to let them muddle through.

You: But why give them anything at all?

Smurd: I suppose it has something to do with demonstrating mercy.

You: That's also an odd thing for a lawyer to say.

Smurd: Don't you like lawyers?

You: Woe unto them.

Smurd: That seems to be an extremist position.

You: What about the non-Christians?

Smurd: The ones who don't obey?

You: Yes.

Smurd: Eventually, they are cut off. They don't get any more distributions. They are even assessed fees for previous distributions.

You: And the ones who obey?

Smurd: They get the same as the Christians who obey.

You: Why should they get the same as Christians who obey?

Smurd: Because of the Trustor's first principle of justice.

You: What is that?

Smurd: Equality before the law.

You: But they can't obey the whole law.

Smurd: Neither can anyone else.

You: But we have Jesus.

Smurd: So do they, if they obey.

You: But that's works religion!

Smurd: No, that's equality before the law.

You: Then what difference does it make if you're a Christian?

Smurd: At the final distribution.

You: So, when do I get my first check?

Smurd: Do you intend to pay 10% back into the trust for operating costs?

You: Do I have to?

Smurd: Yes.

You: What if I don't?

Smurd: Don't expect to receive very much.

You: But I will get some preliminary distributions?

Smurd: Probably.

You: But not big ones?

Smurd: Probably not.

You: So, you're saying that the Trustor wants His cut right off the top.

Smurd: Of course. He's a lawyer.

You: That seems hard to believe.

Smurd: That he's a lawyer?

You: No. That he's a lawyer and takes only 10%.
Smurd: Look, here's the deal: take it or leave it.
You: If I leave it, what then?
Smurd: You lose.
You: And if I take it?
Smurd: You win.
You: That seems straightforward enough. I'll go for it.
Smurd: Fine. Just sign here.
You: The Trustor must be a stickler for legal details.
Smurd: Indeed! He's a Christian Reconstructionist.

FOR FURTHER READING

No book as brief as this one can do justice to the full range of issues raised by the Christian Reconstruction perspective. Critics of the Reconstruction movement have had a tendency to dismiss its main features as if it were somehow deviant theologically. Yet the critics are not always aware of the large body of scholarly literature, not only of Christian Reconstructionism, but also of the Reconstructionists' theological predecessors.

There has been a distinct tendency for those holding dispensational and amillennial views to dismiss postmillennialism as a dead system. For decades, each side has spent most of its time and energy attacking the other. The arrival of theonomic postmillennialism (Rushdoony, Bahnsen, and Nigel Lee) and later of five-point covenantal postmillennialism (Sutton and North) caught both rival groups by surprise.

One argument that has become commonplace among dispensational critics of postmillennialism is this one: "Postmillennialists have never made an exegetical defense of their system." This is an exaggeration. A relatively recent defense is Roderick Campbell's book, *Israel and the New Covenant*, published by Presbyterian & Reformed in 1954 and reprinted by P&R and the Geneva Divinity School Press in 1981. That the critics have never heard of Campbell's book testifies to their refusal to do their homework, not our failure to present our case. Kenneth L. Gentry is now completing a detailed defense of postmillennialism. It should be in print during the first half of 1991. But the criticism is well taken; each generation of theologians has a responsibility to update and refine the received system, applying its insights in new ways. History does move forward. There is progressive sanctification in the realm of systematic theology.

Dispensational Critics of Postmillennialism

The critics are a good deal more vulnerable to this criticism than the postmillennialists are. I think it is time for dispensationalist critics to examine carefully their own dusty bookshelves in search of a single, recent, book-long exposition of dispensational theology. Chafer's 1948 eight-volume set is gone, edited (i.e., expurgated) down to two volumes. Ryrie's *Dispensationalism Today* has not been revised since 1965, and was a brief study at that. No one at Dallas Theological Seminary or Grace Theological Seminary has attempted to present a book-length summary and hermeneutical defense of dispensationalism in a generation. Meanwhile, Talbot Theological Seminary no longer bothers to defend the system publicly.

We need to know what the prevailing, agreed-upon position (if any) of dispensationalism is regarding Israel and the Church, law and grace, the discontinuity between the Old and New Covenants, the Lordship of Christ in the work of salvation, six-day creationism, New Testament personal ethics, New Testament social ethics, natural law theory, the kingdom of God and (if still believed to be separate) the kingdom of heaven, the prophetic significance of the appearance of the state of Israel in 1948) prior to the Rapture (national Israel and the "any-moment coming"), the fulfillment of Joel 2 in Acts 2 (an Old Covenant prophecy of the "Great Parenthesis" Church), the relationship between Amos 9:11-12 and Acts 15:15-17 (the nature of the Davidic throne), the nature of the Melchizedekal priesthood in the Church Age (the restoration of Christ's kingship), Psalm 110 and Christ's reigning from heaven, the number of New Covenants (the Hebrews 8 problem), the restoration of animal sacrifices in Jerusalem during the millennium, the nature of the millennial work of the Holy Spirit with Christ present on earth, and the millennial residence of raptured Christians. A commentary on the Book of Revelation that is intellectually comparable to David Chilton's *Days of Vengeance* would also be appropriate. Perhaps most important of all, we need a statement on the New Testament legitimacy of abortion and the proper response of Christians to legalized abortion. *Roe v. Wade* was handed down in 1973, after all. The professorial silence is deafening.

There is a reason for this silence. Dispensational theology is close to a publicly visible collapse. The received truths from Scofield and Chafer cannot be defended biblically, and today's seminary professors know this. It is an inconsistent system, and each revision places another burden on the shaky structure. But silence is no longer golden. Christian Reconstructionists are addressing these and many other problems. Criticizing our conclusions apart from an equally developed theological system is risky: "Judge not, that ye be not judged. For with what judgment ye judge, ye shall be judged; and with what measure ye measure, it shall be measured to you again" (Matt. 7:1-2).

Introductory Works

Because these is an extensive body of literature on Calvinism and predestination, I have not included it here. A basic work is Loraine Boettner's *The Reformed Doctrine of Predestination* (1933). Martin Luther's classic, *The Bondage of the Will* (1525), is still worth reading, especially by Lutherans.

The easiest introduction to the basic theological issues of Christian Reconstruction is my book, *Unconditional Surrender: God's Program for Victory*, first published in 1981, with a revised edition in 1988 (Institute for Christian Economics).

General Works on the Millennium

Clouse, Robert G., ed. *The Meaning of the Millennium: Four Views*. Downers Grove, IL: InterVarsity Press, 1977. The four major views of the millennium presented by advocates of each view.

Erickson, Millard J. *Contemporary Options in Eschatology: A Study of the Millennium*. Grand Rapids, MI: Baker, 1977. Examines modern views of eschatology, the millennium, and the tribulation.

Works Defending Postmillennialism or Preterism

Adams, Jay. *The Time Is At Hand*. Phillipsburg, NJ: Presbyterian and Reformed, 1966. Amillennial ("realized millennial"), but preterist interpretation of Revelation.

Alexander, J. A. *The Prophecies of Isaiah, A Commentary on Matthew* (complete through chapter 16), *A Commentary on Mark*, and *A Commentary on Acts*. Various Publishers. Nineteenth-century Princeton Old Testament scholar.

Boettner, Loraine. *The Millennium*. Revised edition. Phillipsburg, NJ: Presbyterian and Reformed, [1957] 1984. Classic study of millennial views, and defense of postmillennialism.

Brown, John. *The Discourses and Sayings of Our Lord* and commentaries on *Romans, Hebrews*, and *1 Peter*. Various Publishers. Nineteenth-century Scottish Calvinist.

Campbell, Roderick. *Israel and the New Covenant*. Tyler, TX: Geneva Divinity School Press, [1954] 1981. Neglected study of principles for interpretation (hermeneutic) of prophecy; examines themes in New Testament biblical theology.

Chilton, David. *The Days of Vengeance: An Exposition of the Book of Revelation*. Ft. Worth, TX: Dominion Press. Massive postmillennial commentary on Revelation. It presents the Book of Revelation as structured by the Bible's five-point covenant model. It is both a covenant lawsuit and a liturgy.

Chilton, David. *The Great Tribulation*. Ft. Worth, TX: Dominion Press, 1987. Popular exegetical introduction to postmillennial interpretation.

Chilton, David. *Paradise Restored: A Biblical Theology of Dominion*. Ft. Worth, TX: Dominion Press, 1985. Study of prophetic symbolism, the coming of the Kingdom, and the book of Revelation.

Clark, David S. *The Message from Patmos: A Postmillennial Commentary on the Book of Revelation*. Grand Rapids, MI: Baker, 1989. Brief preterist and postmillennial commentary.

Davis, John Jefferson. *Christ's Victorious Kingdom: Postmillennialism Reconsidered*. Grand Rapids, MI: Baker, 1986. Biblical and historical defense of postmillennialism.

DeMar, Gary and Peter Leithart. *The Reduction of Christianity: A Biblical Response to Dave Hunt*. Ft. Worth, TX: Dominion Press, 1988. Critique of Dave Hunt, and historical and biblical defense of postmillennialism.

Edwards, Jonathan. *The Works of Jonathan Edwards*. 2 volumes. Edinburgh: The Banner of Truth Trust, [1834] 1974. Volume 2 includes Edwards' "History of Redemption."

Gentry, Kenneth L. *The Beast of Revelation*. Tyler, TX: Institute for Christian Economics, 1989. Preterist study of the identity of the beast in Revelation.

Gentry, Kenneth L. *Before Jerusalem Fell: Dating the Book of Revelation*. Tyler, TX: Institute for Christian Economics, 1989. Exhaustively researched and heavily documented study on the dating of the Book of Revelation: *c*. A.D. 67-69.

Henry, Matthew. *Matthew Henry's Commentary*. 6 volumes. New York: Fleming H. Revell, 1714. Popular commentary on the whole Bible.

Hodge, A. A. *Outlines of Theology*. London: The Banner of Truth Trust, [1879] 1972. Nineteenth-century introduction to systematic theology in question-and-answer form.

Hodge, Charles. *Systematic Theology*. 3 volumes. Grand Rapids, MI: Eerdmans, [1871-73] 1986. Old standard Reformed text; volume 3 includes extensive discussion of eschatology.

Kik, J. Marcellus. *An Eschatology of Victory*. N.p.: Presbyterian and Reformed, 1975. Exegetical studies of Matthew 24 and Revelation 20.

Murray, Iain. *The Puritan Hope: Revival and the Interpretation of Prophecy*. (Edinburgh: Banner of Truth, 1971). Historical study of postmillennialism in England and Scotland.

North, Gary, ed. *The Journal of Christian Reconstruction*, Symposium on the Millennium (Winter 1976-77). Historical and theological essays on postmillennialism.

Owen, John. *Works*, ed. William H. Goold. 16 volumes. Edinburgh: The Banner of Truth Trust, 1965. A seventeenth-century preacher and theologian; volume 8 includes several sermons on the Kingdom of God, and volume 9 contains a preterist sermon on 2 Peter 3.

Ramsey, Willard A. *Zion's Glad Morning*. Simpsonville, South Carolina: Millennium III Publishers, 1990. A Baptist defends the postmillennial position.

Rushdoony, Rousas John. *God's Plan for Victory: The Meaning of Postmillennialism*. Fairfax, VA: Thoburn Press, 1977. Theological study of the implications of postmillennialism for economics, law, and reconstruction.

Rushdoony, Rousas John. *Thy Kingdom Come: Studies in Daniel and Revelation*. Phillipsburg, NJ: Presbyterian and Reformed, 1970. Exegetical studies in Daniel and Revelation, full of insightful comments on history and society.

Shedd, W. G. T. *Dogmatic Theology*. 3 volumes. Nashville, TN: Thomas Nelson, [1888] 1980. Nineteenth-century Reformed systematics text.

Strong, A. H. *Systematic Theology*. Baptist postmillennialist of late nineteenth and early twentieth centuries.

Sutton, Ray R. "Covenantal Postmillennialism," *Covenant Renewal* (February 1989). Newsletter discusses the difference between traditional Presbyterian postmillennialism and covenantal postmillennialism.

Terry, Milton S. *Biblical Apocalyptics: A Study of the Most Notable Revelations of God and of Christ.* Grand Rapids, MI: Baker, [1898] 1988. Nineteenth-century exegetical studies of prophetic passages in Old and New Testaments; includes a complete commentary on Revelation.

Toon, Peter, ed. *Puritans, the Millennium and the Future of Israel: Puritan Eschatology, 1600-1660.* Cambridge: James Clarke, 1970. Detailed historical study of millennial views with special attention to the place of Israel in prophecy.

Works Critical of Dispensationalism

Allis, Oswald T. *Prophecy and the Church.* Philadelphia, PA: Presbyterian and Reformed, 1945. Classic comprehensive critique of dispensationalism.

Bacchiocchi, Samuele. *Hal Lindsey's Prophetic Jigsaw Puzzle: Five Predictions That Failed!* Berrien Springs, MI: Biblical Perspectives, 1987. Seventh Day Adventist examines Lindsey's failed prophecies, yet argues for an imminent Second Coming.

Bahnsen, Greg L. and Kenneth L. Gentry. *House Divided: The Break-Up of Dispensational Theology*. Ft. Worth, TX: Dominion Press, 1989. Response to H. Wayne House and Thomas Ice, *Dominion Theology: Blessing or Curse?*. Includes a comprehensive discussion of eschatological issues.

Bass, Clarence B. *Backgrounds to Dispensationalism: Its Historical Genesis and Ecclesiastical Implications*. Grand Rapids, MI: Baker, 1960. Massively researched history of dispensationalism, with focus on J. N. Darby.

Boersma, T. *Is the Bible a Jigsaw Puzzle: An Evaluation of Hal Lindsey's Writings*. Ontario, Canada: Paideia Press, 1978. An examination of Lindsey's interpretive method, and exegesis of important prophetic passages.

Bray, John L. *Israel in Bible Prophecy*. Lakeland, FL: John L. Bray Ministry, 1983. Amillennial historical and biblical discussion of the Jews in the New Covenant.

Brown, David. *Christ's Second Coming: Will It Be Premillennial?* Edmonton Alberta, Canada: Still Water Revival Books, [1876] 1990. Detailed exegetical study of the Second Coming and the Millennium by a former premillennialist.

Cox, William E. *An Examination of Dispensationalism*. Philadelphia, PA: Presbyterian and Reformed, 1963. Critical look at major tenets of dispensationalism by former dispensationalist.

Cox, William E. *Why I Left Scofieldism*. Phillipsburg, NJ: Presby terian and Reformed, n.d. Critical examination of major flaws of dispensationalism.

Crenshaw, Curtis I. and Grover E. Gunn, III. *Dispensationalism Today, Yesterday, and Tomorrow*. Memphis, TN: Footstool Publications, [1985] 1989. Two Dallas Seminary graduates take a critical and comprehensive look at dispensationalism.

DeMar, Gary. *The Debate Over Christian Reconstruction*. Ft. Worth, TX: 1988. Response to Dave Hunt and Thomas Ice. Includes a brief commentary on Matthew 24.

Feinberg, John A. *Continuity and Discontinuity: Perspectives on the Relationship Between the Old and New Testaments*. Westchester, IL: Crossway, 1988. Theologians of various persuasions discuss relationship of Old and New Covenants; evidence of important modifications in dispensationalism.

Gerstner, John H. *A Primer on Dispensationalism*. Phillipsburg,

NJ: Presbyterian and Reformed, 1982. Brief critique of dispensationalism's "division" of the Bible. Expect a major work on dispensationalism in the near future.

Halsell, Grace. *Prophecy and Politics: Militant Evangelists on the Road to Nuclear War*. Westport, CN: Lawrence Hill, 1986. A journalist enters the world of dispensationalist Zionism, and warns of political dangers of dispensationalist prophetic teachings.

Jordan, James B. *The Sociology of the Church*. Tyler, TX: Geneva Ministries, 1986. Chapter entitled, "Christian Zionism and Messianic Judaism," contrasts the dispensational Zionism of Jerry Falwell, et. al. with classic early dispensationalism.

McPherson, Dave. *The Incredible Cover-Up*. Medford, OR: Omega Publications, 1975. Revisionist study of the origins of the pre-trib rapture doctrine.

Mauro, Philip. *The Seventy Weeks and the Great Tribulation*. Swengel, PA: Reiner Publishers, n.d. Former dispensationalist re-examines prophecies in Daniel and the Olivet Discourse.

Miladin, George C. *Is This Really the End?: A Reformed Analysis of* ***The Late Great Planet Earth***. Cherry Hill, NJ: Mack Publishing, 1972. Brief response to Hal Lindsey's prophetic works; concludes with a defense of postmillennial optimism.

Provan, Charles D. *The Church Is Israel Now: The Transfer of Conditional Privilege*. Vallecito, CA: Ross House Books, 1987. Collection of Scripture texts with brief comments.

Vanderwaal, C. *Hal Lindsey and Biblical Prophecy*. Ontario, Canada: Paideia Press, 1978. Lively critique of dispensationalism and Hal Lindsey by a preterist Reformed scholar and pastor.

Weber, Timothy P. *Living in the Shadow of the Second Coming: American Premillennialism 1875-1982*. Grand Rapids, MI: Zondervan/Academie, 1983. Touches on American dispensationalism in a larger historical and social context.

Wilson, Dwight. *Armageddon Now!* Tyler, TX: Institue for Christian Economics, [1977] 1991. Premillennialist studies history of failed prophecy, and warns against newspaper exegesis.

Woodrow, Ralph. *Great Prophecies of the Bible.* Riverside, CA: Ralph Woodrow Evangelistic Association, 1971. Exegetical study of Matthew 24, the Seventy Weeks of Daniel, and the doctrine of the Anti-Christ.

Woodrow, Ralph. *His Truth Is Marching On: Advanced Studies on Prophecy in the Light of History.* Riverside, CA: Ralph Woodrow Evangelistic Association, 1977. Exegetical study of important prophetic passages in Old and New Testaments.

Zens, John. *Dispensationalism: A Reformed Inquiry into Its Leading Figures and Features.* Nashville, TN: Baptist Reformation Review, 1973. Written by a then-Reformed Baptist.

Theonomic Studies in Biblical Law

Bahnsen, Greg L. *By This Standard: The Authority of God's Law Today.* Tyler, TX: Institute for Christian Economics, 1985. An introduction to the issues of biblical law in society.

Bahnsen, Greg L. *Theonomy in Christian Ethics.* Nutley, New Jersey: Presbyterian and Reformed, (1977) 1984. A detailed apologetic of the idea of continuity in biblical law.

DeMar, Gary. *God and Government,* 3 vols. Brentwood, TN: Wolgemuth & Hyatt, 1990. An introduction to the fundamentals of biblical government, emphasizing self-government.

Jordan, James. *The Law of the Covenant: An Exposition of Exodus*

21-23. Tyler, TX: Institute for Christian Economics, 1984. A clear introduction to the issues of the case laws of the Old Testament.

North, Gary. *The Dominion Covenant: Genesis*. Tyler, TX: Institute for Christian Economics, (1982) 1987. A study of the economic laws of the Book of Genesis.

North, Gary. *Moses and Pharaoh: Dominion Religion vs. Power Religion*. Tyler, TX: Institute for Christian Economics, 1985. A study of the economic issues governing the Exodus.

North, Gary. *Political Polytheism: The Myth of Pluralism*. Tyler, TX: Institute for Christian Economics, 1989. A 700-page critique of the myth of neutrality: in ethics, social criticism, U.S. history, and the U.S. Constitution.

North, Gary. *The Sinai Strategy: Economics and the Ten Commandments*. Tyler, TX: Institute for Christian Economics, 1986. An economic commentary on the Ten Commandments. It includes a detailed study of why the Old Covenant's capital sanction no longer aplies to sabbath-breaking.

North, Gary. *Tools of Dominion: The Case Laws of Exodus*. Tyler, TX: Institute for Christian Economics, 1990. A 1,300-page examination of the economics of Exodus 21-23.

Rushdoony, Rousas John. *The Institutes of Biblical Law*. Nutley, New Jersey: Presbyterian and Reformed, 1973. The foundational work of the Christian Reconstruction movement. It subsumes all of biblical law under the Ten Commandments. It includes three appendixes by Gary North.

Sutton, Ray R. *That You May Prosper: Dominion By Covenant*. Tyler, TX: Institute for Christian Economics, 1987. Detailed study of the five points of the biblical covenant model, applying them to church, state, and family.

SCRIPTURE INDEX

Old Testament

New Testament

INDEX

ABOUT THE AUTHOR

Gary North received his Ph.D. in history from the University of California, Riverside, in 1972. He specialized in colonial U.S. history. He wrote his doctoral dissertation on New England Puritanism's economic history and the history of economic thought. A simplified version of this dissertation has been published as *Puritan Economic Experiments* (Institute for Christian Economics, [1974] 1988).

He is the author of approximately 30 books in the fields of economics, history, and theology. Since 1973, he has been writing a multi-volume economic commentary on the Bible, which now covers Genesis (one volume) and Exodus (three volumes). He is the general editor of the multi-volume set, the Biblical Blueprints Series, presently at ten volumes.

He edited the first fifteen issues of *The Journal of Christian Reconstruction*, 1974-81. He edited two issues of *Christianity and Civilization* in 1983: *The Theology of Christian Resistance* and *Tactics of Christian Resistance*. He edited a *festschrift* for Cornelius Van Til, *Foundations of Christian Scholarship* (1976).

He is the editor of the fortnightly economic newsletter, *Remnant Review*. He writes two bi-monthly Christian newsletters, *Biblical Economics Today* and *Christian Reconstruction*, published by the Institute for Christian Economics.

He lives in Tyler, Texas, with his wife and four children. He is a member of Good Shepherd Reformed Episcopal Church, Tyler, Texas.